Scribe Publications
HUMAN RIGHTS OVERBOARD

Professor Linda Briskman is the Dr Haruhisa Handa chair of human rights education at Curtin University. She received the award to deliver the Eileen Younghusband lecture in South Africa in July 2008, for her work on the People's Inquiry into Detention. She is the author of two other books, *Social Work with Indigenous Communities* and *The Black Grapevine*.

Susie Latham is an adjunct research associate at the Centre for Human Rights Education, Curtin University, a registered migration agent and a social worker. Susie has a professional background in engaging general practitioners in a number of health and mental health projects and has volunteered at Melbourne's Refugee and Immigration Legal Centre for over five years. She has also volunteered as an English tutor to refugees and spent more than eight years in various workplaces as a union representative.

Professor Chris Goddard is the director of the National Research Centre for the Prevention of Child Abuse, Monash University. Recognition of his accomplishments include a 2005 nomination for the UN Human Rights Award for journalism. Goddard is the author of two other books, *The Truth Is Longer Than a Lie* and *In The Firing Line*.

HUMAN RIGHTS OVER B ARD

SEEKING ASYLUM IN AUSTRALIA

Linda Briskman Susie Latham **Chris Goddard**

SCRIBE
Melbourne

Scribe Publications Pty Ltd
PO Box 523
Carlton North, Victoria, Australia 3054
Email: info@scribepub.com.au

First published by Scribe 2008

Typeset in 9.5/13.5 pt Sabon by the publishers
Printed and bound in Australia by Griffin Press
Only wood grown from sustainable regrowth forests is used in the manufacture
of paper found in this book.

National Library of Australia
Cataloguing-in-Publication data

Linda Briskman ; Chris Goddard ; Susie Latham.
Human rights overboard : seeking asylum in Australia

Carlton North, Vic. : Scribe Publications, 2008.
9781921372407 (pbk.)

Refugees–Australia; Detention of persons–Australia; Refugee children–Government
policy–Australia; Asylum, Right of–Australia–Government policy; Goddard,
Christopher R. (Christopher Rex), 1947-; Latham, Susie.

323.6310994

www.scribepublications.com.au

CONTENTS

IN MEMORY OF

Those who died attempting to seek asylum in Australia:

On unknown boats

Ayat Saber, 3

Sarti, washed overboard in rough seas while bailing water from his boat with a cooking pan

The Afghan man and the Iranian man who disappeared while trying to get drinking water when their boat was stuck on an island

On the boat SIEV 5

A young baby

On the boat SIEV 7

Hussein Yahia, 30, father of two

Thamer Hussein

Haithem Dawood

On the boat SIEV X

Zahra, daughter of Sondos Ismail, 6

Fatima, daughter of Sondos Ismail, 7

Eman, daughter of Sondos Ismail, 8

Khadija Ismail

Leyla, wife of Faris Kadhem

Zahra, daughter of Faris Kadhem, 7

Zainalabaden Aluomer

Wife of Zainalabaden

Aluomer

Mother of Zainalabaden Aluomer

Sana, wife of Sadiq Raza

Souad Alrimahi, 32

Ahsan Alrimahi, 42

Mahmoud Alrimahi, 6

Moustafa Alrimahi, 4

Fatima Alrimahi, 14

Roukaya Alrimahi, 7

Zaynab Sobie, 31

Donya Sobie, 14

Marva Sobie, 12

Hajaran Sobie, 10

Kaber Khan

Mohammed Khan

Sohki Khan

Salman Khan

Raad Al-Saiegh , 26

Kauthar Raad, 4

Alya Raad, 2

Najla Muhsin, 20

Haydar Muhsin, 22

Karrar, son of Najah Muhsin, 1

Kaltom Al-Battat, 25

Fatima Falah, 5

Batoul Falah, 2

Ali Falah, 1

Wife of Fawzi Qasim, 30

Ayat Fawzi, 8

Noor Fawzi, 6

Fatima Fawzi, 1

Wife of Haidar Ataa, 25

Rem Haidar, 4

Rakem Haidar, 2

Ammar Ismail, 19

Akhlas, wife of Hazam Al Rowaimi, 27

Hamda, mother of Hazam Al Rowaimi, 49

Noor, daughter of Hazam Al Rowaimi, 11

Fatama, daughter of Hazam Al Rowaimi, 8

Nargis, daughter of Hazam Al Rowaimi, 5

Mohammed, son of Hazam Al Rowaimi, 3

Ahmad, son of Kareem Jabar Husein, 8

Dr Kamel Mohsen Al Battat, 40

Aminah Hassan Al Battat, 33

Zainab Al Battat, 4

Mohamad Al Battat, 10

Wissam Al Battat, 8

Zahra Al Battat, 1

Abas, brother of Hussein Jawad, 5

Naima, mother of Hussein Jawad, 31

Raghed Jabbar Al Saadi, 27

Mohammad Al Muntazar Alghazzi, 4

Ali Almurtada Al

Ghazzi, 5

Reyam Al Ghazzi, 10

Yasser Al Helou, 45

Ahmad Yasser Al Helou, 16

Noor Yasser Al Helou, 7

Marwa Al Helou, 3

Doha Yasser Al Helou, 2

Sayed Hassan Al Yassiry, 38

Wife of Sayed Al Yassiry, 30

Fatima Al Yassiry, 5

Zahra Al Yassiry, 3

Abu Yasin

Wife of Abu Yasin

Houda, daughter of Abu Yasin

Muhammad, son of Abu Yasin

Rabab Jawad, 9

Sameeya Al Zohairi, 58

Hadeer Al Zohairi, 15

Hadeel Al Zohairi, 19

Rabih Al Helou, 45

Ahmad Al Helou

Hamza Al Helou

Mostapha Al Helou

Zaynab Al Helou

Batoul Al Helou

Narjas Al Helou

Wife of Sabah Latif Ali

Daughter of Sabah Latif Ali

Amir Al Husseini, 61

Kareema Al Juborie, 27

Mona Al Husseini, 26

Yasser Ali Al Husseini, 10

Mahdi Al Husseini, 6

Asnan Ali Al Husseini, 7

Nasser Amir Al Husseini, 9

Ahmad Amir Al Husseini, 10

Diya Al Saadi, 26

Raged Alzaydi, 26

Ali Diya Al Saadi, 3

Ahmed Diya Al Saadi, baby

Ali Latif Al Saadi, 16

Fatimah Jabbar Alidawi, 32

Mohammed Alghizzy, 10

Hussein Alghizzy, 7

Zahraa Alghizzy, 8

Alyaa Alghizzy, 4

Karima Al Noori

Aliyaa Al Noori, 7

Mohammad Hossein Al Noori, 4

Semira Baceri

Farhare Jezani

Neda Jezani, 19

Noora Jezani, 17

Mohammad Jezani, 15

Reaz Jezani, 13

Mehdi Jezani, 10

Raad Neezar Kawery, 20

Ahmad Tememi, 25

Ali, Yazd village, 20

Abda Rezo Chechan, 22

Kasim Kawery, 22

Mehdi Mandalawe, 18

Mohammad Negmann, 21

Saed Kareem, 35

Wife of Saed Kareem

Abo Salah

Bahar Hadi

Wife of Bahar Hadi

Daughter of Bahar Hadi

Second daughter of Bahar Hadi

Monaf Al Alawy, 25

Fatima Al Alawy, 25

Hassan Al Alawy, 7

Baby Al Alawy

Ahmed Al Alawy, 23

and 219 more men, women and children

Those who died in Australian immigration detention:[1]

The American man who died of liver disease in Villawood in 1998

Viliami Tanginoa, 53

Hai Phuoc Vo, 36

Mohammed Saleh, 41

Avion Gumede

Phuangtong Simaplee, 27

Nurjan Hussaini, 55

Fatima Husseini, 20, pregnant

Thi Hang Le, 33

The person who died of alcohol poisoning at

Leeuwin Barracks in March 2002

Mohammed Sarwar, 20s

Fatima Erfani, 20s, mother of three

Mansur La Ibu, 21

The person who died of drug related illnesses at Maribyrnong detention centre in June 2003

Seong Ho Kang, 37, father of two

Marc Lao Thao, 70s

The person who died of lung cancer at Maribyrnong detention centre in March 2005

Muhammed Heri, 37

Pishevarz Khodaverdi, 64

Those who died having had their applications for asylum in Australia rejected:

The only children, aged six and nine, of an Afghan man, who died when a grenade was dropped on their house after their father was refused asylum in Australia

Alvaro Moralez

Bilal Ahad, 18

Mohammad Mussa Nazari

Yacoub Baklri

Mohammed Sharif al-Saraf

Reginald Jesudasan, 31

Mr Cai

Bill Zhang

Those who died while on a Temporary Protection Visa:

Dr Habibullah Wahedy, 46, father of three, who hanged himself shortly after receiving a letter from immigration offering him $2000 to return to Afghanistan when his visa expired

This book is also dedicated to those volunteers and supporters who gave so selflessly to the inquiry (see Acknowledgements, p. 395).

PREFACE

The Australian Council of Heads of Social Work is proud to be the auspicing body for the People's Inquiry into Detention and to have worked collaboratively with so many passionate advocates who share deep concern about the policy of mandatory detention. The inquiry builds upon the relentless perseverance of the social work heads in protesting asylum-seeker policies over a number of years.

Human Rights Overboard is a stunning example of how social work, a profession of many facets, can contribute to changing public perceptions and to challenging harsh policies that violate core human rights tenets. We are proud that social work has taken a lead, as this endeavour illuminates the heart of social work, which lies in its unswerving commitment to social justice and human rights. This commitment was enacted in many ways during the inquiry process, including the work of social work schools in facilitating hearings, in enabling students to undertake fieldwork placements and for providing support to those giving evidence. The inquiry process demonstrates how social work, despite its diversity of practice modes and organisational constraints, can garner the support of others to challenge human rights abuses.

For the heads of schools, the inquiry is an outstanding example of social work's steadfast commitment to social justice and social action. Under the leadership of Professors Linda Briskman, Chris Goddard and their colleagues, a significant confrontation to government policies was undertaken through a monumental effort across the nation.

The logistics alone were challenge enough, conducting hearings around the country and working with groups in each location to maximise the benefits and to ensure community participation and ownership. The incredible work of an army of dedicated volunteers from all walks of life, with an enormous array of skills, ensured that the process was a success.

The inquiry gave voice to many people who had been silenced. A valued outcome has been that major therapeutic benefits to those directly affected by the policies can arise from such a political challenge. As a result of this effort of the Council the stories of this disturbing era of social policy will be on the record for future generations. May it never happen again.

Professor Margaret Alston
President, Australian Council of Heads of Schools of Social Work

FOREWORD

JULIAN BURNSIDE

Australia has a mixed record in its treatment of refugees. There have been moments of which we can be proud, and others which are less admirable.

During the 1970s, the Fraser Liberal government shepherded into Australia tens of thousands of Vietnamese and Cambodian boat people each year, and helped them become a part of the Australian community.

In 1992, the Keating Labor government introduced a system of mandatory detention for informal arrivals. The boat people, who had hitherto been received with compassion, were now to be locked up, without trial, until their claims for asylum could be determined.

In 1999, John Howard's Liberal government introduced Temporary Protection Visas. These provided protection for only three years, and denied refugees the right to bring their families to Australia. This was a source of great hardship to people who were unquestionably refugees, and was one of the principal reasons why so many women and children died in the SIEV X disaster: families, denied the right to join their husbands and fathers through orthodox channels, tried to get here using people smugglers. On the night of 19 October 2001, 353 people drowned as they tried to get to Australia to be reunited with their immediate family members who had already been accepted in Australia as refugees.

In 2001, refugee policy became a hot political issue. On 26 August, *Tampa* rescued 438 people whose boat, the *Palapa*, had sunk. It rescued them at the request of Australia. It acted according to the tradition of sailors the world over. Apart from the five people smugglers on the boat, the people rescued by *Tampa* comprised for the most part Hazaras from Afghanistan, men, women and children. They were fleeing the Taliban. We knew all this. We also knew that the Taliban were a brutal and repressive regime. We knew that Hazaras, one of the three ethnic groups in Afghanistan, had been persecuted for centuries, but that the persecution had become increasingly harsh under the Taliban who belong to the Pashtun ethnic group.

When *Tampa* entered Australian territorial waters at Christmas Island, Australia sent the SAS and took control of the ship, to prevent the refugees from coming ashore. Ultimately, the people rescued by *Tampa* were sent to the tiny Republic of Nauru in the central Pacific. Australia paid the bankrupt Nauruan government tens of millions of dollars to detain them there on Australia's behalf. During the next two weeks, New Zealand accepted 120 of them as refugees. Over the next four years, Australia accepted many of the others as refugees, but sent many back to Afghanistan after the Taliban had been removed (temporarily as it turned out) from power.

The *Tampa* incident focussed attention on the arrival of boat people seeking asylum in Australia. At the time, the arrival rate of boat people had increased from an average of about 1000 people per year to a peak of 4175 in 1999-2000. By any standards, these were small numbers. Australia receives about four million authorised arrivals each year, most of them visiting for tourism, study or business. An unauthorised arrival rate of one thousand a year, or even four thousand a year, is negligible. Australia's borders are virtually water-tight. Nevertheless, the Howard government took the shameful step of demonising refugees for political advantage.

During the *Tampa* episode, the government closed the port and airspace at Christmas Island to ensure that 'no humanising images' of the refugees would be seen. The *Tampa* episode began on 26 August 2001; Justice North in the Federal Court handed down his decision at 2.15pm AEST on 11 September 2001: just nine hours before the attack on America. The coincidence of events caused many members of the public to blur the two events in their minds, so that terrorism and boat people became part of a single phenomenon.

Mandatory Detention

The Howard government was unapologetic about 'sending a message' to deter refugees who might wish to seek asylum in Australia. As minister for immigration, Philip Ruddock said that '[d]etention is not punitive nor meant as a deterrent'.[2] That is ultimately a matter of subjective assessment. Most people locked up without a trial would probably not agree with Mr Ruddock's view. At the same time, Ruddock applauded the Pacific Solution legislation because '[t]his strategy has been successful in deterring potential illegal immigrants from making their way to Australia'.[3]

The use of detention as a deterrent is not permitted by the Guidelines on Applicable Criteria and Standards relating to the Detention of Asylum Seekers of the United Nations refugee agency, the UNHCR, nor is it permitted by Excom Conclusion No. 44.[4] It is also morally questionable: it involves instrumentalising innocent people to achieve another objective.

Ironically, anecdotal evidence suggests that most asylum seekers who reach Australia have never heard of mandatory detention until they are in it. For them it is no deterrent because they do not know of it. Generally, they do not choose Australia: they get here because they do not have enough money for a people smuggler to take them somewhere else.

Although the Keating Labor government had introduced mandatory detention, the Howard government deliberately exploited the system for political advantage. The wickedness and cruelty of indefinite mandatory detention is at the heart of this book.

Under section 196 of the *Migration Act*, boat people are the only group in our community who can be imprisoned indefinitely, by order of parliament, regardless of the fact that they have not committed any offence and do not present a threat to the community. No court can order that the person should be released merely because the detention is unnecessary, or cruel, or damaging, or pointless.

The *Migration Act* defines 'unlawful noncitizen' as a noncitizen who does not have a visa. The Act does not make it an offence to be in Australia without a visa, but section 196 provides that an 'unlawful noncitizen' must be kept in immigration detention until he or she is granted a visa or is removed from Australia. Sub-section (3) provides, rather chillingly, that 'To avoid doubt, subsection (1) prevents the release, even by a court, of an unlawful noncitizen from detention (otherwise than for removal or deportation) unless the noncitizen has been granted a visa.'

In November 2003 the High Court heard argument in the case of Al-Kateb. Mr Al-Kateb was a stateless Palestinian who had arrived in Australia as a boat person. He asked for protection. His application for a protection visa was refused. He could not bear conditions in Woomera detention centre, so instead of appealing the visa refusal, he asked to be removed from Australia. The government could not remove him, because there was no country which could be forced to take him back. There was an impasse: the only way out of detention is a visa or removal from Australia. Both paths were closed. It would have been a simple matter to create a new visa category to deal with the anomaly exposed by Al-Kateb's circumstances. As it was, the Australian government argued that, in these circumstances, it could hold Mr Al-Kateb in detention for the rest of his life. On 6 August 2004, by four-against-three majority, the High Court accepted the government's argument.

On the same day, the High Court also decided the case of Behrooz, in which it held that, no matter how harsh the conditions in detention, it remained constitutionally valid.

In years to come, it may be that people will ask, how were these things tolerated? A large part of the answer will focus on the fact that the government lied about all of the principal features of Australia's refugee policy. They tagged asylum seekers as 'illegals'; they branded them 'queue jumpers'; they held out the veiled threat that we would be overrun if we did not adopt a deterrent strategy; they demonised refugees as people who would throw their children overboard; they implied that asylum seekers might also be terrorists. The press did very little to correct the record. The lies worked.

International Opinion

Australia's treatment of asylum seekers has been trenchantly criticised by human rights bodies both here and overseas. Amnesty International has been extremely critical of the policy of mandatory detention.

In May 2002, Human Rights Commissioner Mary Robinson sent an envoy to inspect Woomera detention centre. The visit had not been easy to organise: initially the Australian government had refused to allow access to Woomera. In preparation for the envoy's visit, Australasian Correctional Management performed massive renovation work at Woomera. If the renovations were calculated to improve the impression conveyed, they failed. The report which followed that visit contained the following paragraph:

> Justice Bhagwati was considerably distressed by what he saw and heard in Woomera Immigration Reception and Processing Centre. He met men, women and children who had been in detention for several months, some of them even for one or two years. They were prisoners without having committed any offence. Their only fault was that they had left their native home and sought to find refuge or a better life on the Australian soil. In virtual prison-like conditions in the detention centre, they lived initially in the hope that soon their incarceration will come to an end but with the passage of time, the hope gave way to despair. When Justice Bhagwati met the detainees, some of them broke down. He could see despair on their faces. He felt that he was in front of a great human tragedy ... These children were growing up in an environment which affected their physical and mental growth and many of them were traumatized and led to harm themselves in utter despair.

Justice Bhagwati found that the conditions he observed at Woomera involved numerous breaches of Australia's obligations under the International Covenant on Civil and Political Rights, the Convention against Torture and the Convention on the Rights of the Child.

In December 2002 a working group of the United Nations Human Rights Committee reported on Australia's detention system. Its report would shock most Australians. The working group, headed by Justice Louis Joinet, said:

> At the end of its visit, the delegation of the Working Group had the clear impression that the conditions of detention are in many ways similar to prison conditions: detention centres are surrounded by impenetrable and closely guarded razor wire; detainees are under permanent supervision; if escorted outside the centre they are, as a rule, handcuffed; escape from a centre constitutes a criminal offence under the law and the escapee is prosecuted ... During talks with government officials it became obvious that one of the goals of the system of mandatory detention and the way it is implemented is to discourage would-be immigrants from entering Australia without a valid visa ...
>
> The authorities stressed that these practices have the support of most sectors of public opinion. This is no doubt the case, but with the following reservations:
>
> (a) One could reasonably assume that if public opinion were fully and specifically informed about the conditions to which human beings are being subjected in Australia and the negative consequences for the image of a democratic country, public opinion would change.
>
> (b) Australian public opinion must also know that, to the knowledge of the delegation, a system combining mandatory, automatic, indiscriminate and indefinite detention without real access to court challenge is not practised by any other country in the world.

On Human Rights Day, 10 December 2002, Human Rights Watch also released a report on Australia's treatment of refugees. It said:

> The Australian government penalizes asylum seekers who arrive uninvited ... The measures they take to penalize them are also intended to deter future arrivals. They include interception and forcible return to Indonesia; interception and transfer to detention in the Pacific nations of Nauru and Papua New Guinea; mandatory detention within Australia;

and temporary protection visas, with restrictions on the rights afforded recipients.

The Truth at Last

The People's Inquiry into Detention is a remarkable exercise in democracy. The mistreatment of refugees over the life of the Howard government was possible largely because it had bi-partisan support. As a result, the press did not find it necessary or convenient to expose government spin for what it was. We needed a government inquiry into the mandatory detention system. For obvious reasons, the Howard government would not call one, so a small group of academics and activists set up the People's Inquiry into Detention.

This book is the result. It is carefully and fairly written. It is confronting and distressing to read the facts gathered in these pages, the more so because it is all true. Having been closely involved in many aspects of the matters recorded here, I thought I could no longer be distressed by the reminder of what Australia has done to defenceless people, but I was wrong.

This is a profoundly important book. It is an unflinching look at disgraceful events. Too many Australians allowed these things to happen. Our generation will be forever marked with the shame of it. It is not only an epitaph for the Howard government: it is a caution to future generations.

ACRONYMS

ABC	Australian Broadcasting Corporation
ACHSSW	Australian Council of Heads of Schools of Social Work
ACM	Australasian Correctional Management
AFP	Australian Federal Police
BVE	Bridging Visa E
CERT	Centre Emergency Response Team
DIAC	Department of Immigration and Citizenship
DIMA	Department of Immigration and Multicultural Affairs
DIMIA	Department of Immigration, Multicultural and Indigenous Affairs
DOCS	Department of Community Services
DFAT	Department of Foreign Affairs and Trade
FAYS	Family and Youth Services
GP	General Practitioner
GSL	Global Solutions Limited
HREOC	Human Rights and Equal Opportunity Commission
IAAAS	Immigration Advice and Application Assistance Scheme
ICCPR	International Covenant on Civil and Political Rights
IDAG	Immigration Detention Advisory Group
IHMS	International Health and Medical Services
IOM	International Organisation for Migration
MOU	Memorandum of Understanding
MRT	Migration Review Tribunal
PIAC	Public Interest Advocacy Centre
PSS	Psychological Support Services
PV	Permanent Visa
RASSA	Refugee Advocacy Service of South Australia
RILC	Refugee and Immigration Legal Centre
RPBV	Removal Pending Bridging Visa
RRT	Refugee Review Tribunal
SAS	Special Air Service
SIEV	Suspected Illegal Entry Vessel
TPV	Temporary Protection Visa
UAM	Unaccompanied Minor
UN	United Nations
UNHCR	United Nations High Commissioner for Refugees

INTRODUCTION

In February 2005, Cornelia Rau, a permanent resident who had lived most of her life since she was 18 months old in Australia, was discovered in the Baxter immigration detention facility. She had been incarcerated as an 'unlawful noncitizen' for a total of 10 months, six of them in a Queensland prison. Affected by schizophrenia and psychosis, she had told immigration authorities she was a German citizen called Anna.

Following her transfer to Baxter, many refugee advocates heard about 'Anna' and her disturbed behaviour from their asylum-seeker friends and had been lobbying senior immigration authorities, including ministerial staff, for over two months to provide her with psychiatric assistance. But she was only released from detention and given appropriate medical treatment when a newspaper article generated by an advocate described her plight and family members identified her.[5]

Some Australians were shocked when they learned how Cornelia Rau had been treated by the Department of Immigration. But thousands of ordinary people across the country who had formed close relationships with asylum seekers in detention centres were not. For them, her situation was just one more in a long list of appalling stories and shocking incidents inside detention. For them, it was no surprise that someone who displayed bizarre behaviour seemed quite normal in the detention context, or that nothing had been done to help her, despite concerns for her welfare being repeatedly raised with authorities.

When the Howard government announced that former Australian Federal Police commissioner Mick Palmer would conduct an inquiry into the circumstances of Cornelia Rau's detention, the terms of reference were restricted to the circumstances of her detention alone.[6] As Cornelia's sister, journalist Chris Rau, said at the time, her case illustrated a 'shameful double standard':

> While she was an unnamed illegal immigrant, the only treatment she received for mental illness was longer periods in lock-up as punishment for bad behaviour ... Yet, magic! As soon as she became an Australian resident, she was whisked away to a teaching hospital, seen by consultant psychiatrists and medicated. During which leg of her flight from Baxter to Adelaide did she suddenly gain the basic human right to medical treatment?[7]

There were many community calls for the government to widen the terms of reference of the Palmer inquiry to a full inquiry into immigration detention, but these went unheeded. The calls included one from Baxter detainees, who stated:

> *God sent Cornelia here to send our cry to all Australian people. We are all happy that she be free from such a terrible place. We all pray that she will get well. She remains in our minds and hearts as a heroine for ever and ever.*[8]

In response to the narrow terms of reference of the Palmer inquiry, the Australian Council of Heads of School of Social Work (ACHSSW) undertook the People's Inquiry into Detention. This was based on a view that ordinary Australians have an obligation to act when our government is unwilling to do so and that citizen-led inquiries can engage members of the community who are otherwise disengaged from the democratic process.[9]

The People's Inquiry

The People's Inquiry was established as open, independent, transparent and inclusive, to bear witness to events in Australian immigration detention facilities, whose operations were largely shrouded in official secrecy. Anyone with experiences of immigration detention was invited to present evidence about any aspect of the detention regime.

The Response

The response to the inquiry was overwhelming. It travelled around Australia hearing testimonies in Melbourne, Sydney, Perth, Canberra, Adelaide, Launceston, Port Augusta, Shepparton, Swan Hill and Griffith. Most presenters gave evidence to a panel of three, although there have been some private hearings. Almost 200 verbal accounts have been heard and approximately 200 written submissions received. Those who gave evidence to the inquiry include former detainees, their Australian supporters, doctors, nurses, educators, former Department of Immigration[10] officials, detention centre employees,[11] migration agents and lawyers.

The inquiry is extraordinary not just because so many people have felt able to come forward and place on the public record the stories they have carried with them, but also because people all over Australia have volunteered to help. The inquiry commenced with no money, but with a great deal of goodwill, passion, energy and expertise.

Specialist volunteer advisors assisted in the areas of media, ethics, law, publicity and fund-raising. A Melbourne-based steering group planned and organised many activities. Social work and other students on field placements made a major contribution. Universities and community organisations throughout Australia provided venues and other support for the hearings. Volunteer counsellors were available to those giving evidence at all hearings. Actors, artists, poets and musicians performed at the launch of hearings. As the momentum of the inquiry took hold, funding was obtained from a range of sources.

To our knowledge this is the first time that such an extensive citizen-driven inquiry has been conducted in Australia. Its success demonstrates that inclusive and flexible forms of inquiry strike a chord with community members through providing a safe platform to voice their concerns. Many people told the organisers they appreciated the opportunity to tell their stories and wanted to ensure that the policies and practices that shamed a nation are not forgotten.

Changes to Detention Policy

The bulk of information in this report documents the treatment by the Australian government of some of the almost 12,000 people who arrived by boat and sought asylum here between 1999 and 2002,[12] over 11,000 of whom were recognised as refugees.[13] The report traces their experiences over the following years from their arrival, through the refugee determination process, their incarceration in detention centres and their lives after release from detention.

During the time the People's Inquiry gathered evidence, major changes occurred in government policy. When Cornelia Rau's incarceration was discovered, many of those in immigration detention and their supporters were despairing that change would ever occur. Some people had already been held in detention for more than six years.

But in May 2005, federal Liberal backbencher Petro Georgiou, supported by colleagues including Judi Moylan, Bruce Baird and Russell Broadbent, threatened to introduce a Private Members' Bill to soften his own government's detention policy. On 14 June 2005, Mick Palmer presented the Immigration Department with the draft of his damning report on Cornelia Rau's detention.[14]

Three days later, prime minister John Howard announced that as a compromise with his backbenchers, changes would be made to detention policy. Families with children were to be housed in the community, those detained for over two years would be subject to an investigation and report by the Commonwealth ombudsman that would be tabled in federal parliament, initial determinations on refugee claims would be quicker, and applications for permanent residence by holders of Temporary Protection Visas would be fast tracked.[15]

Too Late for Many

These changes saw almost all long-term immigration detainees released and some people granted permanent residence more quickly. By the time the Rudd Labor government was elected in November 2007, just 16 per cent of 493 immigration detainees were asylum seekers,[16] in contrast to 80 per cent of the almost 3000 people in detention in October 2001.[17] The Rudd government also moved to soften some aspects of refugee policy.

But the policy changes have come too late for many. In the past 10 years, 19 people have died in immigration detention. Some people will never fully recover from the physical and mental illnesses they developed during their incarceration. Even those who will cope with the trauma of having been in detention have lost years of their lives before being recognised as refugees, some separated from their wives and children for more than eight years.

Our Purpose

The purpose of the People's Inquiry into Detention is to place on the public record the impact of the policies and practices that unsettled many in Australia, resulted in criticisms from human rights organisations in Australia and abroad, and, most importantly, had a devastating impact on those directly affected. The emphasis in the report is on asylum seekers, but there are other people who are held in immigration detention and the report has included some accounts of their experiences.

The events described in this book primarily refer to the period in office of prime minister John Howard's Liberal-National coalition government. Howard's government lost office in November 2007, after holding power since March 1996. Three immigration ministers served the Howard government, with Phillip Ruddock holding the position for the longest period, followed by Amanda Vanstone and Kevin Andrews. After the Labor government took office Chris Evans was appointed as immigration minister.

In this inquiry, we have endeavoured to ensure that we accurately reflect the hundreds of verbal and written submissions and scores of documents presented. We apologise for any inadvertent omissions or errors. In conducting the inquiry we were inspired by the words of Clive Stafford Smith (in *Bad Men: Guantanamo Bay and the secret prisons*): 'I am under no illusion that I have the skill to do justice to the stories ... but the greatest sin would be not to try.'

METHODS OF INQUIRY & FRAMING OF REPORT

ACHSSW announced the People's Inquiry into Detention in newspapers[18] and through refugee advocate networks. The main inquiry methods were convening public hearings in metropolitan and rural locations and receiving written submissions.

In addition, the inquiry has drawn on other information including official documents, reports, journal articles and media, email and internet sources.

The inquiry gathered a large amount of material from a wide range of sources. While a number of themes ran through the evidence presented – for example, the heavy influence of political considerations on asylum-seeker policy and its implementation, the intimidation of asylum seekers and their supporters and the resilience of those detained – it was difficult to organise the vast amount of material on this basis.

Instead, it was decided to break the material into parts that reflected chronologically the experience of asylum seekers coming to Australia. These are: the journey here and their initial contact with Australian authorities; the processing of their asylum claims; life in detention; and life after detention. The evidence of asylum seekers, supporters and professionals all fit within these parts.

The parts emerged from the evidence presented to the inquiry. For example, the conveners had not initially envisaged writing about journeys to Australia, but included these experiences after hearing the testimony of those who had made them. Within each part, several strong themes emerged from the evidence of different groups of people. For example, the detention part includes sections on assault, mental health, protests, children, deaths and the failure of authorities to stop the human destruction they knew was occurring.

For four reasons, a conscious decision was made not to include material given to the inquiry about the reasons individual asylum seekers left their countries. First, asylum seekers have told their stories repeatedly to government officials, supporters and others. Secondly, almost all asylum seekers kept in long term detention have since been recognised by the Australian government as refugees. Thirdly, publishing their asylum claims could identify individuals. And finally, this report focuses on the actions of Australian authorities, not asylum seekers.

REPORT SUMMARY

The People's Inquiry into Detention heard heart-breaking evidence about the deaths of more than 360 asylum seekers, including 148 children, during boat journeys to Australia in 2000 and 2001. Mostly Iraqi and Afghan families trying to find safety by fleeing regimes that Australia later sent troops to fight, their deaths raise serious questions about the involvement of Australian authorities in trying to stop refugees from coming to Australia, particularly during the 2001 election period.

One man told the inquiry his mother drowned after their boat sank during interception by the Royal Australian Navy and his whole family was forced into the sea:

> *The boats came and took as many people as they could and I was asking them what happened to my family. They kept assuring me they were on the other boat. Then I realised that there was a young woman who had died. My wife and I didn't know anything about our other children and she was crying continuously and asking the officers to find some information about them.*
>
> *They managed to bring the husband of the woman who had died. He told us that your mother has unfortunately passed away, but your children are in the other boat. I was devastated. I screamed, I cried, I*

was very, very sad but I couldn't do anything. As soon as we get into the big boat my wife was running towards our children. She started hugging them and crying with them. I asked the authorities to show me my mother's body and they just show the body from a distance.

The inquiry heard that for asylum seekers who survived the dangerous journey, the relief and joy of sighting Australian land was short-lived. Intercepted by the Royal Australian Navy, they soon learned they were not welcome in John Howard's Australia. Those who were allowed to make claims for refugee status were placed in detention centres, mostly situated hundreds of kilometres from Australian capital cities or on far-flung Pacific islands.

In making claims for refugee status, they faced obstruction and suspicion from the Immigration Department and struggled to deal with an assessment process that the inquiry heard is seriously flawed, subject to political influence and often taking years to recognise claims. Migration Agent Marion Le told the inquiry about helping unaccompanied children on Nauru:

I worked day and night to interview as many people as I could. We were there very late one night and seven young people came in. I looked and I thought, My God, how old are you? One said, I think I'm 14. This is 2004, they had been there over three years, and he thought he was 14. On at least one of the files was written a note from a DIMIA woman officer. 'I have been asked to change this child's age to make him over 18 and because I am asked I am doing it, but I do not agree.' I am guilty of not making a statement about that publicly because I wanted to ensure all of the people on Nauru got off. If I had gone out and talked about the abuses of process we were seeing they wouldn't have been allowed to come to Australia and I would have been stopped from going to Nauru.

The inquiry also heard from numerous sources of shocking conditions inside detention centres – essentially privatised prisons. It was told of people being forced to steal food to feed their children, of assaults on both adults and children, of physical and mental health care so inadequate that many former detainees now have serious, permanent disabilities. The inquiry also learned that between 1998 and 2008, 19 people died in these miserable surroundings and that the agencies meant to hold government to account on such matters were essentially powerless to effect change.

This lack of accountability created a culture of violence and self-harm within detention. Protests were routinely met with armed force. The inquiry was told of people eating glass and gravel and pouring boiling water on themselves, and was presented with images of self-harm too graphic to publish. A boy who spent three years in detention said:

> *The worst thing, I will never forget it, was people cutting themselves. It was horrible. I remember one time a person was harming himself up a tree and his children were crying under the tree. His wife was crying and yelling under the tree. His blood was dropping from the tree.*

The inquiry also heard alarming stories of people being chemically and physically restrained in deportation attempts before being recognised as refugees, and of 10 people who died in other countries after their refugee applications in Australia were rejected.

Once released from detention, many refugees told the inquiry their experiences had irrevocably changed them. Many were unable to forget the violent images they had been exposed to in detention and suffered ongoing mental health problems. Others told how the uncertainty of their temporary visa status compounded their anxiety and stopped them from starting a new life. Still others, unable to reunite with wives and children overseas because they were released on temporary visas, told of relationship breakdowns and their grief at the prospect of never seeing their children again. A refugee supporter told the inquiry:

> *My friend was almost five years in detention, extremely depressed. Now his wife has divorced him and he will probably never see his little six-year-old daughter again. A Sister who met him on his release said he was extremely distressed. He just went into his church and cried and cried.*

Despite the devastation Howard government policy inflicted on asylum seekers, the inquiry also heard moving stories of ordinary Australians who rejected its harsh approach and connected with asylum seekers as human beings through each stage of their journey.

The HMAS *Adelaide*'s able seaman Laura Whittle jumped without a life jacket from a height equivalent to a four-storey building when she saw asylum seekers in difficulty in the water below. Hundreds of lawyers and migration agents offered their services free of charge to assist asylum seekers through the refugee determination process. Ordinary people visited and protested outside detention centres, forming strong friendships with and advocating for those inside. Others started organisations which have raised millions of dollars to assist people released from detention with few government entitlements.

The People's Inquiry into Detention believes that these people embody the spirit with which men, women and children fleeing persecution should be treated and are the people from which the Rudd Labor government should take its inspiration in reshaping immigration policy. The People's Inquiry into Detention recommends that three fundamental changes are needed to address the human rights issues arising from the evidence presented to it. These are to remove racism from, restore human rights to and reinstate accountability for immigration policy. Specific recommendations are included in the final section of the book.

Part 1

TO DETER & DENY:
THE JOURNEY INTO DETENTION

Following an increase in the number of asylum seekers arriving in Australia by boat from 157 in 1997–98 to 4175 in 1999–2000,[19] then immigration minister Philip Ruddock commissioned videos for distribution in countries from which asylum seekers might come. The videos outlined the dangers of the journey, described detention centres and gave information about sharks, crocodiles and snakes.[20] He said:

> When you see them, you might think that they are a little sensational. You may think they're horrific. And that maybe we're trying unnecessarily to scare people from coming to Australia.[21]

Amnesty International, of which Ruddock is a member, considered the videos disappointing, with Refugee Coordinator Graham Thom noting:

> It certainly does nothing to highlight the human rights abuses and violations that these people are fleeing from; the fact that they are being forced to flee, that they're not fleeing just to seek a better life.[22]

The campaign was supported by the Labor Party opposition, however, with shadow immigration minister Con Sciacca saying:

> We would support any moves by the government – and we have up till now – that would act as a deterrent for them to come here.[23]

Six months later, 11 days before Christmas 2000, Ruddock, told the ABC's World Today program that the government would not launch a major search-and-rescue operation for more than 160 asylum seekers feared drowned on their way to Australia. He explained the difference between this decision and previous decisions to authorise wide-ranging and expensive air and sea searches for individual sailors lost in yacht races:

> Well, I'm simply saying they left Indonesia. They have been essentially at sea for more than a week, there's been a tropical cyclone in the area ... those sorts of searches were undertaken in circumstances where ... people had taken proper precautions in terms of using beacons to enable ...pointing ... where you need to mount your search. These people get boats which have little in the way of life-saving equipment, ...inly little in the way of navigational devices, and are a very

high risk. We believe that 350 people were lost in the period of April and May of this year.[24]

In a 2002 speech to parliament, Ruddock again suggested that hundreds more asylum seekers may have lost their lives trying to reach Australia in the period between December 1999 and June 2000:

I lament very much that many people have lost their lives tragically, putting themselves in the hands of people smugglers. Perhaps there were many whom we have never known were travelling and are perhaps lost. That was certainly the case I think 2½ or three years ago when there were suggestions that some vessels that were destined for Australia left and were not seen again.[25]

The People's Inquiry heard from several asylum seekers of deaths during boat journeys. A man who arrived in Australia in late 2000 told the inquiry:

I heard from people who arrived after us that their boat got stuck on an island and they ran out of drinking water. An Iranian and an Afghan guy decided to make up some floating thing and go to the next island and get water. Other people watched them and in the middle of their way they disappeared. After a long time Federal Police came to the detention centre to ask about the Iranian guy who disappeared. I think his family was concerned what's happened to their son.

Another man told the inquiry about the death of a man on his boat:

This individual took our money and said, 'We can send you to a safe place.' There's about 130 of us and they took us to this small boat. When we were in the boat there were some Indonesian families there crying and telling us, 'Don't go by this route because you have children, you cannot survive, it's very dangerous and lots of people have lost their lives.' We didn't listen to them because we had been through so much negativity in life, we had seen so many cruelties we decided to take the risk. We either die or we survive, that's it. It's better than going back to that misery.

  We started our journey at around six and by 12 there was a hole in this boat and there was only two fit men in that boat, myself and another friend called Sarti. There was only two big cooking pans. With them we were taking water from the boat and pouring it outside. The waves were very strong and while Sarti and myself are trying to take the water out of the boat, the boat just moved and Sarti was thrown into the water and he drowned. I couldn't do anything. The women were crying and asking God to help them because no-one else could help them at that moment. Then there was a strong wave that took us close to an island. There was about 100m distance from us and the dry land. One of the boys who was a good swimmer decided to swim from the boat with a rope and he managed to tie the boat in that area.

Despite the risk, asylum seekers continued to attempt the hazardous journey to Australia, with more than 4000 men, women and children making the trip in 2001.[26] They were mainly Afghans fleeing the Taliban and Iraqis fleeing Saddam Hussein – regimes Australia would later send troops to overthrow.

Tampa

On 26 August 2001, the Norwegian freighter MV *Tampa* rescued 438 asylum seekers from a sinking boat just off Christmas Island. Prime Minister John Howard refused the *Tampa* permission to enter Australian territory, ignoring legal advice from the Attorney-General's Department and threatening *Tampa* captain Arne Rinnan with prosecution as a people smuggler.[27] A resident of Christmas Island told the inquiry:

The Tampa would go up and down on the ocean all day and night because it was too deep to anchor. Access to the cove was declared off limits to anyone but the Navy. Helicopters flew over day and night frightening everyone. The SAS, all in black, did crazy manoeuvres in their rubber boats.

According to the *Tampa's* first mate, at least 100 of the asylum seekers had diarrhoea and more than 10 were unconscious from dehydration at any one time.[28] Requests from the *Tampa* for medicines were denied and when it issued a mayday emergency call three days later, Prime Minister John Howard ordered the SAS to board the ship, an operation he followed first hand.[29] A former SAS officer told the inquiry:

You had a poor old civilian skipper who has just rescued 400 people and done a great job. The SAS force that was sent onto the Tampa was the Counter Terrorist Force, which is very much focused on going into a high threat political hostage situation at the last minute when all other options have failed. Its use is approved at prime ministerial level and once that approval is given, its job is usually to rescue hostages using lethal force. To use that force in what was essentially a humanitarian crisis would be quite alarming to people. To people who hadn't seen it before it would be quite shocking.

Second in command of the SAS that day, Peter Tinley, told a newspaper in 2007 that 'he followed his orders with a creeping sense of unease about the use of the military for what he considered a dubious political purpose':

You're talking about armed soldiers on the deck of a freighter. If it had been younger soldiers who didn't have training in ambiguous environments ... if they had got a little bit rough with the refugees, it could have got nasty.[30]

John Howard later declared, 'There were no cases on board the vessel requiring medical evacuation.'[31] Medical officers had examined the 438 people on board in less than 30 minutes, in time for him to make a statement to parliament.[32] A week later, he announced that the asylum seekers would be taken to Nauru and New Zealand, and surveillance of the waters between Australia and Indonesia would be increased.[33]

On the second-last sitting day of parliament before the 2001 federal election, the Liberal government, with support from the Labor opposition, passed six bills relating to border protection. The legislation retrospectively legalised actions taken during the *Tampa* incident. In what became known as the 'Pacific Solution', it also allowed boats intercepted at sea to be towed to international waters and their occupants to be held in detention centres on Nauru and Manus Island, part of Papua New Guinea.

Christmas, Ashmore, Cartier and the Cocos Islands were excised from Australia's migration zone, so that people arriving at those islands could not apply for a visa unless the minister allowed them to. People landing on these islands could also be transferred to detention centres on Nauru or Manus Island and had no access to Australia's legal system. The offshore detention centres Australia established on Nauru and Manus Island were modelled on Guantanamo Bay, where the US has processed thousands of Haitian refugees.

However, there was opposition to the legislation. Liberal MP Petro Georgiou said such a law would have denied sanctuary to Jews fleeing Nazi Germany. David Bitel, president of the Refugee Council, compared it to the case of the St Louis, a passenger ship carrying 930 Jews which in May 1939 was refused entry to Cuba and the US. The Cuban president declared the shipping line and refugees should be taught a lesson about Cuban law and sovereignty. Upon return to Europe almost all the passengers died in the Holocaust.[34]

Operation Relex

The new surveillance operation in Australia's northern waters was named Operation Relex and initially involved five naval vessels and four P3 Orion aircraft. The aim of Relex was to detect and then prevent asylum seekers from entering Australian waters, with the ultimate aim of deterring people smugglers and asylum seekers from trying to get to Australia.[35] Relex's operational decisions were made by the prime minister's People Smuggling Task Force, chaired by the Department of Prime Minister and Cabinet. The 12 boats that entered Australian territory during Relex were referred to by authorities as Suspected Illegal Entry Vessels (SIEVs).[36]

Operation Relex immediately achieved results. Within two weeks of starting, SIEVs 1 to 3 were intercepted and asylum seekers were transported to Nauru on naval vessels when efforts to turn their boats back to Indonesia were resisted. SIEV 3 carried 129 people with no lifejackets, including 54 children and a heavily pregnant woman. They were held on their boat for 10 days before being moved to the HMAS *Tobruk*, on which the pregnant woman gave birth.

Andrew Wilkie, Office of National Assessments expert on people smuggling and border protection in 2001, argued that Relex may have been too successful in stopping boats for a government facing possible electoral defeat. Following the interception of SIEVs 1 to 3, more than three weeks passed without another boat arriving. At this point, two weeks before John Howard called an election, Relex was reviewed. Asserting the government's border-protection credentials, then defence minister Peter Reith announced the 'decision that we've made is to continue the build-up in the north'.[37] However, the government had actually withdrawn one or two naval ships and half the aircraft from the surveillance operation.[38]

Wilkie argues that while this reduction occurred in the wake of the

September 11 terrorist attacks in the US, 'the commitment of ships and aircraft to the war on terror had not been decided upon, prepared for, or announced, at the time Relex was being virtually halved in September'.[39] During the five weeks of the 2001 election campaign, seven boats of asylum seekers were intercepted under Relex.

SIEV 4 Children Overboard

SIEV 4, also known as the 'children overboard' boat, was intercepted by HMAS *Adelaide* on 6 October 2001, the day after the prime minister had called an election. It was carrying 223 people, including 76 children. By 2.30am the next morning, the boat was two or three miles from Christmas Island and ignoring warnings to stop. At 4am the *Adelaide* fired warning shots ahead of the vessel. The log of the *Adelaide* recorded:

0402 Warning 5.56 mm (cannon) shots fired 50ft in front of vessel.

0405 Warning 5.56 mm shots fired 75 feet in front of SIEV-4.

0409 Warning 5.56 mm shots fired 50–100ft in front of SIEV-4.

0414 Boarding party advised by CO that if 50 cal machine gun warning shots do not stop vessel, boarding party is to aggressively board SIEV-4.

0418-0420 Twenty-three rounds of 50 cal (20 rounds of automatic fire) fired in front of SIEV-4.[40]

Able seaman Laura Whittle, who fired some of the shots, told a magazine:

We could see their faces and the screaming was just horrific. They were yelling, 'Help us!' and, at one point, it was more deafening than the 50-calibre machine gun.[41]

Ali Alsaai, who was on the boat, told the Nine Network's *Sunday* program:

It was during the night. We didn't know which way the shooting was going but the shooting was too much. [I was] vomiting, very scary, very sick and my daughter ... too; my daughter very vomiting.[42]

Despite it being perfectly legal for people to seek asylum in Australia, when then minister for defence Robert Hill was asked whether it was appropriate to use force against asylum seekers, he replied:

> Well, we're protecting our borders. There are those who wish to breach our borders, to engage in that illegal activity. We're entitled, and furthermore, we believe it's our responsibility to do our best to protect our borders.[43]

Shortly after the warning shots were fired, a boarding party from the *Adelaide* took control of the boat and its course was changed towards Indonesia. A Senate committee heard from Rear Admiral Geoffrey Smith how the Navy dealt with vessels approaching Australian waters:

> Our policy was to ... turn the vessel around and either steam it out of our contiguous zone ourselves under its own power or ... tow the vessel outside our contiguous zone into international waters. At that point, our boarding party withdrew as we had no jurisdiction in international waters.[44]

The inquiry heard evidence from one of the people on the SIEV 4:

> The Navy personnel intercepted our boat where we were about to reach Christmas Island, but then they shifted the direction of that boat towards Indonesia again. To avoid the anger of the people on board, they assured everyone that they would be in charge of leading and driving that fishing boat to the Australian shore and then when people distanced themselves, they jumped to the cabin and they just destroyed the navigator and the rudder and they just left.

The *Adelaide* reported that passengers were angry and disappointed at being turned north, and that they were 'irate, aggressive and to some extent hysterical'.[45] Some were threatening to commit suicide and 14 jumped overboard. They were returned to the boat and the *Adelaide* then left. Former immigration minister Philip Ruddock described the encounter:

> A number of people have jumped overboard and have had to be rescued. More disturbingly, a number of children have been thrown overboard ... I regard these as some of the most disturbing practices that I have come across in the time that I have been involved in public life.[46]

The following day, Prime Minister John Howard added:

I express my anger at the behaviour of those people and I repeat it. I can't comprehend how genuine refugees would throw their children overboard.[47]

But able seaman Laura Whittle saw it differently. She told a magazine she saw one man hold out his daughter to navy personnel in inflatable rafts:

When I saw that man with his daughter it just made my heart melt. The girl had on a pink jacket and she had curly hair, and it was like the father was saying, 'Take her, take her.' That was the gesture he was making. It was like 'Give her a chance' and it was then that I moved out of work mode and the humanity began to kick in. I thought he just wants to save his little girl. He wants her to have a better life ... That's when I started to think so differently, 'How could somebody be so desperate to head towards the unknown with their children on a rickety boat and to put everything at risk?' They must have been coming from something terrible and it made me think, 'This isn't right, this isn't how things should be.'[48]

Having boarded the asylum seekers' boat, *Adelaide* Commander Norman Banks assessed it as barely seaworthy. However, under Operation Relex his options were limited. He told the ABC's *Four Corners* program:

Our mission was to deter and deny their access to Australia. Taking them on-board Adelaide, *in other than a 'safety of life' situation, would have been a mission failure.*[49]

He then asked permission to tow the boat to safety. According to the *Adelaide's* log:

The commanding officer advised approval from PM of Australia 'to tow vessel to place to be determined'.[50]

Commander Banks told *Four Corners*:

I recollect there were some conversations where the Brigadier took me into his confidence and explained things – that this was important, and it was going to government, and indeed the prime minister, on certain occasions, for decisions to be made.[51]

Rear Admiral Geoffrey Smith told a Senate committee:

Once we had intercepted, everything that occurred after that in terms of major decisions – such as boarding, removal of people or whatever it happened to be – actually came from Canberra.[52]

Military ethicist Dr Hugh Smith says the political interference in naval operational matters was unusual:

Normal military practice was clearly overridden in at least one instance, namely acceptance of the government's requirement for instant reports from HMAS Adelaide *on the situation of SIEV-4 such that its captain, Commander Banks, was compelled to respond to requests in the middle of a difficult operation.*[53]

After 24 hours, the *Adelaide* abandoned its tow and the boat began filling with water. Just before 3pm on 8 October, the boarding party from the *Adelaide* requested that women and children be moved from the boat onto the *Adelaide*. Despite the government's stated concern for the welfare of the children, this request was denied. By 4pm, the water level in the boat was half a metre, having been reduced from a height of 1.2m by the boarding party, which was trying to render it seaworthy. Despite the distress of the asylum seekers, the boarding party began to serve the evening meal. Half an hour later, the boat began to sink rapidly and almost everyone, apart from a few babies and an old woman, was forced into the water.[54] The inquiry heard from a man who had been on the boat:

And then the whole boat just completely collapsed and we sink in the water. We were provided at the beginning to take life jackets. The Navy ship provided a few jackets because they knew from the start that the boat was going to sink. At that time the Navy started to send in small rescue boat, they said they will start in rescuing and saving the little children, but it became too late because people started to swim and to sink and people started to find their way towards that big Navy ship. They took us on board and thanks God that no-one was drowned. The crew of that Navy ship announced that no-one had lost his life. And they announced they have no authority to take us for nowhere. They suggested they will keep us there in the sea until they received an order from higher authority.

Commander Banks told the Senate why he had refused to evacuate the women and children earlier:

Because if I disembarked some to the Adelaide *I would have failed in my mission aim and I might as well have embarked all of them. In my judgment we still had a boat that was still marginally seaworthy and I still had control of the situation.*[55]

The Senate committee expressed concern at the consequences of the government policy of deterring and denying asylum seekers, particularly 'the requirement to avoid embarking unauthorised arrivals onto Royal Australian Navy vessels until the last possible moment'.[56] Despite John Howard declaring, 'I certainly don't want people like that here'[57] when discussing false claims children had been thrown overboard, it was government policy that forced more than 70 children from the boat into the open sea.

The Senate committee noted the relief evident in a signal sent shortly after the rescue by Commander Norman Banks.

All on board are content that their loved ones are with them and it appears, repeat appears, that no-one is missing. An exhaustive search of area has been conducted and only flotsam and jetsam remains.[58]

Military ethicist Dr Hugh Smith has argued:

The effect of government policy here was to put lives at risk, not only those of asylum seekers but also those of naval personnel.[59]

When able seaman Laura Whittle saw the boat begin to sink she jumped 12 metres, about the height of a four-storey building, from the *Adelaide* into the ocean without a life jacket to help rescue the asylum seekers. Almost three years after the boat sank, Whittle said:

I will never forget the look in their eyes. You see desperation, sorrow and helplessness.[60]

The government ensured such images of the asylum seekers were hidden from most Australians. The director-general of communication strategies for the Defence Department, Brian Humphreys, told a Senate committee investigating the 'children overboard' affair:

> We were certainly aware that immigration had concerns about identifying potential asylum seekers, so we got some guidance on ensuring that there were no personalising or humanising images taken of [them].[61]

The asylum seekers from the SIEV 4 were initially taken to Christmas Island, but eventually transferred to Manus Island for processing. One man told the inquiry how people were deceived during the transfer:

> We heard that some people tried to approach us but they just lock the door and prevent anyone from approaching us. Someone came and assured the group that we will be released easily and quickly. There was an interpreter. He suggested we have met the refugee criteria and we will transfer you to the Australian land. They took some photos and our details and we completed forms. We were so pleased and we started to congratulate each other.
>
> They started to transfer small groups, in a very secretive way without the others knowing and mainly in the middle of the night. We were divided into four groups and they started with the single young people because they tried to take first those who are potential troublemakers. Before we were taken on board of that military jet we were heavily checked by army personnel and we didn't really know the purpose of that inspection. After that long journey we ended up with a big surprise.
>
> When we arrived we were struck by the tropical weather, when we looked at the dark complexion of the people we were just struck. We kept wondering, where is the white Australian man? When I looked at the tropical trees and the tropical climate, I had a sense that we were sent back again and we might be in Indonesia. And all our thoughts came in a moment. We found we were in Manus Island in Papua New Guinea.
>
> Later it's been explained to us via interpreter that it is a transit station to assess whether we are eligible to go to Australia or not. Then we suggested to them but someone from you came around before and

said we are going to an Australian land and they said you misunderstood and we doubt ourself to a moment but it's hard to think that 22 people all misunderstood.

Hawraa Alsaai, who was 12 when she boarded the 'children overboard' boat, told a magazine:

They told us we were going to Sydney. And we were dancing and singing. That was the first day we slept because everyone was so relieved. But then they put us on a plane and we were taken to Manus Island.[62]

SIEV 5 – Baby Ashmorey's boat

One week into the election campaign, on 12 October 2001, and after more than a week at sea, a boat carrying 238 Afghani asylum seekers reached Ashmore Island. Unbeknown to them, it had been excised from Australia's migration zone a month earlier. The asylum seekers had run out of food, and water had been rationed from two days into the journey. A young baby on the boat had died. Hours before reaching the island, a woman on board had given birth to her third child. In celebration of reaching land, the mother called her newborn child Ashmorey.[63]

One of those on board told:

Due to extreme happiness the tears were coming from the eyes of all passengers because all of us believed that we finally reached Australia alive. We thought that it was the end of all calamities of our trip. [64]

Shortly after reaching land, they saw the Navy frigate *Warramunga*. But instead of taking the asylum seekers to the mainland, the Navy kept them on their boat for five days while 'the prime minister and some of his closest advisers deliberated on their fate'.[65] As they waited, Ashmorey's mother bled. Ashmorey's father told *Four Corners* that the Navy doctor who saw her tried to get permission for her to be removed from the boat but this did not eventuate.[66] During the wait, government policy hardened.

After the interception of SIEVs 1 to 4, the Navy had been instructed to hold asylum seekers for transportation to a country to be designated. However when it intercepted SIEV 5, Rear Admiral Geoffrey Smith told the Senate Inquiry:

We received new instructions which were to, where possible, intercept, board and to return the vessel to Indonesia.[67]

A woman who was on board the boat told *Four Corners*:

One day, they came and said, 'The Australia government has accepted you.' We were so happy. Then he said, 'We're taking the families to the big ship. The single men will stay on the small boat.'

A man who was on board the boat told:

The Navy people came in our boat and said, 'We are taking you to the refugee camp,' but they deceived us. They separated the families from singles and transferred families to their Navy ship. Then they asked all the singles to come down inside the boat. We requested them it is not possible for 160 persons to come together in a place, which is enough only for 40 persons. They said, 'Only for five minutes, we want to tell something to you.' So all the 160 passengers came down inside the boat, some sat on each other, some were standing.

They kept us down by force for two days where the people cannot breathe, eat or sleep because there was not enough oxygen and there was much smoke of engine. Many people fainted. Each who fainted was taken to upside of the boat like a dead body then Navy people poured water on his face or injected him to become conscious and after he was conscious threw him down in the same tight and smelly place.[68]

Two days later, the asylum seekers were told they were almost back in Indonesia and that the families had 10 minutes to get off the *Warramunga* and back on the boat with the single men.

One of the men who was on the boat told *Four Corners*:

Really, my heart is broken. Then he repeated again, 'Tell the people you have nine minutes.' All the ladies and children cries. Really, I also cried. He announced eight minutes. He announced six minutes. He announced four minutes. Three minutes. Two minutes.[69]

Asylum seekers reported that the families were beaten to force them from the *Warramunga*.[70] One man told *Four Corners*:

When they bring me back to our boat, when I reached there, there was a soldier. Really, he's crying. I was also crying at that time.[71]

Another man said:

By observing this scene some of the Navy people were weeping, one even hit his head to the wall of the boat. Then they broke the engine of the boat, took the oil and generator so we cannot go back to Australia and went by speed boat to the Navy ship which had brought the families, and sailed away.[72]

They were rescued by Indonesian fishermen and taken to the island of Lombok, where 45 of them remained five years later.[73]

SIEV 6

The SIEV 6 sank after being intercepted by HMAS *Arunta* north of Christmas Island on 19 October 2001. A man who was on the SIEV 6 told the inquiry:

It was extremely stormy and every time we thought that the wave could come and kill us. We thought we would die. So with all those difficulties, we see the light and then we see Christmas Island, and every single one starts thanking God and sending their prayers and appreciating that they got to the safe place and everyone was, you should have seen them – we were extremely happy.

And then two or three Australian Navy boats approached us and they break the bad news to us that the Australian government was not allowing any refugees into their land any more. Everyone lost hope completely. They decided to come inside and they found about six individuals who had lost their energy completely. They were fainting, as in they were nearly dying, including my own wife. They were not even able to speak.

They knew that we had nowhere else to go and we didn't have the energy or the methods to go back. They kept us for about four days on that small boat which was broken, which had a hole and people were actually sitting in the corners of the boat because the other areas were completely covered by water.

After about four days they took women and children only. Single men and married men were left in this broken boat by themselves and they said, 'We are going to take you to international waters and then you can go wherever you like.' The wives were pleading, crying and begging them – that's how it is when you are so desperate. You are holding someone's feet and begging for their mercy and that's what our wives were doing, yet they were kicking them and telling them, 'We have to take these people to international waters.' 'You would kill them,' that's the word the women used. 'You would kill them.'

So this big boat was trying to take us to international waters and we travelled for about nine hours. And the hole in that boat became even bigger and the boat nearly drowned. They realised that these people are in desperate need and they allowed them to get into the big boat and join their families.

When the small boat was completely drowned, again they were happy and they were praying and they said, 'They are going to allow us to their country.' We spent another 10 or 12 days on water. They finally came and said, 'We can take you to Christmas Island but we are not going to accept you. We will not allow you stay in Australia, we will take you there only temporarily until the government decides about you.'

The occupants of the boat were eventually taken to Nauru for processing.

SIEV 7

Under Relex, SIEVs 5, 7, 11 and 12 were forced back to Indonesia. On 22 October 2001, the SIEV 7, carrying 215 men, women and children, was intercepted by the HMAS *Bunbury* and escorted to Ashmore Lagoon. They were held for almost a week under open skies without being able to bathe, and many developed conjunctivitis and irritated skin.[74] On October 28, the same day John Howard launched his 2001 election campaign, declaring 'We will decide who comes to this country and the circumstances in which they come',[75] HMAS *Arunta* arrived to escort the boat back to Indonesia. When told they would be returned, some people jumped overboard while others doused themselves with fuel and damaged the boat.[76]

Fearing they would be overpowered, naval personnel used batons and capsicum spray on the asylum seekers. One asylum seeker later interviewed by *Human Rights Watch* reported seeing two naval personnel crying:

I asked them why they were crying, and they said, 'We are also human, but we can't do anything because these are orders from our superiors.'[77]

After the *Arunta* and its boarding party had left, the SIEV 7 ran aground in the dark about 300ms from Rote Island in Indonesia. Many people could not swim, but as the water was not too deep, those who could carried others and children ashore. Some people reported not being able to see clearly due to the combined effect of capsicum spray and conjunctivitis. The next day, three men could not be found. Other asylum seekers did not see Hussein Yahia, Thamer Hussein or Haithem Dawood after the *Arunta* left. One man told the ABC's *Four Corners* program others on board thought they had died:

I don't think they reached the island. The boat was in a horrible situation. Even you can't leave animals on this boat, not people or children or women. This is a kind of genocide. You are killing all these people when you leave them in this condition, in this sea.[78]

SIEV X

On 19 October 2001, despite the Relex surveillance, 146 children, 142 women and 65 men drowned when the SIEV X sank after it left Indonesia. Originally nominated the SIEV 8, this number was later transferred to another boat which did arrive in Australian waters. The Navy learned about the sinking of the SIEV X on 23 October, but had received intelligence about the boat on 14, 18, 20 and 22 October. On 18 October, the minutes of the prime minister's People Smuggling Task Force recorded in relation to two expected boats of asylum seekers:

Some risk of vessels in poor condition and rescue at sea. No confirmed sightings by Coastwatch, but multisource information with high confidence level.[79]

At 10am on 20 October the head of Coastwatch passed on a warning to Defence from an Australian Federal Police (AFP) officer in Indonesia. He warned that the SIEV X was grossly overloaded and in grave danger of sinking.[80] La Trobe University academic Robert Manne has argued:

It is highly unlikely, although not impossible, that if aircraft had been sent to survey the waters south of Java on the morning of October 20, any lives could have been saved. Yet it is also clear that on the morning of October 20, at a time when the government had learnt from an entirely reliable Australian source that 400 asylum seekers were in deadly peril, and at a time when no-one knew whether or not they were still alive, no decision was taken to issue a warning or to mount a search and rescue operation of any kind.[81]

On 22 October, the prime minister's People Smuggling Task Force minutes stated in relation to the SIEV X:

Not spotted yet, missing, grossly overloaded, no jetsam spotted, no reports from relatives.[82]

Some of the 44 survivors rescued by Indonesian fishermen say they saw large boats nearby as they floated in the water praying to be rescued.[83] One survivor gave the following account:

I boarded the boat with 15 other members of my family. Nine drowned and six survived. We clung on to a wooden plank for 20 hours, drifting in the water. Something I witnessed left a very strong impression: a baby with its umbilical cord still attached to the mother was amongst those who drowned. There were 150 children on board – only four are still alive.[84]

Former diplomat Tony Kevin, author of *A Certain Maritime Incident: the sinking of SIEV X*,[85] told the inquiry that the Australian government had admitted that it ran a people-smuggling disruption program in Indonesia during 2000–01. It comprised 10 AFP members and five Department of Immigration members. The then immigration minister, Philip Ruddock, met with the members of the disruption program in Jakarta on 13 June 2001. Drawing on the work of David Marr and Marian Wilkinson,[86] Labor Senator John Faulkner said:

Mr Ruddock allegedly asked in a joking tone, 'Well could we interfere with the boats?' Apparently in response, federal agent Dixon reminded Mr Ruddock of obligations under Australian law. The conversation ended when Ruddock laughed the matter off and said it was just a concept in the air.

Senator Faulkner added:

> *Commissioner Keelty has confirmed that AFP Officer Leigh Dixon,*
> *who was present at the June 2001 meeting, discussed this matter with*
> *his superiors ... According to the government's People Smuggling*
> *Task Force notes on the 12 October, just a week before SIEV X sank,*
> *the taskforce discussed ways of 'beefing up' disruption activity in*
> *Indonesia.*[87]

In evidence to the Senate Select Committee on A Certain Maritime
Incident, AFP commissioner Mick Keelty explained that the AFP had
provided training to Indonesian police in disrupting the people-smuggling
trade. He said:

> *The AFP, in tasking the [Indonesian National Police] to do anything*
> *that would disrupt the movement of people-smugglers has never asked,*
> *nor would it ask, them to do anything illegal. The difficulty is once we*
> *ask them to do it, we have to largely leave it in their hands as how they*
> *best do it.*[88]

When questioned as to whether the fuel and food supplies of boats had
been targeted, if sugar had been put in a fuel tank or sand in an engine,
Keelty stated:

> *I have no knowledge at all of these things occurring, but it is like*
> *anything else I have no knowledge about: I cannot deny that it exists.*[89]

In February 2002, Channel Nine's *Sunday* program aired an interview
with Australian Kevin Enniss. In September that year, Labor Senator John
Faulkner stated in parliament:

> *We know from the* Sunday *program and from evidence given by the*
> *AFP that an Australian by the name of Kevin Enniss was involved in the*
> *people-smuggling disruption program. We know that Enniss worked*
> *for the AFP and that he was paid over $25,000 by the AFP. We know*
> *Kevin Enniss admitted to reporter Ross Coulthart from the* Sunday
> *program that he had paid Indonesian locals on four or five occasions to*
> *scuttle people-smuggling boats with passengers aboard ... How far does*
> *disruption go? What are the limits, if any? ... precisely what disruption*

activities are undertaken at the behest of, with the knowledge of or broadly authorised by the Australian government? I want to know … what directions or authorisations ministers have issued in relation to disruption.[90]

Two months later Faulkner asked Keelty at a Senate estimates hearing if tracking or listening devices were used as part of the disruption program.[91] Keelty initially replied:

… we would not have been involved in listening devices because I do not think it is permitted under the legislation.[92]

He then refused several times to clarify to Faulkner whether he had personal knowledge of any practice to place tracking devices on asylum seeker boats, saying he would take the question on notice. Faulkner stated:

Given that my question is whether the commissioner has a general awareness of this matter – that is, whether tracking devices have been placed on suspected illegal-entry vessels – I am not sure how much this will be able to be advanced since I am asking the commissioner a question about his own awareness. How that can be referred to other people I am not sure …[93]

The following day, Keelty sent a letter to the Senate committee saying that he had decided to claim 'public interest immunity' in refusing to answer Faulkner's questions:[94]

The questions call for an answer which may disclose lawful methods for detecting, investigating or dealing with matters arising out of breaches of the law. The disclosure of [this] would, or would be reasonably likely, to prejudice the effectiveness of those methods.[95]

The SIEV X voyage was organised by Abu Quassey, who in December 2003 was found guilty by an Egyptian court of charges including causing death through negligence of those who boarded the SIEV X.[96] Abu Quassey operated over 1000km from Kupang, the base of Kevin Enniss. However, Faulkner and others have questioned whether disruption activities were directed against Abu Quassey and if they involved the SIEV X:

Before SIEV X departed it was very low in the water and horribly overcrowded, carrying four times the number of passengers a vessel of its size should carry. About 30 Indonesian police were present. They beat some of the passengers and forced asylum seekers to board at gunpoint. The police appeared to be actively involved in the people-smuggling operation.[97]

Tony Kevin told the inquiry:

It has never been made clear how the Jakarta embassy sourced the detailed information it reported by its cable on 23 October 2001 (and Department of Immigration, Multicultural and Indigenous Affairs [DIMIA] officers at the embassy also reported on some of this in separate emails on that day), about the boat's exact dimensions, construction, passenger land itinerary in Indonesia, and passenger statistical details of nationality, age, gender. Such detailed numerical and technical information cannot credibly have come, as was claimed, from talking to one or two SIEV X survivors. It had to have come from a source close to Abu Quassey's people-smuggling organisation.

It is a gross human-rights abuse that the names of those who embarked on SIEV X are still being withheld from public knowledge. There are possibly hundreds of bereaved men in Australia who lost wives, children and other family members on SIEV X, but who still cannot get the psychological closure of official confirmation that their relatives were on the boat. I believe the reason the AFP and DIMIA will not release these lists is because it would raise embarrassing questions for them to explain how they came into possession of such detailed passenger information.

On 27 February 2003, Greens Senator Bob Brown asked Senator Chris Ellison, the minister for justice and customs, whether the AFP knew the names of those who died when the SIEV X sank. He replied:

A list was provided to the AFP from a confidential source after the vessel sank. Provision of any details of that list would compromise that source. It may also compromise a current ongoing investigation in Indonesia. The list purports to contain some details of passengers, but its veracity has not been tested.[98]

Like many of the women who boarded the SIEV X, Iraqi Sondos Ismail had travelled with her three daughters, Eeman, eight, Fatima, seven, and Zahra, six, to join her husband, Ahmed Alzalimi, in Australia. He had been recognised as a refugee but granted a three-year Temporary Protection Visa which did not allow him to re-enter Australia if he travelled to see his family, or to sponsor them to join him in Australia. Sondos survived, but their three daughters drowned, Ahmed learning what had happened after seeing a picture of his distraught wife in a newspaper.[99] John Howard told the National Press Club:

> Like any human being, I was very touched by that tragedy ... and that poor man who lost his three daughters.[100]

However, it was reported in *The Age*:

> John Howard would not brook any bending of the Temporary Protection Visa rules to allow Ahmed to fly to Jakarta and join his wife. Nor would Canberra expedite a visa to allow Sondos to come to Australia. A cowed Labor Party said nothing. It was five months before Sondos and her husband were reunited. They have a new baby daughter but each evening Sondos still makes beds for the three children she has lost.[101]

The day the sinking of the SIEV X became public, ALP leader Kim Beazley told ABC Radio the tragedy was caused by an evil trade:

> We've supported Howard on every proposition he's put forward that deals with that evil trade. And still they come. In some instances that means they sink offshore and die. In other instances it means they come into our area and give considerable trouble, of course, to our officials in handling them.[102]

The SIEV X memorial, coordinated by Steve Biddulph, was erected in Canberra in late 2007. Designed by a Brisbane schoolboy, Mitchell Donaldson, and involving thousands of schoolchildren, church members and community groups, it consists of 353 poles, one for each person who drowned, large for adults and small for children. A plaque there reads in part, 'Love is stronger than fear. Kindness is stronger than greed.'

SIEVs 8 and 9

On 27 October 2001, 31 Vietnamese asylum seekers were intercepted on the SIEV-8 and four days later 155 people on the SIEV-9 reached Ashmore Reef.

Two weeks later, days before the federal election, and in the wake of the 11 September attacks on the World Trade Centre in New York, John Howard drew links between asylum seekers and terrorists, telling a press conference:

> *I choose my language carefully ... I am not saying that in particular cases people on these boats are terrorists or have terrorist links ... What I am saying is that I have no way and unless you have a proper processing system nobody has any way of determining whether or not they are.*[103]

The same day, Labor Party leader Kim Beazley supported the government's harsh policies, and endorsed its falsehood that seeking asylum in Australia is illegal, saying:

> *I don't think it's unhumanitarian to try and keep control of your refugee program. I don't think it's unhumanitarian to try to deter criminals.*[104]

SIEV 10

On 8 November 2001, the SIEV 10 caught fire during its interception by the Australian Navy 24 miles off Christmas Island and everyone on the boat was forced into the water. Two women, 55-year-old Nurjan Hussaini and 20-year-old Fatima Husseini, drowned. A refugee advocate told the inquiry:

> *One was a grandmother and the other one was a young woman, pregnant with her first child. I have witnesses who say that she was frightened of jumping into the water, she was terrified. She and her husband stood and held hands and then finally jumped together. When they hit the water they were separated and she was subsequently found not breathing. She was taken on board the naval vessel where they attempted to resuscitate her unsuccessfully and a day later her husband was shown her body and she was later buried on Christmas Island.*

Afghan asylum seeker Ali Mullaie told reporter Michael Gordon he was with Fatima's husband when he was told she had drowned:

> They wept together and Mullaie remembers an Australian sailor retreating to the upper deck where he, too, broke down, consumed by the tragedy, hiding his tears behind his cap. [105]

Nurjan Hussaini's son, who had travelled with her, his wife and five children, told the inquiry:

> When these two other boats saw us, they started coming close to our boat and they were circling around the boat. Our boat decided to speed up and these two boats were travelling on the sides and I just believed that our boat was travelling as fast as it could, and then all of a sudden we realised that there was a strong fume and then all the boat area was full of smoke.
>
> We had to go on deck to get some fresh air and then we realised that due to too much pressure on the engine, the boat was on fire. People didn't know what to do. Everyone was just completely fearful. I managed to take my youngest daughter, who was six years of age, and jumped in the water with her and she was in very, very bad shape. She had difficulty breathing and she was nearly, nearly fainting.
>
> Her older brother managed to hold her and my younger son jumped into the water with my wife and my mother jumped, either by herself or by another individual. I was completely fearful. You couldn't even hear anyone because the waves were so strong and everyone was screaming.
>
> This other man was trying to save my mother. Her upper body was on top of the water and her head was underneath. I managed to scream out loud asking my son to go and drag the feet under the water so her head can come above the water.
>
> I kept floating or swimming for approximately one hour. The boats were right there but they could not do anything because according to them they were basically waiting for the orders to be received. It was nearly dark, at the dark they received their orders and they decided to save us. At that time I saw my wife only I didn't see anyone else.
>
> The boats came and took as many people as they could and I was very distressed, extremely worried about my family, and I was asking them what happened to my family. They kept assuring me that they are fine and they were on the other boat. Then I realised that there was

a young woman who had died. My wife and I didn't know anything about our other children and she was crying continuously and asking the officers to find some information about them.

They managed to bring the husband of the woman who had died. He told us that your mother has unfortunately passed away, but your children are in the other boat. I was devastated. I screamed, I cried, I was very, very sad but I couldn't do anything and I had to wait till they brought us all together and I had my son and daughter with me.

As soon as we get into the big boat straight away my wife was running towards them. She started hugging them and crying with them. I asked the authority to show me my mother's body and they just show the body from a distance. They said you can have a look when we get to Christmas Island.

The authorities on Christmas Island told me that we should give us our consent regarding your mother's burial ceremony. They said we've got an Islamic cemetery and if you give your consent we are more than happy to bury her in that particular place and I had no other choice so I give them my consent. They took my mother and the other woman to the same cemetery and they were buried there.

I remember having a phone call from the other woman's husband telling me that he was about to go and pay a visit and respect for his wife's grave and he wanted me to go with him. I said I would have loved to do that but it would have cost me at least $4000 or $5000. At the moment unfortunately I can't do that.

A refugee advocate told the inquiry:

There is another fellow and he was on the same boat. He had a two-year-old in one hand and a three-year-old in his other hand, and he had already roped the other family members onto a container to have them float and the little bloke was swamped and had oxygen for a long time and brought him back to life but he has got damage. He is now five or six years old and he has got damage. He said, 'and the boat was there' and then one hour later they still hadn't picked them up and given oxygen.

Despite his intense involvement in Relex, Prime Minister John Howard was vague when announcing the deaths:

By the face of it, it's been quite an unpleasant incident. Quite an unpleasant incident involving children. Er, there may have been a couple of fatalities. Er, I've been told that the vessel was deliberately lit.[106]

The asylum seekers from SIEV 10 were eventually taken to Nauru for processing.

Two days after Nurjan Hussaini and Fatima Husseini drowned, on 10 November 2001, John Howard's Liberal government strode to victory in an election it had looked set to lose before the *Tampa* incident, and during the campaign for which the prime minister had repeatedly stated: 'We will decide who comes to this country and the circumstances in which they come.'[107]

Naval Dissent

But there was far from universal support for the government's actions against asylum seekers within defence ranks. Within weeks of Relex beginning, Commodore Warwick Gately had raised concerns about its potential to contravene the *International Convention for the Safety of Life at Sea*, which requires the Navy to assist any person in danger of drowning and bring them to the nearest port. *The Age* reported that Gately told then defence minister Peter Reith that while the actions of Navy commanders who had transported asylum seekers to safety 'have been questioned', they had acted correctly.[108]

On the day Nurjan Hussaini and Fatima Husseini drowned, Michael O'Connor, executive director of the Australia Defence Association, said that some naval personnel were demoralised by their new role. He said that forcing asylum seekers back into their boats was contrary to their personal training, naval tradition and 'their normal humanitarian instincts'.

They did not join the Navy to man prison ships ... Despite government propaganda that the asylum seekers transported to Nauru and elsewhere were not imprisoned, the sailors know otherwise ... To see the typical asylum seeker as a threat who must not be allowed to land on Australian soil is stretching credulity for the sailors who actually deal with them.[109]

Dr Hugh Smith argued that while military personnel are trained to make difficult life-and-death decisions, these are usually in response to enemy action, rather than the policy of their own government:

Military personnel served as maritime jailers for asylum seekers, sometimes deceiving them as to their final destination, sometimes making promises that could not be kept, sometimes compelling them to go ashore against their wishes.[110]

John Howard acknowledged morale problems amongst naval personnel involved in Relex, stating:

I recognise that this is not easy work, it's not pleasant work. The alternative, of course, is that we send a signal to the world that it's open season for illegal immigrants who come to this country.[111]

But Operation Relex so demoralised some naval personnel that they pretended to be ill or left the defence force rather than participate. Defence documents revealed many faced 'confronting personal dilemmas' in carrying out government orders to detain or turn away asylum seeker boats and many felt they were 'not doing the job they joined up to do'. In addition, in the two months before the 2001 federal election, personnel involved in Relex were banned from sending personal emails to their families – a restriction not even imposed during war.[112] In November 2002, Brigadier Mike Silverstone wrote:

This has the potential for degraded morale which may have serious consequences for retention.[113]

A former SAS officer told the inquiry that his involvement in Relex contributed to his decision to leave:

One minute we were deployed to stop alleged Afghan refugees from coming ashore in Australia, eight weeks later we were in Afghanistan to save people from the Taliban. It progressively eroded my faith in the system.

A senior officer on the *Tobruk* told *The Australian* on election day about his perceptions of transporting asylum seekers from Australian territory:

In the middle of the night I looked down from the bridge. There's two hatches open and it's hot. Through one I could see 100 people lying there on stretchers; I thought, it's like a slave ship. I thought, Jesus, I

*thought we were Australians, I thought we were a great, good bloody
country. On board they don't like to use the word 'prisoners' but they
are. At Ashmore Reef it hit me, shit we're going like South Africa. If
Australia continues down this political path, it will be like apartheid
here and people will think that's what we do here but it's not what we
should do.*[114]

Navy psychiatrist Dr Duncan Wallace spent 30 days at sea on board HMAS
Arunta during Relex in October 2001 and described the actions Navy
personnel were ordered to carry out as morally wrong and despicable. He
wrote a letter to some newspapers saying:

*I participated in the boarding, attempted removal and actual forced
removal of suspected illegal immigrant vessels to Indonesia. Nearly
everyone I spoke to that was involved in these operations knew that
what they were doing was wrong. These actions are ineffective in
deterring boat people in coming to Australia and merely serve to harass,
frighten and demoralise people who are already weak, vulnerable and
desperate ... The hard-hearted who speak loudly about the need for
stern deterrent actions to solve this problem have not seen the faces of
the boat people in their miserable conditions, imploring us for help.*[115]

Stranded in Indonesia

Hundreds of asylum seekers spent years stranded in Indonesia following
Operation Relex's disruption of the people-smuggling trade there, with
Australia paying nearly $3 million a year for Indonesia to accommodate
them. Some had been returned by the Australian Navy, some had had their
money taken by smugglers and could not pay for further passage and some
were unwilling to risk the journey after the sinking of the SIEV X.[116]

There were also other boats, including the one Iraqi Mugdad Saber, his
wife, Rabab, and twin daughters, Megat and Ayat, boarded. Twelve hours
into their journey to Australia, the rickety boat hit a reef. Children who had
been placed in a canoe provided by their Indonesian rescuers panicked and
overturned it. Ayat, then three years old, died. Her father told *The Age*:

*I rescued some other children, but nobody rescued my child. We cannot
forgive ourselves; the cause of her death is us. We chose this way and
she died. We chose this way to build a future for our family, but we paid*

with the life of our child. I have never been able to forget it, every day and every night until now. I miss her very much, every time I look at her sister I see her.[117]

Asylum seekers stranded in Indonesia were unable to work and their children could not attend schools. In February 2006, one man stated:

We lost our hope, our family, friends, relatives and our own life ... We are Australia's responsibility. We came to Australia and asked for asylum and Australia knows this because it pays International Organisation for Migration to provide us with food and shelter ... We do not know how long we will remain here and this causes tension in every individual's mind.[118]

A woman who visited Afghan asylum seekers in Indonesia told the inquiry she and two other grandmothers were questioned by police and International Organisation for Migration officers and were escorted back to their hotel room. Refugee advocate Sue Hoffman, who visited Iraqi asylum seekers in Indonesia, told the inquiry that they missed children they had left behind and worried about the future of the children with them:

Visiting them was reminiscent of visiting detention centres without the guards and in pleasanter surroundings; the sense of hopelessness, powerlessness, injustice, waste, despair.

One man told her:

If Australia punish us, now finish the punishment, six years enough.

In May 2007, following pleas from the United Nations High Commissioner for Refugees, Australia agreed to resettle 120 asylum seekers, including Mugdad Saber and his family, half the total number that had spent more than five years in Indonesia,[119] most of whom have family in Australia. As at 9 October 2007, just 31 of these 120 people had arrived in Australia, the remainder being in the process of having health and security checks completed.

They were initially granted only Temporary Humanitarian Visas, which do not allow for settlement services, family reunion or right of re-entry if people travel overseas to see other family members.

Part 2

PROCESSING OF REFUGEE CLAIMS

People can enter Australia as one of the roughly 13,000 refugees Australia accepts each year[120] in four ways. The first way is that people who are assessed and recognised as refugees while outside Australia can be brought here under the humanitarian program. They are given permanent residence and provided with full settlement services including social security, education, family reunion, work, language training and re-entry to Australia if they travel overseas. They are referred to as 'offshore applicants'.

The second way refugees can enter Australia is by arriving with a valid visa, such as a student or visitor visa, and then applying to be recognised as a refugee. People in this situation make up the vast majority of asylum seekers in Australia. They remain in the community while their claim is being processed and if they lodge their protection application within 45 days of arrival, they are allowed to work and receive income support and Medicare. If successful, they are granted a permanent protection visa.

The third way refugees can enter Australia is by arriving by sea or air in the Australian migration zone without a valid visa and then applying for asylum. People in this situation are automatically taken into immigration detention and remain there until they are either granted a visa or leave Australia. A much higher percentage of them are granted refugee visas than people who arrive with a valid visa. Betweeen 1999 and 2008 if they were recognised as refugees they were granted a Temporary Protection Visa valid for only three years.[121]

The final way refugees can enter Australia is by arriving on Australian territory excised from the migration zone, or being intercepted at sea by Australian authorities, taken to an offshore detention centre and being found to be a refugee. In this case, they may be accepted by Australia.

Mandatory Detention

The bulk of the evidence received by the People's Inquiry concerns asylum seekers who arrived in Australia by boat between 1999 and 2002 and were subject to mandatory detention. Under Australian law, anyone 'reasonably suspected' of being an 'illegal noncitizen' must be detained until they are either granted a visa or leave the country. There are no time limits on the period of detention and it is not subject to judicial review, despite people in detention having committed no crime. It is not an offence to be present in Australia without a valid visa.

In 2002, the UN Working Group on Arbitrary Detention reported that 'a system combining mandatory, automatic, indiscriminate and indefinite detention without real access to court challenge is not practiced by any other country in the world.'[122] The UN Human Rights Committee has criticised mandatory detention in its review of Australia's regular reports under the International Covenant on Civil and Political Rights (ICCPR) and in individual complaints made against the Australian government.

Mandatory detention contravenes a number of international conventions which relate to asylum seekers and to which Australia is a signatory. Numerous Australian and international reports have criticised both the indefinite, non-reviewable incarceration of people who have committed no crime, and the conditions inside Australia's detention centres. In 2005, Amnesty International concluded that mandatory detention placed Australia in breach of the International Covenant on Civil and Political Rights, the Universal Declaration of Human Rights, the Convention relating to the Status of Refugees (Refugees Convention) and the Convention on the Rights of the Child.[123]

Other reports critical of Australia's immigration detention regime include those by the Human Rights and Equal Opportunity Commission (HREOC),[124] former Australian diplomat Philip Flood,[125] the United Nations Working Group on Arbitrary Detention[126] and the Commonwealth ombudsman.[127] In 2002, after inspecting Australian detention centres, the head of the UN Working Group on Arbitrary Detention, Louis Joinet, declared he had not seen a more gross abuse of human rights in over 40 inspections of detention facilities around the world.[128]

In August 2000, the United Nations encouraged states to adopt alternatives to detention of asylum seekers in line with UNHCR (United Nations High Commissioner for Refugees) guidelines.[129] These guidelines argue that the detention of asylum seekers is 'inherently undesirable' and assert the general principle that asylum seekers should not be detained. They argue that the circumstances of asylum seekers differ fundamentally from ordinary immigrants in that they are not able to comply with legal formalities for entry and have often suffered trauma. The guidelines also argue that any detention should be for a minimal period, subject to review, should only take place after a full consideration of all possible alternatives and be reasonable and proportional to the objectives to be achieved.[130]

Progressive Tightening of Refugee Law

Immigration detention was introduced by the Labor government for people who had entered Australia fraudulently or overstayed their visa. Initially they could only be held for 48 hours and then for seven-day periods authorised by a magistrate. Migration agent Marion Le told the inquiry:

> I'm proud I'm on the record as saying right from day one that we should not be opening a detention centre at Port Hedland. To my horror at that time the Refugee Council of Australia went along with that and went up and inspected the place. The Catholic Church did the same and I felt very much I was a lone voice. I do think the fact that the detention centre was in Port Hedland, most of the people were out of sight, out of mind. The detention regime started small and then because not enough people spoke out, it advanced, it went on.

At that time, people seeking asylum who arrived without a valid visa were deemed not to have entered Australia and were held in open areas of migration centres, which they were not allowed to leave.[131]

Between November 1989 and January 1992, 438 Vietnamese, Cambodian and Chinese asylum seekers arrived in Australia by boat. They came following the settlement of 70,000 mostly Vietnamese refugees between 1976 and 1985, the vast majority of whom arrived through family migration after their relatives had come by boat.[132] They also came in the wake of a debate about Asian immigration, to which John Howard had contributed:

> I do believe that if it is – in the eyes of some in the community – that it's too great, it would be in our immediate-term interest and supporting of social cohesion if it were slowed down a little, so the capacity of the community to absorb it was greater.[133]

In 1992, the Federal Court of Australia ordered that the Immigration Department's rejection of 15 Cambodian asylum seekers be set aside. They had been held in detention for almost three years and had applied to the Federal Court to be released. Two days before their case was to be heard, the then Labor government introduced legislation stripping the courts of power to order the release of asylum seekers. Immigration minister Gerry Hand stated in parliament:

> The most important aspect of this legislation is that it provides that a court cannot interfere with the period of custody.[134]

The legislation also introduced mandatory detention, attempting to retrospectively legalise the detention of the people who had arrived by boat since 19 November 1989.[135] A High Court challenge to the legislation[136] found that the detention of the asylum seekers before its introduction was unlawful. In attempting to justify this previous detention, the Labor government relied on Section 88 of the *Migration Act 1958*, which provided for the temporary detention of stowaways until the boat on which they arrived left the country. Justice Mason outlined the government's argument:

> *The explanation for the purported pursuance of s88 is that the vessels on which the plaintiffs arrived will never be leaving Australia. They were, the court was informed, burned. The view was apparently taken by the minister's department that, in a case where a vessel can never leave because it has been destroyed, temporary custody under s88 ... can continue indefinitely.*[137]

Following acknowledgement that asylum seekers could have been detained illegally, the government legislated to cap compensation at $1 per day of wrongful detention.[138]

The *Migration Amendment Act 1992* also imposed a 273-day time limit on detention. Gerry Hand described it as 'an interim measure' aimed at addressing 'only the pressing requirements of the current situation.'[139]

> *The government is determined that a clear signal be sent that migration to Australia may not be achieved by simply arriving in this country and expecting to be allowed into the community.*[140]

Three months later, the Joint Standing Committee on Migration, with the sole exception of Labor Senator Barney Cooney, recommended the continuation of mandatory detention.[141] In 1994, mandatory detention was broadened to include everyone who arrived without a valid visa or who overstayed their visa and the time limit on detention was removed, despite arguments from Senator Barney Cooney and Greens Senator Christabel Chamarette.

The law was also changed to reduce the number of refugees Australia accepted. Previously a family application had been counted as an application for just one of the 12,000 places granted each year.[142] From 1995, each person included in a refugee application was counted as making an individual application for one of the 12,000 places.

In 1996, the new Liberal government further restricted the refugee intake by linking the offshore and onshore refugee programs. Previously the offshore program had allowed about 12,000 refugees to settle here and any successful onshore applications were additional to the offshore grants. From 1996, successful onshore applications offset places offered to offshore applicants. The government then used its own policy change to argue that people who applied for asylum in Australia and were found to have a well-founded fear of persecution were responsible for displacing 'those in the greatest relative need of resettlement.'[143]

Former immigration minister Philip Ruddock told *The Weekend Australian* in 2007:

> For me, the sight of refugees from the Horn of Africa languishing in the Kakuma camp in northern Kenya without hope of resettlement was disturbing. They were forfeiting [asylum] places to those with money who could pay people-smugglers, and that always loomed large in my consciousness.[144]

In 1997, the Liberal government, supported by the Labor opposition, introduced the '45 day rule'. This required onshore asylum seekers who arrived with a valid visa to lodge a protection visa application within 45 days of arrival or lose their right to work and Medicare benefits while their claim was being processed. The next year, legislation prevented HREOC from offering legal assistance or advice to people in immigration detention unless a detainee made a specific request.

In 1998, One Nation MP Pauline Hanson, whose maiden speech to parliament called for policies 'restricting immigration, disavowing multiculturalism and dissolving the Aboriginal and Torres Strait Islander Commission',[145] proposed asylum seekers should be granted only temporary visas. Immigration minister Philip Ruddock told parliament that the government would not consider the idea as it would cause too much uncertainty in people's lives:

> Can you imagine what temporary entry would mean for them? It would mean that people would never know whether they were able to remain here. There would be uncertainty, particularly in terms of the attention given to learning English, and in addressing the torture and trauma so they are healed from some of the tremendous physical and

psychological wounds they have suffered. So, I regard One Nation's approach as being highly unconscionable in a way that most thinking people would clearly reject.[146]

In June 1998, One Nation won 23 per cent of the primary vote in the Queensland state election, causing the coalition to lose its majority in the state parliament. The following year, Ruddock announced that a three-year Temporary Protection Visa (TPV) would be introduced for people who arrived without a valid visa and were found to be refugees. When the visa expired, they would need to prove their need for ongoing protection.[147]

In 2001, on the second-last sitting day of parliament before the federal election, the government passed legislation aimed at restricting the rights of asylum seekers. It excised from the migration zone islands on which asylum seekers most often landed and declared that the overwhelming majority of asylum seekers, those who had spent more than seven days transiting through another country, could only ever access three-year TPVs unless the immigration minister allowed them to apply for a permanent visa.

Judicial review of decisions by the Refugee Review Tribunal (RRT) was also severely restricted, the legislation stating that RRT decisions were final and conclusive and could not be challenged in court. It specifically disallowed asylum seekers from appealing RRT decisions, even on the basis that they had been denied natural justice or that they were so unreasonable that no reasonable person could have made them.

In April 2003, the Full Court of the Federal Court ordered the release of several detainees who wanted to return to their countries, but whose return the Immigration Department had been unable to facilitate. Two months later, the government introduced new legislation limiting the courts from ordering the release of detainees, and in 2004 the High Court ruled in a four-against-three decision that indefinite detention of asylum seekers is legal in Australia.[148] Refugee lawyer Julian Burnside QC told members of the Council for Civil Liberties:

> *The thought of an innocent person being jailed for the rest of his life is shocking. Anyone, even the most hardened, must find it a dreadful thing to imagine the circumstances of a person being held in detention forever when they have not committed any offence. It should be a matter of real concern that a government ostensibly committed to a 'fair and decent society' is willing to argue for the right to jail the innocent for life.*[149]

In November 2003, after 14 Turkish asylum seekers landed on Melville Island, north of Darwin, the Howard government rushed through regulations retrospectively excising it from the migration zone.[150] The following month, the Full Court of the Federal Court ruled that the government could deport asylum seekers to their home country even if they faced certain torture or death.[151]

The Onshore Refugee Determination Process

The bulk of the evidence presented to the inquiry about the refugee assessment process focused on the process for people who arrived by boat and were held in detention centres. The process for people who arrive with a valid visa and are allowed to remain in the community during it is almost identical.

All onshore applications for refugee status are initially assessed by the Department of Immigration. Asylum seekers must show that they have a well-founded fear of persecution for one of five reasons articulated in the Convention Relating to the Status of Refugees[152] (Refugee Convention) and that their government cannot protect them from this persecution. The five reasons for fear of persecution covered by the Convention are:

- race
- religion
- nationality
- political opinion
- member of a particular social group.[153]

Applicants whose claims are rejected by the Immigration Department can appeal to the RRT. At the RRT a sole member, who is not necessarily a lawyer and is appointed by the immigration minister for five years, hears the appeal. Lawyers or migration agents can only make submissions at the hearing if they are invited to do so by the member. If the member upholds the department's decision to refuse a protection visa, applicants living in the community lose their right to work and to Medicare.

After a negative decision from the RRT, asylum seekers can either appeal to the Federal Court or ask the immigration minister to personally intervene in their case under sections 48B or 417 of the *Migration Act*. Ministerial intervention under section 48B allows the asylum seeker to put in a new application and start the whole process again. Intervention under section 417 allows the immigration minister to grant the person a visa directly. The ministerial discretion to intervene in cases is non-reviewable by the courts. The minister does not even have to consider whether or not to exercise this discretion. During the period the case is under ministerial consideration, asylum seekers in the community are granted a bridging visa which does not allow them to work.

Appealing to the Federal and, later, High Courts is also difficult. Courts are unable to consider the merits of an asylum seeker's claim. The Federal Court can only consider whether the RRT has made an error in law in reaching its conclusion. The High Court can only consider whether the Federal Court has made an error in law. The courts are powerless to grant an appeal even if the RRT has made a factual error (for example finding someone is not from a country they can prove they are from) or if new information has come to light which supports the asylum seeker's case. A former detainee told the inquiry:

> I mention my arrest in the initial interview but RRT, immigration they say I mention my arrest only when I have my second interview. I asked for Freedom of Information. They find a note by the immigration officer that I did mention my arrest, but after four years I can't do anything about that. Because they think I amend the story, was a very critical reason to refusing my asylum application.

OUR HANDS ARE TIED: FLAWS IN THE REFUGEE DETERMINATION PROCESS

The inquiry heard evidence from a wide range of sources about flaws at all levels of the refugee determination process.

Immigration Department

Flaws identified at the initial assessment by the Department of Immigration included: 'screening out' applicants from the process on the strength of a brief initial interview; obstructing asylum seekers' access to legal advisors;

the treatment of unaccompanied minors (UAMs); using interpreters speaking different languages or from ethnic groups traditionally hostile to the claimant; inadequately researching country information; using discredited identification methods such as linguistic analysis; making subjective decisions and being influenced by political considerations.

'Screening Out' Applicants

In theory, protection-visa applicants in detention have access to free legal advice funded by the department's Immigration Advice and Application Assistance Scheme (IAAAS).[154] However asylum seekers in detention are not given access to legal advice until after they have been interviewed by the Immigration Department. Whether or not they are offered IAAAS help depends on whether the immigration officer believes they have raised claims of persecution which may meet the Refugee Convention definition. Those 'screened out' of the process are kept in separate areas of detention centres and denied access to legal advice, telephones, newspapers, TV and mail. A lawyer told the inquiry:

> They had new boat arrivals put separately to any other detainees so that there would be no people able to tell them what they needed to do to access legal advice, what they needed to say for an asylum claim to be officially noted and therefore the process to begin. I think the intention of the department was to keep them isolated until they deported them. It's contrary to the Refugee Convention because what they are doing is playing semantic games.

A former detainee told the inquiry how some detainees obtained legal advice despite their isolation:

> After our first interview the manager of the camp came and said to us that we can't have a visa and we have to go back to our country. He said we could hire a lawyer with our own expense, but nobody had any money or access to telephone, fax or mail. Eventually we started to talk to the people in the main compound who were behind two layers of fences 15 metres away. We had to talk quietly because guards were everywhere. People on the other side who had access to phone told us they know a migration agent. They tied his number on a stone and throwed it to us. Most of us talked to DIMIA [the Department

of Immigration, Multicultural and Indigenous Affairs] about getting a
lawyer. The manager came to us angry that how could we get the phone
number.

In May 2005, HREOC found that separately detaining asylum seekers
breached international human rights law. The only communication asylum
seekers were allowed with the outside world was a standard fax saying:

> *This is to let you know that [I] have arrived safely in Australia and*
> *am being detained in immigration detention. I am currently unable to*
> *telephone or write a letter to you but as soon as I can I will be in touch.*
> *I am in good health and being looked after. Return faxes will not be*
> *accepted.*[155]

Even this limited communication was not an option for most asylum seekers
because their families did not have fax numbers, and they could not write or
phone to obtain alternative numbers so they could send messages to them.

People taken to Manus Island were unable to contact family at all.
Hawraa Alsaai told a magazine it was only when she was transferred to
Australia for medical treatment that her mother was able to telephone
her three brothers in Iraq. When she spoke to them after three and a half
months on Manus Island, she was told she and the other family members
in detention had all been presumed dead and given funerals.[156]

Many refugees told the inquiry they had been held in separate areas of
detention centres for periods of up to 12 months. One former detainee told
the inquiry:

> *My brother straightaway he get an interview and he go to other*
> *compound. When my family ask him about me, he say he is in the other*
> *compound, but my family didn't believe it because they say how you*
> *can ring to us but your brother not? They thinks I am to die and they*
> *start to cry.*

Many of those who were 'screened out' lost contact with their families
who had moved by the time they were able to telephone them. Another
former detainee told the inquiry:

> *When I was in Woomera Detention centre for eight months they did not*
> *let us to contact our family. I lost contact with my wife and my children*

and after two years my wife contact me through one of the priest in
Woomera Detention centre, which was the happiest day for me to know
that they are still alive.

Obstructing Access to Legal Advice

Section 256 of the *Migration Act* requires the Department of Immigration
to afford a detainee all reasonable facilities for taking legal advice. On 14
June 2007, the Howard government response to a Senate committee report
stated:

> *Detainees have access to legal representation on request. Upon arrival*
> *at an Immigration Detention facility people are informed of their right*
> *to receive visits from their legal representatives, their right to contact*
> *them by phone and to receive and send material to them via fax or post.*
> *Facilities, such as interview rooms, are available to support access to*
> *legal representatives. Lawyers are generally given unrestricted access to*
> *their clients in immigration detention.*[157]

However Father Peter Norden, a regular visitor and chaplain to
Maribyrnong detention centre, told the inquiry:

> *There doesn't seem to be any systematic process by which people get*
> *access to legal advice and support, it's largely through word of mouth,*
> *through peer referral. I've struck several individuals who, having been*
> *there for weeks, were unclear that they actually needed legal assistance*
> *and how they would access that legal assistance. It seemed to me to be*
> *the first thing that a federal government authority should present to*
> *people in this situation.*

Lawyers and migration agents told the inquiry that the Immigration
Department had actively obstructed detainees accessing legal services. In a
submission to the inquiry, the Refugee Advocacy Service of South Australia
(RASSA) explained that lawyer Jeremy Moore had to issue proceedings in
the Federal Court to access two clients in Woomera, an application that
was initially opposed by the Immigration Department.

A migration agent told the inquiry one detainee's written requests to
speak to his lawyer were consistently refused:

I've got an example here from one person's file. December 6 – this is in writing to DIMIA – 'I want to make a phone call to my lawyer.' And the response was 'You can send a fax.' On December 11 another written request, 'I need to call my lawyer.' The reply: 'You can send a fax or letter.' Another two months 'I want to speak with my lawyer; I want an appointment to see him.' Again, 'You have to send a fax to him, we can't instruct him to see you or talk to you.' Another two months later, obviously not being able to speak to the lawyer, 'I'd like to talk with DIMIA about my RRT court.' And the response: 'You need to speak with your legal advisor.'

A lawyer told the inquiry that legal representatives trying to contact detainees were often met with the same obstruction:

Sometimes they've asked us to have a particular form which you sign to say I appoint this person as my migration agent. In Curtin they wouldn't let you speak to them unless they had that signed form and they wouldn't pass the form on to them.

RASSA's submission to the inquiry also stated:

RASSA is required to write letters to DIMIA seeking access for a visit several days in advance. If a detainee hears about their visit whilst lawyers are actually there, the person is generally refused access to the lawyers. At times permission has been granted and then cancelled abruptly. Lawyers are not allowed entry into the actual compounds so are not able to access detainees who may be ill.

We are unable to provide legal assistance until they sign an authority for us to act for them. If they are unable to sign an authority, due for instance to their mental illness, detainees may never get assistance. On one occasion DIMIA refused to allow us to use a room at Baxter to obtain an independent psychiatric assessment. On occasions detainees have missed critical deadlines for filing appeals due to delays occasioned by DIMIA in faxing relevant appeal notices.

Even asylum seekers who did get legal advice under the IAAAS did not always receive optimum assistance. Solicitors and migration agents contracted under the scheme had to travel to remote locations and, to save on travel and accommodation costs, minimised the staff sent. IAAAS provider David Manne told a study about unaccompanied minors that lawyers had a meeting with the client where they had to explain the process, who they were and how they had been referred the work. They then had to prepare the protection visa application, all through an interpreter, in about three hours when it should have taken double that amount of time.[158]

Migration Agent Marion Le also expressed concerns about the quality of advice provided to the inquiry:

> There are people who are involved in the IAAAS, who are not, in my opinion, properly trained. I have been in the detention centres when some of those teams have gone in. One of these men came up to me one day with a piece of paper in his hand and said, Can you tell me what this is? They said it's a Taskara, what's a Taskara? It's pretty appalling when these people are sitting in detention and have already been there three or four years and something as basic as the identity document that says that you are an Afghan, the equivalent of a birth certificate, and the person says 'What's a Taskara?'

Treatment of Unaccompanied Minors

Between 1999 and 2002, 248 unaccompanied minors (UAMs) applied for asylum in Australia, including two who were under 12 years old and 32 who were 12 to 14 years old. Seven of them were female. About 20 per cent of them, 47 children, were initially refused a visa.[159] Psychologist Harold Bilboe, who worked at Woomera for 14 months told HREOC:

> I was especially concerned about the level of advice and assistance provided to UAMs in the visa process. This appeared to be inadequate and significant anxiety and confusion was expressed to me by UAMs. From my observations, UAMs did not receive any legal advice or assistance until their second interview with DIMIA, which may not have taken place for six weeks after having been taken into detention. At their first interview, when they were screened in or out of the protection visa system, they were not, to my knowledge, provided with representation by a lawyer or other advocate ... They received legal advice for the second interview, but their contact with the legal advisers was infrequent.[160]

A woman who went to Woomera as a support person with a group of lawyers interviewing detainees told the inquiry:

> *They called me into one of the rooms. There were three children – a 15-year-old girl, her younger brother, who was about 10, and another young boy – who were unaccompanied minors. This girl had broken down, she was hysterical because this was the first group of people that had actually shown any interest in their story. The children had been very isolated and I don't need to tell you what was going on in Woomera at the time. They were terrified about what had happened to them and what was going to happen to them. I spent a couple of hours, so we could hear her story and try to reassure her that somebody would be working on her behalf. When I came away from that very traumatising experience I couldn't get those kids out of my mind. I am a mother with two daughters.*

Interpreting

The inquiry heard evidence that interpreters were often used inappropriately. A refugee told the inquiry:

> *First interview, I said I need Kurdish interpreter and they brought a Syrian interpreter. I said I don't understand you. He said don't worry I will write for you a story, I will fix it up, I understand you. I said I don't think you understand me. After two months I had my second interview. Then I get the Kurdish interpreter and they said to me this is what he said and I said no. They interview me for five hours.*
>
> *After four months they let me go to the third interview and at the third interview they say we don't believe you, because you change your story. I said I didn't change. They said okay we will bring the record. Then they said we cannot find it. I said it is not my fault you could not find it. You let me wait for another month in detention.*
>
> *Then I went to the fourth interview and they got for me same Syrian interpreter. I said I want Kurdish interpreter and they let me wait another three weeks and then they got for me Kurdish girl. And the case officer said I don't know why you are here. When he hear my story he could not believe I was put in detention. What Saddam did to the Kurds everyone knows and I had the torture marks on my body.*

A woman who attended Department of Immigration interviews for permanent residency with people whose TPV had expired told the inquiry:

> *I found sometimes they had the wrong language from the interpreter. Sometimes it might be a Dari speaker when they spoke Farsi, and it made the applicants quite anxious because they weren't sure that what they were saying was being translated and presented accurately.*

A migration agent also told the inquiry that some interpreters did not restrict themselves to interpreting:

> *I caught one interpreter. I asked him some simple question to translate right at the front. And the interpreter went on and on and I said, 'What are you telling him?' He said, 'Oh, I told him not to tell you about the part before the Taliban, only the bit about when the Taliban arrived, the early '90s onwards.' I said, 'You keep out of this, you just tell him to tell me about any abuse, any breach of human rights, any discrimination that he has ever suffered and start with that.' And it quietened him down. But I was wondering if people had not been alert for something like that and whether we never got some of the full stories.*

In September 2004, an article in the *Australian Financial Review* examined another issue with interpreters. Most of the Afghan people seeking asylum in Australia were ethnic Hazaras fleeing persecution from the Taliban, who were overwhelmingly Pashtun. However, due to a lack of Afghan interpreters in Australia, the Afghan interpreters used by the Department of Immigration in assessing refugee claims were almost all Pashtun, raising questions about the impartiality of their interpreting.

Researching

Many people told the inquiry that the research undertaken into asylum seeker claims by the Immigration Department was inadequate. A worker in the department told the inquiry that case officers are required to assess 105 cases per year, the equivalent of one every two days, and that their performance is recorded. This pressure means that most case officers rely on country information from Canberra rather than doing their own research.

A high-school teacher who visited detention centres told the inquiry:

I've become a bit of a bush lawyer. I've written several requests for ministerial intervention which have been successful. I'm not a professional migration agent. Nevertheless I've been able to find that you can often overturn the decision by researching a case properly. It is quite incredible the information you can find to support their case.

Several people told the inquiry that case officers appeared to have little knowledge of the countries about which they were making decisions. A nurse who worked in several detention centres told the inquiry:

Once on a flight back I sat beside a case officer. I had travelled in Afghanistan and Iran so I knew about these countries and this person displayed such incredible ignorance. She didn't even seem to understand which country was next to which and I was fairly alarmed. I thought the people who did those investigations were highly skilled and trained.

Migration Agent Marion Le said:

Most of my detention cases in the last few years have been people who have been rejected, sometimes three or four times. When I called for the files and we read them through, you just see the appalling ignorance of the case officers.

A visitor to detention gave the inquiry a specific example of where a case officer had inadequately assessed country information in relation to one applicant:

Even though the asylum seeker explained that he had fled after a military coup in late December 1999, the DIMIA delegate assessed them on a US Department of State Country Information Document published in March 1999. He quoted it saying, 'Ethnic problems in the Ivory Coast are not a significant issue.'

However after the military coup, Human Rights Watch wrote: 'Elections were marred by political violence, which left over 200 people dead and hundreds wounded. Political leaders exploited ethnic tension to repress opponents and incited hatred and fear among populations which had for decades lived in relative harmony.' Amnesty International said a similar thing. This is what I was able to find on my computer at home in a few minutes.

A refugee advocate gave the inquiry another example:

> *He presented his high-school diploma as part of his identification documents. They mistook that for a university degree and said this person has been to university, therefore his claims of lack of education are incorrect. However it's been quickly verified to be no more than a high-school certificate. They just had no idea what they were talking about.*

Migration Agent Marion Le told the inquiry that even when advocates submitted research to the department on behalf of applicants, it was often not considered:

> *We submitted case after case and six months later we discovered they hadn't even put them on people's files.*

A refugee advocate told the inquiry that incorrect information was also recorded on departmental files:

> *In the case of one detainee, inserted in that file we suddenly find that he had spent time in prison – wrong – and that he had escaped and when he was chased he pulled a knife on those chasing him – absolutely wrong. These things would have been held against him. But if you don't know about them you can't even fight them.*

Linguistic Analysis

In late 2003, the Pakistani government refused Australia access to its identity database, leaving the Immigration Department unable to verify the nationality of asylum seekers claiming to be Afghan but suspected of being Pakistani.[161] Many asylum seekers had little or no documentation with them. A former detainee told the inquiry:

> *The government always expect from our people that they need their birth certificates. Birth certificates are not very common in Afghanistan. The people who live in rural area in Afghanistan, most of them don't have any identification.*

A submission to the inquiry stated that some governments use linguistic testing to assess asylum seeker claims to be of particular nationalities. The assumption behind the testing is that clues to a person's origins can be found in their speech. However, linguists around the world have become increasingly concerned at the way this tool is being used.[162]

The submission described the linguistic testing process in Australia. An immigration employee interviews the asylum seeker, who speaks their first language, with the use of an interpreter. The taped interview is then sent overseas for language analysis. A one- to two-page report makes a determination of nationality based only on the linguistic features of the tape recording.

The submission raised several concerns about the testing process. First, there is no guarantee that the asylum seeker and interpreter will be speaking the same dialect, so the asylum seeker may accommodate their own speech to the interpreter's dialect. This concern was shown to be well-founded when a 2003 study by five linguists found Australian cases in which interpreters who spoke different dialects to the applicant had been used.[163]

Second, most analysts are native speakers and not trained specifically in linguistics. Third, some reports make clearly false assertions:

> An example of an erroneous assertion is the claim found in a number of Australian cases that 'Urdu is not spoken in Afghanistan' and thus the use of a few Urdu words is part of the argument that the speaker is not from Afghanistan. The reports appear to ignore the possible effects on an asylum seeker's linguistic repertoire of movement of people between countries with porous borders ... The problematic assumption that an asylum seeker will speak only one language 'uncontaminated' by words or accent from another language is strongly rooted in ideology that sees an individual as 'normally' monolingual.[164]

Fourth, while linguistic features of an individual's speech may reflect a region of socialisation, this has no necessary connection to their country of socialisation, nationality or citizenship.

However Diana Goldrick, former Department of Immigration onshore protection manager NSW, told the inquiry that senior management encouraged the use of linguistic analysis:

> A senior [Immigration Department] officer discovered that one case officer was not using the linguistic reports as part of the evidence in

coming to her decisions. Having obtained excellent overseas linguistic advice, she decided that the method used by so-called overseas experts employed by DIMIA in identifying the nationality of an applicant from a short tape-recording of their interview was unreliable. DIMIA was paying an enormous amount of money to have these very short tapes of interview sent to Scandinavian countries for assessment. I heard this senior officer trying to engage her in an argument and aggressively trying to convince her to accept the linguistic experts' advice as she sat at her workstation typing up a decision. I left my office and stood by her side in order to deflect his attention and suggested he take up the issue with me as her manager rather than directly with the case officer.

In early 2003, five linguists wrote a report to the federal government outlining their concerns about the process. They had found about 120 RRT cases (from the 20 per cent of all its cases that the RRT publishes on the internet) where language analysis was part of a reason for the Immigration Department refusing a refugee claim. It cited examples:

On the basis of one applicant using some 'typical' Pakistani words and Iranian words, it was determined that he lived some time in these countries. Another applicant was deemed to come from Pakistan on the basis of his use of one Urdu word, one Iranian word, and two words spoken with an Urdu accent.[165]

The report concluded that language analysis used in assessing asylum seeker claims of nationality was not valid or reliable and that the practice should cease immediately. A psychiatric nurse who worked in detention told the inquiry:

I had detainees who would come distressed into the medical centre with a letter telling me they had pronounced two words in a way that indicated they were Pakistani.

It also appears that the use of linguistic testing also led to some bizarre practices. A boy who was 12 when detained in Woomera told the inquiry:

They didn't believe if we are Iraqis. So they bring an Iraqi guy. He was talking about the history and somehow he went to the music and told me have you heard this song? I told him yeah. He was like, can you sing it for me? I told him I am not a good singer. He goes, sing it and I said I can't remember it, because I don't want to do it. And I have done it. My brother didn't have to, just me. They have done the same to my mum but not asked her to sing. Asked her different questions.

Subjective Nature of Decisions

A submission to the inquiry from *A Just Australia* stated that in 2003–04, one in eight rejections at the immigration case-officer level was later overturned by the RRT, including almost 90 per cent of the decisions on cases from Afghanistan. Over 50 per cent of the decisions on people from Muslim countries – Afghanistan, Iran, Turkey, Egypt and Pakistan – were overturned by the RRT.

A Department of Immigration employee told the inquiry that the department used to have a culture where some case officers saw their role as gatekeepers and of keeping people out, often suspecting protection-visa applicants of telling lies. She said that the interpretation of the Refugee Convention could be somewhat idiosyncratic, with some case officers approaching their work seeking to refuse cases, while others looked at how they could approve them. She said a hard-line approach was being encouraged within the department in Canberra and by the immigration minister, especially in the period 2000–04.

Former West Australian Labor politician Judyth Watson told the inquiry:

There's a huge variation in how their own views might intersect with their work, how bureaucratic they are. I think I should say how racist some are and how Islamophobic they are. All of those things impact on the way in which they make decisions. You see that when you sit in on interviews with them.

The inquiry heard several examples of decisions that appeared to be affected by subjectivity. A refugee advocate told the inquiry:

There were ten Bedoons [noncitizens of Kuwait] in Melbourne, they all got protection. The ten Bedoons in Sydney were all refused. It's extraordinary.

A lawyer told the inquiry:

> We've just finished a case of a family, one got through and one didn't
> and the persecution was the same and it was linked. We had to take it
> all the way to the High Court and finally the second family won but
> that was after five years of trauma, while the other family is settled, but
> feeling enormous guilt because they don't understand why they have got
> through and the other part of the family hasn't.

A former detainee told the inquiry his story remained the same, but
when he got a new case officer, he was granted a visa after initially being
refused:

> Two persons from same house with same statement, one can get
> rejection and another can get visa. It depends on case officer. When
> I go to interview with another case officer, why he accepted me? My
> statement was the same, I am the same person, but because my case
> officer changes so I also got visa.

A refugee advocate told the inquiry that an interpreter was surprised when
a family was rejected as he had seen many similar cases granted visas.
When he wrote to a minister complaining that the family's treatment was
unfair, the reply stated:

> While the department can sympathise with your belief that the decisions
> made in respect of this family are unfair, it is the law, not fairness, that
> determined the primary decision.

Political Influence on Decision Making

In 2005, after Cornelia Rau's detention became public, an immigration
official appeared anonymously on the *Lateline* program. He said that
blaming her detention on any individual within the Immigration Department
would not be fair because, 'Ultimately everything we do is determined by
the government, and it's determined by right up the top of the government.'
Referring to then immigration minister Philip Ruddock, he said:

> Have a look and see some of the things that he said, describing refugees
> as queue jumpers ... By promoting certain ideas and by criticising

people, in a sense he's given people in the department permission to have those attitudes. People said, 'The minister wants me to reject asylum seekers, so I'm going to reject all these because I know that's what the minister and the government wants.'[166]

Diana Goldrick, former Department of Immigration onshore protection manager NSW, who resigned in 2001, told the inquiry:

Because of the continuing amendments to the Migration Regulations, the interpretation of the Migration Act *and the UN Convention on Refugees has been narrowed to such an extent that the Regulations became an absolute minefield for the case officers. I considered that it was becoming more convenient for the case officers who were junior officers in the department hierarchy to do what they thought senior management and the government wants them to do. Their power as independent administrative decision-makers was being eroded.*

She also told the inquiry that case officers were micromanaged by senior management, with statistics kept of the number and results of their decisions each month. She said case officers were interviewed by senior departmental officers if they did not produce an acceptable number of decisions per month or if they granted an unacceptable number of protection visas.

She heard that shortly after she resigned, case officers were directed to forward all draft decision records to central office for senior management approval. The result was that no protection visas were granted for several months because central office couldn't cope with the additional workload. The decision records were returned to Onshore Protection NSW with the direction that the management team there was to check each decision record before the case officers could finalise the cases. She also heard that a group of asylum seekers in Port Hedland who were about to be granted TPVs, including one who had heard unofficially that he would be released, were refused at the direction of central office.

Diana Goldrick also told the inquiry that refugee case officers were subject to direct political influence, saying:

In 2000, the then Secretary of DIMIA, Bill Farmer, came to Sydney to talk to the case officers. This was most unusual – the Secretary wanted to talk directly to junior officers. They were very excited. Why did the

Secretary want to talk to them? He was like God to junior officers.

I was present at this meeting as were several other Onshore Protection managers. Mr Farmer told the case officers words to the effect that you have to be very careful processing boat people in detention because we don't know who they are. I considered that these words coming from him face to face with case officers carried a very strong message indeed. Be extremely careful in granting protection visas to these people.

Some months later he arrived in Sydney again to speak to the case officers. This was even more unusual. I was not present at this second meeting but was informed of what the Secretary said by a group of case officers immediately after they left the meeting. He told them that the then head of the Department of Prime Minister and Cabinet, Max Moore Wilton, had told him DIMIA would go bankrupt within a few months if the boat people were not released from the detention centres quickly. It was costing the department a great deal of money to keep them there. He stated that if they were not released quickly he would lose his job. He appealed to the case officers to work faster and promised funding would be made available for unlimited overtime.

Another Immigration Department employee told the inquiry that in 2003, when refugees who had been granted TPVs were having their applications for permanency considered, case officers were instructed to be very careful and thorough in reassessing the cases. Due to the huge workload, the requirements gradually became more and more streamlined. In 2005, in the wake of the Cornelia Rau scandal, the government pledged to process all applications within 90 days. Case officers were told to give people the benefit of the doubt, and approvals were encouraged, with interviews and language analysis no longer required.

Refugee Review Tribunal

Evidence presented to the inquiry also identified flaws in the refugee determination process at the RRT level, including: the inappropriate use of interpreters; inadequate research of country information; use of discredited identification methods such as linguistic analysis; subjective decision making; and political considerations influencing decision making. The inquiry heard many comments about how incorrect decisions being made at the RRT resulted in asylum seekers spending additional years in detention.

Interpreting

A refugee supporter who transcribed an RRT hearing told the inquiry about one member's inappropriate use of an interpreter when rejecting the claims of an ethnic Hazara man from Afghanistan, who was found to be a refugee after spending five years in detention:

> *Occasionally he talks for too long at a stretch for the interpreter to be able to quite keep up with translating. Rather than restating the need to pause, she shouts, 'You must stop talking.' At one stage he simply answers 'Yes' to one of her questions. The member says to the interpreter, 'Lovely.' The interpreter says, 'I love your short answers.' The member replies, 'Yes,' and giggles.*
>
> *Member: Okay, you said that you're a Hazara, do you think you look like a Hazara person?*
>
> *Applicant: Yes, I'm Hazara and I look like a Hazara.*
>
> *Member: And what is it about you that looks Hazara?*
>
> *Applicant: From my cheeks, from my eyes, from my nose.*
>
> *Member: Well, what about them?*
>
> *Applicant: Yes, Hazara people have got very small eyes as well as flat nose.*
>
> *Member: But you don't seem to have a flat nose.*
>
> *Applicant: Yes, I'm Hazara and I'm from Afghanistan and I look like Hazara.*
>
> *Member: Well, you don't look like some of the Hazara who I have seen. And what about the shape of your eyes?*
>
> *Member to interpreter: What sort of eyes do the Hazara people have?*
>
> *Interpreter: It's very small and narrow eyes.*
>
> *Member: Aha.*
>
> *Interpreter: Sorry, may I ask you? What is the description for these like, Chinese?*
>
> *Member: Almond shaped [laughs].*

Interpreter: Almond?

Member: Like a nut, you know, the shape of an almond.

Interpreter: Okay, okay. It's important because I face this question and it's hard for me to find.

Member: Yes, but him or lots of people wouldn't know what an almond was in its form so that's how I think of it. [To applicant] We're just having a talk about English words describing shape.

Migration Agent Marion Le told the inquiry about a case in which a man who spoke Kurdish was forced to use an interpreter who spoke Arabic, a completely unrelated language, at his Immigration Department interview and was subsequently disbelieved at the RRT:

> *The RRT decision, from beginning to end, calls him a liar. It says, for example, the Tribunal is of the view that the applicant was uncooperative about how well he spoke Arabic. He claimed the entry interview was conducted in a dialect of a language that he couldn't understand. The Tribunal was not able to listen to the tapes as there was an error in recording and the tape was apparently blank. However the Tribunal is satisfied that there was adequate communication with the applicant when he was interviewed. Now how could you be satisfied, without a tape and when he didn't have a Kurdish interpreter?*

Researching

A former detainee told the inquiry:

> *The members don't have updated information about the respective country. In this world we have the most advanced technology to get any kind of information we want. Eventually they admit they had made an error. The whole time takes six or seven years, the golden years of a man or woman's life.*

The inquiry was told that in one RRT case, the RRT member ridiculed the applicant's claims about Iranian passports, stating:

> *The applicant's evidence became confused and increasingly more incredible as he attempted to explain how he left the country on a*

passport in his own name, but which he claimed was a false passport, and how the Iranian authorities did not know of his departure. He alluded to passports which could be used only once for leaving the country, and claimed that his passport was of such character. He also talked of passports with different coloured stamps in them, 'red' stamps which meant a person could leave but not return, 'blue' stamps which meant the passport could only operate for one year, and 'yellow' and 'green' stamps. It was put to the applicant that his evidence in this regard made no sense and flew in the face of how the passport system operates worldwide, and that I was unconvinced by his evidence in regard to passports generally and his passport specifically.[167]

However, the applicant's evidence was confirmed when in another case the Tribunal member stated:

In its 1996 Country Profile, DFAT [Department of Foreign Affairs and Trade] says: It should also be noted that holding a passport does not confer automatically the right to travel out of the country. When issuing a passport, the Passport Office will enter a green, blue or red exit stamp. Most Iranians receive a green stamp, which indicates permission for multiple exits. The blue stamp indicates permission for one exit and the red stamp also for one exit, but with the caveat that travel details must be provided to the authorities ahead of the journey.[168]

In another case, when an RRT member described an asylum seeker's referral to the Iranian Revolutionary Guards, a government security force also known as the Pasdaran, she stated:

He described the regime as consisting of a revolutionary guard known as 'Past the Run'.[169]

A migration agent told the inquiry that instead of conducting their own up-to-date research into the circumstances in particular countries, some RRT members simply cut-and-pasted country information from the previous decisions of other members.

A refugee supporter told the inquiry that for many years the cases of a minority religious group in Iran, Sabean Mandeans, were rejected after RRT members quoted information from a US anthropologist to reject their claims of discrimination. When refugee advocates located the woman, she was shocked and wrote an extensive document outlining the discrimination Sabean Mandeans faced in Iran:

> *Eventually this was accepted and the minister has let Sabean Mandean cases out. Two years after this document was published and two years after it was available to her.*

The inquiry also heard evidence about several cases in which RRT members rejected an applicant's claims without attempting to verify stories that could easily have been confirmed. A refugee advocate provided the inquiry with one example:

> *The detainee presented a letter from a member of parliament [from his home country]. He claims that his life was in danger because of another political party. The RRT member said he did not believe the letter. The letter was on parliamentary stationery, it had the telephone numbers, email address and the fax on it, yet he completely rejected it without any attempt of verifying that easily verifiable document.*

Migration Agent Marion Le also told the inquiry:

> *He has had acid poured over his body. If you are faced with a person in front of you and you don't believe that he had acid poured over him, don't you think it would be a sensible thing to say, as I did, show me the acid burns?*

Another migration agent told the inquiry:

> *There is a case where the RRT said 'If you go back to your home country you're likely to be imprisoned or even killed, but I can't give you a visa because that wouldn't happen for a convention reason.' On appeal, an expert witness clarified that given the particular warrant that was issued it was a political rather than criminal offence and he was eventually given a visa, but obviously the potential ramifications of that mistake are extremely serious.*

Linguistic Analysis

The linguistic analyses carried out by the Immigration Department were considered by the RRT when reviewing asylum seeker claims. A study by five linguists that criticised their use in the refugee determination process found:

> There is considerable variability in the extent to which different RRT members accept [it]: ranging from finding it to be 'an important investigative tool' and to 'have some evidentiary value' to finding 'that linguistic analyses are not in themselves determinative of an applicant's country of origin.' This means that the weight to be attached to it in determining nationality is dependent on the particular RRT member deciding the case.[170]

Subjective Nature of Decisions

A visitor to Villawood told the inquiry that having one person sitting as a Refugee Review Tribunal made decisions less accountable:

> If that person has some sort of a bias against a particular group, how right and just will his judgement be?

Another refugee advocate, who has been a member of the Social Security Appeals Tribunal, told the inquiry:

> I was used to having three people decide whether people had a minor debt to Centrelink and this parallel tribunal is a tribunal where one member sits on life-and-death matters.

A migration agent told the inquiry she believed one member had made different findings on the same issue in order to reject people. She said that in early 2002, an RRT member rejected the asylum claims of an Iranian woman who said she had been harassed by an Arab-Iranian. The member stated that had this been the case the man would have been arrested straightaway as Arabs were subject to discrimination in Iran, and listed evidence to support this.

However, the migration agent said that when an Arab-Iranian came before the same RRT member six months later and claimed he was discriminated against because of his ethnicity, she also rejected his claims, saying that the Iranian government did not disadvantage or discriminate against Arabs.

In May 2002, Federal Court Justice John Mansfield found the RRT had exercised bias in rejecting a claim for asylum, including through the selective use of evidence. He stated:

> *The Tribunal's approach discloses that it was actually biased against acceptance of the applicant's claim. It demonstrates views which are incapable of alteration.*[171]

Four months later, in another case, he found:

> *I consider, upon careful reflection, that the Tribunal embarked upon its review with a mind fixed upon rejecting the claims … Its doubtful fact-finding does not simply indicate possible legal or factual error. In my view it indicates in the circumstances a failure to attempt in good faith to undertake the review of the delegate's decision with which it was charged under the Act.*[172]

In another Federal Court case, Justice Wilcox stated:

> *It is apparent that the Tribunal member made no real attempt to establish and analyse the evidence given to him by the applicant. Even on critical issues, he did not check the accuracy of his recollection. In the result, he impugned the applicant's credibility by reference to his own faulty recollection of his evidence.*[173]

A former detainee told the inquiry:

> *When they send someone to this RRT member, it means your case is finished. They have a policy not to accept it. She will just trying to make it legally no. I could come two, three people in my room, which member do they have, her – oh, forget it! Really, forget it. We studied in detention. We pull all the cases together and we found some judge 'no', some it's balanced and some it's 'yes'. Really it was there.*

Political Influence on Decision Making

In 1996, three years after it was established, the RRT decided that two women who had been the subject of domestic violence which their government was unable or unwilling to protect them from were refugees, despite the department rejecting their claims. In response, immigration minister Philip Ruddock told *The Australian* newspaper:

The view I take would be if there are tribunal members who have fixed-term appointments who clearly make decisions outside the international law in relation to determining refugee claims, their appointments would be ones I would be highly unlikely to renew.[174]

Professor of International and Comparative Law at Washington University, Stephen Legomsky, wrote:

I spoke personally with a number of RRT members in the months following the minister's public statements. Everyone who ventured an opinion stated the obvious – that many of their colleagues now worried about losing their jobs every time they contemplated ruling against the [Immigration] Department.

The threats from the minister were not idle. Thirty-five of the RRT members whose terms expired in June 1997 applied for reappointment. Sixteen of them were not renewed … One non-renewed member – Mr John Gibson – had had a high set-aside rate[175] of about 30 per cent. Mr Gibson had 'no doubt' that the minister's public statements about set-aside rates left adjudicators feeling 'somewhat vulnerable'. In any event, during April 1997 – the month in which the Immigration Department conducted interviews for applicants for reappointment – the set-aside rate plummeted to 2.7 per cent.[176]

In June 1997, minister Ruddock again expressed anger when two RRT members granted asylum to East Timorese applicants despite being asked by the principal member to defer their decisions. A newspaper report stated the decisions might 'hasten the introduction of government measures giving Mr Ruddock the power to "direct" tribunal members in their handling of cases.'[177]

A barrister told the inquiry:

Whilst the tribunal is claimed to be independent, they operate out of offices owned by DIMIA, they ultimately answer to the same minister, they exercise powers of the minister in making their decisions, they are only appointed for a short period of time, statistics are kept on how many people they let through and how many people they don't.

In 2003, former Refugee Review Tribunal member Bruce Haigh told a newspaper that RRT members would be told by the tribunal's senior member if immigration minister Philip Ruddock wasn't happy about decisions they had made.

> It is supposed to be an independent tribunal, but it is not. People are appointed to the tribunal ... and if they want to have their term renewed, they end up agreeing with certain directions and influences.[178]

He later told a Senate committee:

> There were many applicants who could fall ... either way ... Because of the pressure and the mentality ... within the tribunal, people tended to find against borderline cases rather than for them ... I think it is fatally flawed ... where people are appointed on a contract and that contract is renewable. I think it should be a single contract for four or five years, and that is it. Then you can make your decisions quite fearlessly because you are not getting yourself locked into mortgages, child-care facilities or whatever else that you lock in on when you get $80,000-plus a year, plus a car, plus fuel, plus inner-city parking, plus some of your telephone calls.[179]

He also said there was an unwritten consensus amongst RRT members that only 20 per cent of applicants should be found to be refugees and that at a meeting of 20–25 Sydney RRT members held around the end of 1996:

> The principal member, Shun Chetty, said that the minister had noted that the tribunal had in the past been setting aside around 20 per cent of the cases that came before it and he thought that was a figure that should be maintained ... He also said that the minister was concerned about the productivity levels inside the tribunal and that they needed to be raised.[180]

Haigh told the Senate committee:

> I decided that the only way I could operate was to do each case on its merits ... [Chetty] then sought to use the powers that he had over reviewing my decision making, in the sense that he said it was sloppy and that too many people were being set aside. He sought to apply pressure

like that. I went through all of those decisions and I got separate legal opinion on them, and there was nothing wrong with them. [181]

Between 2000 and 2004, the RRT set aside the Immigration Department's decision to refuse a visa in around 11 per cent of cases. However in the 2004–05 year, the period during which the Cornelia Rau scandal was uncovered, one-third of the department's decisions were rejected by the RRT.[182] The RRT's explanation for the set-aside rate tripling was that there was an increased proportion of cases from Iraq and Afghanistan where TPV holders had been denied a further visa and that about 90 per cent of these decisions were set aside.[183] However in the 2005–06 year, when lodgements by asylum seekers from Afghanistan and Iraq made up just 3 per cent of the RRT caseload, the set-aside rate of all departmental decisions remained at 30 per cent.[184]

Recognising its shortcomings, in 2000 a Senate committee made a number of recommendations regarding reform of the RRT. These included that further training be provided for RRT members in the use of inquisitorial methods, that provision be made for the RRT to be able to sit as a panel of two or three members, that officers from the Immigration Department, the Attorney-General's Department or DFAT should not be RRT members and that members be drawn from a broad cross-section of the Australian community, including the legal profession, with experience in refugee and humanitarian issues.[185]

Courts

Evidence provided to the inquiry also identified flaws in the refugee determination process at the Federal and High Court appeals level, including: unrepresented applicants lacking the language and legal skills to fight their case; applicants receiving inadequate legal advice; and appeal outcomes being influenced by political considerations.

Unrepresented Applicants

A former Woomera worker told the inquiry that most detainees did not have adequate language skills to understand the court decisions and legal correspondence about their case:

They would receive letters and they couldn't read the English so we would get the interpreters to do it and that was considered illegal using our interpreters to do that. So we had to do things like that in secret.

A barrister told the inquiry:

If you want to see a serious miscarriage of justice, all you have to do is go and look at the lists in the Federal Court where case after case of unrepresented person who doesn't speak the language appears before the court. It is easier to get Legal Aid as a murderer than it is to get it as an asylum seeker. The judges try their best to explain to the applicants what they have to look for, but to expect a person who speaks no English, who has no legal training and who is afraid for their lives to isolate the jurisdictional error is just ridiculous.

It is one of the most complex areas of the law and it is constantly changing. The only reason I can argue these cases is because I trained for five years at a very high level and I've practised for ten years at a very high level and that only equips me to do a moderate job at dealing with these complex issues.

These people have no hope, so it becomes a self-fulfilling prophecy that these claims will be dismissed and these people are defamed even more by saying that they are making unmeritorious claims to the court. Focus is shifted away from the real issue which is the injustice of the system that puts them in that position. The judges don't have the time to pour over the applications. It takes at least a day of work to go through a case and identify any jurisdictional error, but many times I have identified jurisdictional error and ultimately been successful.

A man who spent 18 months in Villawood told the inquiry:

They don't help you legally, you have to scrimp if you don't have money, borrow phone cards. When they put a case against you, they have access to everything. If you want to fight it, you don't even have access to the internet to get the information you need.

Another man held in Villawood told the inquiry he had requested access to the internet and a law library so that he could prepare for his court case. The response from the Immigration Department was:

The department is currently considering expanding the reading resources available at immigration detention centres to include reading material of a legal nature, such as the Migration Act 1958. *Consideration is also being given to the feasibility of providing detainees with electronic copies of core legislation and important High Court decisions. However, this may not happen in the near future because of the scale of the project.*

A year after legislation restricting refugee appeal rights was introduced, High Court Justice Michael Kirby said many asylum seekers were in detention, had little English and limited access to legal advice. He told the federal solicitor-general, 'We are here to do justice and you want to take that away from us.'[186]

A former detainee told the inquiry:

I needed a lawyer to go to the Federal Court. I had no contacts. I was given the forms and I did request Federal Court that I have no lawyer and I don't know how to fill the application forms because I don't know how the legal system works even within my country. When I went there he says you have to convince the court that your case is within our jurisdiction and you need to quote from the Migration Act 1958. *He said 'I will give you a photocopy of one page. I give you 15 minutes, read this, write under what clause this court is obligated to hear your case.' I had no idea.*

Another former detainee told the inquiry:

We used to go to courts and hear the judge say in court that our hands are tied and we couldn't understand. I came to you for help and then you say that there is nothing you can do about it.

Inadequate Legal Advice

While many asylum seekers received excellent legal assistance, much of it pro bono, some fell prey to incompetent migration agents or lawyers, many of whom charged for their assistance. A refugee advocate told the inquiry that one lawyer had made one-page applications for ministerial intervention that were almost identical for each person and were subsequently rejected. Another told the inquiry about the experience of one family:

I accompanied them to the court and listened to a very inept lawyer try *to present a case when he obviously knew nothing about refugee law. The case failed and the family were left with lawyer's fees of $2,000 and court fees of more than $12,000. While I was away the family were told they could appeal the case and they panicked and engaged another lawyer.*

The lawyer told the family it was not necessary to be present at the court. I went. The case lasted about five minutes because the lawyer could not give an adequate excuse as to why she was a week late in presenting it. The case was dismissed without even being heard. I wanted to report the lawyer but the family wouldn't, saying she was a single mum and they couldn't do it to her. They were left with barrister's fees of more than $2,000 and a further court bill of $7,000.

My barrister friend helped me write up their case. In February 2004 I sent it to the UNHCR in Canberra. On the basis of the report they opened the case. They suggested I send a copy to the minister because it outlined the issues so clearly. UNHCR told me they had written to the minister recommending the family be recognised as refugees.

Political Influence on Decision Making

In 2002, the chief justice of the Federal Court, Michael Black, asked immigration minister Philip Ruddock to explain his public comments that the court was 'taking a proactive position to undermine the efforts that this parliament supported' in deciding refugee cases:

> *Solicitor-general David Bennett, QC, appearing on the minister's behalf, expressed regret that the court considered that members of the public might construe the minister's comments as intended to apply pressure upon the court in relation to matters which are currently before it for consideration.*[187]

As with the number of appeals succeeding in the RRT, the number of asylum seekers obtaining favourable court decisions also skyrocketed in the period immediately following the Cornelia Rau scandal. Of all RRT decisions appealed to the courts, the Immigration Department in 2003–04 agreed to return to the RRT for reconsideration just 4 per cent of cases. By 2004–05 this figure had doubled to 8 per cent, and in 2005–06 was 23 per cent.[188]

Ministerial Intervention

Evidence to the inquiry also identified flaws in the refugee determination process at the ministerial intervention level: the consideration of intervention not being compellable; decision making not being transparent; and the lack of a complementary protection system. In a submission to the inquiry, UnitingJustice Australia and Hotham Mission Asylum Seeker Project also argued that the ministerial power to intervene in individual cases stifled public criticism of immigration policy. The view of the Human Rights Council of Australia reinforces this silencing:

> *Refugee advocates are conscious that they may need to call privately for the minister's personal intervention in individual cases and are inevitably conscious that public criticism from them may have adverse impacts on individuals they are seeking to assist.*[189]

Non-compellable Consideration

Asylum seekers who ask the immigration minister to intervene in their case take a risk. The Department of Immigration will generally not deport a person from Australia while they have a court appeal pending. However, the minister will generally not consider intervening in a case while court proceedings are afoot. To access possible intervention from the minister, asylum seekers must withdraw from litigation making them liable to deportation should the minister not agree to intervene. Between 1996 and 2003, ministerial intervention was exercised in an average of just 3.6 per cent of cases eligible for intervention.[190] A refugee advocate told the inquiry:

> *It is a very fraught place for people to be because while they remove themselves from the court's protection, they can actually then be deported and we of course know of some cases where as soon as people's legal processes finish, they are taken.*

A migration agent told the inquiry that despite four judges recommending the immigration minister intervene in the cases of two men, no intervention occurred and they were held in detention for five years:

> *Their families had fled from Iraq to Iran when they were children and they initially told Australian authorities they were Iranian as they feared*

being sent back to Iraq. When they confessed they were actually Iraqi six months later, DIMIA and the RRT didn't believe them. They later got evidence to prove it, but by then they were at the judicial review stage and this could not be taken into account. Four different judges said it was likely there had been a factual error and they were actually Iraqi, but as there had been no error of law they couldn't do anything except recommend the minister intervene.

As the men got more desperate in detention they asked for travel documents so they could try and go to another country. At the same time DIMIA was arguing in court that they were Iranian, they provided them with Australian travel documents that I have copies of stating they were Iraqi.

Non-transparent Decision Making

The inquiry heard many stories about cases that would appear to warrant special consideration, but in which successive immigration ministers refused to intervene. In a submission to the inquiry, UnitingJustice Australia and Hotham Mission Asylum Seeker Project told of one case where a mother and child were found to be refugees but the father, who was on a separate application, was not. A request for ministerial intervention was denied and the man was removed from Australia.

A refugee advocate involved with over 60 refugees on temporary visas in a regional town told the inquiry that requests for the men to be granted permanent visas so they could sponsor their families to join them were refused:

One man's wife died of cancer leaving four children. Another man's nine-year-old son was found beaten to death in Afghanistan. He and his wife desperately need to grieve together. He had been in detention three-and-a-half years and is on a TPV with over two years to wait after his son's death. In these and other cases we have asked our federal member of parliament to ask Senator Vanstone for an urgent permanent visa, but they have all been refused.

Former immigration minister Amanda Vanstone also denied Aladdin Sisalem, who spent 10 months as the sole occupant of the Manus Island detention centre during his 18 months of detention, a permanent visa so that he could travel overseas to see his dying father.[191]

However in mid-2003, the Labor Party alleged that Dante Tan, a Philippine businessman whose visa had been cancelled in September 2001, had his visa restored after Karim Kisrwani contacted immigration minister Philip Ruddock's office on his behalf. They also alleged Tan:

> ... made a $10,000 donation to the minister's re-election campaign at a fund-raising dinner organised by Mr Kisrwani, probably on 14 October 2001. Of added interest to this case is that the Philippine authorities laid charges of fraud against Mr Tan in 2000. When Mr Tan was informed that the Philippine authorities were seeking his extradition, he left Australia in 2003.[192]

The Senate Select Committee on Ministerial Discretion in Migration Matters investigated the allegations. Its report stated:

> The committee's efforts to understand why Mr Karim Kisrwani, a travel agent in Harris Park, Sydney, who is not a registered migration agent, should be so apparently successful in supporting candidates for ministerial intervention highlights a number of the issues discussed in this chapter.
>
> Mr Kisrwani is a prominent member of the Lebanese Maronite community at Harris Park. He has connections to Mr Ruddock going back many years, and is known to have supported Mr Ruddock and the Liberal Party both politically and financially.
>
> Over the years Mr Kisrwani has made numerous representations to the former minister in relation to the exercise of ministerial discretion. Figures submitted by DIMIA show that from November 1999 to 29 August 2003, Mr Kisrwani made 56 requests for ministerial intervention in relation to 55 cases. It is clear that he has actively supported cases through the ministerial intervention process – evidence from a departmental liaison officer working in Mr Ruddock's office was that Mr Kisrwani would call the minister's office 'a couple of times a week about a range of cases.'
>
> As at 29 August 2003, the minister had intervened in 17, or 31 per cent, of these cases, with a further 19 cases either still in process or otherwise finalised. Thus, of the cases where a decision had actually been made by the minister before 29 August 2003, close to half had received ministerial intervention. This contrasts with an organisation such as Amnesty International which, according to DIMIA, had made

intervention requests regarding 68 cases, only 11 of which (or 16 per cent) received ministerial intervention as of 29 August 2003.[193]

Correspondence to the Senate committee from a senior departmental official also noted that Philip Ruddock intervened in only about 19 per cent of the cases referred to him by the RRT between 2000 and 2002.[194]

The inquiry heard that one family obtained a permanent visa when the then federal Liberal Member for Adelaide, Trish Worth, advocated on their behalf. Psychiatrist Jon Jureidini told the inquiry:

> *The woman had been lied to during the time that she was in a psychiatric hospital and told that there were no guards around. This was at her husband's instigation as he felt that if she was told there were guards around that would inhibit her recovery. At one stage she saw a guard and took to her bed, pulled the covers over her head and went back to screaming when anybody walked into the room. That happened to be the day that one of the refugee advocates had arranged for Trish Worth to come to visit her.*

The inquiry heard that when Trish Worth sat on the side of the woman's bed and tried to put her arm around her, having heard the family's story from the woman's husband, the woman turned away and sobbed uncontrollably. Being the member of the government then responsible for mental health, she was horrified and could see that the guard's presence was damaging the woman. She had several unfruitful discussions with then immigration minister Amanda Vanstone's office before speaking directly to Amanda Vanstone, who suggested the family could be placed in an 'alternative place of detention' with guards next door. Trish Worth then threatened to make the case public before speaking to Prime Minister John Howard. He told her to come back to him if she couldn't sort it out with Amanda Vanstone. Soon after, the family was given a permanent visa and provided with housing and support through Anglicare, an Anglican NGO.

Another issue presented to the inquiry is that some asylum seekers were found to be in danger of imprisonment, torture or death were they to return to their home country, but not for one of the five Refugee Convention reasons. They were denied a visa and therefore exposed to being returned to those dangers. The only avenue available to asylum seekers whose persecution falls outside the convention definition is to request the minister to intervene in their case.

Many submissions to the inquiry argued that complementary protection should be offered to people in this situation. A barrister told the inquiry:

> *They argue some of the most absurd propositions from a humanitarian*
> *point of view. The case I did in 2003 went like this. Even if we are not*
> *fearful of persecution for convention-related reasons, if we go back to*
> *Iran we will be killed or tortured. The government said, Fine we are*
> *happy to accept all of those facts as made out. Even if they are going*
> *back to certain death or torture, the government argued, successfully,*
> *the legislation requires them to return people. It's an absolute disgrace.*

A Senate inquiry into the use of the ministerial intervention powers recommended: statistics be published on the number of cases referred to the immigration minister, from whom they were referred and why they were approved; an information sheet and application form for use of the discretion be created; that the IAAAS scheme provide legal assistance to applicants for ministerial intervention; that applicants be given reasons for unfavourable decisions; that ministerial intervention applicants be eligible for work rights; and that establishing a system of complementary protection be considered.[195] These recommendations were not implemented.

WAITING & WAITING: PSYCHOLOGICAL EFFECTS OF THE PROCESS

Back to Courts/RRT Time Delays

Another flaw identified in the refugee assessment process at the inquiry is the length of time each stage of the process takes. For asylum seekers in detention, this means lengthy incarceration, while for those in the community it means extended periods without work rights or access to Medicare. In 2003–04, the RRT took 22 weeks to process applications lodged by detainees. By 2004–05, the average time to process an application had grown to 39 weeks.[196] A man who spent 18 months in Villawood told the inquiry:

> *I went to the Federal Court. I'm still waiting for an answer a year later. I waited for my RRT result eight-and-a-half months. If I get a 'no' from the court, it's an appeal. There could be another two years.*

Even if asylum seekers successfully appeal an RRT or court decision, they are not granted a visa but have their case sent back to the RRT for reconsideration. One former detainee told the inquiry:

> *We won that case. It was a big relief for me and I thought, 'That's it, I'm being released.' But no, the Federal Court can only recommend you back to the RRT. I knew from the day I went there that I was refused because of the way the RRT member conducted the hearing. I lost that, went to the Federal Court, won again – all this takes 34 months.*

The inquiry was told about another asylum seeker who spent five years in detention and had his case heard by the RRT four times before he was recognised as a refugee. Refugee advocate Kate Gauthier told the inquiry that a single mother of three children, one of whom was seriously disabled, waited a year in detention for her court case before the department conceded the case on the first day of the hearing:

> *The government kept this family in detention for an additional year, in the hope that she would give up and return to her country.*

A worker in a refugee-assistance organisation told the inquiry:

> *People are told it shouldn't be very long now, maybe two weeks, and then that deadline doesn't get met and they are just so traumatised. They get psyched up, we are going to have a good outcome. It doesn't come and it is throughout the whole system, from people in the detention centre to those on Temporary Protection Visas [TPVs] applying for permanent visas, having to wait.*

Lawyers and migration agents told the inquiry that clients had waited more than a year for the immigration minister to decide whether or not to intervene in a case. One migration agent told the inquiry she knew one family that had waited for an answer from the minister for eight years.

The flaws in the refugee determination process and the time delays involved had a crushing psychological effect on people seeking asylum. A former detainee told the inquiry:

Many people couldn't really bear everything psychologically, especially the visa process and period of time. Others have to get their children's pictures with them, they carry them around.

A man who spent five years in detention told the inquiry:

When I was in Full Federal with three judges, the atmosphere was such that I felt I had done something right and this was my chance, that I was going to be accepted. But then a month later, I got the letter that I had been refused.

Late 2004, Amanda Vanstone asked for a review of all the cases that were left in the camp. I was interviewed and the case officer refused me again. I was astonished at this development. If they were not going to accept me, what was the purpose of sending a case officer, giving me hope and taking it away from me again? I have been into lots of interviews, RRT, court and many times I was hopeful and then the hope was taken away. But none of those has affected me as badly as the very last one because I just don't understand why they did this.

The blow of the very last refusal was so enormous that I could not believe it. I thought to myself, 'They know everything about me. They've got my file. For years they've been talking to me and they have gathered all the information. This interview has to do it.' And yet they refused me. That was something that I could not handle. I was shattered.

Psychiatrist Jon Jureidini told a 2005 court case that a severely depressed detainee's condition 'has been exacerbated by being given the news two weeks ago that he could re-apply for a visa under 48B but then being told this was a mistake.'[197]

A lawyer told the inquiry:

I have been unable to put into words the suffering that I observed as a lawyer. It was common for clients to be so distressed when they gave instructions that they would have difficulty breathing. Towards the end of 2005, the detainees I saw got very low and quiet. They became institutionalised and the idea of ever getting out of detention began to frighten some of them. One person I know had an opportunity to be released but chose not to be because he was too frightened to leave the detention environment.

The inquiry heard evidence that compared the conditions of immigration detainees and prisoners. A man who spent more than five years in detention told the inquiry:

I have been in detention. I got a paper and there was a big article about the dangerous man who was a rapist in Adelaide. He had raped three women, but he was jailed about four years with parole after three years. This is your law – this man is a criminal, he is a serious offence against women, but he has only been jailed for four years. For me I don't know what I have done after five years. I am still waiting and waiting.

A man who spent five years in detention told the inquiry:

I compare myself with people who have committed a crime. They go to court, are dealt with and they get a number of years. At least they know at the end of those years they are going to be free. I never felt that way because I didn't know how long I've got to stay. Am I going to be let out or not?

Father Peter Norden, chaplain to Maribyrnong detention centre with years of experience working with people in correctional facilities, told the inquiry:

In a criminal justice facility, the most difficult regime is when someone is remanded without being convicted. There is uncertainty as to whether they'll receive a custodial sentence, whether they'll be separated from family for short or very long term. It's more likely to incur incidents of self-harm and violence towards others because of anxiety, depression and fear.

The immigration detention facilities effectively replicate the experience of persons on remand, because of the uncertain nature of the outcome and the lack of clear time dimensions. I've noticed, over the last four years at Maribyrnong, people arriving with the expectation that their case was going to be resolved within weeks or months, not realising it could be prolonged to years. The pressures and the anxieties that detainees in immigration detention centres face are greater than in a prison environment.

Lawyer Robert McDonald told a study about unaccompanied youth that he had seen many people who had self-harmed as a result of their distress over the process:

One of the things I saw was a kid who was 19 ... He was leaving the interview room ... that the department would tell people whether they'd got their visa or not. This kid walked out, looked at me with this crazed look in his eyes. Pulled a razor blade out from behind his teeth and just started slashing his wrists. Blood was going everywhere. That's what the process can do to people.[198]

A former Woomera worker told the inquiry:

The first family that was released was really close to me and I was given the privilege to say to them that they have been given their visa. This ended up being a big mistake. Once people found out that they had received a visa, I couldn't enter the compound for about three weeks because they all thought I could give them a visa. When I started to go in the compound after the family had left, people would grab my legs and beg and plead and just say, 'Please get us visas; we'll give you anything.'

Delays in Release

The inquiry also heard that even when asylum seekers were found to be refugees by the Immigration Department or the RRT, they remained in detention for months afterwards while health and security checks were conducted. In March 2005, then immigration minister Amanda Vanstone told refugee advocates protesting outside Baxter:

The simple fact that all too often seems to be ignored is that there are no refugees in Baxter or other detention centres. Where someone seeks protection, regardless of how they arrived in Australia, their claim is assessed and if protection is required, a visa is granted immediately.[199]

However, a submission to the inquiry stated that, in 2004, two detainees waited 10 months in Baxter for their release after being recognised as refugees. The supporter of an asylum seeker family told the inquiry they were held in detention for four months for police checks. A psychiatric nurse who worked at several detention centres told the inquiry that people who had been recognised as refugees often self-harmed due to lengthy delays in their release.

A visitor to detention told the inquiry:

> *A young man was released in October and he had been told early in July that he would be given a TPV, and before he got out he actually tried to commit suicide because he was beginning to think that they had been telling him lies. I had a note from a friend and he was eight months waiting for his. You can see the light diminishing in their eyes as they wait.*

In 2002, Dennis Richardson, director general of ASIO, told a parliamentary committee that of almost 6000 assessments of asylum seekers, not one had been found to be a risk to Australia's security. Labor Senator Nick Bolkus commented:

> *It is interesting when you put that together with the advice we had recently from the commissioner of police at another inquiry that, subject to checking, he thought that there was no-one who had criminality problems.*[200]

Two asylum seekers to have had adverse security assessments from ASIO since then, Nauru detainees Mohammed Sagar and Mohammad Faisal, subsequently had them overturned in early 2007 after waiting in detention nearly 18 months.[201]

Suspension of Processing

Delays in processing were exacerbated by Immigration Department decisions to suspend processing for asylum seekers. Shortly after US troops overthrew the Taliban in November 2001, the Immigration Department stopped processing the refugee claims of Afghan asylum seekers while it reassessed conditions in Afghanistan. By January 2002, processing had not resumed and 189 Afghans held in Woomera went on a hunger strike, 70 stitching their lips together. Twenty-four children, including 11 unaccompanied minors, joined the protest. One person told the inquiry he didn't eat for 18 days:

> *They stopped the processing because the government thinks the war is finished but the war is not finished. Now I got four years visa and war is not finished in Afghanistan. Yesterday 500 soldiers from Britain went to Afghanistan. Yesterday!*

Responding to the protest, then immigration minister Philip Ruddock stated he couldn't say when the processing would resume and asylum seekers could go home if they didn't like Woomera.[202] But by the end of January, the government agreed to resume processing and the hunger strike ended.[203]

The suspension resulted in some people who had been assessed as refugees by departmental case officers not being told about their initial acceptance and later being refused visas. In August 2002, the Federal Court ordered the release of an Afghan asylum seeker held at Curtin detention centre. In November 2001, his case officer requested an urgent police check and on 7 December, just before he left to go overseas, the case officer signed, but did not date, a decision record which found the man to be a refugee. On 18 December, the department received the police check, which showed there were no adverse findings against the man. But a month later the asylum seeker was told that following the overthrow of the Taliban, visa processing for Afghans was being suspended. In April 2002, another case officer refused the man a protection visa, a decision affirmed by the RRT. At least two other similar cases were also brought before the courts.[204]

In August 2004, some Afghan asylum seekers were told they would be released from detention on refugee visas and while some were, others waiting for health and security checks were later told the decision had been revoked because Afghanistan had been deemed safe. A visitor to detention told the inquiry:

> *One visit I made was within a week after that had been revoked. They marched in and we sat around the table. There was no talk at all. For the first 20 minutes it was difficult to communicate. We were trying to talk but they were just quiet. Then three of them, one after the other, started expressing themselves. They did it very forcibly, even though it*

wasn't their first language. They were expressing a lot of anger, a lot of disappointment, very emotionally. They just told how they were feeling, the sense of injustice and their anger and despair. Using expressions like, 'This government is playing with us. They're treating us like toys.'

Another visitor to detention told the inquiry:

One young man said, 'They are playing with our brains. They want to get our hope up and then we get our hope up and then we are crushed.' Two weeks later one of these men had lost 13kg. I couldn't believe it. I would hardly have known it was him, despite visiting him for three years. I said, 'Are you on hunger strike?' and he said, 'No.' He said, 'I try to eat but I put it to my mouth and then I have pain here.' And that's the only thing he said the whole visit. He went outside to have a cigarette and two of his friends came up and said, 'We are so, so worried,' because this man was the strong one. They said, 'He has gone and he does nothing. He stays in his room.'

People who were granted Temporary Protection Visas also experienced delays in the processing of their applications for permanent visas. A worker in a torture and trauma support service told the inquiry that many TPVs expired in 2003, but as most refugees were from Iraq and Afghanistan, the department delayed processing them in the hope the situation in those countries would improve, delaying their ability to settle and sponsor family members.

UNACCOUNTABLE TO ANYONE:
THE 'PACIFIC SOLUTION'

The inquiry also heard evidence about the refugee assessment process for asylum seekers who arrived on Australian territory excised from the migration zone or who were intercepted at sea under Operation Relex between 2001 and 2003. They were taken to detention centres on Nauru and Manus Island, managed on behalf of the Howard government by the International Organisation for Migration (IOM), and processed under legislation introduced in the wake of the *Tampa* incident.[205] The legislation rendered them unable to apply for an Australian protection visa, although the immigration minister can allow such an application if it is deemed in the public interest.[206]

During this period, 1524 asylum seekers were taken to offshore detention centres and 23 babies were born there. The overwhelming majority were Afghans or Iraqis. Some processing on Nauru was initially undertaken by UNHCR, although it quickly ended its involvement.[207] Most asylum seekers were assessed by Department of Immigration officials. Those rejected by the department were unable to access the RRT or Australian courts. Their only option for review was for their case to be reconsidered by another departmental officer.

Refugee lawyer Julian Burnside has argued that the term 'offshore processing' is misleading and that it amounts to a repudiation of Australia's obligations under the Refugee Convention:

> When Department of Immigration officials do the 'processing', they will not be applying Australian law; they will not be applying Nauruan law; they will not be applying any domestic legal rules at all. They will simply be looking to see if an individual satisfies the test under the Convention. They will therefore not be amenable to correction by Australian courts or Nauruan courts … the net result is Australian public servants operating entirely outside the legal system in determining the fate of human beings who have come to Australia and asked for protection … that is an attack on the rule of law. You should not remove people from the protection of the Australian legal system, have them processed by Australian officials and have those officials unaccountable to anyone…[208]

In a submission to a Senate Inquiry, immigration and refugee law lecturer Angus Francis argued the process failed to protect asylum seekers from being returned to countries where they faced danger. He concluded that key elements of a fair process were absent, including:

> …a right of appeal to an independent body, the right to legal assistance and representation at all stages, special consideration given to unaccompanied children, access to impartial and qualified interpreters, an opportunity to present evidence of his or her personal circumstances and country of origin information, and a reasoned, written decision deciding the claim.[209]

Between 2001 and 2004, the period during which many asylum seekers on Nauru and Manus Island had their claims rejected by the Immigration Department, the RRT overturned onshore departmental decisions for Afghans and Iraqis at an average rate of 61 per cent and 53 per cent respectively.[210]

The inquiry heard that many of the flaws in the refugee determination process for asylum seekers on Nauru and Manus Island were the same as those for applicants assessed onshore. They included the department obstructing asylum seekers' access to legal advisors, using interpreters speaking different languages, inadequately researching asylum seeker claims and treating unaccompanied minors as adults.

Obstructing Legal Advice

In December 2002, Aladdin Sisalem arrived on Thursday Island, then within Australia's migration zone, and asked for asylum. He was removed to Manus Island by Australian officials and told to ask the Papua New Guinea government for asylum. According to refugee lawyer Julian Burnside, the government argued in court that he had no asylum claim in Australia because:

> ... the only way you can seek asylum is by filling out form 866, and although he said he wanted to seek asylum, he didn't ask for form 866. Therefore the minister does not have any obligation to consider his claim for a protection visa. And there's no point giving him a form 866 now, because they can only be completed in Australia.[211]

In April 2004, three Afghan asylum seekers including Mohammad Arif Ruhani, who had travelled on the *Tampa* and been held on Nauru since December 2001, instituted proceedings in the Supreme Court of Nauru for release on the grounds that they had been brought to Nauru and were being held there against their will. The Australian government paid Nauru's legal costs engaging Peter Hanks QC, barrister Stephen Lee and Australian government solicitor Tony Fell to argue on Nauru's behalf, at the same time claiming it had 'nothing to do with the matter', and that legal representation in the case was up to Nauru.[212]

Lawyers acting for the asylum seekers, Julian Burnside QC, solicitor Eric Vadarlis and two other lawyers had visas to travel to Nauru. However, when they tried to board the same plane as the lawyers paid for by the

Australian government, they were told that Nauru's justice minister and president had ordered that they not be allowed to board on the grounds there was sufficient legal representation for the asylum seekers on Nauru. Julian Burnside told *Lateline*:

> It's farcical and it's just transparently corrupt ... The last thing they want is for us to win because if they win, Australia stops paying them tens of millions of dollars to lock up 84 children and 200 adults who have fled the Taliban or Saddam Hussein.[213]

He later told *The Age*:

> It is interesting Mr Hanks was only retained to go to Nauru after we had been in court on Friday (morning) and, by 4pm, he had visa, application for admission to practice in Nauru, and was about to arrange a ticket. This same process had taken us about six weeks.[214]

The asylum seekers' case was dismissed by the Supreme Court of Nauru. The High Court of Australia later refused an appeal by the asylum seekers against the decision, a judgement which effectively endorsed the 'Pacific Solution'.[215]

The sheer distance between Australia and offshore detention centres also made it difficult for lawyers to assist asylum seekers held there. In 2006, Julian Burnside secured permission to visit Nauru to assist two other asylum seekers, but said:

> It costs an arm and a leg to get there and there's a very limited number of pro bono lawyers who will be able to afford time off work and the airfares to get to Nauru. I managed to get there for the first time just a couple of weeks ago, but it cost me two days away from chambers, and $5000 in airfares just to get a few hours with my clients. That's absurd.[216]

In 2007, former immigration minister Philip Ruddock told the radio program *PM* that asylum seekers should not consider legal help a right:

> I suspect that most asylum seekers around the world, when claims are made, are not represented by lawyers. The idea that every asylum seeker, wherever they are in the world, is entitled to Australian legal

representation as a right I think flies in the face of what is either reasonable or possible.[217]

The only legal representative allowed to go to Nauru during the pre-Cornelia Rau period was migration agent Marion Le, who represented 282 of the 284 people held there, all of whom were eventually granted visas. Marion and two assistants processed the cases without funding during an 18 month period. However, she told the inquiry that she secured permission to go accidentally:

> *Amanda Vanstone basically recognised me publicly, whether by accident I don't know, but she said Marion Le is the representative of these people on Nauru. That was news to me at that time, but I leapt up and said 'OK, if that's what she said, then I want to go there.'*

Interpreting

Marion Le told the inquiry that Kurds held on Nauru had been made to use an Arabic interpreter despite the two languages being completely unrelated:

> *They didn't speak any Arabic. One person spoke a bit and he was asked to translate so they had no proper assessment and at the end of the day three of them were accused of being non-cooperative with the interviewer because they sat there and said, 'This is a joke, we don't speak this language and you are asking us to tell you about our horrific history and we won't go through with it.'*

Researching

Marion Le also told the inquiry that Department of Immigration officers assessing asylum seekers failed to check easily verifiable claims, resulting in their prolonged detention:

> *There was a man who sewed his lips. If you met him you would be amazed that he would be driven to that because he worked with the UN and had all his documents with him and they just totally ignored his documentation. He had the contact numbers of all the UN and World Vision people he had worked with. I contacted World Vision here, who*

contacted their officers, who said he's our colleague. And the UN people said we have been wondering what happened to him. And there he was stuck on Nauru.

In another case, an unaccompanied minor who was held on Nauru but had family in Australia was disbelieved on the basis of 'body language' when a phone call could have confirmed his story:

He said that one of his brothers was a uni student in Australia and another one was in prison in Iraq. A file note next to 'in prison' stated in block capitals TELLING LIES! BODY LANGUAGE. This is obviously a totally subjective statement by the DIMIA officer, which once placed on the file influenced all other decision-makers who read it. Did the department, saying they don't believe his family connections, ring that brother in Australia? No. And did they ever answer that brother's letters? No.

Unaccompanied Minors

A study into unaccompanied minors raised concerns about the way the department determined the age of children where this was in doubt. It found assessments appeared to have relied heavily on physiological factors including bone density testing and appearance, without consideration of psychological maturity or the child's personal, family and cultural background.[218] Marion Le told the inquiry about disturbing practices involving unaccompanied children held on Nauru:

I think I had six hours sleep over the five days I was there. I worked day and night to interview as many people as I could. We were there very late one night and seven young people came in. I looked and I thought, My God, how old are you? One said I think I'm 14. This is 2004. They had been over three years and he thought he was 14.

On at least one of the files was written a file note from a DIMIA woman officer. 'I have been asked to change this child's age to make him over 18 and because I am asked I am doing it, but I do not agree.' That night I was so tired, I looked at these kids and I just picked up the files and threw them against the wall in total anger. I am guilty of not making a statement about that publicly because I wanted to ensure all of the people on Nauru got off. If I had gone out and talked about the abuses of process we were seeing they wouldn't have come here. I would have been stopped going to Nauru.

She also told the inquiry about a 16-year-old boy who had been interviewed and rejected as a refugee by a UNHCR assessor, a decision that was later reaffirmed by the Department of Immigration:

What I find most offensive about this interview is that the applicant, still legally a child, was repeating again and again that he did not want to join a group that might force him to kill innocent people and the interviewer was totally unsympathetic to the situation. I'm particularly concerned about comments like 'What's the problem, why is that a problem?' I don't hold DIMIA unaccountable for that because that was on the record. We found it; DIMIA should have found it when they got the files from UNHCR.

In September 2005, the International Organisation for Migration psychiatrist treating the 27 asylum seekers remaining on Nauru warned the government they were at high risk of committing suicide. Shortly afterwards, 25 of them were granted visas with the government making no mention of the psychiatric advice.[219]

The Howard government claimed the fall in boat arrivals was a result of its offshore processing system. However, UNCHR figures[220] show that in the five years to 2006, applications to developed countries have more than halved. In 2006, Denmark, New Zealand, the United Kingdom, Norway and France recorded their lowest level of applications in decades.[221]

In August 2003, a Senate committee recommended that the Pacific Solution should be abandoned, with a unanimous view amongst government and nongovernment senators that the detention centres on Nauru and Manus Island should close.[222] In February 2008, the newly elected Labor government closed them, but its policy remained to process asylum seekers who did not reach the mainland outside the Australian legal system on Christmas Island, 2600 kilometres from Perth.

Part 3

DETENTION

Before the 'Pacific Solution' established detention centres in Nauru and Manus Island, the majority of asylum seekers who arrived by boat were taken to immigration detention centres in remote areas of Australia. From 1999 to 2002, Woomera, about 500km north of Adelaide, was the primary centre, accommodating approximately 4100 asylum seekers. Other major centres included Curtin, 2400km from Perth, Port Hedland, 1800km from Perth, and Baxter, 350km from Adelaide. Once detained, some asylum seekers were released months later. For others, however, imprisonment lasted up to seven years.

The 2004 Liberal and National Party policy statement on border protection outlined the aims of the immigration detention regime. These were to protect the community from individuals who posed a health, criminal or national security threat, to ensure that noncitizens who were in Australia in breach of immigration laws were available for removal from the country and to deter prospective unauthorised arrivals. The deterrence aim is acknowledged in the rhetoric of Australia's federal politicians.[223]

For example, in June 2001, the then prime minister, John Howard, justified the detention of asylum seekers, telling ABC TV:

> I wish that we didn't have to detain people, but you cannot run an immigration policy that people can drive a horse and cart through ... the best signal we could send to illegal immigrants is don't come in the first place. We are not a soft touch.[224]

Two years later, he told high school students interviewing him as part of ABC Radio's *Talkback Classroom* series:

> [W]e have a policy of denying entry to illegal immigrants, and detention centres have been part of that policy, and I might say a bipartisan part of that policy for more than a decade.[225]

However, the use of detention as a deterrent is not officially acknowledged by Australia in any forum in which the international legality of its immigration detention regime is under consideration. This is because the first two aims of immigration detention are legitimate under international law, but the last is not. Detaining unauthorised arrivals for the purpose of deterring others involves treating human beings as means to an end, and is a repudiation of the fundamental premise of international human rights law, which is the equal worth of every human being.[226]

Crock, Saul and Dastyari state that it is improper to use the pain and discomfort of some asylum seekers to deter others, and there is little evidence that detention has served a deterrence function. People fleeing persecution are unlikely to be deterred by the comparatively lesser harm of mandatory detention, and some detainees were in fact unaware of where they were going. Moreover, to punish one group of people to deter others sends the message that Australia is not willing to protect people from serious harm.[227]

These concerns are supported by evidence provided to the People's Inquiry that many asylum seekers had little or no knowledge of Australia's detention system. A man who arrived on the 'children overboard' boat and was taken to Manus Island for processing said:

When we asked about the estimated time, we were told it's roughly six months. We were just shocked by hearing such a long period.

Another asylum seeker told the inquiry:

The picture we had in our mind changed suddenly, because the Australian authority started to treat us like criminals. They transferred us to the Detention Centre in the middle of the desert, far, far away from any people. We were just behind the razor wires with security around us all the time, day and night, watching us.

The inquiry heard evidence about the experience of detention from asylum seekers who had been held in Australian and offshore detention centres, professionals who had worked in them and Australians who had visited detainees or supported them in other ways. The evidence was startlingly similar – whether centres were closed or still operating, whether they were in remote locations or metropolitan areas, and whether they were run by the International Organisation for Migration (IOM), Australasian Correctional Management (ACM) or Global Solutions Limited (GSL).

Until November 1997, the Immigration Department and the Australian Protective Service managed Australian detention centres. The management of detention centres was then contracted out to ACM. It held the contract until GSL was awarded it in August 2003. Both these companies specialise in operating prisons and many officers who worked in detention centres also worked as prison guards for ACM and GSL.

In a submission to the inquiry, the Public Interest Advocacy Centre argued that despite official recognition by ACM and GSL that detention was administrative rather than punitive, many of their staff failed to recognise this and treated detainees no differently to prisoners. The submission referred to reports into detention by former diplomat Philip Flood and the Commonwealth ombudsman, noting:

> ACM staff were found to lack cultural awareness, or failed to appreciate that the conditions of detention should not be punitive.

A former detention officer told the inquiry that many officers thought of asylum seekers as criminals:

> I was once told at Maribyrnong you are the cat, they are the rat and don't forget that. The general mind set is the same at Baxter. Officers are not told that it's not against the law to apply for asylum. There is a lot of emphasis placed on control and restraint of people, but I felt that the biggest thing missing was the key issue that these people essentially haven't done anything wrong.

The inquiry heard evidence from many sources that detention centres were prisons in everything but name. Writer Arnold Zable told the inquiry:

> When I entered the foyer of the Maribyrnong Detention Centre for the first time, it was immediately obvious this is a jail. I used to visit prisons teaching, I did this over a decade, and I even visited for three years the maximum security section, and I recognised straight away I was back in a place like that. To call it anything else is deceptive. And I just could not believe that people who had committed no crime, including children, were actually subjected to these kinds of conditions in my city.

General practitioner Dr Aamer Sultan, who spent three years in Villawood after fleeing Iraq, told ABC Radio:

> The migration managers, the language they use is very special. Every time I mention 'Why do we have to wait in this jail?' Then immediately they will stop me and have rude voice: 'Oh it's not jail, it's detention.' And they kept saying it until I really snapped: 'What is the difference between jail and detention? I'm in custody, I can't leave here, I can't

work, I don't have any rights, so how come you're telling me it's not
jail? It is jail.[228]

The semantics regarding detention centres went further in the case of
asylum seekers held in Nauru. In April 2004, the Australian Council of
Heads of Schools of Social Work wrote to Immigration Minister Amanda
Vanstone, raising concerns about detainees there. It received a reply
stating:

The children and other residents in Nauru are not held in detention.
Under Nauru's immigration laws, asylum seekers have been issued with
special purpose visas allowing them to enter and stay there temporarily
on certain conditions, including where they may be accommodated.

According to Oxfam, the Australian government has referred to the
detention centres on Nauru as 'temporary residential asylum seekers'
facilities'. In 2006, immigration officials told a parliamentary inquiry:

The OPC [Overseas Processing Centre] at Nauru is managed by IOM
and is a processing centre, not a detention centre. Security services
provided through IOM at the OPC are largely for safety reasons and
are present to prevent inappropriate or unnecessary access to the centre
by residents of Nauru.[229]

THEY HAD TO KEEP THEM ALIVE:
PHYSICAL CONDITIONS

Having sought refuge in a developed country, asylum seekers were
unprepared for the rudimentary condition of the Woomera, Curtin, Port
Hedland, Manus Island and Nauru detention centres, which housed the
overwhelming majority who arrived by boat between 1999 and 2002. One
man told the inquiry:

We came here seeking safety, security, protection and finding a
homeland where we can settle down. We risk our life. We knew full
well what risks were associated with that journey. But the big shock

that we entered with were the circumstances and the treatment inside the detention centre.

A man on the 'children overboard' boat, taken to Manus Island, told the inquiry:

The camp was fenced and the condition was very hot weather and we were placed in tin sheds where families were screened between each other with curtains.

A man detained on Nauru said:

I had never seen such a place in my entire life. It was scorching hot; you couldn't even see trees. There wasn't enough drinking water and the water itself was completely sour. The windows were covered by plastic, no electricity, not enough food and we couldn't see anything except stone.

A former Woomera worker told the inquiry about the physical conditions for detainees held there:

Eighteen hundred detainees arrived in a couple of weeks. We had to allocate them places to live, which were mainly Bessa block buildings fit for one person and on many occasions there would be six people in one. There was no air conditioning, the temperature would range from easily high 40s and my shirt would be covered head to toe with flies, there were scorpions and snakes and lizards. There were eight toilets for 1800 people. There were two washing machines. There were two taps in the compound. One would often break down so there was very limited access to drinking water apart from meal times. There was hardly any staff. They used to line up for four or five hours in the heat just to get Panadol.

A boy who was 12 when he was detained in Woomera told the inquiry the members of his family were not even provided with a bed each:

They gave us a room, nothing in it, except two beds. When they gave us blankets we had to put them on the ground because it was very cold at night. Me and my little brother had to sleep on the ground or sometimes my mum and my other brother.

The inquiry also heard that, faced with this situation, some of the first Woomera detainees tried to help to organise better facilities:

> When we were taken there the place was in a very shanty condition. We started to organise ourselves to clean the place, do some constructions. We were provided later with some fans, we started to do some electrical switch points to organise ourself.

Arrivals detained at Curtin detention centre were initially housed in tents. A letter written by a 12-year-old girl was provided to the inquiry:

> They put us in a tent without any facility. It was very hot, three millions of mosquitoes and scorpions and tarantulas. After some months they put dongas[230] but they are very small rooms. When I was in the tent the officers didn't let us take our clothes from our stuff and everyone just had one set of clothes. We had to go to the bathroom and we would wear them wet all over and stand in the sun until it became dry.

The inquiry was told that detainees on Nauru had only one hour a day in which water was provided for up to 1000 people to shower. A nurse who worked in detention centres told the inquiry that people in Curtin presented with cut feet because detention authorities refused to re-issue them with thongs if the previous pair had broken within six weeks.

Poor physical conditions in detention centres were not restricted to remote centres. A former Villawood detainee told the inquiry:

> I had a lot of cockroaches in my room where I used to wake up in the morning and there were cockroaches in my chest and in my hair. For three months I asked either to be moved to another room or to have the cockroaches exterminated. They refused.

A visitor to Maribyrnong told the inquiry:

> We were told that the detainees were cold because they only had one blanket per person. We got 30 new blankets; also sent some crocheted blankets. A lot of people had contributed to making those. Day after day we asked the detainees, 'Have you got the blankets?' and day after day we were told, 'No.'

Former immigration minister Philip Ruddock made no apologies for the poor conditions asylum seekers were held in. He said about Woomera:

> We will be briefing people on the nature of the facility, the environment in which it's been placed. It's not a holiday camp, nor should it be seen as one.[231]

A man detained on Nauru told the inquiry about a visit to the camp by Philip Ruddock:

> People are very hopeful thinking that he is going to come and show some sympathy. All the women and children went outside in that scorching weather to welcome him. He doesn't even say hello to us, he just tells us that we will try our best to get you out of this country, because you are the people who came by window. You didn't use the door, you don't deserve to stay here and we will use any method to get you out.

Detention centre operators were not disturbed about the poor living conditions either. Former ACM operations manager at Woomera, Alan Clifton, told *The Age*:

> They [ACM] didn't care. For the first six months they were making $5 million profit per month. For that they had to feed them, contain them, keep them alive.[232]

Asylum seekers in detention were also given inadequate amounts of poor-quality food, forced to work for paltry remuneration if they wished to buy items such as cigarettes and phonecards, and provided with inadequate health care, which in some cases resulted in permanent damage to detainees' physical and mental health.

Food

The inquiry heard evidence from a wide range of sources about the inadequacy of the food that detainees received. A visitor to Villawood told the inquiry that breakfast was served between 7am and 8am, lunch between 11.30am and 12.30pm, and dinner between 4.30pm and 5.30pm, with no food available outside these times. A boy who spent three years in detention told the inquiry:

*The denial of food was everywhere. It was absolutely bad in Curtin.
They would force people to actually steal and children saw this. Parents
couldn't say anything because they needed the food. Small children need
to eat all the time. Each time I get up I just go to my fridge and eat and
that's what makes children, they eat all the time. And this was denied
from them.*

In July 2002, Mark Huxstep, a nurse who worked in detention, told the
Human Rights and Equal Opportunity Commission (HREOC) Inquiry
into Children in Immigration Detention that detainees were only allowed
250mL of milk and one piece of fruit per day. He also said that there
was sometimes not enough formula for infants, due to the bureaucracy
involved in its distribution.[233] A general practitioner told the inquiry:

*A woman told me that she would smuggle milk out of the dining room
for the babies to have during the night.*

The friend of an asylum seeker told the inquiry:

*If the children slept through breakfast there was no food till lunch.
She was still breastfeeding, but gradually she was trying to get the
baby off the breast and they wouldn't give her milk between meal
times. They weren't allowed to bring food back to their cubicle and
anyone knows how much growing children need. She would put some
bread down her front to take back for the children and a guard saw
this and made her take the bread out, then threw it on the ground and
stepped on it.*

The inquiry also heard that the quality of food provided to asylum seekers
was poor. A former Woomera detainee said:

*In a few days they served a very rotten smelly type of meat and people
just got angry and they throw the food for them and said that's not
really for human consumption.*

A detainee's account of Cornelia Rau's time in Baxter submitted to the
inquiry includes this anecdote:

One day she went to the office and told them that she got tired of this

junky food but the officers told her that there wasn't any other food. If she
wasn't happy with it she couldn't eat or she could go back to her country.

In August 2004, the Department of Immigration confirmed that maggots
had twice been found in food served to detainees at Baxter. Minister
Amanda Vanstone responded by saying that Baxter was 'the best detention
centre that I have seen in the world in terms of conditions. I don't have any
evidence of unhygienic conditions in Baxter.'[234]

Attempts by detainees to obtain better food were sometimes obstructed.
A man who spent six years in detention told the inquiry:

> *Due to very disgusting food, I applied from my account to buy some*
> *foods. They didn't buy it. When I ask them why you are not going to*
> *buy some olive oil for me have it with some salads, they said because*
> *it could be used as a weapon. I made the joke that I am going to call*
> *ASIO and let them know that olive oil could be used as a weapon,*
> *they have to be careful. No one knows anything about that, that's big*
> *development.*

Work

Many asylum seekers worked in the detention centres to occupy themselves
and earn 'merit points', which could be used at canteens within the centres
to buy items such as cigarettes and phonecards. They worked as kitchen
hands and cooks, gardeners, cleaners, gym instructors and hairdressers for
one merit point (equivalent to one dollar) per hour.[235] Detention supervisors
chose which detainees could earn merit points. The inquiry heard from a
former Villawood detainee:

> *You only get paid in phonecard and cigarettes if you are lucky enough*
> *to get a job. Otherwise you end up trying to pick up cigarettes from the*
> *floor.*

A boy who spent a year in Nauru told the inquiry:

> *I start working in the kitchen, like 10 hours a day, for free. Nobody had*
> *any money and we all said we are not going to work any more. After*
> *about six or eight months, they said we are going to pay you 80 bucks*
> *a month.*

In October 2005, a Villawood detainee issued proceedings in the Federal Court against the Immigration Department, GSL and the Federal Police in relation to the merits-point scheme. He claimed that detention authorities were flouting Section 235(3) of the *Migration Act*, which prohibits unlawful noncitizens from engaging in work, paid or otherwise, while in Australia, and that the Federal Police had failed to investigate this offence.[236] He argued that he was provided with substandard services delivered by fellow detainees and that it was incongruous for him to be paid the equivalent of one dollar an hour while he was accumulating a debt of around $130 a day for his incarceration. Five months later the government amended the migration regulations to allow detainees who requested employment to perform work within detention centres.

Despite having almost no income, people in detention displayed generosity to others. A woman who was pregnant while held in detention told the inquiry:

> The detainees, I considered those people the best people. I haven't seen in my life people that are so caring about each other. They helped me with food. They had a banana each and they gave all their bananas to me telling me that it is good for your baby and saving every good thing that they had from visit centre to give to me.

A visitor to detention told the inquiry:

> I was having a birthday and one of the quite depressed detainees bought a chocolate cake from Port Augusta and that must have cost a fair bit. He said, 'Don't bring anything today,' when we visited that time. That was really touching.

In January 2004, Baxter detainees donated $2895 to the Australian Red Cross to assist the victims of a December 2003 earthquake in the city of Bam in Iran. They also donated money to victims of the 2004 tsunami. A refugee advocate told the inquiry:

> In Baxter, they decided to put their points together and get them converted to dollars. They raised quite a lot of money and sent it to the tsunami appeal. Even though friends and supporters put out media releases about that gesture, it was not reported in any Australian media.

Health

Another theme that emerged from the evidence presented to the inquiry was the inadequacy of medical care provided to people in detention. GSL sub-contracted health-care providers: International Health and Medical Services (IHMS) for primary and allied health-care services within detention centres; and Davidson Trahaire, trading as Professional Support Services Pty Ltd (PSS), for psychological services. It also engaged general practitioners and psychiatrists on a contract basis.

When ACM ran detention centres, health services were provided by staff directly employed by ACM and those engaged by it on a fixed-term contract basis. ACM health staff consisted of a centre health manager (usually a senior nurse), general and psychiatric nurses and allied health professionals including social workers, psychologists or counsellors. External general practitioners were engaged on a contract basis. All health staff, including doctors, were answerable to the nurse manager who reported to the ACM operations manager and general manager at the detention centre.[237]

A submission to the inquiry argued that health costs are a significant expense to detention contractors, potentially compromising health care provided to detainees. It argued that the employment of health staff by these contractors, the requirement for the staff to adhere to secrecy agreements and the highly isolated clinical contexts in which they worked further heightened the risk of poor care being provided.[238]

Psychiatrist Jon Jureidini told the inquiry a colleague had observed a general practitioner contracted to provide health services at Baxter being threatened by a detention manager:

> *Our worker was involved in a very lengthy case discussion about a particular kid and the GP had expressed that this kid be detained under the Mental Health Act, which is a pretty extreme thing for us to do. This obviously wasn't very comfortable for ACM. At the break in the meeting our worker overheard a senior detention officer saying in a threatening way to this GP: 'Don't forget who pays your salary!'*

The inquiry was told that, in many cases, the only dental care offered to detainees was tooth extractions, with more expensive procedures denied on the basis of cost. A GP told the inquiry:

One man had a painful tooth drilled and a temporary filling put in. When he went back two weeks later the tooth was pulled out – he was told the DIMIA [Department of Immigration, Multicultural and Indigenous Affairs] did not pay for root filling so, unless he had money, extraction was the only option. He continued to have pain in the adjacent tooth and a month later that was extracted. A month later the next adjacent tooth was removed. We now have a 34-year-old man with no molars on his bottom left jaw.

A refugee supporter told the inquiry she paid $400 so a detainee in Port Hedland could access dental care:

Frequent requests to ACM's doctor to allow him to visit the dentist were denied, with expense given as the reason. Finally he was told that if he could produce $400 to pay for his own treatment, he would be taken to the dentist. Are not taxpayers already paying the contractor for medical and dental treatment? I very much resented having to pay this money, but could not bear to think that our young friend was suffering.

A former detainee told the inquiry:

I have heard a nurse speaking to the department that the Chinese lady with infection in her tooth has come to her begging could you do something? 'How long's she going to be here?' 'Oh,' he says, 'maybe a couple of weeks.' She said: 'Oh, if she is being deported we don't need to spend money on her.'

A man detained in Woomera told the inquiry that detainees who needed glasses were also asked to pay $120 for them. Registered nurse Mark Huxstep told HREOC that during the six months he worked at Woomera no detainee was provided with glasses, despite numerous people needing them, because the cost was deemed unnecessary by detention authorities.[239]

Former detention workers who delivered general medical care told the inquiry the care was inadequate. A former detention worker said that Woomera's medical centre was equipped to deal with eight to 10 detainees but had to deal with up to 40. She said that, though untrained, she performed basic medical procedures and gave out medication.

The poor medical care was replicated in other detention centres.

According to Oxfam, at least 40 people were airlifted to Australia from Nauru for medical treatment due to a lack of services on Nauru.[240] In February 2002, the Royal Australian College of Physicians issued a press release calling for the immediate removal of asylum seekers from Manus Island after some of them contracted malaria. The head of the International Health Program at the Menzies School of Health Research warned:

> Asylum seekers and staff of the detention centre on Manus Island with little immunity to malaria are at significant risk of serious illness or death should they become infected.[241]

However asylum seekers were kept on Manus Island until the last detainee, Aladdin Sisalem, the sole occupant of its detention centre for the previous 10 months, arrived in Australia in May 2004.

A nurse who worked at Baxter told the inquiry:

> Five days a week a doctor would attend, but the doctors did not go into the compounds. You couldn't have people from one compound at medical with [those from] another compound, so they finally decided that each compound would have one day. There were six compounds so it was less than a day a week each, and because of this tedious process of driving people back before the next lot could come and much opening and closing of gates through central command, the number of people you could actually process diminished to about 10 in a day.
>
> When a person came to the nurses in the compound you'd say: 'Yes, you need to see the doctor.' You'd look up the computer: 'Your day is Tuesday, well there's not an appointment for another three Tuesdays.' These were things like a foreign body in an eye, things that needed to be seen and so, even though in theory there were doctors available, in practice there really weren't.

In October 2001, the then immigration minister Philip Ruddock said:

> Our approach is humane, people do get a higher level of service and I would say in relation to dental and medical services, the level of service available to detainees would be of a higher order than many people in regional and remote Australia receive.[242]

But a Port Augusta health worker told the inquiry that the difference between official descriptions and the reality of medical services in detention led to a high staff turnover. This in turn further compromised health provision due to poor continuity of care:

> The toxic system affects the staff and not just the staff out at Baxter but contract staff that come in. Already Baxter has gone through three different medical centres. They are up to their last option. One of the biggest complaints that I have heard was that detainees would see a doctor once and then they would never see that doctor again. There were quite a few local nurses who worked out there to start with but I don't believe there's any left. Some left their jobs thinking they would be chasing a gold mine, realised that the gold mine had a terrible underneath to it and now they fly in staff from all sorts of places. They come in for six-week stints and then off they go. So even the nursing staff don't provide continuity of care.

A former Woomera worker told the inquiry:

> A lot of the people that we did employ couldn't cope so they would leave after their six-week secondment. Even though they were offered other contracts they just couldn't come back. So I had to retrain people every six weeks.

A health worker and refugee advocate told the inquiry that health services near Baxter were limited and there was disagreement among them as to the priority detainees should receive for their services. A visitor to Baxter told the inquiry about the consequences of poor medical services for one detainee:

> In May 2003, my friend said 'so-and-so has got a sore back'. The next day he said, 'He's got a really bad stomach as well,' then the next day this guy couldn't go to the toilet and by the end of it he couldn't actually move. He'd asked for the doctor. He'd been to medical so many times. Finally the other guys said: 'Look, if you don't do something we're going to smash the place up – get him a doctor.' So there was a CERT [Centre Emergency Response Team], which is where the officers get in the riot gear, and then at four o'clock the next morning he was taken to Port Augusta Hospital and had an operation to get his appendix removed because it had burst. He had to be transferred to Queen

Elizabeth Hospital in Adelaide because he had developed peritonitis, which can kill you.

A woman who was detained at Port Hedland told the inquiry her young daughter had to wait six weeks to see a doctor after catching her finger in a door:

When I went to see doctor just a little skin was left and they did operation straight away to her but they said we are not sure if the finger is going to work or maybe have to cut down.

The inquiry also heard that medical care was often only provided after detainees fought with detention staff or damaged property. A man who spent two and a half years in detention told the inquiry:

Nurse came in and I asking, 'My finger like this, I have very pain.' One day one Iranian guy was very upset and he say, 'Come with me,' and he used bad words and he said, 'Look his finger and are you human or no?' At that time two weeks already and I have to wait another two or three days doctor came. Doctor saw me and he said, 'When it happen?' I said, 'Three weeks ago.' He arrange for the operation in hospital in Whyalla. He said he knows what is going on in Baxter.

Another former detainee told the inquiry:

I was literally crawling on my elbows to go to the toilet. A person used to carry me on his back to take me to the toilet (as a result of my four discs were bulged). There was one week of struggle, shouting and screaming to get crutches or a wheelchair so I don't have to rely on other people to take me to the toilet.

Regular visitor to Baxter David Leach told the inquiry he witnessed senior detention officers refusing medical care to a detainee who was unable to walk and had been carried to the visit centre by one of his friends:

He was immensely distressed. He was severely mentally ill at that stage. So I said to the guards, 'I want to speak to the centre manager.' They brought the shift manager and a deputy shift manager and by that time things were getting pretty tense and the shift manager said, 'I have seen you walking around.' And he said, 'I have not been walking around,' and 10 men all yelled out, 'He hasn't been walking around!' He was getting more and more upset. We spent the next 10 minutes keeping these strong young men who'd had enough and these stupid couple of guards apart and if it wasn't for two young Catholic fellows who were built like brick shithouses holding back these people, there would have been a full-on riot.

There was terrible language being yelled across the room. So then the man got extremely ill and he vomited into a big bin and he vomited six times. I've seen people vomit and this guy was – phew – he was seriously ill. He was shaking, he was sweating. I thought he was going to die for a minute. The shift manager and the deputy shift manager are still there and I'm saying to them: 'This man needs medical help right now.' 'Oh no, we're not going to get medical help.' I said: 'A riot will start again unless you get medical help.' So the next minute a nurse comes in, a very, very nice nurse comes in, has a look at him, declares him to be very, very ill; arranges for him to go up to hospital immediately in a wheelchair and he needed drugs to control his vomiting and he needed to be sedated that night.

One refugee supporter told the inquiry she knew of two men whose broken limbs were left untreated for weeks. Another refugee advocate, Kate Gauthier, told the inquiry:

A man had a broken ankle. He was taken to hospital where they X-rayed it but they weren't able to set it at that time. He was supposed to come back the next day but they didn't take him back for another 13 days. And that was only after he smashed a light bulb to force the issue.

For some, the lack of medical attention caused permanent damage. After three years of being misdiagnosed and denied medical treatment in detention, 14-year-old Iranian Shahin Adgar was almost legally blind when he came to medical attention.[243] A woman who spent a year on Manus Island told the inquiry that she had made numerous requests for specialist medical assistance without getting it:

Finally when I was released and I succeeded in having a surgical operation to my eye, it has been suggested by the surgeon that unfortunately it is too late to save your vision because the nerve is dead completely.

Australian advocates who tried to assist detainees who needed medical help found detention authorities unhelpful. A lawyer told the inquiry:

We had a case of a minor who was in a terrible situation. He was losing his sight because of the lack of treatment. Medication that he needed for that condition – when they ran out there was no effort made to get more. When we tried to get him transferred so that he could access the medical care he needed the department was very obstructive. They told us it was their policy that a minor could not instruct a lawyer and they couldn't pass on any of our correspondence. I mean that's clearly false, a kid can instruct a lawyer. At the time we were funded by the department to represent unaccompanied minors for visa applications.

Asylum seekers were often handcuffed while undergoing medical procedures, leading some to refuse health services. A refugee supporter told the inquiry:

This young man said, 'I wouldn't go to the dentist, they came to put me in handcuffs.' He said, 'I wasn't going out in the street,' he was too proud to do that.

A doctor held in detention told the inquiry he had twice refused to go to hospital for a heart problem while there because he didn't want to be handcuffed. A refugee advocate told the inquiry about another detainee:

That man had once before had a major operation, and he had come to in recovery handcuffed to the bed. He'd put in complaints and he got a letter of regret from DIMIA over that. So when we are fighting to get his X-rays done, they finally got the appointments and they were going to handcuff him. He said: 'But I don't have to be handcuffed. Here's the letter to say that was wrong that I was handcuffed in the hospital before.' They said: 'If you won't be handcuffed, you don't go,' and they walked out. So he was left for another week with this really bad back.

Detainees who became ill enough to be hospitalised were technically still in detention, and so were guarded by detention officers. A lawyer told the inquiry that one man who was hospitalised weighing just 40kg as a result of being on a hunger strike had two guards with him at all times. A visitor to Maribyrnong told the inquiry:

> I visited a woman from Nauru in Maribyrnong and in hospital and also in a rehabilitation centre. She had spinal trouble so she was in a very, very bad way and yet both in the hospital and the rehabilitation centre there were two officers on duty 24 hours a day. She couldn't move from the hospital bed to the door. She knew no English and she was virtually crying all the time.

Asylum seekers also experienced personal hostility from some of the health providers within detention centres. A former detainee told the inquiry:

> One nurse was really, really racist. We had to go to medical to take the medication. I was sitting there and she told doctor, 'This is dangerous for me, I am scared of this man.' I said, 'What I did to you?' She couldn't tell me anything. After I get really, really angry. I said something bad and just went out, I didn't want to stay there.

A refugee supporter and nurse told the inquiry that on five occasions when she had been on the phone to a detainee she had overheard nurses behaving in an unprofessional manner while dispensing medication. On one occasion a detainee had fitted after being refused his medication because he arrived 'too late' to collect it.

Some detention staff believed sick detainees were faking their illnesses. Wayne Lynch, who worked in Woomera for seven months as a nurse and counsellor, told HREOC:

> A 60-year-old woman with neurological deficits was not transferred to hospital upon advice of medical and nursing staff. Management believed that it was psychosomatic. Eventually this detainee was diagnosed as having had a stroke.[244]

Other detainees reported that detention staff believed Cornelia Rau was faking her mental illness:

> While Cornelia was in the compound they brainwashed everyone to make them believe that she had no mental problem. They said that

*according to the psychologist's report she plays her game very well.
And she's a good actress and she just pretended to be crazy because she
didn't want to be deported.*[245]

A refugee advocate told the inquiry that a Baxter psychologist noted on the
file of a detainee who was losing consciousness and falling onto concrete
in regular panic attacks: 'Informed that many people feel his panic attacks
are not genuine.' Knowing the attitude of detention health staff to his
illness, the detainee refused to have any interaction with them. The refugee
advocate told the inquiry:

> *During one attack, in full view of those witnessing, a senior male nurse
> allegedly exposed this young man's penis and pinched it with his fingers.
> His motive apparently was to prove he was feigning the event. This
> experiment failed, as he was actually unconscious, and he was later
> informed of the incident.*

Health professionals working in external health services were also often
hostile to asylum seeker patients. A former detainee told the inquiry:

> *When there was some protest in Woomera, in support of them I drank
> detergent and they took me to the hospital in Derby. There was one
> woman who told me, 'You came here from the taxpayer' and like that.*

One refugee supporter worked as a cleaner at Woomera Base Hospital. She
told the inquiry that few townspeople, including nurses providing care to
ill detainees, were sympathetic to the refugees. Some nurses were married
to detention officers and others saw the centre as bringing jobs and money
to a town that had little to sustain it. She became a target of suspicion:

> *When I was friendly to two elderly women detainees being treated
> there, one officer told me he was noting how long I spent cleaning
> their room, that I had to leave the door open so he could monitor
> our conversations and that it 'wasn't part of my job to be friendly to
> them.' During this time I was pulled aside for putting fresh flowers on
> the breakfast trays, buying a Cherry Ripe for a teenage girl who was
> in hospital after self-harming, saying good morning in Arabic to the
> elderly women, and questioned on whether I was giving the asylum
> seekers extra teaspoons.*

Later a locum nurse came to share my hospital-supplied house. I was getting phone calls from friends inside the detention centre and she was shocked when I told her what went on in there. One night she came home from work very angry. She had been asked to report to ACM what I was doing at home – who I spoke to on the phone, any visitors I had. She flatly refused. Eventually my boss told me there was pressure from ACM not to have me working at the hospital.

A refugee advocate told the inquiry she was threatened by hospital staff when she tried to inquire about the wellbeing of a sick detainee:

He had in his pocket an authority that the doctor is authorised to talk to us about his condition. When we got to Port Augusta Hospital, we asked if it was possible to see him even briefly with guards escorting us and that was refused. The thing that actually stunned me is that the duty manager of the hospital, when we asked to speak to the doctor, asked us to leave the hospital premises and if we didn't leave immediately she would call the police. She suggested we could even be arrested and I had no idea on what grounds. But it gave us a real indication as to how even the hospital believed the people it was holding in its walls were some incredible danger to society.

However, in this case a detention officer helped her to see her friend:

There was one officer who couldn't believe that we had been refused to even speak to the doctor and she organised quietly to have the guys moved into a room and she snuck us around the back and we could see them through a window. They were very, very happy to see us because they knew then that there were people who knew about them and were looking out for them.

Another visitor to detention also told the inquiry about a kind action from a detention officer when her friend was in hospital:

I rang the hospital and the guard told me I had to ring DIMIA to get permission to talk to him. DIMIA don't operate over the weekend, and this was Sunday night. They wouldn't tell me why he was admitted to hospital. I rang a couple of people in Port Augusta to see how I could find out. It was suggested that I wait about an hour and a half because the officers could change and I might get further with the second officer. The second officer said he wasn't sure whether I was allowed to speak to him, but that he would give him the phone to hold while he went to check.

A LIFE FILLED WITH LITTLE CRUELTIES: MENTAL HEALTH CONDITIONS

Another theme that emerged from the evidence presented to the inquiry was how often those detained were humiliated. Psychiatrist Jon Jureidini, who worked with asylum seekers in Woomera and Baxter, told the inquiry:

Each story on its own risks being dismissed as not very important if you only hear one of them, but when you link them all together you recognise that a detainee's life is just filled with these little cruelties. I think that's one of the things that drive people mad in the detention setting.

A refugee lawyer told the inquiry:

I think the humiliation of detention just can't be overstated – the many and varied ways in which each individual detainee is humiliated from the time they wake up in the morning until the time they go to sleep, and even while they are sleeping they are humiliated.

On entering the detention centres, all asylum seekers were given ID cards and assigned numbers. They each used their number for all official transactions within the centre. A former detainee in Port Hedland told the inquiry:

The first day we were given a number and I was told that from now that's how I will be known. You will be ABC123. That was one of the most difficult things for us because having your normal freedom taken away from you and at the same time you lost your name. One of the most difficult things for me too was that there were three different head counts. There was one at six in the morning, one at midnight and another at two in the morning. No matter who you are, even a baby, they will have to wake you up, you show your card or shout your number loudly.

A man who spent six months in Woomera told the inquiry he tried to protect his children during the head counts:

He poke people with his finger or with a stick to uncover their faces. Sometimes I forced myself to stay awake until they finished their patrol to make sure that the treatment of the children would be in a normal way, to do all that for him, uncover the faces of the children. But unfortunately there is no regular schedule for their visit. You never know when, so you have to be always cautious.

An American woman who was detained in Maribyrnong told the inquiry:

Two guards come in to the women's dorm. One woman, one man counting bodies in beds. I was particularly intrigued that they would send a man into the sleeping area of these women, who are unfortunately mostly Muslim women. If you know anything about Muslim culture, that is one of the least appropriate things you can do.

A former Woomera nurse told journalist Madeleine Byrne that some officers boasted of how they waited until asylum seekers were asleep and then ran their steel torches along the outside of their accommodation to wake them up. She also saw officers shooing children away from drinking taps on scorching hot days, while they sat with Eskies full of iced water.[246] Several former detainees told the inquiry that on hot days officers had eaten ice cream and consumed soft drinks in front of children.

Despite the hostility many officers felt towards them, detainees had to rely on them for their most basic needs. A former detainee told the inquiry:

Even if I want to get a piece of paper, I have to ask them. And they think they are doing us a favour, that's not their job, and we should be very thankful to them.

A man who spent six years in detention told the inquiry:

I know the meaning of humiliation because I have been humiliated.

Not only me. They provoke people, they harass people, they humiliate people and they enjoy that. I never seen their regret or they feel sorry for us. Their job is simply to look after us but we been judged by them, why we came to Australia by boat. We do all the legal things, request form, ask officer for your own rights, which are not privileges. And they will deny you and provoke you. In detention, there is no law. Everything depend on individual officer. Our life depend on his kindness, which should not be.

Several former detainees told the inquiry that some officers deliberately taunted asylum seekers. One said:

They try to play with your mind, they want to make you angry and especially they find what you're sensitive [about]. They push you.

A visitor to Maribyrnong told the inquiry:

I remember one man telling me that the one thing he liked that they got for food was a boiled egg and every now and again they'd get boiled eggs and he would take an extra one. An officer took this boiled egg and held it above the rubbish bin and said 'You beg me for this.' He wouldn't and the officer just threw the boiled egg into the bin.

A visitor to detention told the inquiry they had ordered a birthday cake from a shop in Port Augusta for 80 people in Baxter, but when the shop delivered it they were told it was the wrong time and the cake had to be thrown away. Another visitor told the inquiry she had left a potted rose for a Baxter detainee, but by the time it was given to him several very hot days later, it had died.

In July 2005, the then immigration minister Amanda Vanstone released a report that investigated the mistreatment during 2004 of five detainees being transferred from Maribyrnong to Baxter. Despite initial denial of any wrongdoing by GSL and the Immigration Department, the report found the detainees had been assaulted, denied food and water and had been forced to urinate in the van when officers ignored their requests for help and denied them toilet breaks.[247] GSL was fined $500,000 for breach of contract and the matter was referred to the Victorian police to consider criminal charges.[248]

Regular visitor to Baxter David Leach told the inquiry that an unwell detainee was refused food on a nine-hour return trip to investigate his illness:

> *Three guards took him to Adelaide and it was a fairly warm day. They stopped at McDonald's but they would not get any lunch for this detainee. On the way back they stopped at McDonald's again and this man said, 'Look, can you get me something to eat. I'm very hungry.' He said to them, 'I will give you some money when I get back. Could I just have some chips and Coca-Cola.' That's all he asked for, and they said no. These men sat eating their McDonald's in front of him. He was handcuffed to them. Then he said, 'I'm thirsty.' So they stopped the car at a petrol station and said, 'Go and drink the water out of the hand basin in the toilet.'*

Detainees were also told that all Australians disliked them. A man who spent six months in Port Hedland told the inquiry:

> *From time to time somebody come and say, 'The way you came to this country was an invasion way, not a polite way, so that's why people don't really like you. If anybody wants to go back home then we are more than happy to send them, but don't ever think you are going to get in Australia.' People start to get scared of how they are going to get out, will they be accepted or will they be challenged?*

The inquiry also heard that detention centres were highly regimented, enforcing rules that made no sense. A nurse who worked in detention told the inquiry:

> *There was one family who had three children and a fourth child born in detention, all under six, and they had no photographs. I went to DIMIA and asked if it were possible, even if the nurses funded it, to buy a disposable camera and take a couple of photographs that could be put in their file, so that one day the child would have pictures. They said it was against government policy and when I asked what policy that was, I was told that I was a nurse, could I please leave the DIMIA office.*

Items considered by GSL to pose a risk to security, and therefore banned from entering detention facilities include crochet hooks, Rollerblades, tape recorders, soccer boots, DVDs, wallets, nail polish, pencils and pens.[249] A former detention officer who worked at both Woomera and Baxter told the inquiry that a woman detainee had been using a crochet hook to do craft work. She had been asked by another officer to give it up because it was a weapon. When the woman argued, the officer called for backup and three officers threw her down and handcuffed her to take it away.

As their detention continued, and Australia sent troops to fight the regimes from which they had fled, many detainees had bad news from home. A nurse who worked in detention centres told the inquiry:

> Quite commonly detainees would get news of tragic and hideous deaths of family members. You would hear that [someone's] father had been disembowelled and the body dumped outside the family home in Afghanistan. There was tragedy on tragedy in these people's lives.

A refugee advocate provided the inquiry with information she recorded in early 2003:

> As I write there are people in Baxter grieving deeply and inconsolably for family members they have just heard, through the Red Cross, have been killed. One had his family killed by the Taliban, one by recent US bombing to target the Taliban and the third by members of the current ruling parties under whose leadership the country is supposed to be safe. At the same time as these people receive the news of family deaths, DIMIA officials still apply pressure on them to return home.

Detainees who received bad news got little consideration or support from detention authorities. A migration agent told the inquiry she witnessed an Iraqi detainee being told of his father's death one Saturday morning in the Baxter visit centre, which was full of other detainees and visitors. The distant family members who gave him the news were made to leave the visit centre with other visitors during the officers' lunch break. When they tried to return an hour later, they were initially refused entry because the distraught detainee was 'causing trouble' by refusing to leave the Visit Centre.

In October 2002, Endang Sammaki, the Indonesian wife of Iranian asylum seeker Ebrahim Sammaki, was killed in the Bali bombing. Ebrahim Sammaki had come to Australia because the couple's nine-year marriage was not recognised by Indonesian authorities and neither of their two children had birth certificates. But after more than a year and a half in detention, he had asked his wife to seek legal advice about him returning to Indonesia, and she had travelled to Bali to get it. Suffering burns to 60 per cent of her body following the bombing, she died before her husband could get permission to visit her.[250]

Following her death, Sara and Safdar Sammaki, then three and seven years old, were denied visas to visit their father on three separate occasions. Adelaide Magistrate Brian Deegan, whose son Josh was also killed in the bombing, offered to personally escort the children for a visit, saying:

> All I'm seeking is to take them back with me on a two- or three-week holiday so that they can see their father is alive, so they know they've got a father, and so that he can for the first time in two years just hold his children. I mean ... this is cruel and unusual.[251]

But the then immigration minister Philip Ruddock stated:

> My view is that to reunite him with his children [for] the purpose of a visit without enabling him to remain with them is not really a satisfactory outcome. He is Iranian and he can go to Iran at any time.[252]

Five months later, the then prime minister, John Howard, visited Bali to attend a memorial service for the bombing victims. He was photographed holding hands with Sara and Safdar Sammaki, an image that received wide publicity. A month later Ebrahim Sammaki was granted permanent residency and allowed to sponsor his children to Australia.[253]

The inquiry also heard that ordinary Australians who tried to provide support to detainees in distress were obstructed by authorities. In a 2002 speech, Julian Burnside QC explained how the son of Nurjan Hussaini and the husband of Fatima Husseini, the women who died when the Suspected Illegal Entry Vessel (SIEV) 10 caught fire and sank, were allowed out of detention to attend the inquest into their deaths:

> The last day of it was Friday 8 November which happened to be the 12 month anniversary of the day on which the two women drowned ... a support group had organised a small memorial service to be held in the park immediately adjacent to the Fremantle Court. They got permission from the Court ... from ACM ... from the police ... from the Department of Immigration, that these two men should be allowed to step out of their cells and into the park, under guard, a distance of

20 metres and attend the memorial ceremony for the deaths of their loved ones. Fifteen minutes before the ceremony began, Mr Ruddock withdrew permission for them to attend … I have to say that is one of the most heartless and despicable acts I've seen committed by a Minister of the Crown in recent years.[254]

A visitor to Villawood told the inquiry about her attempts to comfort another detainee:

When she really thought she was going to lose the child, I waited in the Family Court for her. I wanted to give her a phonecard and I wanted to kiss her before she went in and the guard wouldn't let me go close to her. She wouldn't let me give her a little kiss on the cheek to wish her all the best in court.

The evidence presented to the inquiry showed how people's mental health deteriorated with their incarceration. Although they had escaped persecution in their own countries and had therefore experienced trauma and hardship before coming to Australia, most asylum seekers did not have mental-health problems before being put into detention. A man who spent more than two years on Nauru told the inquiry:

The reason my wife is still suffering and having this severe headache is that she ran away from the trauma and tortures of Taliban hoping that she will find a safe haven, but she didn't and they locked us up in the prisons.

A visitor to Maribyrnong told the inquiry:

There was an Afghan woman who was a doctor and had a child in detention. In the beginning she was alive and alert and she was learning medical terms in English from a dictionary that one of her friends brought in. Then gradually this look of sadness and not really caring came over her. I can remember sitting one day with her and her English was minimal so we were sketching. I drew something and she said, 'Mountain,' and I said, 'Yeah.' Then she put in a sun and a sea, some waves and eventually she said, 'Over the mountain, some life for me,' and at that stage she was crying and I was very close to crying. It was just so poignant and that was after several months of her being in detention.

Regular visitor to Baxter David Leach told the inquiry:

> *Out of the four men that I visited, when I first started seeing them nearly three years ago, they were all perfectly healthy, mentally fine people. At the moment three of them are mentally ill. One of them is moderately mentally ill. One of them is slightly mentally ill and the other one is very, very ill and I'm fearful for his life as a result of the psychosis that has come about from being in detention.*

While detention centres employed mental-health staff, they were unable to change the fundamental causes of mental-health problems in detainees. Effective treatment was therefore impossible. In January 2007, HREOC reported:

> *The main way to treat a mental-health concern is to remove the primary cause of the problem. In the case of immigration detainees, detention and uncertainty are amongst the main causes and they cannot usually be addressed by the mental-health professionals.*[255]

Psychiatrist Jon Jureidini told the inquiry that he had never seen such universal mental ill-health outside of psychiatric-patient populations.

> *You could have the Rolls Royce of mental-health services in Baxter and I don't think it would make a scrap of difference, because the environment is so toxic that you can't treat anything meaningfully. Half a dozen of the most damaged people I've ever seen are the adults I've seen in Baxter and Woomera, both parents and single men.*
>
> *It is all caused by being in detention. Provided you get them in time, you take these people out of detention and they're not depressed any more. Of course the interpretation of that from DIMA [Department of Immigration and Multicultural Affairs] is to say they're putting it on: 'Isn't it convenient?' The reason it's going to cure them is because detention is a place that drives people mad and yeah, they want to get out of the place that is driving them mad.*

Another psychiatrist who worked at Baxter, Dr Howard Gorton, told a television program:

> *The people I saw and treated at Baxter were the most damaged*

people I've seen in my whole psychiatric career. Up until that time, I'd never met an adult-onset bed-wetter. I'd never met someone with psychological blindness. And there were also a few physically crippled people who believed they were unable to walk, and this was probably psychological too.[256]

A man who spent 18 months in Villawood told the inquiry that the mental-health problems of many detainees were exacerbated by the way their detention was managed:

> *They started moving people from Villawood to Baxter and this was done by saying to the person that they have an urgent phone call in the office. They would take them and pack up their belongings at three in the morning. So knocks on the door became an absolute anxious moment. They knock on your door dressed in riot gear to move you. When this was happening the place was abuzz. People wouldn't stay in their rooms. They tried to trick the families, saying that there was a family meeting in the dining area, but someone phoned to tip them off and it caused a lot of angst. Not one person was moved to Baxter [after being told] 'Look you are going to Baxter now.' It was all trickery. So this is what you lived with every night.*

Psychiatrist Jon Jureidini told the inquiry that one woman whose husband was very ill in hospital was housed in a motel near the hospital. When she was told she would be taken back to Baxter and realised that her husband might die alone, she threatened to kill herself. Detention authorities initially responded by saying she would have to be taken to Baxter for suicide observations, but later agreed to keep her at the motel, where a torch was shone on her face at random intervals during the night.

A visitor to detention told the inquiry:

> *One time when I was visiting Baxter to tell someone of his mother's death, we had trouble to get the psychologists there when we were telling him. The reason we went to so much trouble was that some other person had also received this sort of bad news a few months before that and had been put in isolation and drugged so heavily that he collapsed. He had a breakdown and has not really recovered from the effects of how he was treated when trying to grieve.*
>
> *We did deliver him the news, but the young man that he had with*

him as a supporter collapsed from the trauma of it himself, so the psych team had to go and help him and it left us to deal with our friend in grief. His friend was carted off to hospital and when he woke up he was handcuffed to the bed.

Mental-health resources provided in detention were woefully inadequate. Former Department of Immigration manager Diana Goldrick told the inquiry that in 2000, ACM employed one psychologist for all their detention centres in Australia. The psychologist told her he was overwhelmed by his workload and that she was the only person from the department to have ever contacted him for information that might assist with an asylum seeker's case.

Journalist Madeleine Byrne, who conducted research on staff in immigration detention centres, told the inquiry:

I spoke to a former nurse who worked at Woomera and she told me that a former cook was conducting preliminary psychiatric assessments of detainees in 2000. Another person at Woomera around the same time saw what she said was a nursing aide dispensing drugs in the mess. Both are good examples of people who were doing things outside their legal responsibilities, and putting people at risk.

In July 2005, it was revealed that two psychologists practising at Baxter had been unregistered in breach of the Psychological Practices Act.[257] A refugee supporter who was corresponding with a man who had been in detention for five years told the inquiry:

He has seen a psychologist who appears to have no clear understanding of the situation. He says that if he is told to breathe and think of something nice and positive one more time he will scream.

One former Woomera worker told the inquiry she had been asked to counsel people despite not having appropriate training:

You are looking at 400 to 500 people. I couldn't possibly reach most of them and the counselling area was under a tree. There was no private area. I would deal with six to 12 people a day self-harming. I was dealing with people tying razor wire around their throats, using razor blades, knitting needles that they would sharpen, rope, whatever they

could access, overdosing on Panadol, detergent, chemicals, gravel – one
person ate a kilo of gravel and perforated his bowel. People climbing
on roofs and trees threatening to jump. I had to negotiate [with] these
people to not harm themselves. I was successful in about 80 per cent
[of cases].

A social worker who visited detention told the inquiry:

I saw one guy who tried to commit suicide and who was then on a two-
minute watch with these completely unqualified officers just literally
following him around all the time. Every two minutes, they would write
something on a piece of paper. I just thought, this would drive me crazy
after half an hour.

The inquiry also heard that people who tried to assist distressed asylum
seekers were faced with hostile attitudes from detention authorities. A
former detention officer told the inquiry that when she raised concerns
with her supervisor about the mental health of a bed-ridden detainee, she
was told to 'tell the fucking lazy bitch to get out of bed and help herself.'
When she emailed her shift manager saying something had to be done, she
was told to 'poke her with a stick to see if she's dead.'

Despite signs of mental illness that would have resulted in intensive
treatment for other members of the Australian community, the inquiry
heard that asylum seekers often received inadequate and inappropriate
treatment. A 2004 study of families in detention found that external
mental-health professionals had difficulties accessing detainees referred for
assessments, which were frequently cancelled by detention officers due to
a lack of transport or concerns about security.[258] Psychiatrist Jon Jureidini
told the inquiry about his experience of assessing one detainee:

This little room was completely closed off and dark. We went in, and
the husband woke his wife, who was asleep. She looked around and he
explained to her that I was there and she began to scream. She screamed
and moaned unrelentingly for the 10 minutes I was there (which felt
like about two hours) as I clumsily tried to say something that might
calm her.

Then I left, partly because I couldn't stand it any more, and partly
because it was clear I had assessed as much as I was going to be able to.
It transpired that she had not been out of bed, except to crawl to the

toilet, for two months. She was unable to walk and was being carried to the shower by her husband periodically. It took a month and a half to get her transferred into a psychiatric hospital.

A submission to the inquiry described how one detainee who had eaten the glass of the light bulb in his room was taken to the detention centre's medical unit rather than hospital. While there he went to the toilet and ate the glass from the light bulb in the toilet. Two days later he ate plastic cups and poured boiling water on his arms, but was still not taken to hospital.

A refugee advocate told the inquiry about another detainee:

Because of his severe mental state he vomited continuously. At times he was vomiting blood. He got to the point where he was chewing his beard, eating the hair and so a lot of delay was made until he [was told] that his mother had died. That left this young man with only his little sister and she was somewhere in Afghanistan, possibly with a friend or distant uncle. Upon the news of his mother's death he became even more distressed. He ended up in intensive care in Port Augusta Hospital.

Despite the fact that mental-health staff could not treat the cause of mental-health problems for asylum seekers in detention, psychiatric medication was often prescribed, mostly by general practitioners who were not mental-health experts. A psychiatrist who assessed people in detention told the inquiry that asylum seekers were wrongly medicated for problems that medication wasn't going to help.

Psychiatrist Dr Michael Dudley said, during a 2005 court case, that he 'saw the primary function of Baxter as being to incarcerate and the medical staff were there to ensure it occurs in the most efficient manner.'[259] The inquiry heard evidence from a range of sources that detainees did not trust health workers because of their close relationship with the management of detention centres.

A former detainee told the inquiry:

One person they called psychology, they run and see what the people got and they pass it to DIMIA, because of that I didn't find anything positive in that field.

In finding that mental-health services in Baxter were substandard, Federal Court judge Justice Finn stated that a detainee's refusal to accept counselling from detention-centre psychologists on the basis of distrust was 'understandable':[260]

> There is clear evidence from the applicants that they distrust the PSS psychologists because of their 'employment' with GSL, there is the evidence of Ms Kannis [Baxter DIMIA Manager] of her easy access to PSS files on individual detainees, and there is Dr Schroff's evidence of the qualified character of the doctor-patient relationship he has with detainees who see him.[261]

A refugee supporter told the inquiry:

> Many detainees, even when ill, simply refuse to see the psychologist or psychiatrist because they don't trust them or they might be put in management. They view the extensive prescription of antidepressant and anti-anxiety medication as a strategy for keeping them under control.

A man who spent four years in detention told the inquiry:

> I got psychiatrists. Always when we talk they supporting GSL; they don't talk about ourself because always their main point is that we be quiet in there. If I make trouble and GSL call the psychiatrist, [the psychiatrist] say if you do this they put [you in] jail or they can make it worse for you. They give tablet for us to be calm.

Psychiatrist Jon Jureidini told the inquiry:

> Every adult we've ever seen in detention has been on psychiatric drugs. In doing that we are dampening down dissent and protest in the detention environment, and we're significantly colluding with an immoral and unethical means of detention. I think that any doctor who prescribes drugs in that environment has to be really careful, and I would find it very hard to justify prescribing.

Psychiatric medication was also administered inappropriately on a number of occasions. A visitor to detention told the inquiry:

> We took with us, the visit before last, a doctor. Of the nine men who were at the visit when the doctor was there, eight of them had

been recently put on an antidepressant. One of the young guys was
hypermanic. Talk, talk, talk and he was really angry. When we left, the
doctor said, 'That young man is overdosed on that drug.'

Registered nurse Mark Huxstep told *Four Corners* that in August 2000 a
detainee in isolation had been held down while he was injected with double
the maximum dose of an anti-psychotic drug despite concerns being raised
about the dose. Still handcuffed, the detainee later had to be resuscitated.
Huxstep's report of the incident disappeared three times.[262]

Regular visitor to Baxter David Leach told the inquiry he witnessed the
inappropriate medication of a detainee:

He found out that his older brother had been killed. He became very
distraught, tearing at his clothes and uncontrollable weeping. Instead of
giving him any psychological help, they put him in a management unit
in solitary confinement. Finally they agreed that I could have a special
out-of-hours visit. He came in with two guards and he was completely
dishevelled. Here is a man who is very clean. He hadn't shaved for three
days. He hadn't showered for three days. He smelt of urine, faeces,
hadn't brushed his teeth. His eyes were all red-rimmed.

As he came over he grabbed hold of me and whispered that they had
just injected him with something. So I sat down with him and he got
really, really shaky and he was crying continuously and he was asking
me if I could kill him. He said, 'Can you please strangle me?' That's
what he actually said.

The shaking got worse and then his whole face went into rigor, his
jaw became clenched and he just went completely catatonic. These two
guards were just sitting there. I said, 'Can you get a doctor, please?'
They said, 'No' and I said, 'Can you get some medical help really really
quickly.' And they said, 'No' and I said, 'Do something now because
I'm going to start putting things through windows.' And I picked up a
chair and I was about to put it through a window.

Then they could see what was happening. His jaws were so tightly
clamped that the muscles on the side of his face were quivering and he
was completely frozen. They called on the radio and two nurses came
into the room and immediately yelled into their radios to get the psych
nurse. The psych nurse came in and barked some orders and they got a
drug which is an antidote to the drug they'd given him.

While they were organising for the psych nurse to come the two nurses just got it for the next couple of minutes because the man was completely catatonic and psychotic. He couldn't hear anything. So I was telling these two nurses that they were a disgrace to their profession and one of them was bawling her eyes out. But the psych nurse that came in, I said, 'This man needs to be in hospital,' which she refused, and I said, 'Then he needs to be in your medical centre,' and she refused and she said, 'He is going back to management until he agrees not to self-harm.'

After three days he went back to his compound. He didn't receive adequate mental care after that. He's a very, very sick young man and he still suffers from psychoses. He regularly goes into catatonic states where he cannot move, cannot talk. The last time was only a couple of weeks ago and his friends found him. Twelve hours or more he'd been on his lounge-room floor. He's in and out of mental hospitals. They have got one young man and absolutely destroyed him.

In her research on staff in immigration detention centres, journalist Madeleine Byrne found that the detention environment sometimes led mental-health staff to act in ways they never normally would. She told the inquiry:

In 2002 at Easter, there was a very violent riot. The two psychologists I interviewed were kept in the medical centre and watched the riot take place. One psychologist says that a little girl about four years old was screaming; she was terrified because they used tear gas and [a] water cannon. The psychologist came out and an officer said, 'Stand back, stand back, officer's orders.' Nothing could be done for this little girl whose mum had run away with some of her other children. Later that night the girl was still hysterical. They had no idea what to do. I don't think the doctor was there and they ended up giving her a chemical sedative. This psychologist said she had nothing else that she could do.

Psychiatrist Dr Michael Dudley has argued that indefinite mandatory detention contradicts Australian government policies on suicide prevention and 'amounts to state-sponsored trauma and child neglect and/or abuse.'[263] He told a rally outside Villawood in 2005 that the government policy of deterring asylum seekers treated mental suffering as acceptable collateral damage.

In 2002, the then immigration minister, Philip Ruddock, responded to UN concerns about conditions in detention centres, particularly widespread depression and acts of self-harm, by stating:

I don't know that you can call it a particularly rampant depression.
Some people suffer depression, and they're treated for it.[264]

A year later he told *Insight* he was not concerned that the department was
not classifying depression amongst detainees as a mental illness, saying:

> *Depression is quite significant in the Australian community and*
> *people are treated for it and I'm not sure that everybody would regard*
> *depression as being a mental illness. You may have some colleges*
> *and world health organisations that will describe it that way, but I'm*
> *not sure it would be seen that way more broadly in the Australian*
> *community.*[265]

Following the publication by mental-health professionals of six studies
reporting on widespread psychiatric disorders in detention centres, the
federal government commissioned a report from psychiatrist Doron
Samuell at a cost of $30,000.[266]

Psychiatrist Louise Newman, an expert on child trauma, told *Lateline*:

> *At a meeting that I had in June of 2004 with Senator Vanstone, and*
> *John Nation and Andrew Kirk, her principal advisers, to discuss the*
> *issues of children in detention … they said, 'Watch this space … your*
> *research is going to be discredited.'*[267]

In February 2005, Dr Samuell told the *AM* radio program:

> *… it's important this message gets out that the research is not robust.*
> *I see that the research they undertook has been an effort at advocacy*
> *rather than a science.*[268]

Professor of psychiatry Derrick Silove, an international authority on the
effects of detention centres on the mental health of detainees, told the radio
program *AM* that Dr Samuell was:

> *… quite unknown to any of us and many other people in the profession.*
> *He's also not a researcher that I'm aware of. I've never seen anything*
> *published by him in research. And he certainly doesn't have any*
> *academic standing that I'm aware of.*[269]

Cornelia Rau – Timeline of Events

The experiences of Australian resident Cornelia Rau while she was held in immigration detention (see Introduction, p. 19) are set out here as they corroborate evidence given by asylum seekers and other immigration detainees to the inquiry of the treatment they were subjected to while in detention. After former prime minister John Howard refused, on behalf of the government, to pay her compensation, in February 2008 she accepted $2.6 million from the new Rudd Labor government for the Immigration Department's handling of her case.[270]

6/10/04	Cornelia Rau is moved to Baxter.
7/10/04	Psychologist recommended assessment by psychiatrist Dr Andrew Frukacz.
6/11/04	Frukacz assessed, 'Diagnosis unclear but possibilities include: 1. Schizophrenia 2. Personality Disorder. Her posturings, bizarre behaviours and guardedness lead me to consider schizophrenia.' Recommended hospital assessment for a clearer diagnosis.
16/11/04	Rau placed in behaviour management unit. Stayed for about two weeks.
24/11/04	Memo sent to six immigration officials that stated: 'GSL case manager believes Anna Brotmeyer [Cornelia Rau] is an Australian Citizen and has advised the Department of Immigration to investigate this matter with the Australian Federal Police through checking missing persons, etc.'
Late Nov/ early Dec	Rau placed in Red One Behaviour Management Compound. Stayed for 94 days.
30/12/04	Psychiatrist Louise Newman visited Baxter and was told about Rau's behaviour by concerned detainees who 'had seen her totally out of control, screaming incoherently, rolling round on the ground, eating dirt, smearing faeces. They claimed she was being roughly manhandled back into her cell. They also said the guards were taunting in their behaviour. [The guards'] culture is to see this as bunging it on.' Newman 'asked was it possible to see her? We were told no, because she was not able to sign a consent form.'

4/1/05	Baxter psychologist asked South Australia's Rural and Remote Mental Health Service for Glenside psychiatric hospital to assess Rau.
7/1/05	Discussion between psychologist, a GP on site, and rural and remote service resolved to keep her at Baxter. However, the same day, the psychologist made a renewed request for her urgent psychiatric assessment.
14/1/05	Refugee advocate Pamela Curr faxed the Immigration Detention Advisory Group calling for the hospitalisation of Anna.
20/1/05	Pamela Curr phoned the Department of Immigration to say Anna was desperately ill and needed care. Department said it was doing everything possible.
21/1/05	South Australian Director of Mental Health Dr Jonathon Phillips contacted a senior Immigration Department officer raising concerns about Rau. The Department of Immigration contacted the Australian Refugee Association in Adelaide to discuss the possibility of an 'alternative detention' arrangement.
24/1/05	Refugee advocate Trish Highfield spoke to the assistant of a senior immigration department official. She asked her to pass on to senior people her grave concerns about Anna's mental health and her belief that she should be in Glenside psychiatric hospital. Highfield also spoke to a staff member of the then immigration minister Amanda Vanstone and asked him to act urgently. She also spoke to Rau's case manager and told him Rau needed to be in Glenside.
24/1/05	South Australian director of mental health, Dr Jonathon Phillips, again contacted a senior Immigration Department officer raising concerns about Rau and offering to facilitate an assessment, voluntary or not, at Glenside.
28/1/05	Anglican chaplain Michael Hillier wrote to Amanda Vanstone about Anna, saying she should be in Glenside.
31/1/05	*The Age* reporter Andra Jackson, informed by refugee advocates of the situation, wrote a story about 'Anna'.

3/2/05	Lunchtime – Rau's parents were shown the story and called police. 3pm – police called Baxter and emailed a photo of Rau to immigration officials. 3.15pm – an email from the Department of Immigration to its staff in Baxter confirmed arrangements made that morning that Rau would be going to Glenside. 4pm – a GP in Baxter signed an involuntary hospital-admission order to start the process of having Rau admitted to Glenside. She was taken from a shower in Red One and brought to Port Augusta Hospital in handcuffs, with only a sheet to cover her, where she was held overnight under guard.
4/2/05	Rau transferred to Glenside.

This timeline was constructed by the University of Newcastle Legal Centre, lawyers for the Rau family, and submitted to the Inquiry into the Circumstances of the Immigration Detention of Cornelia Rau (the Palmer Inquiry).

Management Units

Like Cornelia Rau, the treatment many mentally ill detainees received was being put in solitary confinement 'management units' or in separation-detention compounds. In 2002, psychologist Lyn Bender told *Four Corners* the harsh measures were a result of ACM being desperate to avoid fatalities and the financial penalties that would be imposed if they occurred. She said:

> As the High-Risk Assessment system became increasingly overloaded, the measures used to stop people harming themselves became increasingly crude.[271]

Peter Ostarek Gammon, former psychiatric nurse at Woomera, told the same program that after a riot at Woomera:

> Some of them were not just locked into their dongas, but they were drilled in. The doors were drilled closed. Another nurse and myself actually had to visit one of those guys one day and they had to get an electric drill to open the cabin.[272]

This was confirmed to the inquiry by another former Woomera worker who said:

> Our High-Risk Assessment and Treatment process is where detainees would be locked in a room. These are people that were presenting with self-harm behaviour, and they actually pop-riveted the door so these detainees were locked with a mattress on the floor and they couldn't get out. I had to go in the compound and un-pop-rivet the door to give the person counselling.

Psychiatrist Jon Jureidini told the inquiry that behavioural-management strategies used to deal with detainees in psychological distress were amateurish, primarily punitive and 'completely inconsistent with mental-health management.' He explained that in isolation rooms within psychiatric wards people 'have to be observed every five minutes and if they have been there for more than an hour, then that generates a "critical incident."' However, many asylum seekers were kept in management units for months. He told a Senate committee:

> The fact that they are labelled as behaviour management strategies gives them some kind of credence. It is an extremely punitive program. The program talks specifically about rewards; there are no rewards. People have absolutely everything taken away from them and then gradually get some of it given back.[273]

In June 2004, the then immigration minister Amanda Vanstone admitted that detainees placed in the 'management unit' at Baxter were locked in their rooms for up to 20 hours per day under constant video surveillance.[274] An asylum seeker who spent years in Baxter described the management unit to the inquiry:

> Almost soundproof, there is no window, twenty-four hours there is a light, there is a video camera, there is no privacy. If you go for toilet or shower, they will see. There is female officer there watching everything and this is called humiliation. I been only a couple of times. But I have seen many people there 20 times, 30 times, so because of that treatment I believe people become mentally insane or abnormal.

The Department of Immigration outlines its expectation in relation to the use of management units in *Ministerial Series Instruction (MSI) 403: Transfer of Detainees within Immigration Detention Facilities.* It states:

> It is not appropriate to allow a detainee to remain in a behaviour-management support unit for an extended period of time and alternative measures must be considered after placement of a detainee in a management support unit for a period in excess of 48 hours.

But a 2004 GSL document presented to the inquiry outlines a five-stage management process for Baxter detainees who 'have demonstrated unacceptable behaviour or who have demonstrated behaviour that has threatened the security and good order of the facility.'

The five stages are: placement in the 'management unit' and then through four stages of increasing freedoms, including visits, phone calls, 'time out' of the room, and the ability to earn merit points in Redgum compound. The document states that detainees who 'demonstrate consistent good behaviour [are] rewarded by progression on to further stages of opportunity.' Stages one and two of Redgum compound are reviewed after seven days, stage three is reviewed after 14 days.[275] Stage four lasts for 31 days.[276]

A visitor to Baxter told the inquiry that despite the time frames, the five-stage management process could continue indefinitely:

> If you had another outburst because you were not happy with the meals or the treatment, you had to start the whole process again. He started the process in April and he was not released from there until August. He had to stay in his clothes for those four months through the winter. He had a shirt, pair of trousers and one change. He asked for blankets, he never got one. When he got angry and demanded that they do something, he was put back to stage one again.

Refugee lawyer Julian Burnside QC told a Senate committee there was no legal basis for the further deprivation of liberty inflicted by management units and compounds:

> They do not know when, if ever, they are going to be released. Within that context, the use of solitary confinement without any regulation is an additional problem of very grave proportions ... That stands in marked contrast to the prison system, where even the worst convicted criminal

cannot be put in solitary confinement without a very clearly defined process which is subject to judicial review if misused. It is very hard to see why a private operator of a detention centre should be allowed to put people in solitary confinement without any preconditions at all and, for practical purposes, without any judicial oversight.[277]

One asylum seeker who had been in Baxter told the inquiry he was put in Redgum compound for throwing plastic cutlery on the ground:

They took me with force to Redgum and I have a razor blade with me, hide it in my pocket. I hold the razor blade in my hand and I said I want to talk to the boss. Really plenty officers come. They said, 'Okay we will talk to you. If you throw [out] the razor blade.' When I did they took me to management unit. I spent a few days there and they took me to Redgum again. They said, 'You have to stay two months and one day there.' I said, 'Why?' 'Because this is the process.' I said, 'I will not finish this punishment.' He said, 'It is not punishment.' I said, 'This is punishment, this is punishment.'

Another former detainee described the treatment he received while in Redgum:

In 24 hours you just allow to go out one hour. And the officer is very bastard, very clever. When you are asleep they come and say, 'Do you want to go out?' I say, 'It is four o'clock in the morning,' and they say, 'This is your time.' I have to go out for one hour and then come back. I not going, I lose my hour. They give us lunch for two o'clock or one o'clock or four o'clock or eleven o'clock and we say, 'We are not hungry now.' They say, 'If you want to have lunch have it now, if you don't want it we give you [this] for dinner.'

In 2002, HREOC found that five asylum seekers had been arbitrarily detained in a management block for six-and-a-half days at the Port Hedland detention centre in December 2000. During this time, they were allowed outdoors for a total of 20 to 25 minutes, and only two were given a change of clothes after five days.[278]

Detainees held in management units had restricted access to visitors, with most allowed limited phone contact only. Father Peter Norden, Chaplain to Maribyrnong detention centre, told the inquiry:

I have not seen in a prison situation the same refusal of access to people who have been held in solitary confinement as I have at Maribyrnong. Usually within the prison environment, the chaplain is given notification if someone is in solitary confinement, but I have never been informed [by] the institution's initiative that there was someone being held in solitary, and on several occasions when I enquired about visiting people in solitary I was refused permission.

Psychiatric Hospitals

The Palmer report concluded that 'The mental-health care delivered at Baxter is inadequate by any standards.'[279] However, the official denial of mental-health problems in detention was reflected in the reluctance of detention authorities to hospitalise asylum seekers with severe mental-health problems.

Barrister Claire O'Connor told a 2006 conference that she had to take legal action to compel the Immigration Department to allow a psychiatrist to see her client:

He had self-harmed many times; his stomach was so ribboned with scar tissue that he could no longer be stitched when he cut himself, and he had to have sterile strips instead. Both arms had cuts from the armpit to the wrist and his neck was similarly scarred. He had tried to hang himself in detention, had swallowed shampoo on one occasion, and had cut his feet...

I had a psychiatrist ... who was willing to travel the 300 kilometres to Baxter and visit. DIMIA refused arguing that they were dealing with his health issues appropriately. The GP used by DIMIA and the psychologist who had seen [him] while in detention gave evidence ... they both confirmed that [he] was not eating or drinking and had sewn his lips together. They ... said he did not need any further psychiatric treatment.

After days of evidence, the Judge asked the lawyer for the Commonwealth if it was possible for a doctor to see [him] ... [He] was taken to the Royal Adelaide Hospital, seen by the psychiatric registrar and immediately transferred to Glenside Psychiatric Hospital. He was diagnosed as depressed and suffering from psychosis. He was hearing voices. He self-harmed even while in Glenside, as a result of these voices. He was not released from Glenside, even after he obtained a protection visa, until he had recovered sufficiently to live independently. He still receives psychiatric treatment.[280]

Shortly after Cornelia Rau was discovered in Baxter, her sister, journalist Chris Rau, wrote:

> *One can only assume that when immigration assesses detention-centre inmates, its criteria for mental illness are tougher than those at Glenside, where doctors promptly put her in the intensive care, high-dependency ward under heavy sedation.*[281]

In another court case brought to compel the Department of Immigration to transfer two mentally ill detainees to Glenside psychiatric hospital, the then immigration manager at Baxter, Kaye Kannis, gave evidence that there was a significant mental-health problem amongst long-term asylum seeker detainees. The psychiatrist contracted to provide services at Baxter, Dr Andrew Frukacz, was able to visit Baxter approximately once every two months and had 20 to 30 patients. Frukacz told the court that while he would like the level of psychiatric care at Baxter to be better, he 'would equally like such care to be better in rural and remote towns.'[282] He said one of the applicants was getting 'an equivalent standard of care' at Baxter as his private patients in remote communities, but agreed that being held behind razor wire or placed in Baxter's management unit could contribute to a detainee's mental illness.[283]

The diagnosis and treatment he recommended for one of the applicants in the court case was:

> *A. Major depression. B. Cease Sertraline as getting side effect. Try Citalopram 20 mg daily. Add 500 mg Epilim Nocte to augment efficacy and deal with nightmares and poor sleep. Monitor mood over next 2 weeks. If Citalopram not helping try Efexor XR. However, if these measures not working would need further assessment re in-patient treatment with a view to ECT [electro convulsive therapy].*[284]

In an affidavit to the court he said:

> *Electro convulsive therapy is a more robust form of treatment which is very effective for severe depression … If on review, S needed ECT that would be a reason to move him to Glenside as that is probably the only psychiatric treatment that is not available in Baxter.*[285]

Psychiatrist Jon Jureidini told the court that psycho-social intervention as well as medication was required to treat one of the men, and both these interventions needed to be monitored by a psychiatrist, initially on a daily basis. He added:

> The Baxter environment, along with the hopelessness about his future, are the primary causes of his mental illness. It is unreasonable to expect that he could make a recovery while he remains in Baxter.[286]

Justice Finn expressed surprise at Dr Frukacz's opinion that there was not much difference between mental-health treatment at Baxter and Glenside, noting that:

> Save for one visit to see a patient 'about a month ago', he acknowledged he had not been there since 1982. On his recent visit he did not ask to be shown around.[287]

He also criticised the department's inaction after it received reports by three doctors that the applicants needed care other than that being provided to them in Baxter, and that remaining in Baxter was exacerbating their ill health. He speculated that the reports were ignored because the doctors were seen to be critics of immigration detention:

> The Commonwealth has sought to paint these doctors as advocates of a cause and to impugn their professionalism in consequence. In my view, the lack of professionalism has been demonstrated by others.[288]

In his judgment, Justice Finn stated:

> Having heard the evidence of the medical practitioners concerned, I would if I was required ... prefer Dr Jureidini's view to that of Dr Frukacz.[289]

He concluded that one of the applicants, 'though known to be a mentally ill detainee, was being treated with neglect and disregard',[290] and that Baxter provided inadequate psychiatric services. By the time Justice Finn had delivered his judgment, and in the wake of the discovery of Cornelia Rau in Baxter, the Immigration Department had transferred the two men to Glenside. That year, 2005, 37 detainees were transferred from Baxter to

Glenside, almost four times the total number that had been moved there since Baxter opened in 2002.[291]

But like asylum seekers hospitalised for physical problems, detainees transferred to psychiatric hospitals still felt the presence of detention authorities, with at least two guards assigned to each detainee. A former detainee transferred to Glenside told the inquiry:

> *They took me to Glenside. Anytime we wanted to go walking around, three officer each detainee, they follow us. Actually we were joking, all the doggies coming for a walk. Eighteen officers for six people.*

It is estimated that using guards in this way cost at least $200,000 per month and considerable other costs were incurred. A visitor to Glenside told the inquiry:

> *As they did not work 24 hours a day, there had to be relief staff on hand. Some of these staff came from Melbourne and several were housed in the Arkaba hotel, with transport to and from the hospital in a hired minibus. Many times we observed them playing ball games, having barbecues, watching TV, reading, smoking, all the while being paid to be on duty. A Winnebago mobile home was hired and stationed outside the unit for some weeks. Following this, an ATCO transportable building was installed.*

Concerned about the negative impact their presence had on patient recovery, hospital staff later negotiated for the removal of most of the guards. A refugee advocate told the inquiry:

> *It was the first time I ever saw anyone stand up to GSL and win. The hospital staff couldn't come to terms with the way that GSL just moved in on the hospital and wanted to take it over. It was only a matter of weeks before they insisted that GSL remain outside. Eventually they reduced it to just two officers to monitor the visits.*

PEOPLE JUST LOST THEIR PATIENCE: VIOLENCE & SELF-HARM

Another theme which emerged from the evidence presented to the inquiry was how detention created a culture of violence and self-harm. A boy who spent three years in detention as a teenager told the inquiry:

> Each time you tell them something, they will never do it for you. They will absolutely never do it for you. The only time they actually did it was by people becoming violent.

ACM documents presented to the inquiry show that during a typical two-week period in Woomera in 2001: one person escaped, two people were under regular observation, there were two incidents of damage, nine people were taken to hospital and two to the medical unit, two people self-harmed, one was on hunger strike, one compound mounted a passive protest and restraints were used on 10 people.[292]

Asylum seekers, visitors and people who worked with detainees told the inquiry that complaints about treatment and conditions to detention authorities were largely ineffective. A former Villawood detainee said:

> We had monthly meetings where we brought up things like quality of food, quality of health care and they just ignored it. Ignored it totally. Every month was the same agenda. They did nothing and they made people really uptight and anxious.

A man who was detained in Port Hedland told the inquiry:

> We were seven people in one room and we sleep floor. We ask rooms and they didn't give any rooms for us because we very quiet like innocent, so they don't care. If someone make trouble they arrange for them very quickly. If you ask anything it takes years and months to fix. We have to ask hundred times.

A woman whose son had a fractured foot, and whose repeated requests for him to see a doctor were ignored, told the inquiry:

> Then one day I just got so angry and I said, 'Look, if I am not going

to see tomorrow my number to go in hospital, believe me you have job with me. You not going to have easy day tomorrow.' That is what I said. If you be very quiet you never going to get what you want.

The concerns of detention staff, outside health workers and visitors to detention were also ignored. Wayne Lynch, who worked in Woomera for seven months as a nurse and counsellor, told HREOC he wrote to detention management at least 20 times expressing concern about the mental health of detainees without ever receiving a response.[293] A child and adolescent psychiatrist who assessed and treated children in detention told the inquiry:

I am not used to being a helpless person but I certainly felt that helplessness in a huge way because of my inability to effect any change.

On 31 December 2004, general practitioner Dr Malcolm Richards examined six detainees on behalf of the migration agents acting for them and detained one to Glenside Psychiatric Hospital. He later told Justice Finn in the Federal Court:

[M] was not detained largely through my own naivety of the health service at Baxter Detention Centre ... At the time I believed ... that if one recommended psychiatric review of a person it would be arranged. Subsequent events have shown that a psychiatrist needed to take extraordinary measures to see even the most floridly psychotic detainee at Baxter.

I did detain to Glenside Hospital one detainee who was extraordinarily mentally unwell. If I am absolutely honest I felt that if I detained all the very mentally unwell detainees on that day my visit would have been regarded as a political statement rather than a sober medical assessment and my opinions would be given less credibility. Now on reflection if detention at Glenside Hospital is the only way to get psychiatric care for a detainee it should have been done.[294]

A refugee advocate told the inquiry about her experience of advocating for a family in detention:

She was the only woman in the compound for single men. Her husband was catatonic, her son was in a shocking mental state, self-harming. We were working out a plan for this family to be moved. We got nowhere with the Baxter management and ACM. A senior DIMIA manager approved this plan for them to be moved to the family compound. The son had to attend school every day. This is a kid that was self-harming and screaming half the night, sleeping the days.

I still remember the phone calls I made to that senior DIMIA manager. You'd ring and you'd get the secretary, 'Oh yes, he's looking into this. He'll return your call.' But he wouldn't return the call. In the end I left a message that I really needed to speak to him as the media were ringing within a couple of hours and I was quite happy to give the story out, and 20 minutes later he rang me.

We contacted every organisation; ombudsman, human rights, we did the lot. We got one really good lawyer who was threatening to do a failure of duty of care for this woman. Just before she went in to meet with the lawyer, the DIMIA manager said, 'We're going to move you today.' It took us weeks and weeks.

With formal mechanisms for complaint largely ineffective, and indefinite detention taking its toll on people's mental health, asylum seekers turned to the only forms of protest and expression of frustration available to them – property damage, demonstrations, self-harm and hunger strikes.

Former ACM staff told *Four Corners* that ACM made financial profit from disturbances in detention centres because they billed the Immigration Department for any property damage, and charged an inflated price for extra staff needed to deal with them. Many former detainees told the inquiry that detention officers often provoked trouble. A man who spent 18 months in Baxter said:

Every officer have different rules. They like make people angry. Someone got very bad headache and they have to wait hours to get a Panadol, and some people lose their control and they just start breaking things. They say we don't have enough staff today, you have to wait, and when they start breaking things, within one second nurse and hundred officers around.

Another former detainee told the inquiry:

When I was sick I want to see doctor, my tummy is bleeding. I said, 'I want an X-ray.' And they said, 'Okay, come in two hours.' People, they said to me, 'Go, broke the glasses and burn everything, then they will

listen to you.' I said, 'Why should I do this?' Then I just shout at them,
I get very angry. I never get angry, I always quiet but they make you
angry, they make you just go and do something problem and then they
say, 'Oh this is people in detention.'

Property Damage

Detainees, workers in detention and visitors all told the inquiry that the
only way asylum seekers' requests were met was if they caused problems
for detention authorities. A health worker working with families in
detention told the inquiry:

> *If they needed something for their children or for themselves they would*
> *ask nicely and ask nicely. It wasn't until either something got broken or*
> *the microwave got dropped on the floor, in the next 20 minutes what*
> *they wanted would be there even if they had been asking for months.*
> *Most of the detainees would say you wouldn't train an animal like*
> *that, to not give until it misbehaved. It was so demeaning to put people*
> *through that as well.*

A refugee advocate told the inquiry:

> *A young man told me about his frustration on account of his toothache.*
> *He told me he knew he had to do something bad so he could get*
> *attention, so he threw a chair through a window. In his years in*
> *detention he had never given trouble before, but he had learnt how the*
> *system has to be played. When he was let out of isolation he was given*
> *stronger pain relief. He told me, 'I say to guard ever I or other in this*
> *compound in pain again and not get help, I throw everything and break*
> *everything and give you much trouble.' I expressed surprise that this*
> *tactic might work, but he was very sure.*

A visitor to Baxter told the inquiry her detainee friend was not given some
muscle-building powder she had sent him.

> *They thought it might contain something dangerous. He said, 'It's*
> *sealed and comes straight from the chemist.' After waiting a few more*
> *days, he broke a few windows. Funnily enough, he was quickly given*
> *the muscle powder.*

One man who spent years in a number of detention centres told the inquiry:

> Why when I ask no-one come, when we damage or do something wrong or we want to harm ourselves, everyone come? Why? This is their system like that.

The Western Australian inspector of custodial services, Professor Richard Harding, inspected detention centres in 2001. That year he told a meeting of the International Corrections and Prisons Association:

> It is no coincidence that riots occur in a system that lacks accountability. Anyone who knows the simplest thing about prison riots knows also that unacceptable conditions against which there is no recourse ... are the precursor to riots. We do not have riots in our detention centres because we have a riotous group of refugees. We have them because we run appalling systems.[295]

A man who was in detention for two and a half years explained to the inquiry why he resorted to property damage:

> DIMIA said my application was reject. I was crying in front of DIMIA. DIMIA told me, do you want to talk to counsellor? Psychology nurse came. At that time I was in my compound by myself. Another three guys from my country were in another compound. I already request more than 100 times, please I want to live with people from my country. When I upset, I want to talk to someone and I can feel better. I tried to ring people from my country in the other compound to tell I was reject and can you come to visit me. Main control said we not allowed to give phone call to other compound.
>
> When I was talking with counsellor she asking what I can do for you. I said, 'Please tell them to come to visit.' She told me she can't give visit, but she promised to me when you want to make a phone call you come to office and I'm going to arrange phone call to other compound. I went to office, that officer said she didn't inform us about that.
>
> It is the last 40 cents and I give to one Afghan guy and I tell, 'Please, I want to speak to someone in my language.' He took phone and he said, 'White 3 please.' When control asking what's your name, he said another name. Control ask him from where you calling, and he said

from Sydney. And control said, 'Sorry mate, I saw you in the security camera, nice try,' and he used bad word and he put the phone. After that I was very, very upset.

I got a plastic chair and I just smashed the phone and I hit the door. Guards came behind me and cried, 'What's wrong?' They said to me, 'You should go to Management.' I went there. I did something wrong in the compound and they tried to get a signature for these things. After that psychology nurse came. Same lady spoke with me in my room. When I saw her I was very upset. She said, 'You should sign.' She doing not psychologist things and she not helping the people, she helping the guard.

Another asylum seeker told the inquiry how a riot at Port Hedland Detention Centre started and that the response of authorities exacerbated tensions.

The riot happened because people were really tired. They were trying to move one of the family and the boy, 16 or 17, did resist and said he didn't want my father be treated like that. The boy was taken away; they started beating the boy. People were really unhappy about everything else anyway, so people got really upset and started breaking things and took the hammer on everything and for a couple of hours the officers were not allowed in the compound and a lot of things were broken, the kitchen was destroyed.

A couple of weeks later they brought the police in. We had to go back to our room and there was a security guard in front of every room. Everyone has to get out of their room, and lie down and put their hands on their back for hours. I remember hearing that there was this Palestinian detainee they had beaten and there was a lot of abuses that day, so I think that was another turning point for the time in detention. From that time any little thing that happened, people get really angry.

Demonstrations

A former Woomera worker also told the inquiry the attitude of detention authorities fuelled protests in detention.

In May and June 2000, DIMIA passed on information that they would get their visas if and when they processed them. They came here illegally and they should be bloody grateful they have a compound to live in. That didn't go down well and I was mobbed by over 400 detainees at that meeting, and for the first time I felt unsafe. I had one of the detainee interpreters grab my arm and say to me to get out as there was going to be trouble.

A former detainee told the inquiry:

At the first, normally we did like a hunger strike or sitting there, but normally they make something make you angry, do something more wrong. If you read in the newspaper about what is happening, all of those uprisings or riots. I thought about that. If one person came and about 10 minutes talked with those people, never those happen, but because they need it they make something, make you more angry.

A man involved in the June 2000 breakout from Woomera, in which hundreds of detainees broke through the detention centre fences, told the inquiry:

We started to lose hope completely because we have noticed there is no single individual released from the detention. People had their nerves completely destroyed. People just lost their patience and they started to involve in demonstrations and breaking the fences and the razor wires. I was among those people, and we ran up to the Woomera town. The main purpose is not to go anywhere but to bring the attention of the public that there is people locked here and mistreated. They suggested that soon we go back to the detention centre they will start looking to our cases and release people but, unfortunately, when we get back again they broke their promises.

The former Woomera worker told the inquiry that the way detention authorities dealt with the protest created further problems.

They just pushed down the fence and escaped into the city square. It was winter so it was quite cold. A lot of children and women went as well. The children and women were separated from the men in the town. The men actually spat and threw rocks at me. They were very angry. I don't think it was personally at me, it was that they were desperate people. They were out there for two nights and three days, and part of the ruling was not to feed the men.

However, the children started to show health problems and some of the women were collapsing, and I was asked by immigration to negotiate with the women to return. They felt they could go back, but they had certain conditions and I relayed this back to immigration. They wanted to go back to their same rooms, they didn't want to be separated, they didn't want any punitive action. I was promised that would happen.

When the women and children came back to the compound they had a line of officers in riot gear and as the women and children got off the bus they were taken into a room where they were searched. I had no idea they were going to do this. I was at the other end waiting for the women and children to come out and as they came out they were screaming. They were just hysterical. Many women expressed to me that they were touched inappropriately.

It was four or five in the morning by the time the women and children got back to their rooms. I went home and the next morning came into the compound about nine and I had people begging with me not to be punished because they separated the husbands and put them into Oscar Compound, so there was a betrayal and Woomera was never the same after this.

I went back to the compound two days later and found they had separated women from their children, they had separated husbands from their wives, unaccompanied minors were left to their own devices. The women and children were just screaming, constantly crying and felt betrayed by me and felt that there was nothing good ever going to happen for them again.

From June 2000, the mindset of detainees was totally different. Depression was horrendous, self-harm and daily riots and demonstrations. From seeing six to 12 self-harms a day, I was seeing 20 to 40 a day and more severe self-harming, literally cutting themselves open on their body. Just doing anything they could to get attention, to be taken out of the compound, to be put into a better environment such as the hospital. The hospital didn't have any beds left so some people were sent to Royal Adelaide and Glenside.

Two months later, nurse Mark Huxstep witnessed a Centre Emergency Response Team (CERT) arriving after Woomera detainees had walked around a compound chanting for their freedom. He told ABC Radio:

They were certainly something to behold. They were dressed in dark blue overalls with riot gear and helmets, riot shields, batons. They had covers over their elbows and knees. They were prepared for a full-on conflict. All huge men, and it was just intimidating to witness it, and I was on their side of the fence.[296]

As two detainees, deemed to be the ringleaders of the protest, were removed the incident escalated. Officers fired tear gas and water cannons at the detainees. Mark Huxstep said a guard told him he was sorry he hadn't had the opportunity to use his baton to hit someone over the head. At five o'clock the next morning, a CERT team moved in to remove some detainees. Mark Huxstep said:

I had one lady come and see me subsequent to the riots and talk about the removal of the ringleaders ... The CERT team came in the middle of the night, picked up the wrong person from under the bedclothes and dragged them out, swearing, had them by the back of the pants and the hair, threw them on the dirt, and when they realised it was an elderly lady, told her to, you know what off, and went back inside and got the correct person. She was terribly distraught, describing how her mother was picked up by the hair and clothes, and thrown outside in the dirt in the middle of the night.[297]

Fences were later breached and buildings set on fire. When news of the riot was reported, then immigration minister Philip Ruddock blamed it on detainees whose claim for refugee status had been rejected. He told ABC Radio:

We will not succumb to any pressure in relation to people who had no entitlement to be released into the Australian community.[298]

Another nurse who witnessed the riot told a public meeting:

The riot of August 2000 was a horror I never expected to see in my country. Water cannons and guards with body armour, burning buildings, smoke and stones. The day after I watched the shell-shocked families come wandering out of the rubble, their children skirting around the debris, the tears ... and the guards' recriminations started ... I watched in disbelief as a loud roar shook the earth and an air force bomber flew low over the camp, practising manoeuvres, terrifying those war shattered people. I could have been anywhere except Australia.[299]

Mark Huxstep told HREOC:

During rioting at the centre I was in the company of an ACM officer when he was told by one of his superiors that minister Ruddock had authorised the use of firearms if detainees breached the perimeter of the centre. The guard ... subsequently said, 'We'll shoot over their head to scare them should they breach the perimeter, but we'll aim very low.'[300]

The government also invited media into detention centres to photograph damaged property, prompting media reports such as those following the riots at Woomera in August 2000, when the *Herald Sun* stated:

Illegal boat people saved by Australian authorities have repaid the nation by torching their taxpayer-funded accommodation ... The Woomera rioters must now be brought before our courts. Further, the federal government must take advantage of Labor's offer to back legislation enabling deportation of the rioters.[301]

In May 2001, following a riot at Port Hedland detention centre involving more than 100 asylum seekers, then immigration minister Philip Ruddock said he would not be reviewing the government's mandatory detention policy.

Well, I'm not sure why one would argue that the policy of detention should be reviewed because detainees aren't prepared to observe normal standards of behaviour that we would expect in the Australian community. I mean, that would be like saying that you would close a jail because some people who had been convicted of offences didn't like being detained.[302]

Self-harm

In many cases, detainee frustrations were vented through self-harm. A report by psychiatrist Michael Dudley, the Chair of Suicide Prevention Australia, calculated the men's and women's rates of suicidal behaviours in detention centres as 41 and 26 times the national average, and male rates as almost twice the rate of male prisoners. The report concluded: 'Self-harm in detention ... is driven by the extremity of detention and the detention environment.'[303] Psychiatrist Jon Jureidini told researchers he did not see anyone in detention over 11 years old that had not harmed themselves.[304]

Figures obtained from the Department of Immigration by *The Age* newspaper show that between July 2002 and June 2005, 900 asylum seekers in detention tried to harm themselves. Then immigration minister Amanda Vanstone questioned the veracity of the statistics saying they included multiple acts by the same person and 'very, very minor incidents'.

> *I think (some) people who want to stay in Australia will always resort ... to a very unattractive type of protest in order to draw attention to themselves and hopefully to pressure a government to give them the outcome they want. But Australia has a very good record of not giving in to such protests.*[305]

Despite government attempts to downplay the seriousness of self-harm incidents in detention, Dr Simon Lockwood, the longest-serving medical officer at Woomera, told *Lateline*:

> *Because no-one died, DIMIA or the bureaucrats believed that no-one made genuine attempts, but I can tell you being the doctor that was looking after those people and saving their lives, that that wasn't the case. There was a lot of times where I thought someone was going to die.*[306]

A former detention officer told the inquiry that one night when she was guarding a female detainee and her daughter in an Adelaide motel, the woman went to her room after saying she was going to the toilet. When the officer went to check after a few minutes, she found the woman had attempted suicide by putting herself under a hydraulic bed and dropping the bed down to crush her neck and chest. She was unconscious under the bed and needed resuscitation. This was the woman's second suicide attempt. She had previously tried to hang herself, causing neck damage, and walked with a frame.

A former detainee held in Port Hedland told the inquiry:

> *There was one man from Afghanistan, a bit elder man and he was really, really mentally sick. He has signed more than a year that he want to go back but they didn't send him. He was waiting and waiting. One*

day he just climb on the tree and he jump and he hit the concrete and was bleeding all over. I look and I thought he died. They took him in hospital and then they deport him to Afghanistan.

Another Port Hedland detainee also told the inquiry about the same incident:

Before he jumped he shouted, 'I don't want Australia any more. Thank you, Australia. Thank you, everybody.'

A man who made numerous requests to be held in the same detention centre as his brother told the inquiry:

Even they didn't let me sometimes ring and talk to him. You know what way I could talk to my brother, just take the razor in my hand and I tell them, 'If you not going to let me talk to my brother, easy, I cut myself,' and I did it. If you see here, everywhere I did it. I didn't have anybody in this country, just my brother. Finally after three years I saw him.

A visitor to Baxter told the inquiry:

When I first got involved I used to say, 'We'll do it the right way, we'll contact all the right channels.' I think the time I really learnt was when they had some people in isolation. They left them for weeks, no phone, newspapers, TV and I knew they were going to hurt themselves. I rang DIMIA in Canberra, DIMIA Baxter, ACM Canberra, ACM Baxter, HREOC, Amnesty, the ombudsman, the minister's office, the opposition's office, telling them all to do something. No-one did anything. Then the people cut themselves and a few days later they were out of there – it's just honestly the only way you actually achieve anything in Baxter.

Hunger Strikes

A refugee advocate told the inquiry that for many refugees starving themselves was the only way they could exercise control over their lives.

He felt he had no alternative but to go on hunger strike. This time I could not talk him out of it. He would say, 'It's my right, it's all I have got left.' And I am afraid I had to agree. After a terrible conversation on the phone where his voice was so weak it was hardly audible, I disconnected the phone and sobbed all day. I felt so powerless.

A man who was detained on Nauru told the inquiry that while hunger strikes were an effective means of putting pressure on detention authorities, the consequences for some detainees were serious health problems.

Initially four individuals decided to stitch their lips and nine people went for a hunger strike and later the number increased to 39 people, including myself. I was on a strike for 29 days. During the hunger strike I passed out three or four times and they took me to hospital and then I would come back and start again. Some of them who passed out, even after they were receiving medical treatment, they were not able to walk. Still they wouldn't break their strike.

They waited until the 29th day and then they started to interview people. That was the interview in which 70 per cent or 80 per cent of the people were accepted. I had some friends and nine or 10 of them are still suffering due to that strike. They are having severe stomach problems and kidney problems; their physical condition has been badly affected.

The inquiry also heard that medical treatment was administered against the will of the hunger-striking detainees. One former detainee said:

I continued a hunger strike until they called a doctor to the camp. They tied my hands and feet to the legs of the bed and through the tube that was put in my nose into my tummy, they tried to feed me and break my strike. They did whatever they wanted to. Even when the doctor was trying to run the tube through my nostril I told him that if any problem comes up, then you will be responsible and he told me we've got permission through DIMIA to do this.

A lawyer told the inquiry a hospital was more prepared to follow Department of Immigration requests than the instructions of her client, their patient.

The response from the hospital was they had to do what the department wanted because this is a detainee so he had less rights than a regular person in the community. That was a real eye opener for me. When

I was trying to say he doesn't want this tube inserted, I was harassed by the guards who said they are trying to save his life and you are trying to stop them from saving his life. Obviously I didn't want to see him die. I wanted him to start eating but there was a different way of doing that which was give him a bridging visa and don't put him back into detention, which is what happened eventually through a lot of pressure.

Escapes

Other detainees escaped from detention centres. Some had help from Australians and many found sanctuary after their escape in safe houses provided by refugee supporters. At Easter protests at Woomera in 2002, about 50 detainees escaped when protesters helped to breach the fences. By October 2005, 11 had still not been located. A refugee advocate told the inquiry about her first impression of these escapes:

People from inside the detention centre were dropping over and through the fences, helped by people who had come to protest. The first thing I saw was a number of men running desperately up the dirt road towards our campsite, being pursued by police on foot and on horseback. Some were dragged to a waiting paddy wagon.

Another refugee advocate told the inquiry about her involvement in helping escapees:

Everybody said that they would rather die than go back to Woomera and asked for our help. We ended up harbouring six escaped refugees taking them with us in a car. It was a pretty hopeless cause, we were very unprepared to be dealing with that and we got arrested. The people we got arrested with said it was their best day in Australia ever. They said it was the first time they felt they had been treated like human beings.

Many people showed us their scars of self-harm. By the end of the day in the jail cell people had become quite distressed about going back to Woomera. One man started hitting the wall until his hand was quite bloody. Other people were trying to stop him, but they said this happens all the time, when people can't cope they hurt themselves.

They wrote: 'We prisoners/refugees really appreciate the people of

Australia who are demonstrating for us and the time we passed in jail together is really unforgettable.' It was an outdoor compound that we were in and it didn't have razor wire and they spoke about seeing the sun go down without razor wire as a really beautiful thing.

The inquiry received a detainee's account of his short-lived escape when he was taken to the dentist in Port Augusta. Despite being handcuffed, he jumped out of the toilet window and climbed to the top of the Port Augusta Town Hall.

It was difficult to climb with handcuffs, but my adrenalin was flowing, and I found a strength I thought I had lost. I took some deep breaths, looked around and realised that I was gazing at a horizon. In Baxter, horizons are never sighted. I noticed the sea and the ranges, the plains, the homes and everything. I could hear voices of the local policemen pleading for me not to jump. I reassured them I was safe and negotiated a five-minute extension of time on top of the building in return for my safe climb down. I thank the police officers for granting me this wish.

A crowd had gathered. Each person was looking up at me. I had a pen and notebook in my top pocket, so I began to write notes and throw them into the crowd. I scribbled messages like: I am not a terrorist; I love Australia; I yearn for freedom; I am an innocent detainee; Please release me. I could see that the notes were being picked up and read. I took several deep, final breaths of the sweet, fresh air. It was much more difficult to come down. Many in the crowd were cheering for me. Some were crying. Some came forward and hugged me. Some asked my name and number and promised to visit me at Baxter.

Once in the community, escaped detainees found themselves in a difficult position. They could not legally work, access health care or education, and lived with the constant fear of being caught and re-detained. Several escapees eventually turned themselves in to the Immigration Department. Others managed to leave the country. A refugee supporter told the inquiry:

Some activists were arrested for arranging false passports to help asylum seeker escapees to get out of Australia. Would I break the law and risk going to jail if I could save some asylum seekers from four years in Australian detention? I honestly don't know what I would do if the

risks were high, but I do know what I think the gospels would ask of
me and what I believe would be the right moral choice.

The government tried to minimise publicity about escapes from detention. Refugee advocate and journalist John Highfield told the inquiry that immigration officials lied to him about an escape from Villawood.

My wife said, 'We've got a DIMIA compliance team here who are demanding entry, there are about a dozen of them and they have been doing kung-fu exercises on the driveway.' The officer in charge explained that it was necessary to search our house because that morning at 3.20, nine adults and six children had escaped from Villawood and they were looking for these escapees. They thought they might be at our house because we were on the visitors list for one of the people who had escaped.

She explained that she couldn't let him in until she had spoken with her husband and he said, 'Well, ring him now,' and she said, 'I can't, he's on the air at the ABC.' His face fell about 5ft and he dashed out punching numbers into a mobile phone. He went through the house in about 45 seconds.

As a journalist, I was suddenly confronted with a reasonably good story that there had been a break-out at Villawood that morning. So I rang a senior departmental official. I said, 'I believe there has been an escape at Villawood.' And he said, 'I don't know where you get that idea from. I don't think that's the case, but I will get one of my senior people to ring you straight back.'

It took nearly an hour for that person to ring me back and he said, 'No, you are mistaken, there's been nothing,' and I said, 'That is a lie.' He said, 'What do you mean? Are you accusing me of being a liar?' and I said, 'Yes, I am, because at 3.20 this morning nine adults and six children escaped.' And he said, 'Where did you get that information from?' And I said, 'One of your squads has just raided my house looking for them,' and his response was, 'Oh shit, I've got to go.'

Fires

In late December 2002 and early January 2003, detention centres in Woomera, Baxter, Port Hedland, Christmas Island and Villawood were severely damaged by fire, with estimates of property damage reaching more than $9 million.

A refugee advocate told the inquiry that after the fires all the single men in one compound at Baxter were given a letter telling them to pack and be ready to be deported. Some men who had earlier requested to leave Australia packed their bags and lined up outside the office. The detainees told her:

> We sang, 'We want freedom, we did not do violence.' But about 50 guards came in riot gear and sprayed tear gas into our faces. We could not sleep, our eyes were so hurting. Since then, they punish us. They take our mattresses, everything except four walls they take. We have no newspapers, phone and visits. On 4 January, early in the morning, crowd of guards came in riot gear and dragged the men out of their beds, some had no clothes on and were not allowed to dress. Then they had to sit outside for hours like this. This very shame for us.

Following the fires, detainees were refused access to phones and other communication with anyone except their lawyers or human rights organisations – some for up to six weeks. More than 132 men were also strip searched.

Strip Searches

In September 2001, amendments to the *Migration Act* allowed children over 10 to be strip searched. The then immigration minister, Philip Ruddock, issued directions outlining the strict conditions under which strip-search powers could be used. These acknowledge:

> The power to strip search a detainee is necessarily intrusive and can be an extremely embarrassing experience for the detainee. As such, it is a measure of last resort. It is not a power that will be used lightly nor as a routine procedure. [307]

The instructions state that strip searches must only be authorised and conducted on the grounds of a reasonable suspicion that a weapon or other thing is hidden on an individual detainee or in their clothing, and that a strip search is necessary to recover it. The grounds for a reasonable suspicion can be a search, screening procedure or other information such as witness statements that a detainee is hiding something, or the visible outline of 'something weapon-like hidden in the person's clothes that the detainee will not reveal on request.'[308]

However, following the fires, mass strip searches were conducted on 77 Woomera detainees and 55 men held at Baxter. An angry Daryl Williams, acting immigration minister at the time, stated:

> They [strip-searches] will be used more widely. They have been done at Baxter. I think they have been done at Woomera, and they may well be done at other centres as well.[309]

In early 2003, Steve Davis, a senior Department of Immigration official, told a Senate committee that three groups, consisting of all adult male detainees in particular compounds damaged by the fires at Baxter, were strip searched. Groups of detainees were also strip searched at Woomera and Villawood. He said:

> The authorisation was for the whole group. The requests were authorised by the acting secretary at the time. Within that authorisation, the individuals who were to be strip searched were named in the request. Therefore, in authorising the group, it was authorising a group of individuals.[310]

Later that year the National Community Legal Centre Conference passed a resolution demanding an end to strip searches in immigration detention centres, labelling them sexual assaults.[311] The inquiry heard evidence about how strip searches had affected detainees. A refugee advocate provided the inquiry with a letter from a detainee shortly after the fires:

> I never used handcuffs in my whole life. When they put me in handcuffs and sit me under the hot sun I cried. I cannot control myself after that strip search in front of two officers. It is a very shameful thing for me; I cannot eat for two days.

The inquiry also heard how detainees were humiliated by being kept naked on other occasions. A refugee advocate told the inquiry:

> The tears dropped down his face as he described the shame of being stripped naked and left standing with no underwear, and then having to wear only a special gown while kept on 24-hour watch.

A former detainee told the inquiry:

> When I escape from detention centre and they catch me, they pushed me on the ground and one officer put feet on the back of my neck and they tie my hand with leg together from the back, then they sent me to isolation room. They took my clothes and they, behind the small screen window, a couple of officers make fun.

Jail

Some detainees were charged with property damage or escaping from detention and sent to jail. In 2002, the Inspector of Custodial Services for Western Australia, Richard Harding, told ABC *Radio National* that detention centres were worse than prisons:

> The detainees who commit an offence and end up in the prison system all prefer it in terms of the human interaction, the location, the relative respect with which they are treated by staff.[312]

Father Peter Norden told the inquiry that the facilities, staff and services in criminal justice facilities are far better than those in detention. This was supported by other evidence to the inquiry. A former detainee jailed for escaping said:

> The jail was better for me because I used to go to English class every day. I knew I have to stay for seven months, that's it, but in detention I didn't know. The people in jail have more rights. They had the right to study and contact the university, was organised time for everything. It was library, internet, you could get some information.

Another former detainee told the inquiry:

> I was treated in jail better than detention, really. The food was good, the officers was all right but some prisoners was really good. I say to my lawyer, can you send me to the jail again, because I had my study and my English there getting improve. In detention we didn't have anything.

A visitor to Villawood told the inquiry:

I remember a couple of years ago talking to a 14-year-old boy and he allegedly had some part in leading the riot. He was sent to a youth training centre for a time. I asked him when he came back how was it and he said, 'Oh it was much better than being here. The officers respect you and you respect the officers and there is something to do all day.'

Some detainees were held in jails as places of immigration detention. An asylum seeker who initially arrived legally, and subsequently overstayed his visa after losing his refugee appeals, told the inquiry he was placed in jail for 14 months when he presented himself to the Department of Immigration. He was subsequently granted a refugee visa.

SHE SHOWED ME THE SCARS ON HER FEET:
ASSAULTS

Another theme emerging from the evidence presented to the inquiry was that of detainees being physically assaulted while in detention. A visitor to Baxter told the inquiry:

I was talking to the men we visited last Sunday and I told them I was coming to this inquiry. I said I knew that some people had been assaulted and they looked at me and said, 'Everyone's been assaulted at some time.' One man told me that he had one hand handcuffed to his ankle and one wrist handcuffed to the other ankle at one time when he was in management. A woman told me that she and her husband and child were dragged by their feet and she showed me the scars on her feet from that incident.

In a study on the impact of detention on families, 86 per cent of adults alleged they had been assaulted by detention officers.[313] Port Hedland officer Graeme Hindmarsh was convicted of assaulting a handcuffed 47-year-old Iranian detainee in 2001.[314] In October 2004, former Baxter officer Paul Leavai received a two-month suspended sentence after kneeing a detainee in the stomach. He then went on to work at a refugee camp in Nauru.[315]

In 2005, *The Bulletin* published photographs of Port Hedland detainees injured during December 2003 protests. Professor David Wells, from the Victorian Institute of Forensic Medicine, concluded that the injuries had probably been caused by a baton or stick, saying, 'To produce injuries like that in a person who is otherwise healthy does require a significant amount of force.'[316]

A young man who spent six months in Woomera as an unaccompanied minor told the inquiry he had witnessed detention officers assaulting a detainee:

> *There was one person, mentally he was not well. He threw a chair – which is not good – but other people should look at his situation and why he is doing this. About five or six ACM officers grabbed him. They got some karate and they pushed him to the ground. There was no-one except the ACM officers and that person, and I was there. When they pushed him to the ground, one ACM officer put his knee on his neck and was saying, 'Now are you okay, now are you okay?' I was really shocked and I ran and told other people to come. But when we came, there was no-one there. They took him away, I don't know where.*

In 2005, 24-year-old Baxter detainee Peter Mode complained about the food. Another man threw it against the wall. Shortly afterwards they were watching a video when Peter left the room briefly. When he returned, up to 12 guards were taking the other man away. Peter claimed that, when he objected that the man had just had a kidney operation, Peter was held down by guards while one of them deliberately twisted his leg until it broke, after which he was made to wait an hour before being taken to hospital. The incident was referred to South Australian police.[317]

The inquiry was presented with a 2002 ACM stocktake of armoury and equipment at Woomera. Despite immigration detention being described as administrative rather than punitive, ACM held, at that time, 48 standard ring batons, 48 'grenade grip' batons, 55 riot helmets, 48 riot vests, 48 riot shields and 48 each of guards for legs, forearms, elbows and groins. It also held 54 pairs of handcuffs, 32 'rescue tool' knives, tear gas, 85 gas masks, 2 cameras and 3 video cameras. The equipment was used by officers in CERTs.

The ACM policy on the use of force and restraints for Woomera's residential housing project, in which only women and children were detained, states:

Where a situation arises that requires deployment of riot equipment, unobtrusive and non-intimidatory video filming of the subsequent event must take place ... Instruments of restraint, such as handcuffs, chains, irons and straightjackets are never to be applied as punishment ... Cuffing belts are only to be used with the consent and direction of the Centre Manager ... Where equipment is issued or used it is to be orally reported to the DIMIA Business Manager within one hour.[318]

A visitor told the inquiry that she had witnessed the CERT officers training at Baxter before expected Easter protests by refugee activists:

We were in the visitors' centre when we heard this big military manoeuvre going on – we looked through the little crack in the corrugated iron and there were about fifteen of them and they all had their riot gear on and were just marching around in formation shouting, 'Hup, two, three.'

Many assaults on detainees occurred in the context of disturbances in the detention centres. An asylum seeker who spent six years in detention told the inquiry:

When people break a window or something out of desperation, security guards come with the full riot gear. Many times we have seen fellow detainees bashed by them. They bashed us, they threw even some sort of gas. They put us on the ground and our hands be locked and they put us in the management unit.

Water cannons were also used in detention centres – the first ever use of them in Australia.[319] A refugee advocate told the inquiry:

In September 2001 I went to a protest at Woomera Detention Centre. We had big sheets that said 'Freedom' and people inside detention were standing on top of the buildings and waving banners at us and there were people up on the fences waving. Somebody came out with a mattress and lit it and then a water cannon was rolled up and the people behind the fences, including the kids, were all water-cannoned and they threw tear gas.

A 2003 ACM training manual on the use of the Westfire Gas Gun says the spray must be dispensed directly into a person's eyes and nose and can cause severe physical reactions lasting up to 45 minutes. These include involuntary closing of eyes, respiratory inflammation, coughing and shortness of breath, skin inflammation, nausea, a burning sensation on the skin, anxiety, panic and disorientation. It instructs officers to restrain people by making them lie down for handcuffing. It also contains a warning, however:

> *Due regard shall be given to the positioning of a person affected by chemical agents when restraining due to possible asphyxiation. This is due to the greater need of oxygen and the increased cardiovascular and respiratory activity. This is particularly true if the person is lying face down, which does not permit easy breathing. This combination of factors can lead to death through the person's inability to breathe.*

Even those not involved in disturbances suffered the consequences when officers retaliated. One man told the inquiry:

> *One day there's a big fight. Many officers came and they couldn't take control. The police came and beat everyone and the manager locked all the compounds. Then they came to each room, banged the door and said to get down, and they put their leg in my face, the police and the officer. Then one officer said, 'He is not trouble,' and he took his leg off my back.*

A boy who spent three years in detention told the inquiry:

> *I was seeing these big fights against officers and that was really bad, those people getting hit, women getting hit, children getting hit, so it was horrible.*

A former detainee told the inquiry that detainees supported each other when faced with officers in riot gear:

> *I protected my friend because my friend has a problem mentally. He applied for a tablet and they put it in the water. He didn't like this and all of the officers attacked him. I said, 'He is an ill man, you are not allowed to act like this to him.' That time all of the detainees got angry. Two shifts of guards tried to take us, but the other detainees protected us by taking us to a room.*

A visitor to detention presented the inquiry with a letter from a detainee in Baxter:

We have one person he living in detention centre for long time and he missed his mother two months ago. He gone to medical to receive his medicines but the nurses didn't give him. He take a razor and cut his leg (he cut hands, chest and more of his body before) and start breaking the glass. When the people were sleeping all the officers take on the guard clothes. They came into our compound and wanted catch him but we never let them do that, we resist guards men and they beat us very nice (this is human right in Australia).

The inquiry also heard that some officers used critical incidents to exact revenge on detainees. A former detainee said:

The officer tried to find some chance to hit you because sometimes you get angry and you say something nasty. Officers keep it in mind and when the ten officers were coming they said that it was a good chance. They put the gas in my eyes. One officer sat on my leg. I screamed and all of my friends just started to cry. That time they put me in management and I said I needed the police. The police never comes because when you are in detention, you never have a right. When you shout nobody hears you.

Several visitors to detention told the inquiry they had seen evidence of assaults by detention officers on asylum seekers. A refugee advocate told the inquiry that her life was changed after witnessing an assault on a female detainee during a protest at Woomera:

A woman in a long garment and a head scarf came to the fence near us and began to call out. We could not understand her words, but at some basic human level we understood her. She was calling for help. She was pleading. We tried to call something back hoping she would understand us the way we understood her. Then we saw a man in uniform fully kitted up with a helmet and visor and a heavy riot shield. He tried to drag her back from the fence. We started yelling for him to stop.

She stayed at the fence calling out to us. The guard became more and more violent. He began hitting her with his riot shield. She was totally unarmed and a smallish woman. All she was doing was trying to make human contact. We yelled at him to stop as he gradually beat her to the ground with his shield. All of us were crying, even the men. We were powerless to do anything and he dragged her through the dust into the building.

Another refugee advocate told the inquiry:

We were in Curtin just after the riots. We saw evidence of physical abuse on the adults, bruising and cuts.

Another one told the inquiry:

I got a shirt covered in blood delivered in the mail. A guard started to beat one of the people inside the detention centre and that guy got a light globe and held it to his neck and said, 'If you don't stop beating me I will cut myself.' They kept beating him and he cut himself quite badly and that was the trigger incident in the riot and it was his shirt that I got sent in the mail. They smuggled it out and sent it to us because they wanted to have a physical record of what had happened. I got a phone call about that incident at about 10 o'clock at night. I heard screaming in the background and halfway through the conversation the phone lines cut out.

Despite evidence of assault, action was almost never taken against detention officers. A former detainee told the inquiry:

They put handcuffs on my hands and if you move, it is going to be tighter, and I had a four months mark around my wrist. I told them, 'Who is going to take responsibility for this? I need to talk to the police.' 'No you cannot talk to the police,' they said. But if I do something to the officer, straightaway the police is coming for me.

Other detainees and supporters thought that if they reported assaults they would be seen as troublemakers. They were worried they could be victimised further and that their visa process could be jeopardised. A visitor to detention told the inquiry:

I saw the bruises on the chest of a female detainee who had been assaulted by a female officer. I sought the advice of her legal representative and documented this assault but, in the context of her overall best interests, did not pursue this matter further.

Another refugee advocate told the inquiry:

There was a very, very bad riot. He had tear gas sprayed directly into his face. He was beaten by the guards. They came in riot gear to remove him from the compound and when he was taken to management, they threw him against a wall so severely that he couldn't get up and he had difficulty walking for some time. About a year later they finally decided that he needed surgery. He was obliged if he wanted to make a complaint to do so in front of GSL officers. It was considered a security risk to leave him in a room with a policeman on his own and he knew that if he did that he would very likely get some kind of retribution, so he refused to give evidence.

Despite the fact that detention centre staff have, on rare occasion, been charged with assault and dismissed, there are some instances where police refused to even investigate detainee allegations of assault. Visitor to Baxter David Leach told the inquiry:

When they had the Baxter convergence, one of the young men that I visit climbed on the roof to see what all the fuss was about and when he got up there, he had a look for a minute or two and then he came down and they beat the crap out of him. A couple of weeks after he showed me the bruises and he was really badly hurt. I said, 'Do you want me to do something about it?' and he said, 'No, I'll get in trouble. It's not worth it.' But over the next few weeks, each time he was still in a lot of pain, I'd ask him, 'Do you want me to call the police?' In the end he said, 'Yes, call the police.' So the next day I rang the police in Port Augusta and the police said, 'We're not going to do anything about it. We're sick of going down there. We've got more important things to do. I don't want to know about it, mate,' and put down the phone.

A lawyer told the inquiry that the Department of Immigration was aware of the frequent assaults on detainees:

There will be many individual stories about guards mistreating detainees and I wouldn't want that to be explained away as, 'Well you can't stop individual instances like that.' It became clear to me that this mistreatment of asylum seekers is institutional, because I spent over a year of my life communicating directly with the minister for immigration and her department. For them to have failed to respond to our concerns about breaches of human rights can't be explained away as an oversight or an accidental occurrence. It's a deliberate policy.

GUARDS TAKE MY MUMMY:
CHILDREN

A further theme in the evidence presented to the inquiry was the devastating way in which detention affected children. The Convention on the Rights of the Child states:

No child shall be deprived of his or her liberty unlawfully or arbitrarily. The arrest, detention or imprisonment of a child shall be in conformity with the law and shall be used only as a measure of last resort and for the shortest appropriate period of time.[320]

More than 2000 children were kept in Australian detention centres for an average of one year and eight months, including 'one child locked up for five years and five months before he and his mother were deemed to be refugees (the outcome for 93 per cent of families).'[321]

In June 2003, the Full Bench of the Family Court ruled that it had jurisdiction to make orders against the minister for immigration, including ordering the release of children from detention if it was in the best interests of the child. The minister for immigration appealed the decision, but on 25 August 2003, the Family Court ordered the Bakhtiyari children, on whose behalf the case was argued, be released from detention immediately pending the final outcome of appeals. In April 2004, the High Court of Australia ruled that the Family Court had no jurisdiction over children in immigration detention, effectively ruling that children can legally be detained indefinitely in Australia.[322]

The UN Human Rights Committee investigating the detention of the Bakhtiyari children found that:

... in this case children have suffered demonstrable, documented and ongoing adverse effects of detention ... up until the point of release ... in circumstances where that detention was arbitrary and in violation of ... the Covenant ... the measures taken by the State party had not ... been guided by the best interests of the children.[323]

In 2004, social work academics Chris Goddard and Linda Briskman described the detention of children in Australia as 'organised and ritualised abuse' by the Australian government:

We use the term organised abuse to mean that those children are being abused by many perpetrators who are acting together in ways that they know can be extremely harmful. And we use the term ritualised abuse to mean that the children are subject to formal and repeated acts of abuse carried out under a belief system that the government uses to justify such cruelty.[324]

In 2001, *Four Corners* aired a video secretly recorded in Villawood by the parents of then six-year-old Shayan Badraie. The video explained that Shayan would not eat or drink and had become mute after witnessing acts of violence and self-harm, including discovering a man who had just slashed his wrists. He was admitted to hospital and rehydrated eight times and later diagnosed with post traumatic stress disorder.[325]

In early 2007, the New South Wales (NSW) Supreme Court awarded him $400,000 in damages.[326] The same day, the Department of Immigration granted his family permanent residency in Australia.[327] It had fought for 63 days in court before settling, spending more than $4 million in legal costs.[328] In August 2005, Shayan's lawyer told the Australian Broadcasting Corporation (ABC):

Given the severity of his symptoms now, the seriousness of his psychiatric diagnosis, I think that Shayan will find it very difficult to develop as a normal adult, to be able to form normal relationships and to hold down employment and interact with the world as a normal adult.[329]

A study on the impact of detention on families found that children had witnessed self-harm and suicide attempts, including people cutting themselves, jumping from buildings and attempting to hang themselves. Some had witnessed self-harm by their parents or their parents being struck with batons.[330] According to the Human Rights and Equal Opportunity Commission:

> Between July and December 2001, the department recorded 688 major incidents involving 1149 detainees across all detention centres. Of these incidents, 321 were alleged, actual or attempted assaults (19 involved children), 174 involved self-harm (25 involved children) and about 30 per cent involved 'contraband, damage to property, disturbances, escapes and protests.' Almost 75 per cent of these incidents occurred in the Curtin, Port Hedland and Woomera centres, where the largest number of children had been detained for the longest periods of time.[331]

For children, witnessing a threat to their carer is the most potent predictor of the development of post traumatic stress disorder.[332] All the children in the study were diagnosed with at least one psychiatric disorder and 80 per cent were diagnosed with multiple disorders. Almost all the children had major depressive disorder, half of them were diagnosed with post traumatic stress disorder and many wet themselves three or more times a week. Over half had suicidal thoughts and many thought it would be better if they were dead. A quarter had self-harmed.[333]

Another study of families found that all 10 six to 17 year olds, had post traumatic stress disorder. One of them had witnessed her mother cut herself and write on the wall in her blood, while another one had seen his mother attempting to set fire to herself while psychotic.[334]

Although child protection is a state responsibility in Australia, the Department of Immigration has responsibility for children within detention centres. Many health professionals and visitors to detention raised concerns about the abuse of children in detention, including social work academics Chris Goddard and Max Liddell who reported suspected abuse of children in Woomera to South Australia's child protection service in March 2002.[335] Early childhood professional Trish Highfield told the inquiry:

> If I saw the same level of abuse, neglect and distress in the children in the service in which I work, and I failed to make a mandatory notification, I could be prosecuted. Yet I have made mandatory notifications on so many children in detention and they have gone nowhere.

In defending itself in the Bakhtiyari case before the UN Human Rights

Committee, the Australian government argued there were effective domestic remedies for their complaints:

> *There is a comprehensive federal system of family law, complemented by rigorous child protection laws in States and Territories. These laws apply to persons in immigration detention (except as inconsistent with federal law).*[336]

However it failed to point out that in its view, later confirmed by the High Court, inconsistency with federal laws meant the Family Court was unable to release children from immigration detention. State and territory child protection authorities were also effectively hamstrung, being unable to compel the minister for immigration to remove both children and their families from detention.

In one case, although 20 child protection notifications were made, the Department of Immigration refused to remove the child and his family from detention.[337] Then minister for immigration Philip Ruddock explained:

> *If the professional advice is that it is in the best interests of the child to be in the community fostered and not with their parents and that advice was given to us, we would take it. But we have had advice directly to the contrary. The advice is that when faced with the choice, and it is a choice, of in the community but without family or in detention with family, the decision has always been to date that they should remain in the latter situation.*[338]

In June 2003, high school students interviewed Prime Minister John Howard as part of ABC Radio's *Talkback Classroom* series. When asked about children being held in detention centres for extended periods, including one who had been in Port Hedland for five years, he said:

> *Look, I would wish it were otherwise but unless you completely abandon the policy of detaining people who've come here illegally, which the Australian community plainly does not support, well, you have to have some kind of detention and you try and make the process of assessment as quick as possible.*[339]

Other politicians also justified the detention of children as a deterrent to others. Refugee advocate Kate Gauthier told the inquiry:

I recently had a lobbying session down in parliament. We showed them evidence of the mental health implications of detention, especially for children. We showed them evidence that detention constitutes child abuse and we said, 'Do you believe that child abuse is justified?' And they said, 'Of course not, there's absolutely no justification for child abuse, but we have to stop the boats.'

In a 2005 speech, refugee lawyer Julian Burnside QC told members of the Council for Civil Liberties:

Mr Howard has made it clear that the mandatory detention system, and the iniquitous Pacific Solution, are designed to 'send a message'. What does this mean? It means that we treat innocent people harshly to deter others. The punishment of innocent people to shape the behaviour of others is impossible to justify. It is the philosophy of hostage-takers. Any society which is prepared to brutalise the innocent in order to achieve other objectives has stepped into a moral shadow-land.[340]

Parenting

The Immigration Detention Standards state that parents remain responsible for the health and welfare of their children in detention, and that they can be assisted to care for their children through the provision of parenting training.[341] However a study on the way detention impacted on family relationships found that detention itself undermined the role of parents:

Detention takes away from both personal daily routine and the normal family environment. Parents' authority is undermined by that of the detention staff, and they are unable to adequately protect their children from violence, isolation, boredom and loss and grief … [This] may lead to feelings of guilt, depression and a loss of self-esteem, with adverse effects on parents' mental health. Where parents are forced to surrender their roles, due to their ill health, it is often left to their children to take on adult roles and responsibilities.[342]

A child and adolescent psychiatrist who assessed and treated children in detention told the inquiry it was inevitable that parents lost responsibility for their children in an institutional setting like immigration detention:

In the housing project, the women had to get the knife to cut up the carrots from the guards, or a child wanted to cut paper with scissors and that had to be a requisition form. These little impeachments on everyday life inevitably bring about the sense that you can't conduct life in a way you want to as a parent.

Parents in detention centres were unable to make up bottles for babies, cook meals, choose what their children ate, set mealtimes, decide sleeping arrangements or manage their children's illnesses. Registered nurse Mark Huxstep told HREOC that a child with an ear infection and his mother had to queue for three hours in the rain to receive his medication from the main medical centre.[343] A general practitioner who worked in a detention centre told HREOC:

This boy's diabetes had always been managed by his mother and had been well controlled. During his time in detention, his mother was not allowed to care for the boy's illness, and his diabetes worsened. When the boy was hospitalised, his mother was allowed to manage his illness and his diabetes stabilised rapidly. This occurred a number of times.[344]

A child and adolescent psychiatrist told the inquiry the disempowerment parents felt in detention had a destructive effect on the relationship between them and their children:

For children, seeing the daily humiliation their parents experienced was incredibly demoralising. Seeing their parents tearful and despairing is the most frightening experience for a child and many of the children I spoke to said they were really, really worried about their parents. They would stop talking to their parents because they knew their parents were totally preoccupied with their visa applications and were incredibly burdened. This created a real chasm between kids and their parents.

Both the deterioration in the mental health of their parents and the conditions of detention itself, exposed the children held in detention to trauma. Psychiatrist Jon Jureidini told the inquiry:

You couldn't really design an environment more destructive to child development than immigration detention. The other main abuse that the children were subject to was the witnessing of unrelenting violence, not just the spectacular stuff that happened during the riots but people cutting themselves and writing their names in blood and the kinds of comments that their parents were making to them, like, 'I'm dead, do your best to be a good girl and get on with your life.'

The inquiry was given a paper which outlined the ways in which chronic stress could have long-term effects on children:

Stressful events that are uncontrollable and/or experienced without the child having access to support from caring adults can have an adverse impact on brain architecture. In the extreme, it may result in the development of a smaller brain. Less extreme exposure can change the stress system so that it responds at lower thresholds to events that might not be stressful to others, thereby increasing the risk of stress-related physical and mental illness.[345]

A child and adolescent psychiatrist told the inquiry that the Department of Immigration's response to parents' despair and the damaging effect this had on their children was to attempt to put children in foster homes. A refugee advocate told the inquiry that a young mother who climbed onto a low roof at Villawood in a protest with her three-year-old daughter, suffered severe consequences:

She was sedated, restrained and locked in solitary management. The next day she was transferred to the psychiatric unit of Bankstown Hospital and scheduled. At no time was she deemed psychotic. The daughter was placed with an unknown family at an undisclosed location. The child was returned bruised and dirty one week later. We never knew where this little girl was taken, we couldn't find out.

A man who spent a year in Curtin as the sole carer of his five- and six-year-old children told the inquiry they were left alone in the detention centre when he served a four-month prison sentence for involvement in a riot:

Everyone had been involved in that demonstration but they targeted a selective group, and I was misfortunate enough to be among those. My mind was completely occupied by thinking about my children in Curtin. After one month imprisonment they allowed the children to visit me once a month via video conference. At the time I was in prison they granted my children a visa and released them to Perth and I was advised about that later. They sent them with an Iraqi family I didn't know. When I heard that my children were released that was a little bit of relief for me. Because then I felt they are in a safe place.

Babies

From 1 January 1999 to 26 December 2003, 71 babies were born in detention to mothers who arrived by boat.[346] Professor Chris Goddard, Director of Child Abuse Research Australia at Monash University, visited an eight-month-old girl born in detention in 2003. He later wrote:

As part of my work, I have seen prisons and secure units. I have seen children dying of child abuse, with fractures too many to count. I have seen children torn apart by sexual abuse. I have seen things I had to see, that I will never forget, that I found impossible to understand. This time I have seen something that I should never have seen. I have been to see an eight-month-old girl, small for her age, smiling at her parents, soon to be walking, her every move watched by guards. I have seen an infant behind grey wires and electric fences, in a high-security prison on the edge of Australia's dead heart. I have seen her parents found guilty, without trial, of wanting freedom. I have seen parents so proud of their first-born, but so close to despair. I have seen an infant given a number. I have seen a baby girl kept in a cage.[347]

Giving birth, stressful under the best of circumstances, was particularly traumatic for women in detention. A visitor to detention told the inquiry:

She had recently given birth to her daughter and told me how she was taken to hospital in a van and escorted by female officers who stayed with her during the birth. She was crying while she was telling me that they treated her like a criminal even in labour.

Women in hospital after giving birth wanted to see their families, but this was often obstructed by detention authorities. A woman who had previously given birth to premature triplets that later died, gave birth to twins at 26 weeks gestation while in detention. Her husband told the inquiry:

When my wife was at the hospital, she told the interpreter and doctor 'Bring my husband to visit me.' She was very worried, but ACM said 'We can't do anything because we not have enough staff.' Maybe two or three times we visit hospital. My children were crying everyday, 'Do we go and visit mother?' ACM said 'afternoon' and in the afternoon ACM said 'evening' and 'tomorrow'. It was very hard for the children because they are crying and worry about their mother. It was the first time they were separate from her.

A visitor to detention told the inquiry about another woman:

His wife had quite a difficult pregnancy and ended up having a caesarean and almost dying. She was still in hospital three and a half weeks post-birth. Her doctor had rung and begged for him to be able to come down and actually offered to pay to fly him down and put him up, but of course that could not happen. But he made such a fuss that it was agreed that he would be driven by the guards and three days in a row he was driven to Adelaide to see his wife and then driven back to Baxter.

Babies of mothers taken into detention from the community also suffered. Refugee advocate Trish Highfield told the inquiry she had to fight detention authorities to stop a five-month-old breast-fed baby from dehydrating after the mother, who spoke no English, had been picked up from her work at a chicken factory and taken into Villawood. Another advocate alerted Trish to the situation, which was confirmed by a sympathetic officer inside Villawood:

We rang Villawood very early in the morning and I said I needed the manager. An hour later the manager rang me and I said, 'You've got a mother in there with engorged breasts. You've got a breast-fed baby that's been abruptly weaned. I am a mothercraft nurse and I know what that means. The baby is rapidly dehydrating.' The baby was lethargic and I expressed my absolute disgust that anyone could rip a baby from the mother's breast.

I said to him, 'What are you going to do about it, because you don't need a dead baby on your hands.' He said, 'I'll get the case manager to ring you.' I said 'Something's got to happen fast or do I ring Canberra.' And he said, 'No it's a local issue, let me deal with it.' That baby was refusing a bottle so it was becoming dangerous. I waited one hour and 15 minutes. I got straight on to a senior person in Canberra and told him the situation. At 4.30 that afternoon the mother was released. But we were told by a professional on the inside that in that hour the manager was supposed to ring me back, he was busy trying to deport the mother.

Toddlers

Living in detention profoundly affected children's development. A child and adolescent psychiatrist told the inquiry:

Children really can't wait for things to get better because we know from brain development that the first three to five years of life are critical in terms of your adaptation, your growth intellectually, socially and we know that permanent damage can come about from toxic environments.

A former Woomera worker told the inquiry:

I really, really worry about children who have been incarcerated in detention centres because I have seen the change in them. I have seen babies born and when they are two years old they are not a normal two-year-old child.

A case study presented to the HREOC Inquiry into Children in Immigration Detention outlined one mother's experience of being separated from her family for four weeks before having her baby delivered by caesarean without her consent or knowledge, being separated from her new baby for days and being told not to breast-feed him. One week after delivery she was returned to detention where her wound wept for six weeks. The long separation from her two-year-old child led to a deterioration in his behaviour:

During the interview she was expressionless and almost mute, occasionally tears coursing down her face … The toddler was … angry and disruptive. He threw any offered toys away and spat at people, he attempted to eat bits of foam that lay on the floor. He repeatedly tried to leave the room and when he succeeded, wandered quite far from the room until returned by a guard. His father said: 'You see his behaviour? It is because we are sad and weeping all the time. He has lost his trust in us … We came here hoping to be free but this is worse. There is a big possibility that I will kill myself here. I am a dead man, every day I am dying. I have brought my family to hell' … The infant (at a developmental stage when most babies interact socially at every opportunity), made no attempt at eye contact and looked profoundly sad.[348]

A refugee supporter told the inquiry one child in detention was banned from kindergarten:

On the child's report, because he was seen to be difficult, it said he was not a good ambassador for his country and needed to learn some social skills.

A psychiatric assessment of children and families in detention found that eight of 10 pre-school children assessed displayed developmental or emotional disturbance. Of the pre-schoolers assessed, 70 per cent had spent at least half their life in detention. The study cited the following example:

In the richer environment in which assessment occurred, 'A', aged three, moved busily from one activity to another, eagerly seeking to use toys in a way that suggested he had never before seen a puzzle, or scissors, and that he was uncertain what to do with a picture book. His mother initially smiled and then wept as she watched his pleasure at exploring the toys and the room.[349]

Refugee advocate Trish Highfield told the inquiry about a three-year-old girl born in detention:

I saw the little thing put her hands through the inner wire. So deprived was that environment that a thistle growing outside the wire was something new and different. I had been advocating for five months to get her released two hours a week to attend a playgroup because she was having no respite from that shocking environment. She was so frustrated she was banging her head. I saw bruises on her forehead and lumps on her head.

She was so disturbed. I was playing with her and she was a little way away from her mum who was chatting to some other visitors and the whole time she was playing with me she was on alert. She was checking where her mother was the whole time because she had been separated from her before. That little child has suffered terribly in there and someone is responsible in this bloody country.

A submission to the inquiry told how medical reports on a three-year-old boy blamed environmental deprivation and the depression of other family members for his sadness:

His mother reported that on one occasion he obtained a piece of string and executed his truck. He said to his mother, 'I have killed my truck because it is tired of being sad.'

One woman whose family was held in Port Hedland told the inquiry her two-and-a-half-year-old son could see a playground and other children playing on the other side of the detention centre fence:

He keeps saying to me, 'Mum can I go and play with that little girl or that little boy?' And I couldn't explain why [not], but he is getting angry with me and he's biting and scratching and kicking me because he thinks I'm the one who doesn't let him go.

Very young children were not shielded from distressing events such as assaults on their parents. A refugee advocate told the inquiry:

One of the most poignant moments I experienced was when a three-year-old curly-haired child who could barely speak, interrupted my conversation with his father with the words, 'Guards take my Mummy.'

But refugee advocate Trish Highfield told the inquiry about one incident where an early childhood worker's kindness to a toddler in Villawood had been appreciated by his father:

The early childhood centre there is the most deprived, pathetic little environment I have ever seen – I think they were given two hours a couple of times a week. The father said that one day he woke very late and took his little boy for this session and the session was already over. And he said to me he would never forget that day because that early childhood worker, she was just about to lock the door and leave when he arrived with the little boy, but she took him in and she gave him two hours of lovely time. And he said to me with tears in his eyes, 'I will never forget what she did for my child that day, I will never forget it.'

School Children

Evidence presented to the inquiry indicated that the experiences and responsibilities of school-aged children in detention were inappropriate for their age. A boy who was 11 when detained on Nauru for three years told the inquiry:

I felt like my childhood was being washed away by detention. It's like watching an R-rated movie you are not supposed to watch. It included sexual content, very coarse language, violence, suicide and every horrible experience that you can imagine. Children experienced the grown-up world when they are not ready for it.

Former West Australian Labor politician Judyth Watson told the inquiry she had helped to settle a family on their release from detention, when the oldest boy was about 13:

I was trying to explain about power points and plugs, pretty basic stuff, but if you are from an Afghan village you need to start with electricity and gas and safety, and he made it very clear to me that in detention he had seen men putting knives into electric points to shock themselves and into light-globe fittings. He had also seen a man cutting himself.

These experiences had profound consequences for individual children. In 1999, a nine-year-old Chinese boy who had been held in Port Hedland Detention Centre for six years was forcibly fed tranquillisers to control his behaviour.[350] The inquiry was presented with a letter from a doctor working in detention regarding a 12-year-old girl who had started to wet her bed and was sleeping with her mother again.

A study of families in detention stated that a 12-year-old boy drank coffee to try and stay awake all night to protect his depressed mother and psychotic father.[351] The inquiry also received a copy of a letter written by a psychiatrist about a child in Baxter. It reads:

> *His mother described one episode where guards came in full riot gear and beat up a detainee. He became very distressed by this experience. He remains hypersensitive to any sign of distress in his mother. When I met with his father, he lay on the bed with him for some of the time and held him, apparently wanting to comfort him. He is now reluctant to go to the visitor's centre because he does not feel comfortable leaving his father. He is also not having visits from any peers. The stated reason for this is that the compound he is in is not a suitable place for children to visit!*

A boy who was 12 when detained in Woomera told the inquiry he and his younger brother were left alone in the camp when another brother and their mother were taken to hospital:

> *I was scared because at night I was by myself with my little brother. He doesn't listen to me and was missing his mum and that was bad. But after two days, she came back.*

Adolescents

The inquiry also heard evidence about the particular impact of detention on adolescents. A refugee advocate said:

> *The older children talked about how sad their parents were and how hard it was to sit and be with their parents, because of the depression and lack of hope. The children were with families they didn't know as well as ACM officers. They didn't have a space to just be who they wanted to be. They always felt that they were being watched.*

When sent on excursions out of detention, the children were under even more intense scrutiny. A boy detained on Nauru told the inquiry:

> *I remember they took us to a school dance, and cops were everywhere around us. I wanted to go to the toilet and the cops went after me to the toilet.*

The inquiry heard evidence about the distressing events adolescents had witnessed. A boy who spent three years in detention told the inquiry he found it difficult as the oldest male in the family not being able to protect his single mother:

> My mother was beaten one time and it really hurt my pride. It is my cultural value to protect the family but I just couldn't. I didn't get physically hurt but mentally I went through a lot of problems.

An adolescent who was in Woomera for six months told the inquiry:

> Sometimes they gave us meat and we could see the maggots. So the whole restaurant was throwing the food. One time my little brother went into the toilets and he saw a guy cutting himself with a sharp knife. When the strike happened, there was a big line and they said, 'Nobody goes into the restaurant. If somebody goes there we will kill you.' And did you see the guy in the newspaper? He got up and he threw himself on that – I was standing there. He was bleeding fast.
>
> The same day, people started walking around the camp and saying they wanted freedom. The officers were throwing gas into their eyes. Me and my family were sitting next to the caravan and this officer just threw two next to our room. My mum had to put us in the room but the gas was in the room. We couldn't see anything, we were coughing. Mum was in very bad condition. My dad told her not to come 'cos he has been in the same camp. But she couldn't live in Iran by herself.

A boy who spent three years in detention told the inquiry:

> The worst thing, I will never forget it, was people cutting themselves. It was horrible. I remember one time a person was harming himself up a tree and his children were crying under the tree. His wife was crying and yelling under the tree. His blood was dropping from the tree.
>
> I didn't leave my room for one week. I just didn't want to see the outside. I didn't even open the curtain in front of my room. I would never imagine a person of my age would go through these things. You can't blame that person because I have seen the calmest of people turn to violence. That place was breeding this type of people.
>
> I hated this country, I absolutely hated it. Most people really hated their own government but even I hated this country far more because

it hurt my family, hurt myself, hurt my brother, hurt my other brother, hurt everybody around me.

Some adolescents dealt with their problems by using drugs. In August 2003, three Australians working for the International Organisation for Migration, which ran the detention centres on Nauru, were charged with drug offences amid claims of drug dealing in the centres.[352] A boy who spent a year on Nauru told the inquiry:

Over there I used to smoke two packs a day to just keep myself busy. I did drugs, I want to be honest, to just get my mind out of it. You don't have hope. You don't know what's going on. We were just so worried about what was going to happen to us and just the way they treated us. They are torturing you, but they have smiles on their face. I've come from where there is nothing, but nobody ever treated us like that.

School

Despite the Immigration Detention Standards stating that children in detention should have access to appropriate educational services and materials, former teacher at Woomera Tom Mann told the inquiry:

With insufficient teachers and classrooms and an ad hoc curriculum, it was impossible to run anything but a tokenistic program. In July 2001, we were five teachers for over 300 children aged five to 17 and more than 1000 adults who needed to learn English. Children were lucky to receive two hours of teaching per weekday. Most children showed a willingness to learn in their early days at Woomera. However, with the onset of severe depression and self-harming episodes, learning became less of a priority for both parents and children.

Katie Brosnan, a former teacher at Port Hedland Detention Centre, told *The 7.30 Report* that the education provided to children in detention was 'a joke':

There is no curriculum ... there is no syllabus, there is no program, there is no accountability ... within this environment. It's solely dependent on the teacher. And, in my opinion, this is an absolute disgrace. It's a farce.

ACM are obliged to provide education to the detainees and they do so in reality, it's a very, very different practice.[353]

The inquiry heard from a child who was in Woomera for six months, that different levels of English proficiency amongst detainees in the same class made it difficult to learn:

They teach us English and there were some boys that knew English from before, so I started to leave it because there was no interpreter there. During the day I play marbles, just marbles. I hate them now.

Children in Baxter were unable to attend schools in Port Augusta until early 2003, and even then it was amid deep hostility towards them from the local community. A refugee advocate living there at the time told the inquiry:

The department called a public meeting where they presented slides telling this economically deprived community about the fantastic facilities and services asylum seekers got in Baxter. The meeting was full and most locals, including the mayor, opposed the kids from Baxter going to the schools. When a nun said that the people in Baxter weren't animals, someone yelled that they were and that was the general atmosphere.

However, a teacher who visited detention told the inquiry that even when children could attend mainstream schools, it could not ameliorate the effects of detention on their education:

These two children had spent the last four years out of touch with freedom of any kind, except that for the last six months they had been on day release to go to Port Augusta High School where in the morning they were bussed in, and bussed out immediately when classes ended. I find it difficult to believe that had been a considerably normalising experience for them, knowing that at the final bell, they were back into the bus to Baxter.

Refugee advocate Trish Highfield told the inquiry that even on the school bus, asylum seeker children were treated differently:

This day I rang and the guard was very gruff and he said, 'She is in a meeting.' I said, 'What do you mean, a meeting?' He said, 'She's in a meeting with all the other children. Ring back in an hour.' Finally she came to the phone. She said, 'We had to go to a meeting because on the school bus you are not allowed to laugh and talk and we were laughing and talking and some of the big kids were shaking the fence when we got back to detention.' Well, why wouldn't they? They had been out, they had been free and they were shaking the fence.

And she said with such distress, 'It wasn't the little kids, it was the big kids, but we had to go to the meeting as well.' I said, 'What did they say to you in the meeting, how did they treat you?' She was nearly crying and she said, 'They were rough, they were so rough.' As soon as I got off the phone from her, I rang a senior officer in the Department of Immigration because I was so disgusted that a six-year-old child in my country was being bullied and there was nothing I could do about it.

A refugee advocate who worked with Vietnamese children held on Christmas Island told the inquiry that children were taken to school under guard and attended school with children of the guards. She said there were playground fights and pressure was placed on teachers who tried to go further than their normal responsibilities to support the children. The children at school said they were scared of the 'children from the prison'.

A regular visitor to Maribyrnong told the inquiry:

Children were dealing with other kids at school knowing they came from the detention centre, seeing the kids being brought to school in a van with blacked-out windows. One of the little girls gave me a story she had written and she said that she had been asked why she was living in a prison.

But Hawraa Alsaai, who attended Footscray City College while in Maribyrnong Detention Centre, told a magazine she kept the fact that she was living in detention secret from her school friends because she thought they would stop liking her, and that she often returned from school ashamed and in tears.[354]

The inquiry received a submission that explained how a six-year-old girl who had been in detention for two and a half years, couldn't go in her school skipping race because she didn't know how to skip. She was not allowed to have a skipping rope in detention so she could learn, because of fears she or someone else could use it to hang themselves.[355]

A boy who spent three years in detention and attended school while in Baxter told the inquiry he was also acutely conscious of the difference between him and his friends at school:

> The worst thing about it is having friends at school but the only time you could actually see them was at school. My friends talked all the time that they were going to do this and that, and for me as a 16-year-old that was really painful.

Despite having the option of going to school, some children were too damaged by detention to attend. The inquiry received a copy of a letter written by a psychiatrist about a child in Baxter. It reads:

> The family were told that if they wished to be moved to a family compound they would need to meet certain requirements such as him attending school. I thought I had successfully negotiated with ACM staff two weeks ago to terminate this program, but it seemed he still felt under pressure to attend. There are at least two reasons why he is reluctant to do so: 1. He fears for the wellbeing of his mother and father. 2. He does not believe that he would be able to cope with the process of being searched on returning from school.

Others who wished to attend were not allowed as they were considered too old. A visitor to detention told the inquiry:

> During those four years, he'd been deprived of schooling, though he had consistently requested to be able to continue his education. A few months prior to our visit, arrangements had been made for the children to attend school. He, with great joy and delight, applied to attend school but was told that, as he was over 16, he wasn't eligible.

A migration agent told the inquiry about a 17-year-old boy who was not allowed to go to school but whose younger brother did attend:

> The younger brother was making friends. He even found a girlfriend and went to school all dressed up. But the older brother shuffled around the centre stooped over in old tracksuit pants and started taking antidepressants.

Unaccompanied Minors

The Department of Immigration website states that the Australian government takes its obligations towards unaccompanied minors very seriously. However, under the *Immigration (Guardianship of Children) Act 1946*, the minister for immigration, the same minister responsible for mandatorily detaining them, is the legal guardian of any children who arrive in Australia alone.[356] The minister is also the opposing party in any asylum-related litigation.

In July 2001, there were 143 unaccompanied children in detention. Until January 2002, when most unaccompanied children were transferred to foster homes, they were detained in the same manner as adult asylum seekers.[357] About 55 were sent to Nauru and Manus Island.[358] A study of 85 unaccompanied minors who sought asylum in Australia found that 55 were detained for three months or longer, 36 were detained for six months or longer, three were in detention more than a year, four in detention for more than two years and seven in detention for more than four years.[359]

Parents of unaccompanied minors had often sent their children from danger in their home countries hoping they would be safe. However, in a submission to the HREOC Inquiry into Children in Detention, mental health nurse Roshanak Vahdani described the situation of a 16-year-old Afghani boy held in detention for six months:

> *He cried continuously, expressing hopelessness about living and repeatedly telling me that he wanted to kill himself. He reported being depressed and agitated ... for weeks ... He had thought about self-harm continuously since the Red Cross had told him that they could not help him find his parents ... He had classical symptoms of a major depression ... and severe agitation and anxiety. He refused to let me tell the authorities as he felt that he would be punished by being put on suicide alert. His father was taken by the Taliban three years ago as a political prisoner ... The boy's older brother ... went missing, so his mother sent him to Australia to protect him from further persecution.*[360]

Children in detention alone also had to deal with bad news from home. A refugee advocate told the inquiry about one 17-year-old:

> *His mum died and his brother couldn't tell him because he didn't know how he would take it. His mum had been dead for two years before his*

brother told him. And his brother only told him because he thought he was going to be deported. I went to the detention centre the day he found out and he was just sitting by himself crying. I went and sat with him and he said, 'I wanted to show my mum that I was a good boy,' because I think he had been a bit of lad.

Migration Agent Marion Le told the inquiry how the detention of a boy who arrived alone at the age of 14 had affected him:

I met him because a lot of the Afghans came and asked me to help. He was a very slim, cute little boy that any mother would have loved to have taken home. When I last saw him I stayed in the detention centre one day only. I couldn't bear it any more. I was supposed to be there for three days. Someone like me who's been in and out of detention centres for all these years often, was moved to tears. That day I had to get out and get a plane home. I saw that boy go from a cute little kid to an obese quivering mess who says to me, 'I just want to get out of here and go to Glenside because I hear the nurses there are nice and they treat you like a mother.'

He's still in Glenside. He's been released from detention but he's now detained there under the public health system. We're asking the minister to grant him a permanent visa because the doctors say the only thing he wants is to know that he'll never have to return to Afghanistan and that he can have permanent protection to hopefully be able to reunite with his mother and siblings.

He deserved our protection and our care. Instead he's now seriously and perhaps irrevocably damaged by his time in detention and his experiences within a flawed destructive system which lacked compassion and decency in dealing with a minor unaccompanied by any adult relative or friend.

Residential Housing Projects

One option for women as well as children under 14 years of age held in detention is a transfer to one of the department's residential housing projects, which currently operate in Sydney near Villawood and in Perth near the Perth detention centre. The department describes Residential Housing as offering 'a more domestic and independent living environment'.[361]

In June 2004, then minister for immigration Amanda Vanstone claimed accommodation at the Port Augusta residential housing project was a 'rolled-gold' alternative to Baxter describing it as 'better housing than a lot of Australians have.' But a refugee advocate who lived in the Woomera township told the inquiry the housing project there was surrounded by a fence with security cameras:

> The women and kids couldn't go anywhere without guards. They could only see husbands, fathers and brothers once a week. Often the men and boys would suffer greatly from the separation and deteriorated mentally and emotionally.

Another refugee advocate told the inquiry:

> We have a government which is always talking about family values, yet it has a policy of separating families. The minister's statement that these houses are just like any other house in any street in Australia is so wrong. Where else are the houses with six-foot fences, with spotlights and guards at the gate, where no-one can visit? Where, at 11pm, is it completely shut down and every window and door must be closed?

Former prime minister John Howard acknowledged the difficulties for families with fathers and older boys having to remain in the detention centre, telling high school students interviewing him on *ABC Radio*:

> We don't like having to detain anybody ... in relation to young children, we have tried to provide alternative community housing arrangements, that has not been taken up a great deal. One of the reasons ... is that people are reluctant to see their own families divided with the father remaining in detention and the mother and children going into some kind of community housing arrangement.[362]

A former Woomera worker told the inquiry this was the reason many women refused to move to the housing projects:

> We set up a community in Woomera for women and children to live in and I thought it was a fantastic idea. I really wanted it to take off and I put my blood and guts into it. But the women couldn't leave their husbands, they couldn't.

A refugee torture and trauma service told a Senate committee that the arrangements could increase family stress as children and women felt guilt and responsibility when leaving other family members in detention.[363] A child and adolescent psychiatrist told the inquiry:

> A lot of them regretted going to the housing project. Their children had a bit more freedom, but the effects of being separated from the father and the burden of care that the mothers felt was really enormous.

Some families were also placed together in ways that were inappropriate. A visitor to detention told the inquiry:

> I know one family who was made to share with another family who belonged to the religious group from which they had fled. They continually suffered the indignity of being considered unclean and unworthy. Where everything they touched or sat upon was wiped down with disinfectant. Where one woman refused to cook in the same kitchen the other woman used, and cooked in another house.

Assaults on Children

In a study on the impact of detention on families, 37 per cent of children alleged they had been assaulted by detention officers.[364] A migration agent who visited Woomera told the inquiry:

> On one occasion I was stunned to see a tall young female guard kick a small boy aged about four because he was having fun near the compound gate.

A former detainee told the inquiry that once tear gas was used in Curtin despite a six-month-old baby being present. Psychologist Harold Billboe, who worked at Woomera for 14 months, told HREOC:

> I saw tear gas used two to three times on groups that included children. I also saw water cannon used four to five times on groups involving children during demonstrations. On one occasion ... a water cannon drove through a fence while women and children were present. I also saw adolescent children cuffed behind their backs and carried by their elbows.[365]

A refugee advocate provided the inquiry with a letter written in detention by a 12-year-old girl. It reads:

> *Officers use the tear gas and it exploded in front of women and children. Our eyes were burning and I could not open my eyes and because of too much burning in my skin. I couldn't touch my face. All people, especially women and kids, were screaming and crying and I did too.*

Refugee advocate John Highfield told the inquiry about an incident which the UN Human Rights Committee found breached the rights of both a three-year-old child and his father, who were placed in an isolation cell together.[366]

> *They took part in a hunger strike at Villawood. At two in the morning a removal team forced their way into the recreation room and took all of the people out, including him and his three-year-old son. One of the officers tried to legcuff and handcuff the little boy who was screaming, being woken from a sleep by strange men in riot gear attacking them. One of the other officers was so moved by the little boy's writhing that he stopped the officer doing it and said, 'You can't do this to a kid.'*
>
> *They flew them over to Port Hedland, the father and the son, in the early morning hours. They kept them locked up for thirteen days in this isolation cell. They would only let them out once or twice a day for ablution and toilet. The father explained that he had to let the little boy defecate and urinate on a pile of clothing in the corner of the room because there wasn't a toilet provided and the guards wouldn't respond to his pleading to let the little boy go out to the toilet.*
>
> *He would take the clothes out when they were allowed out once or twice a day and wash them and dry them – they would dry very quickly – and then put them back and the little boy would have to use that. On the first day they were not fed or given water from the time they left Sydney until well after they arrived at Port Hedland which was about 15 hours.*

Staff who took action to try and stop assaults on children were discouraged from reporting incidents and had their complaints ignored. A nurse who worked at Woomera in 2000 told a public meeting that children were subject to the same punitive behavioural management strategies as adult detainees and that she had seen a 12-year-old boy assaulted by guards, with no further action being taken by the Department of Immigration or ACM despite a complaint being filed.[367] A former Woomera worker told the inquiry:

> A lot of my reports never went through to organisations they were supposed to. A lot of my reports on children were stolen, went missing. One incident was two young boys sleeping in their beds with their mum and dad, and two officers dragged them in their boxer shorts across the compound which is gravel. Their feet, their body, their legs were cut to smithereens.

Wayne Lynch, who worked in Woomera for seven months as a nurse and counsellor, told HREOC:

> A 10-year-old boy was physically abused on two occasions by guards. After no action was taken against the guards by management, I recommended that it was a case of child abuse which should be reported to Family and Youth Services. I was advised by management that if I did this, I would find myself in a lot of trouble.[368]

Evidence presented to the inquiry showed that reports to detention and policing authorities of assaults on detainee children were met with the same disinterest as those about assaults on adult detainees. A child and adolescent psychiatrist told the inquiry about a family who had spent four years in detention:

> The father brought out pictures that the Federal Police had taken of his older children with facial bruising and he described how their heads had been pushed against desks by guards, but he felt that the investigations hadn't brought any sense of justice.

In December 2001, Zihar Sayed, a 13-year-old unaccompanied boy, was dragged by his neck from a room by three guards in riot gear. A nurse, doctor and female guard all witnessed this and the female guard tried unsuccessfully to prevent the child being taken. Once outside, the guards allegedly demanded the boy identify people rioting in another compound. When he refused, he was bashed in the face and shoved back into the room where witnesses said he was sobbing and shaking violently,[369] reportedly telling a detainee who tried to comfort him, 'See what they do to us? Is this what Australia is about?'[370]

Within minutes of the assault, Dr Dominic Meaney examined him and reported bruising around his neck and a welt on his face. The next day his injuries were photographed, but the photos later went missing. Federal Police were at Woomera on the day of the incident but did not interview Dr Meaney until several weeks later. In March 2002, the three guards were sacked after an ACM investigator found the boy had been assaulted, but were reinstated after the intervention of ACM's Sydney headquarters. Dr Meaney told a newspaper:

> It is outrageous that this could happen in Australia. I was deeply appalled that such a young boy could be assaulted and that those responsible not be severely dealt with.[371]

By October 2002, the case had gone to court twice, but each time the guards failed to appear. The Department of Public Prosecutions and the Australian Federal Police both claimed the other was responsible for finding the guards, and ACM refused to deny they were still employed by the company.[372] In early 2003, Steve Davis, a senior Department of Immigration official, told a Senate committee that of the three charges against the three officers, two had been withdrawn due to insufficient evidence and one was being pursued.[373]

A visitor in contact with a family in Villawood whose eight-year-old intellectually disabled son was allegedly sexually assaulted at the time by a visa overstayer kept in the family compound, told the inquiry:

> In October 2003, the mother went into the recreation room to find her son in tears and one of the detainees feeding him chocolate biscuits. She took him away. He told her he had been assaulted. She then went to the officers. They spoke to the alleged perpetrator who said it had been an accident. The mother talked to the child a bit more. She said she was not convinced it had been an accident. The child was quite detailed in what he told her and other people in a consistent manner. She went to the ACM supervisor. They finally agreed to take the perpetrator to the single men's compound. However, she wanted the case investigated more.
>
> The child went to school and told the same story to his teacher. The teacher phoned the Department of Education. The Department of Education contacted DIMIA. An adult daughter in the family asked to see the head of DIMIA. She was refused. Only when the teacher

contacted DIMIA were they approached by some middle-ranking DIMIA officials. They said they would report the matter to the police. That afternoon they saw a police car arrive and police officers go into DIMIA. About half an hour later they left without speaking to them. The police officers apparently said the Department of Community Services [DOCS] were involved.

I phoned DOCS and had a series of telephone calls. They told me, and this went on for over a week, they were negotiating with DIMIA to interview the family. Because the NSW police had told me they had no jurisdiction, I phoned the Federal Police. After being referred to several officers in Melbourne, Sydney and Canberra, I was eventually told that they had no jurisdiction either.

I made an official complaint to the Department of Community Services. On the seventh day, the family rang me in shock to tell me that the alleged perpetrator had been returned to the family compound. I was able to get in contact with a priest. He sorted it and the alleged perpetrator was removed the following day.

About a month after the event, they were taken out of Villawood to go and see DOCS. They said they did not even ask them directly about the matter. About six weeks after the incident, the family was released. They said they did not want to carry the matter forward. They wanted to restart their lives.

One of the reasons the police said they couldn't investigate further was because of language difficulties. The child does have communication difficulties, not only because of language but because he is intellectually disabled. However, the mother feels he was sufficiently able to communicate to get this information, as does the teacher, and there was consistency in the story. I was phoned up by DOCS to follow up my complaint a couple of weeks after the incident. They said they had tried to do their best. I gave them a bit of a blasting. I did not think that what they did was sufficient. They were not prepared to cross DIMIA or ACM.

A Record of Interview investigating an allegation that a detention officer had hit a seven-year-old boy on the legs with a baton during the Easter 2002 disturbance at Woomera, was presented to the inquiry. The boy's bruises had been seen by a doctor, but the boy was unable to identify his attacker because he was wearing a gas mask. His mother told the ACM manager conducting the interview:

It is not important that we know who the guard is. I don't care about that. ACM treats us badly and that is what I care about. I am told that in Australia, family is important and that women and children are not treated badly. ACM should not use the gas when we do not do anything. We were going to our room. We were not doing anything bad. Some of the men had sticks and tin and were fighting, but we were not. I have spoken to Human Rights and United Nations because we were treated badly. I don't care who was the guard who did this thing.

Self-harm Amongst Children

In a submission to the HREOC's Inquiry into Children in Immigration Detention, Suicide Prevention Australia documented cases in which 21 children in detention had made medically serious suicide attempts.[374] These included a 17-year-old boy slashing his throat when his father was not allowed to attend the dentist without being handcuffed, a 13-year-old unaccompanied boy drinking shampoo and a 10-year-old girl whose successful hanging was narrowly averted. A former detainee told the inquiry:

Children copy other people. Too much people go crazy inside. People standing on the fences, wanting to jump – the children look at these people.

A study of families in detention found that all 10 children studied, who were aged between six and 17, had thought of self-harm, with eight actually harming themselves, some by potentially lethal means. In contrast to community samples where self-harm in pre-adolescent children is rare, those who had self-harmed in detention included a seven-year-old, a 10-year-old and an 11-year old.[375]

An ACM incident report provided to the inquiry shows that on 7 April 2002, a 12-year-old and a 14-year-old boy attempted to hang themselves in Woomera. It states:

Both boys are solid friends ... at 1640 hours Officers were alerted by other children that two children were at the playground equipment and [A] had a green sheet tied around his neck. Officers observed [A] on top of the monkey bars with a green bed sheet tied to the bars but not around his neck. Detention Officer ... spoke with [A] and told him to

*come down he refused and stated that he was not coming down unless
he got a VISA. At this he wrapped the bed sheet around his neck and
started to climb down the rail he was grabbed by officers before the
sheet became tight.*

*[B] tried to walk away from officers stating that he was going to cut
himself with a razor. As Officers spoke with [A] and started to escort
him to Medical, [B] climbed up on to the monkey bars and wrapped the
sheet around his neck. Officers spoke with [B] and asked him to come
down but he refused the bed sheet was wrapped around his neck but
was not tied with a knot. Officers had placed themselves around him
with a number of other residents at some point he slipped and Officers
grabbed him as he fell. Officers stated that at no time did the sheet
become tight around the neck of [B].*

When children self-harmed it was deeply painful for their parents. A father
told the inquiry he felt powerless inside detention:

*I can't control my son. He tried to hang himself. My son drank shampoo
two times. He drank bleach two times. He was brought by ambulance
to Woomera Hospital.*

A visitor to Maribyrnong told the inquiry:

*Perhaps the most poignant visit was the time an Iranian man in tears
told me that his daughter had attempted suicide the previous day. He
was shattered, wracked with guilt and deeply distressed. The other
inmates were also deeply affected by this shocking incident.*

Psychologist Harold Billboe, who worked at Woomera for 14 months, told
HREOC that by the time he left, self-harm was almost universal amongst
unaccompanied minors.[376] Children also took part in hunger strikes. A
refugee advocate provided the inquiry with a letter written in detention by
a 12-year-old girl. It reads:

*We are in a hunger strike because we lived in Curtin Detention since
two years ago and we are tired. My brother sewed his lips by his hand
and we have not eaten anything for thirteen days. My father is in hunger
strike too because he wants to support us. He has pain in his heart and
kidney but he still does it. I have bad feeling and even I cannot walk*

because of hunger, nobody listen to me and my brother.

About five months ago they didn't give us a room to accommodate in. I would sleep in another room, my father in single persons, my mother in her friend's room, my brother in another compound. Suddenly my father became angry and broke a fluorescent lamp and put under his neck and he threatened them to obtain a room and he said if you don't give it to me I will kill myself. My mother and I were crying and wanted him to stop it. At last they gave us a big donga but we must live with other family. It doesn't have any drawers and must be all the stuff on the ground.

DIMIA refused us in three interviews and they said you will be refused again and must be deported to your country. When they understood that I am on a hunger strike they didn't allow me to go to my High School. Why I have to stay in prison two years, why my brother and I are called with a number. It is not justice. I am sad most of the time.

A nurse who worked at Woomera, Barbara Rogalla, has argued that the Australian government's treatment of children in detention meets the definition of torture:

Government policy places children into these conditions of pain and suffering. Systematic government involvement in such practices could amount to torture, as defined by the Convention against Torture and other Cruel, Inhuman or Degrading Treatment or Punishment. Australia is a signatory to this convention, but Australian domestic law ensures that prosecution for the crime of torture may occur only in very limited circumstances. [377]

In 2004, the Australian Democrats moved an amendment to migration legislation to limit the detention of children to 12 weeks. This was not supported by either major party.[378] The following year the Australian government told the UN Committee against Torture the number of children in detention was:

… as limited as possible, that children are only detained as a last resort, and that those who are detained are well cared for. [379]

The 2004 HREOC report on children in immigration detention concluded that children were subject to 'cruel, inhumane and degrading treatment'. In response, Phillip Ruddock and then minister for immigration Amanda Vanstone rejected its major findings in a joint media release, describing it as 'unbalanced and backward looking':

> The HREOC report is very disappointing. In proposing that there should be a presumption against the immigration detention of children, and that family unity should be preserved, the report recommends a model that would in practice encourage the inclusion of children in people smuggling operations.[380]

But the inquiry heard that government policy, particularly the introduction of Temporary Protection Visas (TPVs), was responsible for an increasing proportion of women and children undertaking boat journeys to Australia. Between 1997 and October 1999, when TPVs were introduced, the proportion of children as total passengers on asylum seeker boats averaged approximately 8 per cent.[381] In November and December 1999, children accounted for almost 16 per cent of passengers, and during 2000 and 2001 made up at least 20 per cent of all passengers, including 36 per cent of those on the SIEV X (Suspected Illegal Entry Vessel X).[382] Refugee advocate Sue Hoffman has argued:

> By disallowing family reunion, the effect of TPVs was to create a new market for people smugglers ... ever-increasing numbers of women and children attempted the dangerous journey.[383]

She notes that Department of Immigration employees were aware of the changing demographic of asylum seeker arrivals. The former DIMIA Manager at Woomera, Anthony Hamilton-Smith, told the HREOC Inquiry into Children in Immigration Detention:

> The accommodation including the new compounds was designed with single men in mind. The composition of the camp increasingly included women and children because of the conditions of the TPV which prevented family reunion.[384]

The department's Infrastructure Manager at Woomera in 2000 told HREOC:

The intended use of the WIRPC [Woomera] for processing
(predominantly) single men was based on the demographics of the
asylum seeker population who had arrived as unlawful noncitizens in
the period prior to the establishment of the WIRPC. However, because
of the removal of the ability to seek family reunion for those holding
Temporary Protection Visas in 1999, these demographics changed and
increasingly women and children arrived in Australia unlawfully seeking
Protection Visas.[385]

An Iraqi man on a TPV who lost his wife, his four-, seven-, eight- and 10-
year-old children and nine other members of his family when the SIEV X
sunk, told an Arabic newspaper shortly after the tragedy:

If they allowed us to bring our families this would not have happened
… I had lost hope of seeing my children because of the cruel condition
of TPVs. There was no other way but the sea to bring my wife and four
children.[386]

A former detainee told the inquiry:

A friend of mine was in Woomera. He got the TPV and he has four
kids. He thought he could be reunited with his family here but found
out from that visa he can not meet again with his family. So he gets his
family to come by boat and unfortunately his family were among those
who died on that boat. Until now he hasn't got the visa yet and his life
is just shattered.

MY JOB IS TO UNWIND HIS FINGERS:
DEPORTATIONS

Article three of the Convention against Torture, to which Australia is a
signatory, says no country should expel, return or extradite a person to
another country 'where there are substantial grounds for believing that
he would be in danger of being subjected to torture' or which shows a
'consistent pattern of gross, flagrant or mass violations of human rights'.[387]

Once asylum seekers had exhausted court appeals, they were liable to
be deported. A former detainee told the inquiry:

Do you think anyone is able to have a rest? Twenty four hours we were ready to be deported. During the night going by the complete dressing to the bed, knocking the doors of the neighbours. I need to have their lawyer's numbers and they need to have my lawyer's numbers. We need to contact the people outside. One man he got deported, we are phoning and the people start to work hard and they stop his deportation. We still were thinking: Who is the next one? The mental problem that we had. Who is the next one?

A worker in a torture and trauma support service told the inquiry:

Of my own personal case load, I can think of a number who have said that when they were in detention the thing that upset them most was waking up in the morning and finding that somebody had been removed.

Deportations were carried out secretly, to minimise resistance from both asylum seekers and their Australian supporters and lawyers. They often occurred in the early hours of the morning or after someone had been deceived into going to a part of the detention centre isolated from other detainees. A refugee supporter told the inquiry:

After four years of detention, all his supporters were hopeful he would soon be released. We were devastated when we heard of his deportation and shocked when we heard how this had been carried out. He was called away from the Sunday Service on the pretext there was a message for him. That was the last anyone saw of him.

An ACM memorandum provided to the inquiry outlines how detention authorities isolated detainees being deported from potential sources of assistance:

Detainee will be escorted to the DIMIA interview rooms at 0400 hours. Upon being informed of his removal by DIMIA, detainee will not be permitted access back into the compound or provided with any telephone calls.

A GSL document, *Security Assessment for Carriage on Aircraft*, provided to the inquiry states:

The [Villawood] psychologist has been consulted, and in his opinion he will try to have his removal stopped at any cost, including self-harm. This detainee has a large support group in the community. If they have any prior knowledge of this removal they will almost certainly mount some sort of campaign.

However, things did not always go the way detention authorities planned, with both other asylum seekers and ordinary Australians providing resistance. A former detainee told the inquiry:

About 11.30pm, the officers started gathering to take him. We were that time really united in the centre. I asked the other detainees that we will protect this person. We asked the officers that if you have to take this person, you have to kill us all. We told this guy that he should tell them that they should not come near him. He broke one of the windows, had one broken glass in his hand and he threatened he will kill himself if they come near him. The whole night there was negotiations that he should come into the administration area. Once a person is in the administration block, no detainee could help. About six o'clock, they drag him inside.

A detainee who helped others with legal advice told the inquiry how he helped to delay a deportation:

I went to the telephone, asked the Federal Court, 'Is there any way that the person is being deported tonight, the Federal Court can intervene?' A person says, 'I'm going to fetch you a form, you just fill it and fax us back.' I said, 'Could you please make sure you call the department and tell them this is urgent and you're giving us a call in 10 minutes, because they won't let you pass this paper to us.' She was kind, she said, 'I can do that.' We filled in the form and faxed it back. We managed to stop this boy. At that day, they did not deport the person.

Another former detainee who has now been recognised as a refugee told the inquiry:

Every morning I used to go to the clinic for medication at a quarter to six. At that time the immigration officer is not supposed to be there. They call me. I judge it quickly. I say, 'Okay let me take my medicine,

I'm coming.' I look. There is not much people around. I went to that office, I saw the immigration and I saw four security guys. They give me a letter signed for deportation. 'Okay, can I have a phone?' They say, 'No.'

When I was trying to talk to him, I jumped, I ran. I was faster than them and I get to the public. When they saw me running, all the people come to me. They stop the boss of immigration. When they back up, I phone my lawyer. We phone here, there. It's like a state of alert. All the people started gathering, they don't like any more security to get in our place.

Once asylum seekers notified their supporters and lawyers of a deportation, they swung into action, organising protests at airports and seeking court injunctions to stop the deportation. A refugee advocate told the inquiry about an attempted deportation:

The judge ordered that he be removed from the plane. He was, of course, a nervous wreck. He was able to give us a very clear outline of his forced removal and that included the fact that people were videoing the whole event, that they tried to inject him and he resisted. Those videos are there but you will never get them. I would love to see a court manage to extract anything from DIMIA when it says it can't find it.

Refugee advocates also organised legal assistance for many asylum seekers who had represented themselves throughout the refugee determination process, aiming to prevent mass deportations. One told the inquiry:

There was a weekend in August 2003 when it became clear that they intended to deport a whole heap of people. One team of people went through all who we knew were in Baxter and found out who was out of process. Another team was watching the gates. Another team was looking up all of these people's RRTs [Refugee Review Tribunals] and faxing them off to lawyers. It was a whole weekend of phones ringing and stress where about 14 people at risk, ended up in two deportations.

Another advocate told the inquiry:

In late 2004, the Uniting Church put together a project which we called the Baxter Project because there were about 48 people who were at risk of imminent deportation. All of those people got proper migration and legal advice and were actually all able to put in an application under section 417 of the Migration Act. *Apart from two people who were deported that we couldn't stop, one of them because they were so mentally ill they weren't competent to instruct a solicitor, all of those people are now out of detention. We do feel a sense of achievement and pride in the fact that we were able to facilitate some of those people becoming recognised as refugees after the process, which is such a faulty process, failed in every other aspect.*

When all other efforts to stop their deportation failed, some asylum seekers appealed to members of the public for help when they were on the aircraft. A submission to the inquiry included an account by a man, who was eventually deported in January 2005, of a previous attempt to deport him:

I stood screaming and asking for help from passengers. Those escort officers beat me fiercely with kicks all over my body, especially my genitalia. The nurse, trying to inject in my leg, missed my body to hit the plane seat where the needle got bent. But he didn't change the needle and injected me again with that contaminated needle. I continued to scream and ask for help until few passengers cried and combined with each other to relieve my oppression.

In October 2006, the Immigration Department responded to a Question on Notice about deportations, stating:

If physical restraint is required, escorting officers may use physical holds or instruments of restraint, such as flexicuffs, handcuffs and security belt (which allows a person's hands to be restrained at waist level). It is departmental policy … that medication must not be used as a means of restraint.[388]

The policy referred to in the answer is contained in Ministerial Series Instruction (MSI) 408, which came into effect on 1 November 2005. The inquiry asked the Department of Immigration whether the MSIs it replaced did permit the use of chemical restraints, but no response was received. However, the inquiry heard numerous stories of deportations in which asylum seekers were forcibly injected or made to take tablets. One former detainee said:

I heard my name on the speaker and I was escorted to meet the immigration officers. I said let me talk to my lawyer and they said no. They locked me in the isolation place. I was feeling very scared. Then I start to harm my hand. If my hand is injured they will take me to clinic. If they take me to clinic the other detainees will see me, they will ring my lawyer.

Then I found maybe 16, 17 officers around me. They hold my legs together and they bend the big belt and kicked my chin and bound my hands together. They stood over my body and the nurse have an injection and Valium tablets. I said I don't want an injection. I don't want tablets. They tried to do it maybe 20 minutes. I was very angry, screaming, and they couldn't. My muscle was very tight because I was frightened. And then they forced me.

I was in this airplane. I said, 'I need a piece of paper to guarantee, with stamp with signature, when I go to my country nothing will happen to me. Don't say it to me with your mouth, give me a piece of paper.' Suddenly the immigration officer heard his mobile ringing from Federal Court. He said to me, 'You are lucky, you go back.' I was wearing the garment of the mental hospital as well. I said, 'I want to ring my lawyer.' They said, 'Okay, you have a right.' I say, 'Why now I have a right, before no?'

A submission to the inquiry also included an account of an attempted deportation:

The doctor entered the cell carrying an injection with four tablets, asking me to choose either the injection or the tablets. I refused both. The doctor offered the security officers to do their job, and he and the officers laid me down on the floor and sit on my back, took my pants down. Then I accepted to receive the tablets. They didn't work, so they force me to take a fifth tablet at the airport. They got me on the airplane with a wheelchair accompanied by a nurse, two companions and three other ACM officers, with three types of handcuffs and ties of leather, plastic and steel around my hand and belly that gathered my arms to my trunk. Since then I haven't consulted any medical personnel in detention since losing the trust in any who works for this ACM.

Another submission to the inquiry included an account of a deportation by a former detention officer:

We have an 'extraction', he's high risk, whatever that meant. I didn't know anything then. I just followed orders. We get this guy out of bed early in the morning. We pull the sheet off him. He's in his pyjamas. He clings on to the bedstead. This is a steel bedstead. My job is to unwind his fingers, struggling, shouting he won't go. There are nurses. First time I'd seen a 'chemical restraint' used. They must have broken about three needles on him. I'm thinking there must be a better way, this bloke's not an animal.

We put him in the fishbowl, that's like a cage. There were about six big blokes like me. Another tries to get these injections into him. But it's not working. He's shouting he won't go back. Anyway, we get the handcuffs on him. We get him out of the cage and into the van to the airport. He's saying, 'I want my shoes.' His T-shirt is torn. He's saying, 'I can't go without my shoes.'

When we get him into the aircraft, we handcuff him to the seat. But he pulls the whole seat out of the floor. That was it. We got him off the plane and took him back. Next week we did it again. This time he went quietly. 'Just give me the tablet,' he said, 'don't inject me with that.'

On 13 December 2004, Australian environmental consultant Sonia Chirgwin witnessed a deportation on a flight from Sydney to Thailand. She told ABC Radio:

There was an enormous amount of noise, of metal scraping on metal ... then two big ... security guard–looking people dragged onto the plane a man who was in handcuffs and leg cuffs with chains to a ... leather restraint thing around his waist. Probably the most alarming sight was he was gaffer taped around his mouth, all around the back of his head, several times, so that he could not make any noise whatsoever and he looked terrified. They put a flight mask over his eyes ... The man that I spoke to said that he was so uncooperative that he'd been screaming for eight hours.[389]

Acting immigration minister, Peter McGauran, told ABC Radio:

The person being removed would have had full access to all aspects of refugee determination, and I don't believe this person was being removed to a place that would place he and his family at risk. Restraints are rarely used, and only when necessary to prevent a person harming themselves or others. It's the behaviour of the person being removed that determines the measures that have to be used. I'm sure it wasn't pretty for the observers on the aircraft, but it was necessary and entirely brought about by the person himself.[390]

Some asylum seekers were deported from Australia when they were mentally ill. A series of Department of Immigration emails provided to the inquiry outline preparations for deportations. In one deportation attempt, an immigration staff member tells another:

Due to the psychologist's report, we have cancelled the commercial arrangements and he will be transferred by charter.

A worker with a refugee legal service told the inquiry about the deportation of a man who had claimed asylum on the basis of his Christianity:

He had been worn down by detention to the point where he actually refused to believe that any of his appeals could be rejected. He had lost complete touch with reality and honestly believed that even though he had his rejection papers, Australia would not deport him because he was a Christian, so why would a Christian country deport a Christian.

Deportations were also carried out despite requests from the United Nations not to deport particular individuals. In one case, an asylum seeker who had spent five years in detention was returned to Australia, at a cost of 'tens of thousands of dollars' after three days in transit when new information about his case was received from the UN.[391]

Alarmingly, the inquiry also heard of a number of cases of people who the Department of Immigration initially attempted to deport, but later recognised as refugees. A refugee advocate told the inquiry of one such instance:

He was seeing some visitors when the riot people arrived in the visitors' centre and removed him to Villawood for deportation. There was actually a seat booked by DIMIA on an Emirates flight at 6pm that night. He was in such a state they thought they had better admit him to a psychiatric unit to see if he was fit to travel. We went and visited him and he was in the locked ward in a foetal position on the floor, unable to speak, with two GSL guards. He subsequently was taken back into Villawood and was on 14 separate pills, very physically ill.

A worker in a refugee assistance organisation told the inquiry about the attempted deportation of another man who was later recognised as a refugee:

> *He decided that he couldn't go back but would kill himself. He said he felt his spirit was crushed and when he was taken to the Perth Airport he swallowed 35 to 40 sleeping tablets and lost consciousness. He miscalculated when they would be working because he actually had vomiting and diarrhoea with his distress, so he absorbed the sleeping tablets quicker. He lost consciousness before the plane took off, so they took him to Royal Perth and pumped his stomach. In his pocket was his suicide note. This letter was actually addressed to me, thanking the Uniting Church and us for all our care, very polite, beautiful letter. 'Now I am dead you have to tell the government not to do this any more. I will die myself for no-one else to suffer from this.' It's the most moving and confronting piece of information that's come to me, ever.*

Deportations also resulted in the forcible separation of families. Australian citizen Vivian Solon was separated from her children when she was wrongly deported to the Philippines, for which she later received $4.4 million in compensation.[392] One of her sons was placed into foster care when she failed to collect him from a Brisbane child care centre.

Russian asylum seeker Kristina Nievens, later allowed to remain in Australia, was threatened with separation from her nine-month-old Australian son after a Family Court injunction failed to stop her pending deportation in 2002. Justice Richard Chisholm ruled that the *Migration Act* overrode her baby's best interests. He stated:

> *While I feel great sympathy for the mother and child, the law does not allow me to make the order sought by the mother.*[393]

On hearing the decision Kristina was inconsolable, saying:

> *Just make me have a baby and leave it behind. I would rather die.*[394]

Fijian mother of five, Seseana Naikelekele, overstayed her visa and lived in Australia for 15 years before spending more than two years in Villawood. She was deported to Fiji in 2004, taking her three-year-old child but leaving behind her other children aged from four to twelve because she believes they will have a better future in Australia. Three of her children are Australian citizens. More than 100 children from the school her oldest children attended wrote to immigration minister Amanda Vanstone asking that their mother be allowed to stay, but they received no reply.[395]

In 2001, the UN Human Rights Committee found that the deportation of the parents of a 13-year-old girl, who had been born in and spent all her life in Australia, interfered with the right to family life.[396]

A submission to the inquiry also cited the case of a woman who overstayed her student visa and spent a year in Villawood. While there she married an asylum seeker and became pregnant. She was separated from her husband and deported when she was eight months pregnant, despite the couple having told authorities they were prepared to leave Australia voluntarily together after the birth of their child.

Bakhtiyari Family

One of the most high profile deportations was that of the Bakhtiyari family. Ali Bakhtiyari arrived in Australia in October 1999 and was granted a Temporary Protection Visa (TPV) in August 2000.[397] The Department of Immigration concluded:

> [He] displayed knowledge of Afghanistan, [he looks like] a person of Hazara ethnicity. Based on [his] knowledge of Afghanistan, his fluency in the Dari language and, in the absence of any evidence to the contrary, I accept that [he] is a national of Afghanistan.[398]

His wife, Roqia, their five children and Roqia's brother, Mazar Ali, arrived in Australia in January 2001 and were detained at Woomera. Roqia claimed her husband had been arrested two years earlier in Afghanistan and she had not seen him since. Her visa application was refused on the grounds that she claimed her husband had been arrested two years prior when the Immigration Department knew he was now in Australia, and on the basis of linguistic analysis which concluded she was Pakistani.[399]

A year into the family's detention, reports outlined the damaging effect it was having on the Bakhtiyari children. The reports described self-harm, including 14-year-old Alamdar and 12-year-old Montazar stitching their lips together, slashing their arms and going on hunger strike.[400] In an incident that received extensive media coverage, Roqia's brother Mazar Ali threw himself into Woomera's razor wire to draw attention to the family's situation.[401]

A month later, a minute to then immigration minister Philip Ruddock regarding the possibility of him intervening in the case stated that Roqia was an Afghan citizen and her children were born in Afghanistan. Other considerations it listed included advice from an ACM psychologist that Alamdar:

> ... is also reported to have drawn a picture of a Taliban soldier holding the decapitated head of a child, which strongly suggests that he has been witness to gross acts of brutality and continues to suffer severe post-traumatic-stress reactions ... He has clearly suffered traumatic periods in his life and aligns these early experiences with his present state, which he views as imprisonment.[402]

The psychologist also advised that Montazer had cut himself with a razor blade on his arms and legs. The minute stated:

> Indefinite detention of the children may constitute breach of the Convention on the Rights of the Child. It would not be in the children's best interest to remain in the detention centre environment for a prolonged period of time.[403]

On 25 March 2002, the Bakhtiyari family lodged a complaint with the UN Human Rights Committee claiming that their treatment amounted to a breach by Australia of the International Covenant on Civil and Political Rights. One week later, Philip Ruddock refused to intervene in their case.[404] The same month, a linguistic analysis of Ali Bakhtiyari concluded that his dialect, while mainly spoken in Afghanistan, was Pakistani.[405]

The Australian government told the UN Committee investigating the Bakhtiyaris' concerns that:

The standard of medical care available at the Woomera facility is 'very high', including continuous cover by a general medical practitioner and nurses, including a psychiatric nurse, as well as availability of psychologists and counsellors, dentists and an optometrist. A range of recreational and educational facilities are available to assist in the maintenance of mental health and to foster individual development. As to the issue of release from detention, the State party did not consider such a course would be appropriate.[406]

In May 2002, the High Court of Australia agreed there was an arguable case that Roqia and the children should be granted visas on the basis of her husband's acceptance as a refugee. While the family was waiting for the High Court case to be heard, Alamdar and Montazar were among 30 detainees who escaped from Woomera in June 2002.[407]

In a widely reported incident that embarrassed the Australian government, three weeks after their escape from Woomera, Alamdar and Montazar sought asylum at the British consulate. This was refused and they were returned to Woomera. Shortly after, lawyers for the family applied to the Family Court in Adelaide for the two boys to be released from detention and examined by a psychologist.[408]

On 5 December 2002, Ali's visa was cancelled and he was taken to Villawood,[409] the Immigration Department claiming that Ali Asqar Bakhtiyari was actually Asghar Ali, a man identified as Pakistani by the Pakistan embassy.[410] Under Pakistani law, the wife and children of Pakistani citizens are deemed to be Pakistani also.

On 4 February 2003, the High Court refused Roqia and the children's application to be granted a visa based on Ali's initial acceptance as a refugee.[411]

A submission to the inquiry stated that despite linguistic analysis determining her to be Pakistani, when Roqia was five months' pregnant (in June 2003) she was offered the option of completing an Afghan passport application form and of obtaining the Afghan reintegration package of $10,000 if she obtained the passport and travelled to Afghanistan.[412]

The family once again made news across Australia two months later when the Family Court ordered all the Bakhtiyari children released from detention immediately. In October 2003, the UN Human Rights Committee found that the detention of the family violated the International Covenant on Civil and Political Rights. It recommended that Roqia be released, and that both she and the children be granted compensation.[413]

On 29 April 2004, the High Court overruled the Family Court decision to release the Bakhtiyari children[414] and they were taken with Roqia into a house designated as an 'alternative place of detention' in Adelaide under the care of welfare organisation Centacare. Ali remained in detention in Baxter.[415] In the early hours of 18 December 2004, Immigration Department officials visited the house and took Roqia and her six children into detention in preparation for their deportation to Pakistan.[416]

The next day, the Identity Checking Unit of the Afghan Interior Ministry in Kabul, which is funded by the Australian government, made an interim report on the Bakhtiyari family with potential to embarrass the government in its high profile campaign to discredit the family. The report asked for more time to investigate claims backed by local officials that Roqia's cousins had vouched for her Afghan identity.[417]

On 23 December, the Afghan embassy in Australia released a statement which noted that the evidence regarding Roqia's nationality was inconclusive and the Identity Checking Unit needed more time to verify it, saying:

> At least a few local inhabitants of the Jaghuri district of Ghazni province have identified Mrs Bakhtiyari to local authorities as someone who is apparently connected to this district.[418]

The Afghan Ambassador to Australia when the Bakhtiyaris were deported, Mahmoud Saikal, told journalist Paul McGeogh the statement was made to clarify things for Australian agencies following rumours of the family's imminent deportation:

> Also, as a national of Afghanistan, we didn't want her to come

back to us later to ask why did we do nothing about it. We were
saying that the file was still open.[419]

However, a statement released by the office of the then immigration minister, Amanda Vanstone, said:

The minister noted that the Afghan embassy had today advised
that Mrs Bakhtiyari's nationality needs further investigation
and remains 'inconclusive'. [But] the government has written
confirmation from the Pakistani authorities that Mr Bakhtiyari,
Mrs Bakhtiyari and the children are all Pakistani nationals. This
puts the matter beyond doubt.[420]

At 1am on 30 December 2004, Ali, Roqia and their children, ranging in age from one to 16, were woken and deported to Pakistan,[421] 12 days before the Identity Checking Unit delivered a final report concluding Roqia was in fact an Afghan. The deputy head of the Identity Checking Unit told McGeogh, 'Mrs Bakhtiyari is Afghan – we wrote a reply telling the Australians she was Afghan.'[422]

However, almost a year later, the Department of Immigration responded to a Question on Notice stating:

DIMIA has not refused to accept that Mrs Bakhtiyari is an
Afghan national. The fact is that the Afghan authorities have
never confirmed that she is Afghan and are continuing to
investigate. However, that aside, the Pakistani government
has confirmed her right to enter Pakistan as a national of their
country.[423]

The head and deputy head of the Identity Checking Unit told McGeogh their team had spent 37 days in the field verifying Roqia's identity, but they were unable to say whether or not Ali was Afghan.

A 2005 media release by then immigration minister Amanda Vanstone stated that the government had spent more than $3 million on legal costs, detention costs and removal expenses on the Bakhtiyari family.[424]

Memorandum of Understanding with the Iranian Government

On 12 March 2003, Australia signed a memorandum of understanding (MOU) with the Iranian government in which the Australian government claimed 'Iran agreed to the return of failed Iranian asylum seekers in Australia.'[425] However, immigration minister Philip Ruddock refused to release the MOU, saying it was a confidential agreement.

A letter sent to Iranian detainees in April 2003 offered individuals $2000 (up to $10,000 per family) to accept voluntary return within 28 days, but stated:

> You and family members accompanying you in Australia should consider carefully your options for voluntary return to Iran. If you choose not to accept voluntary return within the 28 days, plans for your involuntary removal will begin, and you will be removed from Australia as soon as practicable.

The belief held by many detainees and their supporters that the Australian government was bluffing over the contents of the MOU was supported by the leaking of an internal Immigration Department document. The document was written to then minister Philip Ruddock and senior officials by a senior bureaucrat in the department. It reads:

> The department's experience suggests that, for all but the hard-core detainees, the key to ensuring voluntary departure lies in the creation of a credible threat of involuntary removal. The Iranian Embassy has suggested that we negotiate arrangements to secure the involuntary removal of 'emergency cases', that is those who are disruptive and uncooperative. We believe the enforced removal of a group of difficult detainees, irrespective of the number, is likely to make it easier for others to choose to depart voluntarily. We will seek to define the 'emergency' group as broadly as possible. In particular, we would be seeking to include those who have attempted self-harm or committed acts of violence within the centres.

Despite scepticism about the MOU, distribution of the letter to the detainees had a profound impact on their morale. A visitor to detention told the inquiry:

I visited Baxter soon after the letter had been given out and the change in mood was palpable. People just sat in silence. It was like being at a funeral. The people I visited were worried and I was worried too. It suddenly made it more real that they could be taken at any time.

The MOU also concerned the United Nations Commission for Human Rights. The head of its Working Group on Arbitrary Detention, Louis Joinet, asked the minister to explain what the MOU contained, particularly in relation to protecting those who returned. He told ABC Radio:

There'll be no guarantees as to what will happen once they're in Iran ... Experience has shown us that in certain countries, people who are repatriated, even those who have returned voluntarily, once they're back, they're called in by the authorities and asked 'Why did you flee the country?' ... and that very act of fleeing takes on a political complexion ... a further reason is that the Working Group has just visited Iran ... And one might reasonably believe that there are risks if the MOU contains no guarantees about preventing the risk of persecution in Iran ... It has to be recognised that the situation relating to basic freedoms in that country is of concern.[426]

Immigration Minister Philip Ruddock responded to the concerns by saying:

I don't think it's a matter of asserting to any country quite frankly ... that they're required to give such an assurance ... The asylum process deals with the very question as to whether or not a person has a well-founded fear of persecution ... if people had reasonable grounds for believing that they would be persecuted on return, those issues should have been advanced during the asylum process.[427]

Only six of the 85 Iranians offered voluntary return had accepted by June 2003.[428]

Voluntary Returns

Pressure was also put on asylum seekers of other nationalities to voluntarily return to the countries they had fled. In total, about seven per cent of people who arrived in Australia by boat between July 1999 and August

2001 were eventually deported or removed from Australia.[429]

A much higher proportion of those processed on Nauru and Manus Island volunteered to return home because they had no access to the Australian legal system to appeal departmental decisions not to accept them as refugees. Once they had been refused by the department, they had no hope of the decision being overturned and faced indefinite detention in shocking conditions.

According to Oxfam, about 31 per cent of asylum seekers processed offshore between 2001 and 2003 voluntarily returned to their home country, including more than half of all Afghan applicants.[430] During 2001 to 2002, the RRT set aside 62 per cent of departmental decisions for Afghan applicants processed onshore, with 32 per cent set aside in 2002 to 2003 and 90 per cent the following year.[431]

One man who was detained on Nauru told the inquiry:

> *Every Friday there was a meeting by DIMIA reminding us that we will organise something to take you out of this country. Finally they decided to have an interview – they said people have to prove they are refugees. If they are refugees they will be granted a visa, if not they will be given 28 days to make a decision, take $2000 and go back home.*
>
> *When they had this interview, a very small number of people got accepted and the rest were rejected, including my family, but still we decided not to go. They went through several times. They did interviews, they accepted a small number of people, and they kept warning the rest of the people that's the last chance. Finally I told them, 'Look, I don't have anywhere else to go. I am either staying here or dying there.'*

The inquiry also heard reports that raised questions about the informed consent of some detainees agreeing to voluntary removal. Of the roughly 55 unaccompanied children sent to Nauru and Manus Island, 32 volunteered to return to Afghanistan in 2002 to 2003.[432]

A visitor to Maribyrnong told the inquiry that one man who agreed to leave Australia had severe mental health problems.

> *There was an Iranian man who was okay mentally when I first met him but then got into an absolute form of paranoia. He would pull me aside and start whispering at me in very, very broken English, so the whispering was quite odd because I didn't know what he was saying but he was so, so tense and he was always shaking. Eventually he asked*

to go back and I have no idea what happened to him, but certainly he left Australia in an absolutely powerless situation in terms of health.

One former detainee told the inquiry he sought the assistance of refugee lawyer Julian Burnside QC for a fellow detainee who signed a paper after being assured it was not important.

It was consent that, 'I agree to withdraw my claims of refugee application and I volunteer myself to be removed from Australia.' This young boy who could not speak English, just keep on crying the tears. I said, 'Don't worry, we'll do something.' I took the boy out and Julian wrote a note on that letter saying: 'I was misled, misinformed, I was tricked by this particular manager and I disagree with this.' Now, how many people would have a chance to speak to a person like me or would have a chance to have Julian Burnside there?

A woman whose husband was taken into detention told the inquiry:

The second day my husband was in detention I told him not to sign any papers. I was sitting with him and a girl came up with a paper and said, 'Sign this.' And we said, 'What for?' and she said, 'Just sign it, it's just a formality.' When I read it, it was permission to deport him within two days.

Some who returned voluntarily did so under extreme duress. An unaccompanied minor who spent months in Woomera before being released into community detention told the inquiry he was given the choice of returning to Afghanistan briefly so he could be granted a student visa and permanent residence in Australia, or being re-detained.

It was completely uncertain to go back there and come back because when we go to the airport they were helping us to process our application and to look after us. They were forcing us in the airport to be quick, to get into the car and go because they were also scared. If you say to some people we will put you in detention centre and then you sign a letter that okay, I am ready to go back, and then they still say this is volunteer. Well if you said to me, I won't put you in detention, I will sign it? I won't sign it.

Some of the people who left Australia voluntarily were sent to third countries on short-term visas, leaving them in a precarious position. The inquiry was given the account of one man:

> He was told by DIMIA that he would be safe to live in Syria and he would be given documents. So he became a voluntary removal. He got his travel documents and visa 15 minutes before the plane landed in Damascus, and to his horror the visa was limited for a couple of months. It had largely expired and it was stamped that he had to report to the public security department. He again became stateless.

A refugee advocate told the inquiry:

> I met a guard at Port Hedland who was talking about how deportations were usually okay but there was this one time he went to Syria and it was quite scary because these people came with guns to pick the people up. I asked what happened to the people and he said 'Oh, I don't know. I've got no idea.'

Deaths on Return

Some people whose claims for asylum in Australia were rejected were killed when they returned to the country they had said they feared persecution in. In July 2006, researchers working on the *Deported to Danger* report[433] interviewed asylum seekers who returned to their home countries, mostly after spending years in detention. The researchers were told that nine people had been killed after their return to Afghanistan and that one man's only children, aged six and nine, were killed when a grenade was dropped on their house four months after he returned from Australia. A Pakistani newspaper reported the grenade attack as:

> One of many attacks on Afghans who return to their homeland from Western countries. These Afghans who come back to Afghanistan after spending years as refugees face constant abuse, their house robbed, and in some cases murdered, forcing them to leave the country again.[434]

Their father, who spent 16 months on Christmas Island and Nauru, told the researchers, 'My children died so that John Howard could win an election.'[435]

Alvaro Moralez

In September 2002, Colombian Alvaro Moralez was shot and killed by paramilitaries after the RRT rejected his asylum application and he voluntarily left Australia for Argentina, where he was again refused asylum. The Argentinean government deported him to Colombia.[436] Commenting on his death, the then attorney-general, Daryl Williams, told a newspaper:

> Australia was not responsible for what happened to that person. He wasn't deported. He went [to Argentina] voluntarily and what occurred after that was really his own responsibility.[437]

A submission to the inquiry stated:

> The federal government claims that Australia is not responsible for what happened to Alvaro Moralez because his was a 'voluntary' departure from detention. The choices given to Alvaro were to leave voluntarily or face deportation.

Bilal Ahad

In late 2002, 18-year-old Pakistani Bilal Ahad was killed within weeks of being deported from Australia. He had come to Australia on a temporary visa and later claimed asylum on the basis that his family was involved in an anti-drug organisation and that his grandfather and uncle had been killed by drug smugglers as a result. The RRT found he was a 'highly unreliable witness.'[438]

A refugee advocate told the inquiry that the former immigration minister refused to accept he had been killed:

> Philip Ruddock said that this 18-year-old died of a heart attack. This was ridiculous because we had adequate information about how he died, but Philip Ruddock stuck by that story. He knew lots of young people who had just suddenly died of a heart attack. We gave all the information about what the doctor had said about the froth coming out of his mouth, about his aunt who had seen him go out with strange men, who saw him come in and almost die in front of her. They raced him to the hospital. It was quite clear that he was murdered, but Philip Ruddock just rejected that.

Mohammad Mussa Nazari

Afghan Mohammad Mussa Nazari returned to Afghanistan from Nauru in early 2003. Before he left he wrote to an Australian supporter:

> At first the IOM and DIMIA and UNHCR [United Nations High Commissioner for Refugees] were saying the people to go back to Afghanistan, and they were saying that there is peace in Afghanistan now. And they said if we will not go back they will send us back by force ... If I am sent back by IOM I will be killed by name of a communist. Haven't I the right of life as a human?[439]

In August 2003, it was reported that he was shot dead by Taliban forces while riding his motorbike.

Yacoub Baklri

Yacoub Baklri, an ethnic Hazara, also returned to Afghanistan from Nauru and was gunned down by local militia commanders. It was reported to the inquiry that his death was confirmed by family members.

Mohammed Sharif al-Saraf

Iraqi man Mohammed Sharif al-Saraf was recognised as a refugee after he arrived in Australia by boat in 1999 and was granted a TPV. After four years in Australia, during which he could not bring his wife and children, he was found to have no further need of protection because Saddam Hussein's regime had been overthrown. He left Australia in 2004 and was murdered months after arriving back in Iraq, having been accused of being a spy for Australian forces stationed there.[440]

Reginald Jesudasan

In September 2006, the naked body of 31-year-old Sri Lankan Reginald Jesudasan was found dumped beside a river in Colombo bearing marks of torture. The Catholic priest with whom he lived while he sought asylum in Australia told a local newspaper he was a quiet and sensitive man who was forced to return to Sri Lanka in 1997 and was a target for years after. A Department of Immigration spokesman said the government was not responsible for the well-being of people because they had at some stage spent time in Australia.[441]

Mr Cai

In 2005, Greens Senator Kerry Nettle raised in parliament the case of Chinese man Mr Cai, who died three months after being deported. She stated:

> I am aware of a Chinese detainee, most recently at Villawood, who needed a form of kidney dialysis. It was self-dialysis, rather than being on the machine the whole time, so he changed the bags several times a day. He was subsequently deported to China. I understand there was discussion before he left, that he might not be able to access the same level of kidney dialysis as he was able to access here. I am aware that upon his return he was not able to receive that access and he passed away.

The then immigration minister, Amanda Vanstone, replied:

> In some cases, for example, it may appear that someone has come here quite deliberately to access the health system ... We do not have a principle in the migration system or a sentence we go by that says: if you can get better health treatment in Australia you can stay. I tell you what: the whole world would be here.[442]

Bill Zhang

On 14 June 2008, a Chinese pro-democracy activist known as 'Bill Zhang', who had been deported to China from Australia the year before, threw himself from the sixth or seventh floor of a housing estate. Having spent 10 years seeking asylum in Australia, the last two in Villawood detention centre, according to a report in *The Age* on 21 June 2008 he was jailed for 15 days and tortured on his return.

His application for asylum in Australia was rejected by the Immigration Department and the RRT found he was 'not a credible witness'. Six requests for ministerial intervention to former immigration ministers Amanda Vanstone and Kevin Andrews were rejected. When Labor won government, refugee advocates asked the new minister Chris Evans to allow him to return, but no action was taken.

Refugee advocate Frances Milne told *The Age* Zhang had told her that if he could not return to Australia and he was either killed by Chinese authorities or committed suicide, she should publicise his death to highlight the flaws in the refugee system so that others would not suffer needlessly.

Deportation of a Child

On 23 July 2003, seven-year-old Massoumeh Mastipour, an Iranian whose father Mohammed had had custody of her since she was two years old, was removed from Australia without his knowledge while he was held in the management unit at Baxter. She had been in detention with him since 2001 and was deported despite being a party to an appeal pending in the High Court.

In a Federal Court case concerning her removal, Mohammed claimed:

> ... *that she was removed ... to place pressure on him to abandon his attempt to get a protection visa and to pressure him to return to Iran voluntarily.*[443]

In February 2003, allegations of child abuse from an unknown source were made against Mohammed to South Australian Family and Youth Services (FAYS). Massoumeh was removed from Baxter for two weeks while these were investigated. She was returned when FAYS found no evidence of abuse. Refugee advocate Kate Gauthier told the inquiry:

> *FAYS had made repeated investigations of this child previously and found that it was in her best interests to remain with her father because of their close and loving relationship, despite the fact that meant that the child had to remain in immigration detention. They found it would be more traumatising for her to be removed from her father than to remain with him.*

As the unsubstantiated allegations became known to other detainees, Mohammed asked that he and his daughter be moved to another detention centre. On 8 July 2003, he began a hunger strike to protest the failure to transfer them. Trish Highfield, an early childhood professional in contact with Massoumeh, told the inquiry:

> One day I rang for our regular talk and she whispered into the phone, 'My daddy hasn't eaten for many days now,' and I said, 'Darling, you must go to the dining room, you must eat.' She said, 'No, I can't leave my daddy. I have to look after my daddy.' She said, 'The guards bring food to my door,' and I said, 'Are you going out and playing with the other children? You need to get fresh air.' She was very angry. She said, 'I know about fresh air. I can't leave my daddy, I have to look after him.'
>
> I could hear her father talking very loudly in the background and I said, 'Your daddy is awake now; could I please speak to him.' She said, 'No, he's not awake, he's talking when he's sleeping.' I started to panic because my perception was that he was delirious and I thought, my God, here is a child holed up in a room with a father on hunger strike; she's having no respite from this shocking situation.
>
> I talked to her for some time; she didn't want me to get off the phone. After we had calmed her down, I rang immigration in Baxter and immigration in Canberra. I rang Child Protection because I was in touch with the Baxter Crisis Team from Family and Youth Services in South Australia.

On 14 July 2003, Mohammed was taken to the management unit. Trish Highfield told the inquiry:

> Guards went in and brutally separated her from her father. She jumped on the back of one the guards and tried to stop what they were doing to her father. They were trying to order him to strip search in front of her. He would not do that. She was hysterical. We had this report from a female detainee who was outside trying to coax her to come out. He was dragged to Management, she was taken to medical.

While held in the management unit, Mohammed was allowed to

see Massoumeh in the visit centre at around 5pm each day for 90 minutes, although he complained that the visit was often only 45 minutes. On 17 July, he refused to sign a behaviour management plan that stated he had assaulted two officers. He was told that if he did not sign those papers, he would not be able to visit his daughter. He was also told by Ms Terrina Wallis that if he signed the paper she would give him recent photographs of his daughter.[444]

It was reported to the inquiry that on 23 July, as his daughter was on her way to her mother in Iran, Mohammed complained about the curtailed visits with his daughter and was promised he would be allowed the full 90 minutes. About 5pm that day, when he was due to visit with his daughter, he was told that his daughter was shopping with Greg and Terrina Wallis, the manager and deputy manager of Baxter, and that he would be able to visit her later. About 7.30pm he was told that there would be no visit as Terrina and Greg Wallis had taken his daughter to their house. He became upset and asked to speak to his daughter by telephone, but this was refused on the grounds that he hadn't signed the paper.[445] On 24 July at about 5pm, Greg Wallis came and told him that he had sent Massoumeh back to Iran. When Mohammed said that he did not believe it, Greg Wallis said he could call her in Iran, which he did at about 7.30pm. Massoumeh asked him, 'When are you coming?' Trish Highfield told the inquiry:

> *That little girl was deported without being able to say goodbye to her father who had been her sole carer. Without father and child being able to hold each other for the last time, that is unforgivable. Within 24 hours of her being deported I was finally allowed to make contact with her father in management and he was a totally broken man.*

In a 2004 decision of the Full Court of the Federal Court, Justice Lander summarised the circumstances of Massoumeh's removal:

> *[His] case was that he had been subjected, for no apparent reason, to the humiliation of being warned that he would be strip searched in the presence of his daughter; handcuffed in her*

presence; removed to the management unit against his wishes; threatened with the loss of visitation rights to his daughter unless he signed a false confession; and deprived of his daughter under the cover of a lie all because he had asked to be removed with his daughter from Baxter to another immigration centre because of his concerns about false allegations...[446]

He also acknowledged that Mohammed's allegations of deceit in regard to Massoumeh's removal were substantiated saying:

Gregory Wallis is the DIMIA Manager of Baxter. His wife, Terrina Jane Wallis, is the Deputy Manager at Baxter ... Neither denied that Mr Mastipour had been placed in the management unit in the circumstances deposed to by him ... Neither contradicted Mr Mastipour's claims in relation to his detention in the management unit and his claims of deprivation ... Neither denied that Mr Mastipour's daughter was removed from Australia in the circumstances deposed to by him and, in particular, as Mr Burnside QC put it 'under the cover of a lie'.[447]

Justice Lander refers to a report written by Department of Immigration psychiatrist Dr Howard Gorton, who was informed that Massoumeh had been deported, but that he was not to tell Mohammed during a 24 July consultation.

Dr Gorton's report supports Mr Mastipour's claim that he was actively deceived in relation to the return of his daughter to Iran. It is unfortunate that Dr Gorton became embroiled in the deceit which was practised upon Mr Mastipour ... It would appear that Mr Mastipour's daughter was removed from Baxter knowing that would cause Mr Mastipour to deteriorate further ... On 25 July 2003 Mr Mastipour told the Case Manager that 'he had no reason to live as his little girl had gone'.[448]

Trish Highfield has spoken regularly to Massoumeh since she arrived in Iran. She told the inquiry:

She was distressed, she was very worried about her father and I said to her, 'My darling, we didn't know where you were, we were so worried about you.' And she said, 'Trish, they told me it was a secret. I couldn't tell anyone.'

One of the first things she said to me in that very first phone call with such urgency, was, 'You must tell Keely and Amanda that I will never be coming back.' They were her best friends at the Willsden School and she said, 'They will wonder what happened to me; you must tell them where I am.'

It took a long time for her to build up a relationship with her mother. Her mother said, 'She doesn't know how to play with children, she doesn't know how to form relationships.' Three weeks ago, her Mum said she still has moments where she stares into nothingness and she said, 'I don't know what's going on in her head.' She said, 'Those times she looks like a very old woman and she's only nine.' She said, 'I need to know what happened to her in detention.' She wants me to send material about what has happened to her. I said, 'It will make you weep,' and she said, 'I know that, but I need to know.'

Refugee advocate Kate Gauthier told the inquiry that in this case the Federal Court had ruled that immigration detainees retained their civil rights and that Mohammed Mastipour therefore had the same parental rights as any other person in Australia. To arrange the return of a child to a guardian in Iran, an application must be made under the *Family Law Act*, and factors such as the best interest of the child and the effect separation from either parent would have on the child would need to be considered:

DIMIA have claimed that Family and Youth Services supported their moves to remove Massoumeh in the manner in which they did. I find it difficult to believe that a government agency mandated to protect a child's welfare would agree that it's in the child's best interest to be removed without saying goodbye to her father, without being prepared for the removal and without assessing whether or not the mother was in fact the best parent to raise this child. I find it difficult to believe they would agree that the Department of Immigration had the knowledge, expertise and even the lawful mandate to make that determination.

After Massoumeh's removal, Mohammed remained in the management unit, still requesting to be transferred to another detention centre. During the Federal Court case, Greg Wallis said he would not move Mohammed to another detention centre because he did not believe he had been harassed by other detainees as there were no complaints on the department's records to this effect. Justice Lander commented:

I am not sure why the absence of a report would establish the absence of harassment. More relevantly, [Greg Wallis] said: 'Transferring the applicant to a facility located in Melbourne or Sydney is not a viable option. There are a whole list of issues that must be addressed before we would transfer a detainee to another facility. We do not just transfer people because they want to be transferred. We do not believe that there is significant justification to transfer this detainee to another facility as his needs can be adequately met at the Baxter detention facility. We also believe that to transfer him would create a precedent which other detainees would want to pursue.'

Mr Wallis does not give any reasons why it would not be viable to transfer Mr Mastipour to a facility located in Melbourne or Sydney. One gets the impression from Mr Wallis' affidavit that there is a resistance to moving Mr Mastipour because it is his wish that he be moved ... Both Mr Wallis and Mrs Wallis assert that Mr Mastipour can be accommodated within Baxter. They do not address the uncontradicted psychiatric evidence, including the Secretary's own evidence, that it would be in Mr Mastipour's best interests to be accommodated at a Detention Centre apart from Baxter.[449]

Mohammed was finally transferred to Maribyrnong in late 2003 and released two years later when he was found to be a refugee. In the Federal Court case, Justice Selway noted that despite there being no legal guidelines as to what mandatory detention could entail, the case raised issues for consideration including:

> ... *whether there was an 'administrative' power to detain Mr Mastipour in the management unit; whether that power could be exercised without affording Mr Mastipour a right to be heard; whether there was an 'administrative' power to separate Mr Mastipour from his daughter; whether that power could be exercised without affording Mr Mastipour a right to be heard; whether there was a power to send Mr Mastipour's daughter back to Iran without some judicial determination that Mr Mastipour did not have lawful custody of his child; and whether that power could be exercised without affording Mr Mastipour a right to be heard.*[450]

HE FELT HIS HEART WOULD BURST THROUGH HIS MOUTH:
DEATHS IN DETENTION

Another theme that emerged from the evidence presented to the inquiry was that inadequate care in detention in some cases led to death. The inquiry has documented a total of 19 deaths in Australian immigration detention, 12 of them between January 2001 and June 2003. The inquiry has included deaths that occurred during Operation Relex and Department of Immigration compliance raids. The inquiry has also included the death of a detainee held in Nauru on behalf of the Australian government.

Between the introduction of mandatory detention (in 1992) and 1999 only one death occurred in detention. On 10 May 1998, an American who had been in Australia for one day died of liver disease in Villawood. Between 2000 and 2008, 18 people died under the care of the Immigration Department, a 1700 per cent increase.

Viliami Tanginoa

An ACM policy document presented to the inquiry shows that detention operators recognise the risk of deaths in detention centres.[451]

However, Viliami Tanginoa, a Tongan who had lived in Australia for 17 years after overstaying his visa, deliberately dived to his death at Maribyrnong detention centre on the day he was due to be deported, 22 December 2000. Before his death he had spent eight hours perched on top of a basketball hoop in the rain. The inquiry obtained a copy of Victorian State Coroner Phillip Byrne's Record of Investigation into that death. It states:

> I remain puzzled why virtually no-one appreciated Mr Tanginoa was at imminent risk of some form of self-harm ... It may be due to a fundamental misjudgement of this gentle, quiet, apparently uncomplicated man ... Mr Tanginoa's response to an endeavour to place further mattresses is graphically depicted on the audio-visual tape in evidence. He stood up and became quite agitated. Quite frankly, it should have been patently obvious and management should have been alerted that great risk of self-harm was by this time, very probable. It should be noted that this was almost two hours before Mr Tanginoa plunged to his death ... [452]
>
> I do not see any strategic, informed, cohesive, active structured management plan ... In fact what I see is a haphazard, unmethodical, wholly inadequate approach ... If one action epitomises the ineptitude of the approach adopted by ACM, it is the action of ... bouncing a basketball in the courtyard in the vicinity of Mr Tanginoa ... If expert negotiators had been involved, I am satisfied the tragic event would have been prevented. Whilst the immediate cause of Mr Tanginoa's death was his own action ... Another cause was the inaction of centre management. [453]

Hai Phuoc Vo

The following month, on 24 January 2001, 36-year-old Hai Phuoc Vo died at Western General Hospital after suffering an asthma attack in Port Phillip Prison, where he had been held as an immigration detainee. The Victorian coroner found that he died from pneumonia, which followed from a chest infection related to persistent sinus. The Department of Immigration failed to answer questions from the inquiry regarding why Hai was being held in Port Phillip Prison and how long he had been in prison as an immigration detainee.

Mohammed Saleh

On 21 January 2001, 41-year-old Palestinian asylum seeker and father of three, Mohammed Saleh, was placed in Juliet, the isolation area of Port Hedland detention centre, for alleged involvement in a riot. No charges were laid against him and a senior Department of Immigration manager told the coronial inquiry that he posed no behavioural management difficulties in detention.[454] Labor MP Colin Hollis visited Juliet Block while Mohammed was held there. He told *Insight*:

> *It was dark. It stank. There were, I don't know how many cells and that's because they had iron doors, locked doors and behind these doors were people looking at us with the most pitiful, sorrowful look I have ever seen in my life.*[455]

While in Juliet, Mohammed and the other detainees were allowed out of their rooms for one or two hours each day.[456] Thirteen days later Mohammed was released from Juliet Block in a severely depressed state. In the seven weeks after his release from isolation, he had a mental breakdown, was unable to physically care for himself and sought medical attention 22 times.[457] He was admitted to Hollywood Private Hospital in Perth in early April for severe depression with the probability of psychosis.[458]

While in hospital he was accompanied by an ACM guard at all times.[459] It was discovered that he had a tumour in his stomach, which required surgery.[460] Mohammed, who had been born in the al-Yarmouk Refugee Camp in Syria, expressed his fears in his personal writings:

> *Another doctor said that I needed an operation. Oh, God, help me. My wife and children should be present. What if I die? It's a big operation.*[461]

Doctors waited two months for his depression to improve so they could operate on his tumour,[462] eventually giving him electric-convulsive therapy, an option they had tried to avoid because he had previously been tortured by electric shock.[463] He died from complications following the surgery on 23 June 2001, eight months after his arrival in Australia.[464] *The Australian* newspaper reported:

Five weeks after Saleh's death, an Immigration Department official wrote to one of the department's lawyers 're Mohammed Saleh. It's likely we have not heard the end of this man's story, as there is a Palestinian organisation very actively pursuing issues relating to his death. Also HREOC have now written to us asking heaps of questions about him, his applications before the department, his treatment at the Port Hedland IRPC [Immigration Reception and Processing Centre], his illnesses and treatment thereof, circumstances of his death and results of the coroner's enquiry. Don't be surprised if litigation hears more and is possibly involved at some later stage.' Nine months later ... the department claimed the documents were missing.[465]

Avion Gumede

The following month, on 26 July 2001, Avion Gumede, a Nigerian man with a wife and child in South Africa, hanged himself hours after being taken to Villawood. He had been in Australia on a tourist visa, which was cancelled after he was found working illegally. In October 2002, South African High Commission diplomat Rashida Adam told the *World Today* that Avion had left a suicide note and that he had been exploited in an immigration racket where white South Africans brought black South Africans to work in Australia in 'slave labour conditions.'[466] The next day she told *PM* that consular officials had interviewed Avion's brother, who had confirmed this exploitation.[467]

The day after Avion's death, then immigration minister Philip Ruddock told *PM*:

Mercifully we've been free of the tragedy of deaths in custody in detention centres. I think we've only had one previously while I've been minister, but it's to me a very, a very regrettable incident, although perfectly explicable.[468]

Less than a year later he told *Lateline*:

In terms of the centres like Woomera, Curtin, Port Hedland, I don't believe there have been any suicides there ... There have been seven deaths in detention and we don't know that any of them have been suicide.[469]

Phuangtong Simaplee

On 26 September 2001, a month before Philip Ruddock praised the medical services in detention, as being 'of a higher order than many people in regional and remote Australia receive',[470] 27-year-old Thai woman, Phuangtong Simaplee, died at Villawood detention centre after being held there for three days. Phuangtong had been brought to Australia as a 12-year-old sex slave and was taken into detention after immigration authorities raided a Sydney brothel.[471] Despite slavery, sexual servitude and child prostitution being offences under Australian law, immigration authorities did not notify Australian Federal Police of Phuangtong's allegation that she had been working in the sex industry for the past 15 years.[472]

When brought to the detention centre, she weighed just 38kg. A report to the NSW State Coroner by forensic pathologist Allan Cala was presented to the inquiry. It shows that Phuangtong told detention staff she was a heroin user, and that they believed she could experience withdrawal while in Villawood. She was observed vomiting more than 16 times and her weight fell to 31kg in three days. Barrister Georgina Costello, who appeared at her inquest, has written:

> She was given a bucket and, as the withdrawal symptoms intensified, she vomited, defecated and urinated in that bucket, too weak to walk to the bathroom. Three days after her arrival at Villawood, without having seen a lawyer, social worker or friend while in detention, she died face down in a pool of vomit.[473]

The inquest into her death summarises some of Dr Cala's concerns about her treatment:

> I have concerns that over the three-day period from the time of her admission to death no person has made a decision that this woman was too ill to be in a detention centre and needed ongoing care in a hospital ... There are a number of public hospitals within 30 minutes of the centre ... Had this woman been recognised as requiring hospitalisation, and treated with simple measures, she may well have survived.[474]

Fatima Husseini and Nurjan Hussaini in Operation Relex

Two days before the federal election, on 8 November 2001, Fatima Husseini and Nurjan Husseini drowned off Christmas Island after their boat was intercepted in Operation Relex. The circumstances of their deaths are explained on pp. 49–52 of this report.

Thi Hang Le

On 8 January 2002, 33-year-old Vietnamese woman Thi Hang Le, who had been hospitalised for wrist slashing before escaping from a psychiatric ward and being returned to Villawood, stood on a stair rail and launched herself headfirst three metres onto the concrete. Refugee activist Cyrus Sarang told the *Sydney Morning Herald*:

> When they brought her [back], within two to three hours ... she went to the balcony and she was shouting, crying and she was saying 'Send me back to my country.' Nobody was listening and she jumped from the balcony.[475]

She died in Liverpool Hospital five days later. She had been in detention for four months after overstaying her student visa. She was picked up by immigration authorities in a brothel and was also alleged to have been trafficked to Australia for prostitution.[476]

The Person who Died of Alcohol Poisoning at Fremantle Hospital

The Department of Immigration informed the inquiry that an immigration detainee died of 'alcohol/methanol poisoning' on 16 March 2002 in Fremantle Hospital, having previously being held at Leeuwin Barracks, an army base in Western Australia. While the department stated that the case had been referred to the West Australian State Coroner's office, it failed to answer questions from the inquiry regarding whether an inquest had actually been held; the person's gender, nationality and age; the length of their detention at Leeuwin Barracks; why they had been detained there; whether they had been detained with other people there and, if so, how many; which organisations had responsibility for immigration detainees there; and the circumstances leading to the person's death.

Mohammed Sarwar

On 26 August 2002, as asylum seekers on Nauru prepared to celebrate the one-year anniversary of their rescue by the *Tampa,* one of them died. Afghan Mohammed Sarwar was in his late twenties, with no known health problems. One of his friends wrote to a refugee supporter:

> *... if you would see him you would think he is a teenager, although he had left his young wife with his small son and small daughter waiting for him ... He was cancelled his claim for asylum after one year waiting to countries who are outwardly the human rights protectors. He waited for exactly one year after his saving by the Tampa with hundred kinds of psychological pressures and finally went to God's perpetual asylum.*[477]

Another letter one of his friends wrote to an Australian refugee supporter was presented to the inquiry:

> *After my second interview DIMIA told us that all the cases has been closed and nobody is going to be accept. All the people they are too much disappointed. And one of our friend died – his name was Mohammed Sarwar. Because of too much depression on his mind. DIMIA told us we have only 28 days for deport.*

While immigration authorities wanted to bury him on Nauru, his friends and a relative in Australia organised for his body to be sent to Kabul so his wife and children could bury him.[478]

Fatima Erfani

The inquiry heard from lawyer Judith Quinlivan about the January 2003 death of her client, a young asylum seeker and mother of three, Fatima Erfani, who had been detained on Christmas Island. Just before Fatima's death, Afghans on Christmas Island had been offered a repatriation package to return to Afghanistan and told that if they did not accept it they would be transferred to Nauru where they would be detained indefinitely. One man told researchers working on the Edmund Rice Centre's *Deported to Danger* report:

> *We were forced to leave. A man from DIMIA told us they would drop*

us in a camp where we would not be free for many years. He told us: 'You will be in prison.' He said we would never see our families again.[479]

Judith Quinlivan told the inquiry:

There was enormous pressure for them to return to Afghanistan. Fatima had been diagnosed with high blood pressure, she was on medication. She was young. During this period her blood pressure was getting quite high and then they made the decision to return to Afghanistan. Fatima's whole life kind of collapsed. After two or three days of these blinding headaches, she got taken up to the Christmas Island Hospital and saw a doctor and he thought she was in some migraine cycle. Her blood pressure at one point was 220/120.

The ACM nurse could see that it was getting worse and, according to her statement to the coroner, she went back to the hospital and said she's not getting any better. About the fifth day, she collapsed and didn't regain consciousness. A plane was brought to take her to Perth and she was admitted to Sir Charles Gairdner Hospital. By that stage she was brain dead basically.

I fronted up at Sir Charles Gairdner where her husband was keeping vigil and I wasn't allowed in. He was begging them inside, please let my friend in to stand with me, but there were ACM guards at the door. They had to turn the life support off. He had to make this big decision and he wanted me there. In the end I was removed from the hospital because I was just so angry.

I rang DIMA in Canberra and they said you are not going. They said something like it's the minister's orders that you are not to go in. Ali Reza said afterwards, he said his pain was so great at that time by his wife's bedside, that he felt as though his heart would burst through his mouth, and he just wanted me with him because I was at that stage his only friend.

He went back to Christmas Island and her body was to be returned to Afghanistan with him but the body was mishandled. We saw him off at the airport and it was just the most tragic thing. This young man with his three children going back to Afghanistan to nothing. And he rang a day later from Dubai saying Fatima's body has just been left on the tarmac in the sun at Dubai airport. He could see it from where he was. The kids, one of them was three, and they could see their mother's coffin on the tarmac.

Mansur La Ibu on Darwin Harbour

On 26 February 2003, Indonesian fisherman Mansur La Ibu died on Darwin Harbour. The circumstances of his death are explained on pp. 277-78 of this report.

The Person who Died at Western General Hospital

The Department of Immigration informed the inquiry that an immigration detainee died 'following numerous hospitalisations for ongoing drug-related illnesses' on 19 June 2003 in Western General Hospital, having previously being held at Maribyrnong detention centre. While the department stated that the case had been referred to the Victorian State Coroner's office, it failed to answer questions from the inquiry regarding whether an inquest had actually been held; the length of the person's detention at Maribyrnong; why they had been detained there; and the circumstances leading to their death.

Seong Ho Kang

In July 2004, 37-year-old South Korean father of two Seong Ho Kang, who had overstayed his visa, died when he ran from Department of Immigration compliance officers who visited his home late at night. He told them he was a visitor in the house and needed to get his passport and visa from another nearby house. He went outside and ran to the road, chased by two of the officers. He was then hit by a taxi and died three days later. A coronial investigation revealed that none of the compliance officers, including the team leader, had finished their compulsory two-stage training program.[480]

Marc Lao Thao

On 29 August 2004, a French man in his seventies, who had been held at Villawood, died of a brain haemorrhage. A visitor to detention told the inquiry:

> When I saw Marc he had just been operated on for a hernia and was back from the hospital. The younger detainees worried about him because he was vomiting every night. Marc was taken to the hospital

only when he collapsed. I went to see him in Liverpool Hospital. There were two guards to look after an unconscious sick man. He never regained consciousness and died the next day.

A spokesperson from the French embassy in Canberra told *The Australian:*

Frankly, we are appalled at the way our citizen was treated. Consular officials were not told he was in detention for five months and only knew he was in hospital because an Australian doctor alerted them to his condition.[481]

The Person who Died of Lung Cancer at Western General Hospital

The Department of Immigration informed the inquiry that an immigration detainee died of lung cancer on 25 March 2005 in Western General Hospital, having previously being held at Maribyrnong detention centre. While the department stated that the case had been referred to the Victorian State Coroner's office, it failed to answer questions from the inquiry regarding whether an inquest had actually been held; the length of the person's detention at Maribyrnong; why they had been detained there; and the circumstances leading to their death.

Muhammed Heri on Darwin Harbour

On 28 April 2005, Indonesian fisherman Muhammed Heri died on Darwin Harbour. The circumstances of his death are explained on p. 279 of this report.

Pishevarz Khodaverdi

On 13 January 2008, 64-year-old Iranian man Pishevarz Khodaverdi died of heart failure after collapsing on the steps of St George Private Hospital on his way to an appointment there two days earlier. He had been held in Villawood for the previous three months after being assessed as unfit to be deported. Volunteer human rights advocate at the Brimbank Melton Community Legal Centre, Charandev Singh, stated:

He continued to be detained at Villawood even after it was
acknowledged that his condition was so serious that he could not fly,
making deportation impossible. How then could the Department of
Immigration continue to detain such a frail and vulnerable individual
in the Villawood Prison instead of releasing him to be cared for in the
community?[482]

A man held in Villawood at the time of Pishevarz's death told the inquiry:

I wasn't surprised. You could tell he was on his last legs. The man had
to struggle up the hill to get his medication. He used an umbrella as a
walking stick. We told the GSL officers this man shouldn't be in here.

WE PUT ON A CHARADE:
ACCOUNTABILITY

A key issue that ran through the evidence presented to the inquiry
was concern about the lack of accountability for the treatment of
people in detention. The Immigration Detention Standards, developed
by the Immigration Department in consultation with HREOC and
the Commonwealth ombudsman, are a schedule to the contract the
department enters into with detention centre operators. The Immigration
Detention Standards outline the quality of care expected in detention
centres and cover areas including education, visits, infrastructure and
assaults. However, as detainees are not a party to the contract they have
no legal rights to enforce the standards. In a submission to the inquiry that
recommended the rights and conditions of detainees be enshrined in law,
the Public Interest Advocacy Centre (PIAC) stated:

PIAC notes that convicted criminals have the benefit of minimum
standards in relation to imprisonment, which are guaranteed by
regulations. PIAC is unable to understand why asylum seekers and
other immigration detainees are denied such guarantees.

Both the Palmer Inquiry and the Australian National Audit Office have
concluded that measures to assess compliance with the Immigration

Detention Standards are lacking. The contract between the Department of Immigration and the operator allows the operator to be fined up to 5 per cent of the value of its contract for breaches. The PIAC submission to the inquiry argued this may act as a disincentive for detention providers to report incidents of failure to comply with the Immigration Detention Standards.

The Detention Services Contract recognises that, despite operational responsibilities being contracted out, the Immigration Department is ultimately accountable for the management of detention centres:

> *The department, and particularly departmental staff in the facilities, have an ongoing role in monitoring the provision of services.*[483]

However the PIAC submission to the inquiry argues that departmental staff in detention facilities are susceptible to being compromised by their close contact with detention operators, and self-interest:

> *It is a case of the agency delegating the accomplishment of its formal goals and the discharge of its responsibilities to others. Failure by the delegates is tantamount to failure by the agency itself. All criticism is akin to self-criticism. The regulator is the principle operator, thus has a vested interest in its delegates appearing to be doing a satisfactory job.*[484]

In October 2002, the inspector of custodial services for Western Australia, Richard Harding, made the same point when he told *Background Briefing*:

> *When one went into Curtin, one was greeted by people climbing up trees and doing symbolic hangings of themselves because ... they could not make themselves heard ... Who should have been listening? It should have been DIMA. But they weren't because DIMA and the operators in this Gulag situation in the middle of nowhere, were each interested in ... just keeping the whole business under wraps ...*
>
> *They are of course very much under the direct political influence in this regard. It's always the government that wants to cover these things up. The governments are the ones who, in the end, always have to take the blame. When private providers don't perform, it's because governments are enabling them not to perform. The department is not capable of looking after the interests of detainees, children in particular, adults also.*[485]

One area where the contracting arrangement has resulted in substandard service being provided to immigration detainees is that of mental-health care. To satisfy its contract to provide health services to detainees in Baxter, GSL contracted two companies, Professional Support Services and International Health and Medical Services (IHMS). IHMS in turn contracted a Port Augusta medical practice and a private psychiatrist.

In a 2005 court case about the adequacy of mental health care provided to two detainees, Justice Finn expressed surprise that the Baxter psychiatrist had not been consulted about how mental-health services might be improved. He also said:

> ... one can only register surprise ... at [Department of Immigration manager] Ms Kannis' statements that she would 'go on the advice' of the GPs as to the adequacy of the levels of psychiatric services at Baxter in January 2005, but that she did not speak to any of the GPs in that period.[486]

He found that:

> ... the Commonwealth has, for the most part, put itself in the position where it has relied in substance upon its own mental health care service providers to advise it as to whether it is in fact discharging its duty to care for the detainees in rendering the services provided by those providers. The hazards of its so doing are self-evident and are manifest in these proceedings.[487]

He concluded that there was an:

> ... inadequate level of psychiatric care in Baxter for detainees with serious mental illness ... Given the known mental conditions of the applicants, the Commonwealth permitted its contractor to provide an inadequate and, on the evidence, poorly functioning mental health care service to them.[488]

According to the government, organisations other than the Immigration Department also have a role in monitoring detention centres. In February 2002, then immigration minister Philip Ruddock told a newspaper:

> Visits are made by the Human Rights and Equal Opportunity

Commission, state and federal parliamentarians, the Red Cross,
the Commonwealth ombudsman, and parliamentary committees.
Journalists and photographers from many media organisations have
participated in tours to detention centres arranged by the department
... visits to the centre by external bodies average more than one a week
and this demonstrates that the immigration detention program is among
the most closely scrutinised of government programs.[489]

However, former Baxter chaplain Father Arno Vermeeren told *Insight* that
in his experience of visiting Woomera and Baxter:

... none of these bodies that are scrutinising them have the power to
do anything to change anything, and the ones who do have the power
don't seem to have changed anything. It was only with Cornelia Rau
that anything, as far as I could see, has happened.[490]

On the same program, Pamela Curr, from the Asylum Seeker Resource
Centre, said she had contacted the ombudsman, HREOC and the
Immigration Detention Advisory Group (IDAG) to try and get help for
Cornelia Rau, before she was identified as an Australian resident:

I knocked on all those doors for Cornelia Rau for six weeks and nothing
happened. Nothing happened because it can't happen. Father Arno is
quite right. Those people can walk through, they can look, but they can
do nothing.[491]

Evidence provided to the inquiry by a range of sources criticised the
ability of the ombudsman, IDAG and HREOC to have any impact on the
conditions and practices within Australia's detention centres.

A refugee supporter told the inquiry about a letter the ombudsman sent
to an unaccompanied minor. The boy had not been provided with official
notification that he had been recognised as a minor or consulted about
the assignation of a nominal birth date. Developmental reports supposed
to be completed were not done. However, the inquiry was told that the
ombudsman wrote to him after he had turned 18 saying:

Unfortunately there is nothing more that I can accomplish for you in
relation to this particular complaint as DIMIA no longer recognises
you as a minor. I apologise for not providing you with an update

on my investigation at an earlier date but hope you understand my investigation was reliant upon DIMIA providing me with accurate and complete information, which they didn't do.

A lawyer told the inquiry she complained to the ombudsman when the Department of Immigration refused to pass her correspondence to an unaccompanied minor she was representing over a health issue, because it was department policy that a child could not instruct a lawyer:

The ombudsman came back saying they couldn't do anything except lobby the department to change their policy, which is just outrageous given that it's legal nonsense. We were so shocked. Whenever you get a department within our system that starts to go a little bit haywire you do usually have someone else to go to, but on numerous occasions the ombudsman, with all the best intentions, was not able to pull them into line.

In February 2008, Ombudsman John McMillan recommended the Immigration Department apologise to a former detainee for failing to provide the detainee with video footage which he claimed showed an ACM officer punching him in the face and kicking him in the legs, after which he lost consciousness. He had wanted the footage to substantiate a complaint to HREOC over the assault, but had waited four years with his request still not met. The period for a damages claim over the assault expired after two years.[492]

A former detainee told the inquiry about a chance encounter with a representative of the ombudsman at Maribyrnong:

After one year and 10 months of detention I saw this man from ombudsman walking around. I said, 'What are you doing here?' He said, 'I come every month or two months, we hold meetings here with your representatives.' I said 'Who is our representatives?' He said, 'Some of the detainees.' I questioned him about the living conditions, the food, the treatment of the detainees, the climate control, the building being contrary to occupational health and safety standards and he says, 'All these things are beyond my powers.' I did ask him, 'If you have a little bit self respect, you should not work in this position. If you think it's beyond your power and you cannot correct, you cannot protest, you should not work on this position.'

The Department of Immigration's attitude to bodies such as IDAG, which were supposed to make government more accountable for immigration detention policy, was revealed in a June 2007 speech by the secretary of the department, Andrew Metcalfe. He told the Australian and New Zealand School of Government:

> For a number of years, we didn't always recognise the benefits of working positively with these stakeholders, and sometimes tended to argue issues through the media rather than engage constructively with them. One of our key strategic reforms has been to devote senior-level resources to implementing a specific stakeholder engagement strategy, with a view to building stakeholder and community confidence in our work. For instance, we have been working constructively with the Immigration Detention Advisory Group. This key group was appointed in 2001, and provides advice to the minister on the appropriateness and adequacy of services, accommodation and amenities at immigration detention facilities.[493]

Refugee advocates also told the inquiry they found IDAG unable to assist detainees. One said:

> One time when I and other people were very distressed about something that was happening in Baxter, we were told that IDAG was visiting Baxter later in the week and if we got our concerns to them in writing they would look into it. We went to a lot of trouble to put in a submission. It cost us $60 to airfreight it to arrive in time. It arrived at the immigration office and the courier could not deliver it because the officers there didn't know anything about it.

At a press conference on 15 July 2005, responding to the findings of the Palmer Inquiry into her sister's detention, Chris Rau argued, 'IDAG has kept its concerns about detention practices so private as to be ineffectual.'[494]

In November 2000, HREOC found the human rights of two Chinese men, held in separation detention and denied legal assistance at Port Hedland detention centre, had been breached and recommended they be paid $15,000 and $20,000 compensation.[495] These recommendations were ignored by the Immigration Department.

The United Nations has also made several inspections of detention centres and investigated detainee complaints through official committees, finding on six separate occasions that Australia's immigration detention regime is arbitrary and a violation of the right to liberty.[496] In 1997, the UN Human Rights Committee found that the detention of a Cambodian man for over four years in Port Hedland violated the International Covenant on Civil and Political Rights. The Howard government responded by saying:

> [T]he government does not accept that the detention of Mr A was in contravention of the covenant ... Consequently, the government does not accept the view of the committee that compensation should be paid to Mr A.[497]

In mid-2002, the United Nations Working Group on Arbitrary Detention visited Port Hedland, Woomera, Baxter, Villawood, Maribyrnong and Perth detention centres. It concluded:

> The Working Group is particularly concerned with regard to the detention of vulnerable persons, particularly children; about the whole legal process governing the detention of asylum seekers, and about the lack of adequate information given to the detainees. Other matters of concern ... are the lack of proper complaints mechanisms and the implications of the management of the detention centres by a private company.[498]

In response, a media release issued by the former minister for foreign affairs, Alexander Downer, and then immigration minister, Philip Ruddock, stated:

> The report is a very disappointing effort. It contains fundamental factual errors, misrepresents Australia's policies and demonstrates significant confusion about the relationship between international and Australian law ... The report makes recommendations about the length of detention. People in immigration detention are under administrative detention, they are not in prison. They are generally free to leave detention and return home at any time ... the government takes its ... human rights obligations very seriously. It does not accept that our system of immigration detention is inconsistent with our international obligations.[499]

In 2002, the UN Human Rights Committee found that the rights of Roqia

Bakhtiyari and her children had been violated and that they should be compensated.[500] Instead, they were later deported.

In July 2002, Australia was the only Western country to vote against a new UN protocol against torture, which called for independent visits to prisons as a way of combating torture. The Australian government's refusal to endorse the protocol was widely seen as a mechanism to stop UN inspectors from entering its detention centres without prior authority.[501]

The inquiry also heard evidence from former detention-centre workers, visitors and detainees that detention-centre staff were informed ahead of visits from inspecting bodies. A nurse told the inquiry:

> There was quite a show put on for the arrival of HREOC when I was in Curtin. They potted plants all over the place. In 2002, after the riots in April, somebody had decided that detainees would be issued all food in plastic takeaway containers and the dining room furniture had been packed up. But the day before HREOC arrived, the tables and chairs were all put up again and the detainees were told to sit there. They recognised this was a show and they said, 'No, thank you, we'll just take our food as we always have,' and there was a lot of anger verbalised towards them.
>
> Also there was a brochure that ACM put out which had an amazing photograph of child detainees at Curtin on bicycles, with their helmets on, in front of a swimming pool, with a whole lot of potted palms in the background. The pool was in the staff quarters, the potted palms were in administration, the bicycles came for four days whilst the children had bike ed and then were returned, so these things had been combined in a very attractive way for a brochure.

In the book *Acting from the Heart*, psychologist Lyn Bender describes a visit to Woomera by UN inspectors:

> When the UN delegation was due to arrive to inspect the camp, there was a flurry of activity. Seedlings and flowers were planted. Now the officers were 'permitted' to play cricket with the children, in the compound that was most visible. Now visitors would see and hear the sights and sounds of happy children playing.[502]

A former detention officer told the inquiry:

*When Amnesty International comes through, there is plenty of warning
that's going to happen. It would probably be better to have a mole
planted there for a month to see what is really going on.*

Former operations manager at Woomera, Allan Clifton, told *Four
Corners*:

*We always knew in advance that they were coming ... The place was
dressed up. It was made to look like yes, services were being provided.
So for ... however long they may have been there, we put on a charade.
There were activities that were being reported as having been carried
out for detainees – being taken out of the centre or whatever – when
you knew those things hadn't happened ... ACM was being paid for
that. It was one of their contractual obligations to provide the required
number of hours in all different areas. More often than not we weren't
providing that service.[503]*

Detention authorities did not like it when visits did not go according to plan.
Labor MP Colin Hollis visited Port Hedland as part of a parliamentary
delegation. He told *Insight* detention authorities were reluctant to allow
them to visit Juliet Block, the isolation block there, particularly the upstairs
area where detainees were held in dark, smelly cells behind iron doors:

*During our meetings people, especially the men, raised the question ...
'Are you people going to visit Juliet Block?' This was the first that most
of us had heard of Juliet Block ... they were so insistent and when we
put this to the officials, they hesitated and started to say 'Well, why do
you want to visit that?' ... They were very, very reluctant to have us
visit it. We were told, 'Well, why did you want to go upstairs?' and the
officials actually argued with us and tried to persuade us not to go.[504]*

Refugee advocate Kate Gauthier told the inquiry:

*I have travelled to the Baxter Detention facility five times since it was
opened, both in the capacity of a private citizen and as the immigration
policy adviser to Senator Bartlett. In both capacities they have made
our visits problematic. They have tried to deny access to certain areas,
they have tried to deny us access to certain people. The first time visiting
with Senator Bartlett, many of the Afghan men who were on our list*

were offered, for the very first time, an outside soccer trip as a way of encouraging them not to be available to us during the visiting times, some of whom took it.

In July 2005, Australian Greens Senator Kerry Nettle was refused a visa to visit the remaining 32 asylum seekers on Nauru on the grounds that Nauru was reviewing its policy on the detention centre, including that of access to it.[505]

The PIAC submission to the inquiry also argued that outside scrutiny of detention centres is tightly controlled by the Department of Immigration. It stated that GSL must report the presence of media or protestors at a detention centre to the department within one hour. This is the same time frame in which it must report a detainee's death, a mass breakout, a bomb, fire, cyclone or earthquake. Media or protestors at a detention centre must be reported to the department faster than a suspected case of unlawful detention or a minor being on hunger strike.[506]

During the 2002 riots and hunger strikes at Woomera, police ordered media to retreat from the centre fences and stay 200 metres away. ABC journalist Natalie Larkins was arrested when she questioned this, and other journalists and photographers were threatened with arrest if they did not move. One newspaper stated that 'the scenes at Woomera on Saturday night would not have been out of place in the countries from which the asylum seekers have fled.'[507] But Prime Minister John Howard denied press freedom had been curtailed, saying:

> *People who pretend that because of what happened in Woomera yesterday that there's some attempt being made by the government to cover up what is occurring in detention centres, I mean that is just ridiculous.*[508]

However, the inquiry heard that when detainees did complain to outside bodies about their treatment, they sometimes suffered consequences for doing so. One former detainee told the inquiry:

> *In the beginning we didn't know there are organisations that we can approach. Then we were told you've got to say anything about immigration, write to this committee and that's what I did. It started from 2002 and continued to 2004, then I gave up. This had two effects, sending correspondence to various organisations. First of all because*

they did not do anything for me, it emotionally affected me. I thought I don't have anybody to help me and that wasn't easy to handle. Secondly, because immigration knew I was writing a letter, they were trying to put pressure on me as well.

Another man who spent 18 months in Villawood told the inquiry:

They came and said to me why did I go to the ombudsman and I said, 'Well I wasn't getting any luck with you people.' And they said, 'Well we can make life pretty difficult if you do that. Next time, speak to one of us.' I said, 'Well that is what I have been trying to do.'

Even members of the monitoring organisations were subject to pressure for their scrutiny of detention centres. HREOC Commissioner Sev Ozdowski told the June 2008 Human Rights Law and Policy Conference about then immigration minister Philip Ruddock's reaction to its decision to inquire into children in immigration detention:

After HREOC approved the Terms of Reference for the Inquiry I met with Minister Ruddock and informed him of the Commission's decision. The minister in response expressed his utmost displeasure in no uncertain terms. The minister simply told me that: 'If you dare to conduct the inquiry there will be no job for you as long as I sit around the Cabinet table.'

The inquiry also heard from a worker in a refugee-assistance organisation that asylum seekers they helped were asked to keep silent about their treatment in detention:

We actually signed confidentiality agreements with DIMIA in order to get people out of detention. All the people coming out to us had to agree that we wouldn't do media.

As well as poor conditions being hidden from public view, descriptions of conditions they were supposed to enjoy but didn't added to detainees' frustration. In December 2002, an article published in News Limited newspapers in Sydney, Brisbane, Adelaide and Melbourne described conditions in detention centres as 'five star', citing Immigration Department claims:

Detention centres around Australia provide asylum seekers with everything from DVDs and pay TV to classes in yoga, flower arranging and driver education.[509]

A refugee supporter told the inquiry one detainee had asked her: 'If this place is five-star accommodation, why is it a prison?' Another former detainee told the inquiry:

We used to shout and speak loudly in every consultative meeting for all the rights for detainees which they propagate on their website. I asked them, 'Your website said that you take us out for outing once a week, or month. I'm here for such a long time, when it's my time?' They laugh, they said, 'Oh, you know it's all bullshit propaganda.' But no Australian people know that this is propaganda.

A worker from a refugee assistance organisation told the inquiry about his experience of being involved in such a meeting:

My role was to sit there and hear the debate between detainees and the DIMIA manager, the centre manager and a fairly high number of officers. I have from time to time thought that it is a waste of time my agency being represented there but I've also felt as if our role is to witness what is not happening. We have no power to make it happen.

Professionals and organisations that tried to offer asylum seekers effective assistance were also thwarted by detention authorities. A worker in a refugee torture and trauma service told the inquiry that although officially it had a contract to provide mental health services to detainees, no-one in the service was aware of it for the first year and no detainee had been referred under it in two years.

A study of families in detention found:

In each case, comprehensive mental health assessment of children and parents resulted in recommendations that adequate treatment was not possible while they remained in the [detention] environment. In no case was the primary recommendation implemented by the detention authorities.[510]

A child and adolescent psychiatrist who assessed and treated children in detention told the inquiry:

> When a report was given that management didn't agree with, something like: the patient will continue to be suicidal unless they are taken out of that toxic environment, the report would be written off. At one stage we were directed that we were not allowed to make recommendations in our report on children in immigration detention about them living outside detention.

Mick Palmer's investigation into the Cornelia Rau case found that the failures in the Immigration Department were not the responsibility of low-level bureaucrats. He described it as a 'strongly hierarchical' department with 'a high degree of vertical control'. He found a culture of denial and self-justification that was 'pervasive at senior executive management level'.[511] Journalist David Marr argues:

> Such organisations do not grow by accident. By and large, Australians have been happy with this cruel and dysfunctional department guarding our borders. It's a system that's developed under two governments. For Howard, in particular, it's been a winner.[512]

THEY HAD THE POWER TO CHANGE THAT POLICY:
GOVERNMENT INACTION

Ordinary Australians in contact with detained asylum seekers wrote letters to, rang and made appointments to see members of the government to voice their concerns about the impact of its refugee policy. However, many told the inquiry their representations were ignored. One refugee advocate said she had written 20 letters to Immigration Minister Amanda Vanstone over two years and received one reply. Another told the inquiry that while public servants had advised her to take a case to the minister, she was unable to arrange either a meeting or telephone conversation, despite strenuous efforts.

Refugee advocate Trish Highfield told the inquiry:

We have brought the most shocking damage to these children. There are many people in the Department of Immigration who have to take responsibility for the abuse and neglect – and I use those words very strongly – of children in detention. But let's be very frank here. It's come right from the top and we all know who is responsible. I take it to the very, very top and I will never, ever forgive them for what they have done. There have been children emotionally murdered in detention.

In the years that I have been advocating for children in detention, I have rung Philip Ruddock's office, I have rung the prime minister's office so many times and I have hit a brick wall. No one has acted and I think that is absolutely disgraceful. When people like me were going into detention and were seeing this damage and were notifying them, they had the power to change that policy, to hear people like me.

I have worked as an early childhood professional for over 30 years and to not be able to keep children physically and emotionally safe in detention, children I know were suffering, has been the most shocking, brutal thing that's happened in my life and I will never forgive this government. I will never forgive those in a position of power who refuse to act. I am sorry – I feel like I need to explode on this issue. It is disgraceful and despicable.

Many refugee supporters told the inquiry that members of parliament, most of whom had never visited detention centres nor had personal contact with people detained there, displayed ignorance about the plight of asylum seekers. One supporter said:

I went to a member of parliament and I was told that all of these people were liars, they were queue jumpers and that nobody had been in detention for four years. That was when Peter Qasim was in detention for seven years and he was on the front page of the paper, and this politician kept telling me what a nice place Baxter was.

In April 2003, then immigration minister Philip Ruddock publicly refuted claims of poor conditions in detention centres, telling *Meet the Press*:

Let me make it very clear, there are people out there who are intent on demonising the system itself and seek to portray it as being inhumane, as if we're involved in breaching people's fundamental human rights.[513]

Refugee advocate and journalist John Highfield told the inquiry that despite him notifying the acting immigration minister of an incident which he felt had endangered a detainee's life, his complaint was ignored. Even more disturbingly, he was warned not to pursue his concerns:

In June 2001, at the Curtin Detention Centre, people started to self-harm when they were locked in isolation cells and a 27-minute ACM or DIMA video of that incident found its way into the hands of the advocacy movement.[514] *They subsequently managed to interest the* Lateline *program in that and it went to air on the 22 April 2002, in which a very small amount of the total video was used.*

Many of us were convinced that a man was dying on the floor and he received no medical attention, despite the fact that two nurses were present. You could clearly see them in the video, standing well back from this man who was cyanosed on the floor and his friends were so distressed that one of them attempted CPR himself. The nurses just stood there with no-one impeding them and you could see it all clearly on the video.

The next day in federal parliament there were questions during question time on this and the acting minister for immigration, minister Ellison, made a statement that information had been provided by DIMIA and others present that the nurses were prevented from rendering medical assistance to the injured detainees. So I rang the minister's office as a journalist who had seen the whole video tape several times. I informed the minister's office that either the minister had been grossly misinformed or he was deliberately distorting the truth, because the video clearly showed the two nurses making no attempt whatever to render medical assistance.

The response came in a late-night telephone call from Canberra, asking me if I had a home fax machine. When I said I didn't, they said we will courier the minister's response as he has an urgent letter for you. When I received that letter the next morning it was a caution, that if I had access to a copy of the entire video footage, or was aware of which individuals or organisations are in possession of the video or copies of unlawfully obtained Commonwealth material, it would be in my best interests to hand it over without delay. I didn't have the material and didn't do anything about it. But I believe he was warning me that if I pursued the angle in a story, there could be serious consequences.

The attitude of government ministers was also reflected by senior immigration officials. While Dr Simon Lockwood was providing medical care to detainees in Woomera, a 12-year-old boy tried to hang himself and a woman wrote a suicide note in blood. He told *Lateline*:

> *I saw so many proud and fantastic people just break down to a level that you would find hard to believe, grovelling on the floor in my clinic room saying, 'Please help me get out of here.' I found that really difficult to cope with. I'd sometimes go home towards the end there and I'd cry myself.*[515]

But he initially decided not to go public with his concerns about the mental health of detainees, instead spending two hours briefing a meeting of immigration bureaucrats in Canberra. He told *Lateline*:

> *Towards the end of the meeting one of the bureaucrats said to me, in front of everyone there, 'That sounds all well and good to us, Simon, but we don't want to make it so nice for them in detention that they won't want to leave.' I knew that I'd spoken for two hours probably for nothing.*[516]

In February 2004, Julian Burnside QC described the acts over which the International Criminal Court has jurisdiction and which the Australian Criminal Code recognises as constituting crimes against humanity. With then immigration minister Amanda Vanstone in the audience, he stated:

> *Our government is engaged in a continuing crime against humanity when assessed against its own legislative standards. I accuse Mr Howard and Mr Ruddock of that crime. I accuse Senator Vanstone of that crime. I expect that they will ignore this accusation, since the only person who can bring charges is the attorney general of the Commonwealth ...*
>
> *Our prime minister, who regards himself as walking in the footsteps of Robert Menzies and calls himself a Christian, is in fact immoral, hypocritical, un-Christian and – as a proponent of mandatory detention – a criminal. He must take personal responsibility for the Pacific Solution, which is the most disgraceful and cynical enterprise ever*

undertaken by an Australian government.

Mr Ruddock clings to his membership of Amnesty International, in the face of sustained criticism from that organisation; he chants the Liberal mantra of family values whilst locking families of innocent people behind a 9000V 'courtesy fence' at Baxter ... He is responsible for instructing counsel to argue that we do not have solitary confinement in detention centres, but if we do the courts must not interfere; that we must send terrified people back to torture or death; that we can lock them up for the rest of their lives.[517]

In 1988, when John Howard was promoting a reduction in Asian immigration, Philip Ruddock, immigration minister in the Howard government between 1996 and 2003, crossed the floor of parliament to vote with the Labor government on a motion condemning racial quotas in immigration.[518] This principled action and his role in establishing a parliamentary branch of Amnesty International placed him at odds with many of his colleagues. According to a newspaper article, fellow Amnesty member Eric Sidoti once asked him how he could remain with a party that seemed so out of step with his values. Ruddock replied:

I have spent my life in opposition. I want to be in government.[519]

In a 2003 article, journalist Phillip Adams described another conversation with Ruddock:

Shortly after Ruddock became minister for immigration and multicultural affairs, I sat in his Sydney office expressing some concern for his behaviour. It was long before the scandals of asylum seekers and the international shame of our response to Tampa *– but Ruddock was already implementing policies he'd long opposed. Why? His answer was absolutely simple and utterly honest: 'I've been waiting to be a minister for 20 years.'*[520]

Only a few politicians were prepared to jeopardise their political futures by taking a principled stand on the treatment of asylum seekers. In May 2005, federal Liberal backbencher Petro Georgiou, supported by colleagues Judi Moylan, Bruce Baird and Russell Broadbent, threatened to introduce a private members' bill to soften the government's mandatory detention policy. They and Senator Judith Troeth also opposed the government's

2006 attempt to excise the whole of Australia from the migration zone. Newly elected Liberal MP Russell Broadbent declared:

> *If I am to die politically because of my stance on this bill, it is better to die on my feet than to live on my knees. Some warn that any dissent is a form of political death. [But] it is not the office of the federal member that is important; it is what you do when in office.* [521]

In 2006, Moylan argued:

> *In considering this legislation we need to ask the questions in this place: What values do we place on the rule of law? How can we in all conscience legislate to consign people to a place where they are out of sight and out of mind? I for one cannot remain silent.* [522]

SOMETHING EVIL IS HAPPENING: REFUGEE ADVOCACY

As the *Tampa* waited for permission to enter Australian waters shortly before the 2001 election, Prime Minister John Howard said:

> *We are a humane people, and others know that and they sometimes ... try and intimidate us with our own decency.* [523]

Opinion polls taken shortly after the SAS boarded the *Tampa* showed that 77 per cent of Australians agreed or strongly agreed with the government's policy of preventing asylum seeker boats from entering Australian waters while 18 per cent to 20 per cent disagreed or strongly disagreed. By 2004, 54.4 per cent agreed or strongly agreed with the policy of turning back boats while 28 per cent disagreed or strongly disagreed. [524] This change can be at least partly explained by the increasing involvement over this period of ordinary Australians with asylum seekers, and the advocacy they undertook on their behalf.

In January 2002, 13 refugee supporters set out in a bus for a seven-week tour of Australia's detention centres. Based on the 1960s Freedom Bus in which activists drew attention to the plight of Aboriginal Australians, it visited all detention centres except Woomera. One of those on the Freedom Bus told the inquiry about its visit to Curtin detention centre:

I wasn't allowed to visit but the manager told the people inside that we decided not to visit them. They had been waiting for us for a couple of months and had written submissions for us and nominated people to talk to us. People called us quite angry, saying why have you decided not to visit. Four of us tried walking in and they stopped us and said they couldn't get a decision on whether we were allowed because the manager had gone fishing. We told that to the people inside by phone and they said, we spoke to him five minutes ago and then they went into his office and said they weren't going to leave until we were allowed to visit. They said that we could visit, but on Monday, which was the day after we were scheduled to have left.

So two of us stayed behind. They took us to an abandoned airport, picked up five of the six people that we wanted to visit and bussed them over. They pat-searched us and they had the five people with a guard standing right behind them, a guard standing to their right with a video camera and somebody sitting at a table 2m away taking notes. The person they didn't bring out was their translator.

Refugee advocate Kate Gauthier, who travelled on the Freedom Bus's second trip around Australia, told the inquiry:

The first thing I noticed was the incredibly heavy police presence as we travelled through Western Australia. We would go into a town and the police would meet us 50km outside of town and drive us all the way through to make sure we didn't stop. We would have repeated random breath tests. They would stop us and check the bus over for defects. We stopped in Geraldton to have a public information night. Only 10 people turned up, but the police walked around the car park and wrote down the licence plate of every local who came.

As we arrived in Port Hedland, we had a police escort of six vehicles. They had blocked off access to the detention centre with a mobile arrest van so we had to walk down. When you left the detention centre to go to the bathroom or the store, a police officer would follow you. When we went to Curtin we had a police escort the entire 850km journey from Port Hedland to Derby.

People on the Freedom Bus gathered the names and numbers of detainees thrown to them over fences. One said:

> *I painstakingly tried to write down foreign names to line up with the numbers. The people didn't give their names first up. They just told us their numbers. The memory still makes me cry. It was truly shocking.*[525]

Around the same time, other Australians concerned by the government's refugee policies organised grassroots action. Lawyers, political activists, church workers, health workers and thousands of ordinary Australians developed detailed knowledge of Australia's refugee assessment process and detention centre operations as they tried to assist the asylum seekers struggling with them. Some networked informally, advocating for a few individual asylum seekers and finding themselves working with people they would not otherwise have met. Others established organisations.

Anne Coombs, Susan Varga and Helen McCue formed Rural Australians for Refugees, which attracted 500 people to its inaugural meeting in Bowral and established more than 90 groups around the country. Kate Durham set up Spare Rooms for Refugees, allowing people to offer a room in their home to a refugee. Mariana Hardwick and Eva Sallis formed Australians Against Racism. National lobby group A Just Australia was established in July 2002 and is supported by 120 nongovernment organisations, 70 prominent Australians and 11,500 other individuals.

Ordinary people who wanted to do something to protest against government policy and assist those affected by these policies contacted these and other organisations, which linked them with asylum seekers in detention. They wrote, telephoned and visited, developing relationships that would change their lives, both through the rewards of their personal contact and what they learnt in dealing with the detention system. The stories of many of these relationships are described in the book *Acting from the Heart*, in which over 50 Australians document their involvement with asylum seekers.[526]

Most refugee advocates were linked by email communications and the internet. Through newsletters, petitions, calls to action and websites, those involved had access to knowledge of the larger movement.[527]

Australian supporters of asylum seekers told the inquiry how they had come to be involved in the refugee issue. One said:

> *I first became interested in the refugees when we watched the evening*

news with horror to be told that children were being thrown overboard. I had been to the Middle East a lot and I know that no Arab woman would throw her child into the water; no mother, Jewish, Arab, Christian – so we knew we were being sold something that was insidious and the horrible part is that there was an election coming up and the public went along. I went to my local synagogue and our rabbi said: something evil is happening in this country and if I were you, I would get out to Villawood and see what's happening. He said, I am going out, I'm wearing my kippah to let them know who I am.

Another told the inquiry:

I was asked on an email to help donate things for babies because there were four Muslim women coming out of Woomera about to deliver babies and there were no supplies for them. I rang and checked that this email was legitimate only to be told the story was even worse than I had imagined. I filled up my boot with nappies and various baby items and that was the beginning of my involvement.

Writer Arnold Zable, whose mother escaped the Nazis and tried but failed to obtain visas for her parents, brothers, sisters, nieces and nephews, all of whom were subsequently murdered, described his reason for demonstrating outside Maribyrnong detention centre:

I was there for one simple reason. I am alive today because my mother was a 'queue jumper'. As I know from my mother's story, when it is time to run, there is no queue. Asylum seekers do what many of us would do if faced with a similar fate.[528]

The inquiry also heard many stories from visitors about their experience of the policies and procedures applied within detention centres. The two main themes that emerged from the evidence were of unreasonable rules, and of rules constantly changing. One visitor told the inquiry:

One time we visited with another couple and the woman wasn't allowed to visit. She had to go back and sit in the car for the three hours because she didn't have the right type of shoes on. She was wearing sandals instead of covered-in shoes and yet the detainees were coming over in sandals. It just didn't seem to make sense.

A daily visitor to Baxter told the inquiry:

> You could take paper and then you couldn't. You could take a cane basket and the next day you couldn't. They wanted to count photos on the way in and on the way out and one time I'd taken photos in which they hadn't counted, but on the way out they insisted they had to count them even though they didn't know how many had come in. The latest thing about the photos was that I could take photos in, but not photos with me in them. Someone else could take in a photo of me, but only if I wasn't there. They would seriously tell you this stuff and you just have to stand there.

A visitor to Maribyrnong told the inquiry:

> Unless one could spell exactly the person's name that you wanted to visit they would go through some funny game saying, 'Could you just have another go at Mohammed, this person's name is not quite spelt that way.' There are several ways in which one can spell Mohammed, so you had to keep on playing that game until you got it right or else not be able see that person.

Another visitor said:

> I think I took a tape recorder in and out about seven times before it was actually allowed to come in. The first time it was at the wrong time of the day, the next time you could only bring new ones, so I didn't have the actual receipt even though it was obvious that it was new, and so on.

Many visitors to detention also told the inquiry they had witnessed detention centre staff treating detainees or other visitors in a racist manner. A regular visitor to Villawood told the inquiry:

> The clerk at the desk was yelling at a couple of men who could not speak much English. She dismissed them after hours of waiting in the sun and called the next person. I asked them what was the problem and they said she wanted telephone numbers. They told her that they did not have a telephone. I took their pen and created imaginary phone numbers and they waited submissively to be called. My friend and I were called instead so we reminded the clerk that the two men were

ahead of us. Her tone completely changed. She called them over and was just so polite.

Another visitor told the inquiry:

If you are Chinese you have no show unless you have a passport and something that indicates where you are living, like an electricity bill. Whereas white faces like mine who have been going for so long, many of them will let you in. I had my wallet stolen and I didn't have an up-to-date driver's licence and they said, 'Don't worry, just put your old one in.' Some are good, some are absolutely horrible and if you have not got a white face you have great difficulty.

The inquiry was given an email from a visitor to Maribyrnong, which stated:

I was waiting in the security line-up at Maribyrnong. A Vietnamese family was standing in front of me. The guard said to the family, 'What date did she arrive?' They replied in very broken translation, 'Tuesday.' The relative then started counting the days of the week on his finger as the guard flipped through an admissions log. The relative then said, 'I mean Wednesday.' The guard then picked up the log book and threw it across his booth. It was very intimidating. He then said, 'Well make up your f***ing mind, was it Tuesday or f***ing Wednesday?'

Another visitor told the inquiry:

After treating someone in an incredibly humiliating way in front of me, some guards would look at me in complicity and roll their eyes to ridicule the person. They assumed I would agree with the behaviour because I was a white Australian. The environment was so insular they thought their behaviour was normal.

However, the obstruction of visitors by detention staff was not limited to people of different cultures. Even Father Peter Norden, who has worked as a chaplain in a maximum security prison and was appointed the Catholic chaplain to Maribyrnong, told the inquiry he sometimes had difficulty entering the centre:

When I was first appointed by the Archbishop I contacted the State Director and received approval to visit and made an appointment to meet the local manager. When I arrived the manager came outside and told me I wasn't welcome to visit because members of his staff felt that I might be a troublemaker. So I went to my car and spoke to the state director of immigration and the Victorian secretary for the Department of Justice and within half an hour they were phoning me full of apologies.

On two occasions since, I've been refused to celebrate Mass there on the basis that I was bringing into the facility alcoholic substance. The alcoholic substance was a very, very small thimble of altar wine and on both occasions I said you can't celebrate Mass without altar wine. Despite that I was refused entry and it created quite a scene and quite an emotional upset for several detainees who were waiting to participate.

The inquiry also heard many accounts of people being allowed to visit, but being processed extremely slowly so that the amount of time for the visit was curtailed. Processing entailed visitors filling in forms, producing identification, having plastic bands placed on their wrists, invisible stamps put on their hands and being screened with metal detectors. Once this process was complete, detainees would be told the visitor was there, after which they also needed to be screened and transported to the visit area. One visitor told the inquiry:

They were really slow processing us. We got in at quarter to seven and we waited and waited and nobody came. It just seemed really bizarre. In the compound overnight there had been a bit of a skirmish, so I think the message had been passed on to the other guards, and our friends just haven't been told. One of our young men knew that we always come. He kept going and saying, 'We have visitors.' 'No, we haven't called for you yet.' And in the end he lost it and was sent to the isolation unit. At 10 to eight they finally allowed them to come and they say to us, 'You're late tonight.' And we say, 'No, we've been waiting here.' It was just game playing.

Another visitor said:

The number of times we have spent half of the visiting time waiting for someone to present. The number of times someone has come in the last half hour and said that no one passed on the message. There are many, many ways that power can be used and there are many ways that it can be used inappropriately.

Visitors who questioned the rules learned there were consequences. One visitor to Baxter who argued when told she couldn't book a visit although there were places available told the inquiry:

Then I said, 'I'd like to talk to the supervisor about it,' and he just looked at me and said, 'Oh, I see. You think you're going to go over my head. Well it doesn't work like that, I'm in charge here.' The supervisor let me book, but the next time I came to visit, I was outside waiting at the gate with the camera zooming in on me and they said, 'He's busy, you have to wait.' It was really hot out in the sun and he made me wait for 25 minutes. It was a lesson to me that these people have got enormous power over something that's very important to you, and they are quite prepared to use it.

However, despite the rules and laborious security procedures, many visitors managed to circumvent them and deliver 'contraband' items such as phone cards, mobile phones and documents to detainees. A visitor to detention told the inquiry:

I would take the phone cards in and I wasn't supposed to be doing that but I used to hand phone cards under the table.

A refugee advocate told the inquiry:

Mobile phones did not officially exist although it was possible to call those who had one late at night when they were unlikely to be discovered using them. Full marks to those who smuggled them in (usually women) and to the detainees who successfully hid them.

Many visitors described meeting asylum seekers face to face as something that changed their lives. They described feelings of shame and grief at the situation of the people held in detention and guilt when enjoying freedoms not available to asylum seekers. Once they met people, they felt they had to become more involved in advocating for them. One visitor explained:

I have to be honest and say that I went to have a look. It's like everybody who's been visiting. You go once and you can't not go again, even though it's so awful. I know what we experience is nothing compared to what our friends do – but visiting Baxter has cast a dampness on my whole life. Peter has never visited and once I started this – Peter asked, 'Would you like me to come with you?' and I said, 'Actually, no. I need you at home so that when I come home and cry all night,' as I do, 'I need somebody who hasn't been there that doesn't – I need support.'

We've got three late-teens, early-twenties, boys, and they're just exactly the same as these guys. One of my boys got engaged and I was so thrilled, but at the same time I felt almost guilty and sad that these guys we visit, they should have that experience and they don't. They are supposed to be working, meeting people and all those kinds of things. A couple of our young guys, every visit it's, 'but there has to be more.' I sit and I think, I don't know what else I can do unless I write another letter. What am I going to do? That's really, really hard.

Refugee advocates also reported that feeling powerless to help asylum seekers had affected their mental health. One woman said:

Once you've been into Baxter it takes over your life. It's like nothing else is more important. That obligation keeps you going beyond your burnout and I think you'd have to say that that equals a mental-health problem. That's a combination of things – sadness, shame, lack of sleep, anxiety, absolute fear that your friends will be deported and there's nothing you can do.

One visitor to Baxter told the inquiry he would never forget one visit:

One young gentleman that we visit regularly – one particular time as we were leaving, I will never forget this – he hung on to my wife and started sobbing. Sobbing so loud that everybody in the visitors' centre at the time knew and could see it happening and we had to separate them before we could leave. We went into the office and you could see him through the glass window still crying, he went down on the floor and then he eventually got up and went into the toilet out of sight.

A visitor who attended a Christmas church service in detention told the inquiry:

I was able to go to the Christmas service and the passing of the peace and two women, who I had never met before, with children broke down and cried and cried. The men were just so quiet. And then I left and went out to have lunch with friends and I couldn't eat.

A Year 11 student who later became involved in the fight to free children from detention told the inquiry how visiting a family in detention affected him:

The older child of the family reminded me of myself in some ways and this made me feel very attached to him. When we had to leave it was very upsetting and I cried for a long time. It was seeing them across the glass and that I couldn't take them and help them and I had to leave them there in that horrible situation.

Once they became personally involved with individual asylum seekers, Australian supporters found themselves drawn into a world of frantic activity aimed at seeing their friends released from detention and making their time in detention more bearable. They organised legal assistance, wrote submissions, initiated protests, negotiated with detention authorities and networked with other refugee supporters. A man told the inquiry:

That's at the forefront of the supporter's mind, what we are doing in regard to this situation. It's just ongoing. You wake up having dreamt it. I would turn up to work absolutely exhausted, every day. I'm one of the 'new wave' of refugee supporters. With a sense of shame, I can say that a few years ago, I knew nothing about refugees. But when you come face to face with them, that was a different experience. And then it's impossible to just forget about it and move on. Because these are real human beings who have come from terrible experiences, but then to get to my country and being treated just unnecessarily terribly and unjustly. In some ways it's a sense of duty. Absolute duty.

I recently was involved in an interview by a researcher who was looking at refugee supporters and how they've sprung up all over Australia and the sort of things they have experienced. And it wasn't until halfway through that interview that I realised maybe I was carrying around an awful, great weight myself, psychologically underneath, because halfway through the interview, I just broke down and cried, and couldn't stop it. You don't get through this and then it's all finished and everything's hunky-dory. It continues on, so, for me, it's just get your feet in the door and bingo, you're into another world and it stays there.

The relationships some visitors established with detainees culminated in marriage. Between March 2001 and December 2003, at least 21 marriages were held in detention, mostly between detainees and Australian citizens.[529] Many other visitors established strong sibling- or parental-type relationships with those in detention.

Some refugee advocates told the inquiry they became so involved in advocating for asylum seekers that their friends and relatives who were not involved did not understand the intensity of their involvement and these relationships became strained. However, many also explained that they had found great comfort from other refugee supporters, people from walks of life they would never otherwise have come across. One told the inquiry:

> *There's two main people I support and we got some really bad news for one of them and I got a text from somebody that just said, 'You must be feeling terrible, it's like a death in the family' and it is. You can't explain that to people. It's like a mad bubble which we are all in and the rest of the world isn't in and people within the mad bubble were incredibly supportive.*
>
> *I found this one of the most difficult periods of my life, but also some of the most positive in that they are wonderful people, not only detainees but some activists as well. I have never met so many really, really good people before, coming together with something that is wrong and actually doing something about it, and I do believe that we have turned things around a bit by enough people in the community saying this is not OK. For example, in the first year that he came out things just weren't in place for him to be supported and there was a group of people in the community that all gave $5 a week into a bank account, and that helped him in that initial period.*

Visitors also spoke of the way the asylum seeker issue had increased their political awareness. A man told the inquiry:

> *Since 2001, I have had to move from believing that the worst excesses were overseas or back in history, and come to an understanding that Australians are as capable as anyone on earth of bigotry, racism and the*

ability to ignore injustice. Australian politicians are just as capable as any of lies, half-truths and blindness to atrocities done in their name. I am 63 years old and many of my contemporaries developed their social conscience during the Vietnam War. I have to say I have left my run a bit late, nevertheless that doesn't detract from my conviction at the moment and I am also really delighted to see the younger people and it gives me a good hope for the future.

After one of the Baxter convergences in 2003, Mike Rann, the South Australian premier, complained about the ferals and meatheads at the protest. I was there and I spoke to young people and I didn't come across any that would go by that description, because where he saw rabble-rousers I saw wisdom, maturity and understanding, and courage too.

A GP told the inquiry:

I attended the Easter demonstrations and was disgusted at the behaviour of the police. I always thought you were allowed to peacefully demonstrate in this country – apparently not if you are rallying to support refugees. I experienced being charged by mounted police while standing 100 metres from the electric fence in a group and singing. I witnessed people being plucked out of a group at random and taken to the police station at Port Augusta – one was a journalist from The Australian *who was released of course, but not the others.*

Some detention staff were among those who tried to help asylum seekers, but the inquiry heard evidence from a range of sources that staff who showed compassion toward detainees were pressured and ostracised by other staff. Detainees recognised that officers who were kind to them suffered, while those who were cruel tended to be promoted. A former detainee told the inquiry:

There were some good people and if those guards were friendly with you they suffered. Some of them were good, but they hurt them. And if they were bad they could go up.

An ACM memo presented to the inquiry outlines how one detention officer was counselled after being reported by other officers for being too friendly with a detainee.[530] A nurse who worked at Woomera in 2000 told a public meeting in 2002:

At one stage some of us had our names, addresses and telephone numbers translated into Arabic and Farsi so that we could give them to the people we'd gotten to know and care about and support them on their release. We had to have them in Persian and Arabic so the guards couldn't understand what it was if they saw it. More than one nurse lost their contract for this reason. ACM's response ... was to completely ban all nurses from saying goodbye to anyone when they were given a visa ... We were also told our phones would be tapped and ASIO was watching us. God it was bizarre. The paranoia and suspicion were incredible.[531]

Registered nurse Mark Huxstep told HREOC:

Written complaints were often made by ACM officers about medical staff. Complaints were regularly made that medical centre staff were too familiar with detainees. Complaints were also made that medical centre staff were spending too long with patients ... During my first contract, a conversation between myself and other nursing staff over dinner at the local restaurant was taken down by an ACM officer and given to ACM management.[532]

Working in detention centres affected the mental health of staff who showed compassion to detainees. Sharon Torbet was employed as an activities officer at Woomera and described a hunger strike there where women and children lay on mattresses in the desert heat:

As I moved around the group I came to Roqia Bakhtiyari, an Afghani. I had worked extensively with her five children aged 14 years to five years. I had filed numerous reports and referrals on the family ... she lay on a mattress too weak to sit up; I knelt beside her, the other women told me she had not eaten for days. Roqia's lips were stitched from corner to corner (this is a sight I will never forget), her eyes held no life. I placed my hand on hers and cried; when I looked up, all present were crying.[533]

Torbet was later diagnosed with post traumatic stress disorder (PTSD) and compensated. Nurse Mark Huxstep was also diagnosed with PTSD and found it hard to work in a normal setting after Woomera:

I tried to come back to my old job, but I couldn't cope with all these fat white people wanting elective surgery while there were people being tortured in the Australian desert.[534]

A former Woomera worker told the inquiry:

The Australian government should be extremely ashamed to allow what I witnessed to happen in Australia, it's just insane. I believe I worked in a war zone. I am three years away from the detention centre and I still have weekly counselling to live with my part of it.

Pro Bono Lawyers

Anger at the injustice of government policy drove ordinary Australians to establish hundreds of community organisations which offered support to asylum seekers. Of key importance were those which offered legal and immigration services free of charge to those in detention. Hundreds of lawyers and migration agents offered pro bono services through organisations which include: Spare Lawyers for Refugees, the Refugee and Immigration Legal Centre, the Asylum Seekers Resource Centre, the Refugee Advocacy Service of South Australia, the Refugee Advice and Casework Service, CASE for Refugees, SCALES community legal centre, the Woomera Lawyers Group and the Legal Services Commission of South Australia.

A refugee advocate told the inquiry she worked with lawyers to assist those in detention to access legal advice:

We were able to set up language-based networks to find out who were asylum seekers and ask for them to come out. The ones that tend to be unknown to us don't speak English. We are operating with pro bono barristers and solicitors who want information all the time. The last time I walked into detention I had batches of questions I had to ask people and the person looking through my papers said, 'What's all this writing about, who are you seeing, what are you asking them about, why are you doing that?' So we are starting to feel the cord tightening.

They are aiming to make sure as few of us as possible can have any sort of significant contact with people who might benefit out of what we can offer. The ones that stay in a long time are the ones who get adequate information to know what to do next. The ones that move through quickly are ones that they can get in and out without us knowing about them.

A barrister who provided pro bono advice told the inquiry:

I would spend at least 15 and possibly 20 days in court a year on these cases. The normal rate I would charge would be about $2500 a day and so every day that you spend on one of these cases is a day that you can't earn an income to meet your expensive outgoings. But those are the sorts of equations you don't really make when somebody is being faced with deportation. Once you're in, you're in. There's lots of barristers who are doing exactly what I am doing.

Despite government attempts to restrict legislation and asylum seekers' access to legal advice, refugee lawyers did have some success in assisting asylum seekers, and the government subsequently targeted them. In March 2005, then immigration minister Amanda Vanstone announced legislation which ordered courts to consider the imposition of personal costs against lawyers and migration advisers who brought cases 'which have no reasonable prospect of success.'[535] In a submission to a Senate committee, Australian Lawyers for Human Rights argued:

Lawyers are already bound by a professional obligation and a duty to the courts not to pursue causes of action that have no reasonable prospects of success. The imposition of specific costs orders appears aimed at intimidating lawyers rather than improving access by asylum seekers to proper legal advice as to the merits of their claim. The risk of a costs order will inevitably dissuade advocates from pursuing difficult but valid cases where there is a real issue to be determined.[536]

Amnesty International lawyer Maria Lamattina argued:

This Bill effectively intrudes into judicial powers and undermines applicants' fair and equal access to the courts by deterring lawyers and migration agents from providing representation.[537]

Other Refugee Support Groups

Other community organisations that supported asylum seekers in detention were created by ordinary Australians. The organisations ranged from informal groups that met in halls, cafés and homes across Australia, to organisations with paid staff and offices. A visitor to detention told the inquiry how people in her country town formed a group to take action on the issue:

> Some years ago my next-door neighbour said she was going to call a public meeting in the Country Women's Association Hall in case people were interested in what was happening to people in detention, and would I go. Lots of people turned up. I was quite surprised actually. After that a number of people got together and became a member of Rural Australians for Refugees. We started meeting in one of the members' homes.

Another refugee supporter told the inquiry how her local group had begun:

> We are members of a group of 20. It started at the end of 2001, when one of our parishioners was really upset about the Tampa and she called a group at a café and now they meet at the church every fortnight. We raise money by trading tables, concerts, bridge afternoons, raffles – probably about $8,000 a year.

A submission to the inquiry explained that 70 Circle of Friends groups had been set up since mid-2002. These groups provide practical support to individual asylum seekers in detention and on release, including by members making a small weekly financial commitment.

Some refugee advocates also organised local public protests. One man told the inquiry he helped to organise a 30-hour fasting vigil in Launceston's Civic Square to raise awareness about asylum seekers in detention:

> We could not feel that our integrity was intact if we continued to be totally private about our concerns in this whole matter. Soon after returning from Baxter two close friends at church responded to my sense of great frustration and anxiety, and it was agreed that some sort of public vigil should take place. We wanted to challenge people of conscience and appeal to all Australians to act as agents. This was two days before Christmas. Everybody was in a hurry, and yet 171 people stopped to write in the books.

A refugee told the inquiry:

> *We are always appreciating support of the Australian people and when we were in detention centre, they helped us. We will never forget that.*

However, a refugee advocate told the inquiry that the energy and resources volunteers expended on providing services that should have been provided by the government came at a cost to the Australian community:

> *I had over 600 supporters on my database. The cost to Australia in terms of tying up thousands of volunteers in trying to redress serious problems caused by government policies is huge. If not engaged in this work, doubtless they would have been involved in other voluntary work in their communities.*

OTHER PATHWAYS INTO DETENTION

While the bulk of the information presented to the inquiry concerned asylum seekers, the inquiry also heard evidence about other groups of people held in detention centres. People other than asylum seekers kept in immigration detention include: foreign fishermen intercepted in Australian waters; people who originally entered Australia with a valid visa but later overstayed or had it cancelled; and people like Cornelia Rau, detained due to error by the Department of Immigration.

Foreign Fishermen

Under the *Fisheries Act*, foreign fishermen intercepted in Australian waters can be held for seven days, after which they are classified as illegal noncitizens under the *Migration Act* and can be held indefinitely. Once intercepted, they are brought to Australia against their will for prosecution.

One local fisherman told historian Dr Ruth Balint:

> *For the amount of miles these boats would have covered, the people are either desperate for food or desperate for money. You just wouldn't risk*

your life in a lot of these boats, that's for sure … you wouldn't catch me in them.[538]

Up until late 2005, intercepted fishermen were kept anchored in Darwin and not allowed to leave their boats, sometimes for months. Food and water were provided by Kerrawang Pty Ltd, trading as Barefoot Marine, a company majority owned by the family of federal Liberal-Country Senator Nigel Scullion. In his maiden speech to parliament in February 2002, Scullion praised the government's policy on foreign fishermen:

If you come to steal, we are prepared. You will be caught. You will be prosecuted and it is very likely you will lose your vessel and your equipment.[539]

That financial year Kerrawang was paid a total of $1.3 million by either the Australian Fisheries Management Authority (AFMA) or the Commonwealth government, and Senator Scullion received over $47,000 in salary.[540] Section 44(v) of the Australian Constitution prohibits a person who benefits financially from an agreement with the public service of the Commonwealth from serving as a senator. Legal advice on Senator Scullion's position concluded that neither the AFMA nor the Commonwealth government were technically the public service of the Commonwealth. However, in May 2002, Senator Scullion sold the three shares he owned in the company (from a total of eight) to his wife, who already owned another three shares.[541]

Mansur La Ibu

On 26 February 2003, 21-year-old fisherman Mansur La Ibu died on a small boat with no navigational equipment on Darwin Harbour. Less than a month earlier, the boat had been intercepted by HMAS *Fremantle* 52 nautical miles inside Australian waters. No fish were found on the boat but 'some scales from fish were found.'[542] The captain of the boat told the boarding party they had caught about two kilograms of red fish. As they had no Australian fishing licence, they were towed to Darwin Harbour and moored next to 12 other Indonesian fishing boats.

On 5 February 2003, the captain of the boat pleaded guilty to illegal fishing. He was released with a $3000 fine and a five-year good behaviour bond. He was allowed to sail his boat back to Indonesia, but the crew waited three weeks, confined to the boat as illegal noncitizens, for rough weather to abate. The boat contained no running water, no toilets and no means of communication. The only shelter from the wet-season storms for seven men was the sleeping quarters, described at the inquest into Mansur's death as:

> *Height-wise it would probably be ... three and a bit feet in height ... and ... wide, about four and five feet ... Length-wise approximately about five or six feet.*[543]

The federal minister for fisheries at the time, Senator Ian Macdonald, told Dr Ruth Balint these are:

> *... certainly not boats or conditions that I or most Australians would want to live on, but these are village people from Indonesia, they've already lived on the boat for a long period of time and they feel comfortable there.*[544]

The night Mansur died, 'the weather was described by the investigating officer as cyclonic.'[545] As the men lay on the floor of the boat, Mansur became sick but his crewmates yelling, turning on the motor and cutting their boat loose failed to attract the attention of Barefoot Marine employees for up to an hour. When they finally did arrive, Mansur was unconscious but still breathing. Twenty minutes later, he was dead. The inquest into his death could not determine a cause.

Mansur's family was told they would have to pay for the body to be sent back to Indonesia, which they could not afford. They asked that he be buried in accordance with Muslim tradition, which stipulates burial should occur within 24 hours. However his body lay in the morgue for about four months while the Australian and Indonesian governments argued about who should pay for his burial. Eventually the Indonesian Consulate and the Northern Territory government paid for it. Coroner Greg Cavanagh stated:

> *Whilst living seamen are repatriated by DIMIA, DIMIA did not take responsibility for the body or the repatriation or burial of the deceased ... The deceased was held by federal government agencies for some weeks against his will, as a virtual prisoner without charges being proffered against him, without trial and without access to judicial review.*[546]

Two years after Mansur's death, his father travelled by fishing boat to visit his son's grave. Also intercepted and towed to Darwin, he spoke to Indonesian consular officials and was able to spend a few moments at his son's graveside, leaving all he could afford – his tobacco – as an offering to him.[547]

Muhammed Heri

On 28 April 2005, 37-year-old Muhammed Heri, a second fisherman, died on Darwin Harbour after being held on a 20-metre boat in rough seas for seven days. A coronial inquest into his death heard that the failure to give him a medical examination after he was detained contravened Department of Immigration guidelines.[548] Although Muhammed was alive when help reached him, his boat was moored 1.5 nautical miles from the Barefoot Marine base and bad weather made his transfer from the boat to the speedboat and the wharf slow. He was dead from heart failure by the time ambulance officers reached him. His family received his body two days after his death, the costs of transportation being met by the Australian government.

Further Developments

Following the deaths of Mansur and Muhammed, arrangements were made for fishermen to be held in the Northern Detention Centre. In November 2006, HREOC visited the centre. It found that many foreign fishermen were held for longer than two weeks and that services were inadequate. Particular problems included: no specialist staff to cater to children; inadequate mental-health services; overcrowded dining and accommodation areas; inadequate education and recreation programs; insufficient reading material; and no access to public phones or computers. It was also noted that HREOC posters had been put up two days before its visit.[549]

When HREOC visited the following year, it found that children detained after being found on fishing boats were housed in a motel from which the Department of Immigration permanently booked nine rooms. One room was used as a recreation room and one as an officer's station.[550]

In 2005, about 2500 foreign fishermen, mostly Indonesians, were either jailed or deported.[551] They can be fined up to $70,000, which for second-time offenders who cannot pay, is paid off at $100 per day in prison.[552] In 2006–07, 1437 foreign fishermen were taken into immigration detention, including 212 minors.[553] *The Australian* newspaper has claimed that foreign fishermen will make up almost one third of the Northern Territory's prison population by 2009.[554]

In November 2007, three Indonesian fishermen, their wives and 10 children were intercepted 650 kilometres west of Darwin. The men had reportedly been arrested previously for illegal fishing and were seeking economic asylum with their families because restrictions on fishing in Australian waters threatened their traditional livelihoods.[555]

A May 2006 Department of Immigration information paper stated that detention of foreign fishermen would be 'scaled up significantly' with additional funding of $49.6 million provided for the cost of their detention and removal from Australia.[556]

As part of a $389 million 'tough on illegal foreign fishermen' package in the 2006 Federal Budget, the government leased the 98-metre ACV *Triton*.[557] It can hold up to 30 illegal fishermen for more than a month at sea; Navy and Customs boats fill it to capacity before transporting people to the Northern Detention Centre in Darwin. As illegal fishermen can only be held for seven days under the *Fisheries Act*, in effect it will be a sea-based detention centre and has been called a 'floating prison'.[558]

Visa Overstaying

As at 31 December 2005, approximately 46,400 people had overstayed their visa to Australia, including over 39,000 visitors, 2,700 students and 2,300 temporary residents. People from countries that have the largest number of visitors to Australia make up the largest number of overstayers, with most being from the USA, the UK, China, the Philippines and Korea.[559] People who overstay their visa may be taken into immigration detention and removed, but can also be given temporary lawful status through the grant of a bridging visa.[560]

The inquiry heard evidence from an American woman who was detained when she inadvertently overstayed her tourist visa:

> I came to Australia to reunite with my partner. I came on a tourist visa with the understanding that I was to start university the following year, but I hadn't seen this man for more than nine months and wanted to check things out before I committed. Things did work out pretty well and I decided to stay and was accepted to university.
>
> You have to leave the country to apply for a student visa. My return

ticket to the United States I allowed to lapse because we had this plan to go to New Zealand, and I was going to apply for my student visa from there. For reasons that have a lot to do with my ability to organise myself, my tourist visa lapsed without my knowledge before I left the country. They don't stamp when this electronic visa actually expires, so I wasn't too sure when it was.

I was golfing and had my camera and my Pennsylvania driver's licence in the pocket of the camera case and the camera fell out of the golf bag. The next day the police station rang to tell me that they had found my missing camera and I should come at my earliest convenience to pick it up.

I said, 'I'm here to pick up my lost property,' and the police officer comes back five minutes later and says, 'We're just trying to get the paperwork in order, I just need to take you out the back to sign the papers,' and he led me straight into an interrogation room. He said, 'I regret to inform you that you are an illegal noncitizen and you have no legal rights whatsoever.' I'm not allowed to contact a lawyer, I'm not allowed to do anything except go with these people. I was pretty upset, shocked.

They told me they were going to take me to Maribyrnong and I didn't know what that was. I didn't cry until they put handcuffs on me. I remember I was upset that they would not help me buckle my seatbelt. So we get to Maribyrnong, and it's a prison. There is no other way to describe it.

They took my property, my passport, some cash and they took my photo. The whole time they were saying, 'We're just going to put you in short stay tonight because we don't expect that you are going to be here for too long,' and they could see that I was visibly upset. But after they registered my property, they led me to my room – I'm a native English speaker and I can read – and they led me right past the door that says 'short stay' and they led me into the door next door that says 'isolation'.

The people at the police station had told me that I was going to get to call my partner and speak to immigration when I got there. I asked to speak to immigration and they said, 'It's after midnight and there is no-one here. You will be able to talk to them first thing in the morning and you're not allowed to use the phone until you speak to DIMIA.'

They brought in my breakfast and I said, 'When am I going to speak to immigration?' I don't know how many times I asked to speak to immigration and they told me, 'A little bit later.' The on-site immigration *person did come and see me but it wasn't an official meeting. I was meant to meet with a case worker and this is just the on-site woman. She came in and said, 'What do you plan to do?' and I was saying, 'I want someone to tell me what's happening because I don't have a clue why I am here.'*

She said, 'You have two choices: you can leave Australia voluntarily or we can force you to leave,' and I said, 'Obviously I am going to leave voluntarily, I don't want to cause any trouble, I just want to go and collect my things.' She said, 'You misunderstand me; by leaving voluntarily that means without restraints on. We are still going to escort you from here to the airport and put you on a plane.'

After that it started to get that frustrating and what they had told me had been a lie. I didn't get to call anyone when I got there, I didn't go to short stay, I didn't get to speak to a case officer, so I was starting to get really upset and I started banging on the door and yelling.

They sent me to the psychiatric nurse. The first thing she said was, 'I understand you're a little bit upset, can you tell me why.' I'm like, 'You must be joking, I have no idea why I am here and what is going to happen. They are telling me I am going to leave straight from here to the airport, I'm supposed to be able to call people, I'm supposed to have a case worker. It's past one o'clock, what the hell is going on?' About 20 minutes later someone came and said, 'You are going to the women's dorm.'

I got treated really nicely; they allowed me to make calls to mobiles when that is against the rules. The guards talked to me a lot more than they were talking to anyone else. They treated me differently too. There was this implicit understanding that because I'm a white American woman I don't belong there.

When I went to see my immigration case worker I went into the interview room and the window was open and I was a bit chilly and I asked him if he'd mind if I closed the window and he said, I'll never forget this, this is verbatim, 'Yes. I like to have it open because sometimes it smells of Indians and Chinese in here.'

He produced this file with all this information about me. He had all the details of where I had been living, information about things that my mother had shipped from the United States. He told me it was DIMIA's contention that I had planned to attend the University of Melbourne without a visa and to remain in this country unlawfully and all this ridiculous crap.

I'm freaking out, and he's like, 'Calm down, we'll sort this out.'
So he started to fill out the interview, and he's writing everything for
me. He said, 'Everybody knows that this place wasn't built for people
like you.' I was only there for Monday evening, Tuesday and most of
Wednesday.

According to the Department of Immigration many people recorded as overstayers simply remain in Australia for a few days or weeks longer than permitted and leave voluntarily.[561] But about one third of visa overstayers have remained in Australia illegally for more than 10 years.[562] In other sections, this report documents the death in Maribyrnong detention centre of Viliami Tanginoa, a Tongan who had lived in Australia for 17 years after overstaying his visa,[563] and the deportation of Fijian mother of five Seseana Naikelekele, who lived in Australia for 15 years before spending more than two years in Villawood detention centre.[564]

Visa Cancellation

People initially granted a visa to Australia can have it cancelled by the Department of Immigration in a range of circumstances. These include: failing to abide by the conditions of the visa; the breakdown of the business or personal relationships that led to the granting of the visa; the use of fraudulent documents in obtaining the visa; and the failure to meet character requirements because of a criminal history. A person is usually notified of the department's intention to cancel their visa and given a period in which to respond. They are also able to appeal the cancellation unless it is cancelled by the immigration minister personally. In 2006–07, the department cancelled 20,673 visas, an increase of 11.4 per cent on the previous year.[565]

An immigration officer can detain someone whose visa they know or suspect will be cancelled, and who they reasonably believe would otherwise attempt to escape or be uncooperative with investigations, for four hours of 'questioning detention'. After this period they must release them or cancel their visa and detain them.

If on appeal a cancelled visa is reinstated, it is deemed never to have been cancelled. However, if the person is detained between the cancellation and the reinstatement, the detention is lawful and the person is unable to seek compensation for it. Further, they are liable for the costs of their detention.

Spouse Visa

An Australian woman whose husband was taken into detention when his temporary spouse visa was cancelled told the inquiry:

We were asked to come in to DIMIA – it said in the letter 'finalising of a visa' and we were so excited. We were there seven-and-a-half hours, deprived of drink, toilet or any break whatsoever. There were two women, one would scream at us for an hour and a half, the other would come in and speak softly to us. The lady who interviewed us said she was an investigation officer; she played like the CIA, slamming the desk.

My husband, who has been tortured, slowly slunk down under the desk crying and this was interpreted that he was guilty. When I tried to explain why he was being like he was, I was told if I didn't shut my mouth, they would shut it for me. My husband was taken away by four men in handcuffs after being belted, which I witnessed. When I objected to them handcuffing him, I was escorted by the police out of the building.

We went to court twice while he was in detention to get his visa back, twice, 'Yes, he can get out.' The second time I was told to take $10,000 to DIMIA. I raised $10,000 and a girl came out and said, 'Oh no, he can't see you today,' and I said, 'But I'm supposed to go and get my husband, here's the $10,000.' He wouldn't even come down and speak to me and I went home and rang him. I said, 'What's going on?' He said, 'I don't like his character.' I said, 'But you've never met him,' and he said, 'I'm sorry, I'm not happy with that tribunal decision.'

When he was pulled into detention he was working at a hospital and going to university. Both those things were cancelled and left us in great debt because then we had no income at all. We had to pay for a solicitor to go to these tribunals. Finally, we went to court and that day the lady gave us a decision. She was really angry at the immigration lawyer because he said to her, 'If he'd asked, we would have given him a protection visa.' And she said, 'Why didn't you tell him that, sir?' and he said, 'It's not for us to say,' and she said, 'Well how does he know he could get a protection visa and where is it now?' 'Oh, we don't really want to give it to him now.'

He was whipped with an iron cable, he's got whip marks all over, he had to undress at the last court case right down to his undies and the judge was just looking at all these marks all over him. She couldn't believe it. Usually it takes three weeks, the judge stood up and said, 'I'm going to give my decision now.' The immigration lawyer said, 'You can't, Ma'am,' and she said, 'I will. He's out.'

Six months in the detention centre. I now have a bill for over $25,000 which I was told to pay within a week of him getting out. I said I didn't have that money and they said they wanted two-and-a-half thousand deposit and I didn't have that. Now we are paying it off at $50 a week and we have to have it paid within five years. I was only on sickness benefits before this, and we lived on that for three years. Mr Howard, Senator Vanstone, the opposition leader, all of them have all received a letter from me outlining everything and not one of them has answered me. Not one. I wrote because I don't know why I have to pay it or he has to pay it. He didn't break any laws, they cancelled his visa.

I want to put it on record that I have a Federation Medal for Services to the Armed Forces, I have a Humanities Medal and a Long Service Volunteers Medal. I am an ordained minister, I have worked for many years with St John's as an officer. I've given this country seven children, I served in the army for three years as a paramedic and I was a chaplain in the Navy and the country has gone and just put their fingers up at me. I had a nervous breakdown over this and I ended up for three weeks at a psychiatric hospital and then another three weeks later because I just couldn't cope with this treatment. I think it is disgusting, because all I asked was to be happy with the person I had picked to live the rest of my life with, which is not much longer at my age.

Student Visa

A submission to the inquiry stated that student visa cancellations account for a third of all visa cancellations[566] and that Australia is the only country in the world to incarcerate some of its full-fee-paying international students. In 2007, roughly 80,000 international students were studying in Australia.[567] Almost 6,500 student visas were cancelled in 2006–07.[568]

Between January 2001 and July 2005, almost 2500 former student-visa holders were held in detention centres, of whom about 20 per cent were female. The reasons for detention included: nonattendance, unsatisfactory performance, failure to commence the course, overstaying the visa, withdrawing from study and work breaches. Detained overseas students came from 83 countries, with students from China, India, Vietnam,

Indonesia and Thailand being most frequently incarcerated.[569]

An Indian student who had paid about $40,000 for his education in Australia and had one subject left to complete for his master's degree was caught working extra hours so he could pay for a lawyer to extend his visa. He spent a year in detention trying unsuccessfully to have his visa reinstated.[570]

In December 2002, Bangladeshi student Muhabab Alam was at home when immigration officers came to his home looking for his housemate. When they had finished questioning his housemate, they also conducted a search of Muhabab's room. When they found a payslip stating that he had worked two hours more than the 20 hours a week he was allowed to work, he was taken into detention, where he remained for three weeks. The Magistrates Court and three judges of the Federal Court later found that the department had wrongly cancelled Muhabab's visa in a decision that hinged on the definition of a week. One of the Federal Court judges, Justice James Allsop, told *PM*:

> *My reaction to it ... frankly, is outrage. The idea that Immigration Department officers could come to private premises without a search warrant and without even any reason to suspect that this respondent lived there or had done anything wrong, and ransack his belongings, and on the strength of that, take him away involuntarily, I ask myself if that is something that is tolerated?*[571]

Humanitarian Visa

In April 1999, the war in Kosovo resulted in large numbers of civilians fleeing to refugee camps in Albania and Macedonia. The pressure placed on these camps prompted the UNHCR to issue an appeal to the international community to participate in an international effort to evacuate ethnic Albanian Kosovar refugees from the former Yugoslav Republic of Macedonia.[572] Australia responded to this appeal and agreed to accept 4000 refugees, introducing temporary 'safe haven visas' and establishing eight 'safe havens' around Australia. According to a research paper developed by the NSW Service for the Treatment and Rehabilitation of Torture and Trauma Survivors:

> *Kosovars were first accommodated at the East Hills Defence base where they underwent health screening by the NSW Department of Health,*

were issued identity cards and new clothing and received more detailed information about Australia. After approximately four days they were transported to the longer-term accommodation. Haven Centres were established at the Department of Defence bases at Puckapunyal (Victoria), Bandiana (Vic.), Portsea (Vic.), Singleton (NSW), Hampstead (SA), Brighton (Tas.), and Leeuwin (WA), with East Hills also becoming a Haven Centre for the last group. Services provided at the Haven Centres included: food, health care, education for the children, survival English language training for adults, recreation facilities, small weekly allowance, family tracing service (Red Cross Tracing Service), and professional counselling.[573]

The inquiry heard evidence from a woman whose family arrived in Australia as part of the airlift of refugees from Kosovo. When they arrived here, her two-year-old daughter had a dislocated hip. The woman told the inquiry that her daughter initially received medical treatment, including three operations, but when the family refused to return home and was taken into detention, that ceased. As a result, the child now walks with a permanent limp.

She was in plaster from legs to neck. We have to carry her and she was in lots of pain. Then she had to have every three months an X-ray to make sure she was going well. She had two X-rays but then the third X-ray she couldn't have because suddenly things changed. Immigration decide after 10 months not to give visa any more to us. There were two choices for us: to go back in the country or to go in detention. We decide to go in detention but we didn't know what 'detention' mean.

Immigration minister come for a visit to explain, 'Nobody can stay here and you have to sign voluntarily to go back.' I took my daughter and we all went outside waiting for him. My daughter was in plaster just after her second operation and he come straight to me and he said, 'What happened to your child and why she is in plaster?' And I said she had two operations and she had a dislocated hip but I am very scared because you came to tell us to go back, my place is not safe and my children are so little and he said, 'Don't worry, we are not sending children back who need medical help.' I was so happy. I trust him. But after that all so different happened. And finally we got to Port Hedland.

My daughter, she always crying about her hips pain, but they said we can't do that here. So then I request can I have the phone number so I can phone her surgeon. They said no, but we can organise one appointment so you can talk through the phone with us with him. Three weeks later it was that day. When I went there they already talked to the doctor without me by telling him my daughter is okay. I said why you just talk with him and I wasn't there to listen to what you saying and then I was so angry and I start to scream and swearing.

I said you do not have right to talk for my child because I am a mother and you are not father, you are just the DIMIA person here. You don't know nothing about my child. I said I going to fight, this is not right. And I said if I am going alive from here I will tell the whole world what you been doing to innocent people and how you treating them.

I was outside and crying and crying. I didn't know what to do. But I remember, I had somewhere in my property her doctor visit card and then I write request to get my stuff from property. When I went there I was scared to ask I was looking for my doctor visit card, but I keep saying to ACM not in that bag, not in that bag till I find the right one and I got that piece of paper and I was hiding in my hand so that if they going to see they going to took.

I called the doctor and he asked me who give you my number? I said I had your visit card. And he said they told me from immigration you are not allowed to give your number, and I said don't worry I just had your visit card so you are not in trouble.

I explain what's happen and he write a letter and he forced them to make X-ray but they cancelled three appointments by just lying, we don't have car to send you, doctor is not in hospital. Finally again I ring the doctor and he said I am going to send another letter to make an urgent appointment. It took me five months to get another appointment. I got really crazy, just to keep fighting for everything and then we saw X-ray again. The nurses they look at X-ray in other room. And then I went inside in room without asking them and I saw her bones just look down and her hips was out of place and that's why she was limp and was in lots of pain.

Now I am secure here but still I can't forgive the Australian government; why I was treated like that without committing any crimes, without doing nothing wrong to this country? Just I spent six months in jail and gave my children more suffering.

Cancellation on Character Grounds

In 1999, the Howard government amended section 501 of the *Migration Act 1958* to increase the powers of the immigration minister to deport long-term Australian residents. Previously people who had lived in Australia for more than 10 years could not be deported, even if they had not taken out Australian citizenship. In the three years between 2002 and 2005, 233 permanent residents were deported from Australia, almost double the number deported between 1995 and 1998. Many of these people had arrived in Australia as infants and were unaware that they could be deported,[574] with some not even aware they were not Australian citizens.[575]

The amended section 501 contains a character test which noncitizens must pass if they wish to come to or remain in Australia. Those who fail the test can have their visas refused or cancelled. People automatically fail the test if: they have been sentenced to one term of imprisonment of at least 12 months or if they have been sentenced to more than one term of imprisonment, the totals of which are more than two years; they are or have been associated with others involved in criminal activity; their past and present criminal or general conduct is considered to render them not of good character; or there is a significant risk that they will commit crimes or disrupt or endanger a segment of the Australian community.[576]

When a person fails the character test, immigration officials consider the protection and expectations of the community, the best interest of any children involved and the extent of the person's links to Australia in deciding whether or not to refuse or cancel the visa. People whose visas are cancelled because of their criminal record or conduct are permanently excluded from Australia.

Appeals against decisions to cancel or refuse visas on character grounds can be made to the Administrative Appeals Tribunal (AAT), unless the decision was made by the minister personally. Whether or not people appeal to the AAT, they can appeal to the courts against such a decision.[577] In 2006–07, the department cancelled 116 visas under Section 501 and removed 55 people from Australia.[578]

In 2006, a Senate committee heard that the 1999 amendments to section 501, supported by both major parties, had been introduced following government decisions to deport people under section 201 of the *Migration Act 1958* being overturned by the courts.[579] Under section 201, the power to deport is restricted, with people who have lived in Australia for more than 10 years only able to be deported in exceptional circumstances.

The committee was told by the Department of Immigration that the broader powers to deport in the amended section 501 effectively superseded the provisions of section 201. It said that between 2000–01 and November 2005, 293 people had been removed under section 501, while only 18 people had been deported under section 201.[580] However, the Senate committee stated:

> To accept the proposition would be in effect to bypass the role of the parliament in the debate and passage of laws which affect the fundamental rights and interests of Australians ... The abolition of a significant safeguard against deportation of people who are, in all practical senses, Australian is a matter of serious public policy. Section 201 is the current Australian law in relation to criminal deportation of permanent residents and the abolition of the 10-year rule, if it is to occur, must be repealed by the parliament not by administrative practice.[581]

The Senate committee heard that many people whose visas were cancelled under section 501 had no legal representation and expressed concern about the 'apparent disregard for the welfare of Australian residents.'[582] The department told the committee that people deported under section 501 with special medical needs or who were destitute were referred to a medical facility or provided with a small allowance to purchase food and obtain accommodation upon arrival in the other country.[583] However, the committee recommended that section 501 should not be applied to people who arrived in Australia as minors and stayed for more than 10 years.[584]

A man who has lived in Australia for over 10 years and who was sentenced to more than 12 months in jail for nonviolent offences told the inquiry he was a first-time offender who only became aware that he could be deported while serving his sentence:

> No-one ever told me. I was never warned. I thought I was a permanent resident, then I get some letter from immigration and I'm thinking, 'What the hell is this?' I'd just about finished two years in jail when I got the letter. I haven't had a moment's peace in almost six years, because if I haven't been dealing with jail, I've been dealing with the prospect of being deported.
>
> I was handed a list that said what would be taken into account. The three considerations were devised to weigh against you. Two of

them, protection of the community and expectations of the community will almost certainly go against you. Best interests of the child may go in your favour but the minister or the tribunal will say that you are outnumbered by the other two and cancel the visa. The general manner in which these people make such serious decisions is shocking.

When you're sentenced for a crime, the sentence reflects society's need for protection and at the end of your sentence that need is discharged. I haven't reoffended and I'm no risk to reoffend either. I've lost a family as a result of my actions and I still live with the shame and guilt of my past.

After I was released, I was living in the community for over a year. I was working, I was living my life. Then someone in an air-conditioned office who never met me said I'm a risk to society based on crimes that I did the time for. What do we need the courts for? In such a serious matter, the rules of evidence do not exist and the minister and the tribunals can (and do) completely ignore that which casts a person in a better light.

Some people wonder why an American would be in detention for so long when he could go back to a country where he would be at no risk of being harassed by the government. But wouldn't you stay and fight for your two-and-a-half-year-old son? If I lose, I may not ever see him again, and the High Court has the nerve to tell me this isn't punitive. Despite a court giving me contact orders to see him, the minister and the tribunal were of the belief that long-distance telephone calls are sufficient. I have to be able to show him in maybe 20 years (if I see him at all) that his dad did all he could to stay and raise him. Even if it means an undignified existence in detention, he's worth it.

Australians protested for Hicks. I'm watching these people on TV and thinking to myself, 'How many of you drove past Villawood and Maribyrnong to get to a protest against detention without charge on the other side of the world?' Just because our conditions may be better than Hicks' does not excuse detention without charge and no judicial oversight.

He also told the inquiry that two people currently in detention after having their visas cancelled on character grounds had lived in Australia for over 50 years.

Stefan Nystrom

Stefan Nystrom was born in Sweden when his Swedish-born Australian-citizen mother was there on a holiday. He arrived in Australia 27 days later. His mother did not apply for Australian citizenship for him, so under Australian law he remained Swedish, although he lived in Australia all his life until deported as a 32-year-old with a serious criminal record. He had served eight prison terms for 87 offences including intentionally causing serious injury, armed robbery[585] and aggravated rape.

Held in immigration detention while he fought his deportation, Nystrom won an appeal against it in the Full Court of the Federal Court in July 2005.[586] Judges in the majority decision, Michael Moore and Roger Gyles, said Nystrom's behaviour was no worse than that of many other Australians:

> *The difference is the barest of technicalities. It is the chance result of an accident of birth. Apart from the dire punishment of the individual involved, it assumes that Australia can export its problems elsewhere.*[587]

While dissenting from their decision, Justice Emmett stated:

> *I share the disquiet expressed by their Honours concerning the circumstances in which a man who has spent all of his life in Australia and who has no knowledge of the Swedish language will be removed to Sweden and banished from Australia because of what must be characterised as an accident of history and an oversight on the part of his parents.*[588]

In November 2006, the High Court overturned the Federal Court decision and confirmed the minister's power to deport long-term residents.[589] Nystrom was deported on 30 December 2006.[590]

Robert Jovicic

In November 2005, 38-year-old Robert Jovicic, a convicted burglar and former heroin addict deported to Serbia the year before was found destitute, sleeping on the steps of the Australian embassy in Belgrade. He was born in France to Serbian parents and had lived in Australia since he was two. He had visited Serbia just once in his life and was unable to speak the language.

When he was deported he was under the impression he would be getting a Serbian passport. Instead, he entered the country on a seven-day visa, after which he was rendered stateless when Serbia refused to recognise him as a citizen. This left him unable to work. After publicity about his case, the Australian government organised accommodation and medical tests for him. These showed that he could need back surgery for degenerative disc disease and that he may also have prostate cancer. Jovicic told *Lateline*:

> *Knowing that there is a family back down there that care for me is just the only thing that's keeping me going for the moment. But that even is fading too. I've suffered enough. I think I've paid more than enough and I want to just come back home.*[591]

In March 2006, then immigration minister Kevin Andrews allowed him to return to Australia on a one-month temporary visa, a condition of which was that he not receive medical assistance. He was also required to seek Serbian citizenship. His sister told ABC radio that after prison he had stopped taking drugs and started his own business:

> *Why would someone, who believes they're Australian, has lived here nearly all their lives, want to apply for a nationality somewhere else? ... He was on a new road to a different life and then this deportation happened.*[592]

In February 2007, Jovicic was granted a visa to stay in Australia for two years, with no certainty about his future after that.[593] One year later, new Labor immigration minister Chris Evans used his ministerial-discretion powers to grant Jovicic permanent residence.[594]

Mohamed Haneef

On 2 July 2007, Indian doctor Mohamed Haneef was arrested and held in police custody on suspicion of terrorism-related offences. Haneef was held for 12 days without charge under Australia's anti-terror laws. On 14 July he was charged with 'recklessly' supplying a mobile telephone SIM card to his second cousin whose brother was involved in the failed Glasgow attack in June 2007. Having been charged, Haneef applied for bail and was brought before the Brisbane magistrate's court on Friday 13 July. The magistrate remanded the matter over the weekend and on Monday 16 July granted Dr Haneef bail. Three hours later the minister of immigration,

Kevin Andrews, revoked Dr Haneef's visa on 'character grounds', stating that:

> *I have a responsibility and a duty as minister under the Act to turn my mind to the question of whether Dr Haneef passes the character test.*[595]

Mr Andrews said that based on Australian Federal Police (AFP) advice he was satisfied that Dr Haneef was involved in criminal activity and therefore failed the character test. It later emerged that the AFP and a senior Immigration Department official had corresponded by email over the weekend to plan for the possibility of Dr Haneef getting bail. The email correspondence said in part:

> *Contingencies for containing Mr Haneef and detaining him under the Migration Act, if it is the case he is granted bail on Monday, are in place as per arrangements today.*[596]

While the detention of people whose visas have been cancelled is technically to facilitate their removal from Australia as soon as possible, in Haneef's case the purpose was clearly to keep him in custody, prompting refugee lawyer Julian Burnside to accuse the minister of misusing his power.[597]

In December 2007, the full bench of the Federal Court confirmed an earlier decision that Haneef's visa had been wrongly cancelled by Kevin Andrews, ruling that he had misinterpreted the character test by too narrowly considering Haneef's association with his relatives.[598]

In 2006, the commonwealth and immigration ombudsman, Professor John McMillan, investigated the department's use of Section 501 of the *Migration Act 1958* and made several recommendations, including: that other than for exceptionally serious offences, people should be issued a warning prior to visa cancellation; that consideration of 'the expectations of the Australian community' refer specifically to the compassionate expectations of the community; that an independent assessment of the possible impact a parent's removal would have on a child be undertaken; that the seriousness of the crime and likelihood of repeat offending be considered; and that the health of the visa holder or family members be considered.[599] He concluded:

> *The investigation has highlighted many deficiencies in the content and application of policies and procedures for cancellation of long-term permanent residents' visas under s501. The majority of cases examined*

had at least one, often several, significant omissions or inaccuracies in the information provided to decision-makers. The standard of procedural fairness provided to those liable for cancellation was inconsistent and often fell below that which might be expected given the gravity of the decisions. The outcomes for affected long-term permanent residents can, in many instances, be characterised as unfair and unreasonable.[600]

Departmental Error

In 2005, the Australian government referred 248 cases of wrongful detention to the Commonwealth ombudsman for investigation. The inquiry received evidence regarding two cases where people had been detained due to departmental error. A submission to the inquiry from an asylum seeker living in the community told how she was wrongly detained at a Department of Immigration office before being taken to hospital by ambulance:

I went to the DIMIA office for permission to obtain a tax file number so I could get Medicare. I was made to stand there for more than 30 minutes. Then I felt a man standing next to me. He asked me to come to the compliance office. Then he started to tell me that I am an illegal and he will have to lock me up. I started panicking.

At the compliance office another officer ordered me to get into a room. She closed the door and proceeded to interrogate me, repeating that I was illegal and had to leave the country. I started perspiring and shivering and to get a severe pain in the chest and thought I was going to die. I asked her to get a doctor to see me but she refused.

Another officer joined her and they told me I was illegal because their system showed so. I told them there is something wrong as I have a pending court case. They insisted I sign papers, which I refused to do. I repeatedly asked the officers to check with the court about my status but they refused, saying they did not have to check anything. I gave the officers the name and phone number of the minister's lawyers. After some time the lady officer said she was going to lock me up in the room. I started screaming for help and crying. My mobile phone then rang and the minister's lawyer said she had explained the matter to the DIMIA officers.

A refugee advocate told the inquiry how two young children were taken from their primary school and placed in detention for four months:

I was rung by a mother to say, 'I need some counselling for my child. My child went to school today and his best friend was taken by DIMIA out of primary school.' Two immigration officers turned up at the Stanmore Primary School. The assistant to the headmistress came out to see what they wanted and they said, 'We want these children.' It was a brother and sister, two little Korean children, one 11 and the other six. The 11-year-old commenced school there and the six-year-old had just started.

The assistant to the headmistress was very traumatised and she went to the headmistress and said I've got two people from immigration who want to take these children. The headmistress said I can't release children to any old person, so she rings up the Education Department and the Education Department says you have to let them go. That whole class was completely traumatised.

I got in touch with a lawyer. They were trying to deport them that night. There was a Korean Airlines plane at the airport. The lawyer managed to get an injunction that afternoon. They had already picked up the mother and the mother was in Villawood when they got there. We got them into the court processes.

In the time they were in Villawood, the older child witnessed three major suicide attempts and he said, 'There are crazy people in here. They are always trying to hurt themselves.' The assistant to the head teacher was so traumatised by that she rang me and said, 'I've done the most dreadful thing, I feel like a Judas. I've handed them over.' That little school was totally traumatised, the parents were traumatised, because they thought you send your child off to school in the morning and suddenly a stranger can turn up and just take a student.

We managed to get them out on a bridging visa only to discover that there had been a mistake. They never should have picked them up in the first place. There has never been any form of apology. The younger child is apparently not very well. She's had a lot of missed school days.

COSTS OF DETENTION

As well as the human cost of the Australian government's policies on asylum seekers, there has been widespread criticism of the financial costs associated with them. Costs associated with Australia's mandatory detention laws include: the costs of interception by Australian authorities; the costs of building, maintaining and operating detention centres; the costs of transporting detainees, lawyers and departmental officials to remote locations and the costs associated with legal appeals.

As the contracted provider of health, welfare and security, ACM was paid more than half a billion dollars to manage detention centres between 1998 and 2003.[601] In March 2006, *The Age* reported that on completion of ACM's contract to run detention centres, the Department of Immigration paid it more than it was contractually obliged to pay. The Australian National Audit Office found:

> DIMIA was not able to provide evidence of the criteria it used to ... pay ACM $5.7 million in contract completion payments. The basis on which DIMIA made these payments was doubtful.[602]

GSL took over the running of detention centres from ACM in February 2004. The GSL contract ran from August 2003 to August 2007, with an option to extend for another three years. The Australian National Audit Office expected the total costs for the four years to exceed $400 million.[603]

A submission to the inquiry from the Public Interest Advocacy Centre (PIAC) stated:

> PIAC contends there is no evidence that the privatisation of the operations of immigration detention has resulted in more efficient and economic provision of these services. On the contrary, it has resulted in a large number of costly inquiries and the expenditure of millions of dollars in pre-tendering processes, tender evaluation, contract negotiation and termination payments. More disturbingly, it has resulted in breaches of the human rights of detainees, and a decrease in the accountability and transparency of the provision of immigration detention services.

Detention costs are made up of fixed costs to keep a detention centre operational and the daily costs of accommodating detainees. The daily cost varies depending on where the centre is, the total capacity of the centre and how many people are held there. As at February 2004, detention costs ranged from $111 per day at Villawood to $2,229 per day at the Port Hedland residential housing project.[604] The cost of holding people in the

Christmas Island detention centre is estimated at $1830 per detainee per day[605] and the new detention centre there has cost about $400 million to build.[606]

In 2007, a Senate committee was told it had cost almost $94 million to keep Australian detention centres open in 2005-06, as well as extra costs of up to $189 per detainee per day.[607] The costs included $14.9 million for six months when the Nauru facility was empty[608] and more than $25 million to detain 31 people in Baxter and the Port Augusta residential housing project.[609] In August 2007, 80 guards were employed for 11 detainees held at Baxter and two held at the nearby housing project.

Detention costs do not include the expense of moving detainees between detention centres, deporting them, or funding litigation to oppose asylum seeker cases. A barrister told the inquiry:

> The government will fight every single point. They have private law firms acting for them who behave as though they are engaged in commercial litigation. They fight every case very, very hard which racks up the costs and the time involved.

In April 2007, two Chinese men who had been in detention for seven years were deported at a cost of about $45,000. This included the costs of six police, immigration and medical staff and airfares for 35 seats purchased to create an 'exclusion zone' on the aircraft.[610]

In contrast to the costs of holding asylum seekers in detention, asylum seekers who arrive with a valid visa and who are processed while living in the community can work to support themselves, or may be eligible for assistance through the government funded Asylum Seeker Assistance Scheme. Managed by the Red Cross, the scheme provides roughly 89 per cent of Centrelink's Special Benefit payment to each asylum seeker. In 2001, it assisted 2691 asylum seekers and cost an average of just over $4000 per person.[611]

The high cost of detaining asylum seekers in immigration detention centres was acknowledged by the secretary of the Immigration Department, Andrew Metcalfe, when he told a June 2007 gathering it had.

> ... started implementing a new, more cost-effective Onshore Detention Strategy. This strategy provides for a range of placement options for people who are detained. It moves away from the previous 'one size fits all' approach where being in immigration detention was synonymous

with placement in a detention centre ... There are clear savings to government as additional centres will not need to be built.[612]

Pacific Solution

Australia's offshore detention strategy consumed exorbitant amounts of taxpayer's money. An August 2007 report concluded that the 'Pacific Solution' had cost more than $1 billion over six years. During this period less than 1700 asylum seekers were processed, an average cost of more than half a million dollars per person.[613] In a speech in February 2004, refugee lawyer Julian Burnside QC stated:

> *We could have bought each of them a house in Adelaide or Brisbane for what it has cost us to dump them on Nauru, and we would have created a lot of goodwill by doing so. Instead, we have simply destroyed their hope and their lives.*[614]

Additional costs include charter flights to move asylum seekers offshore, which amounted to nearly $5 million in 2005-06, and the cost of flying lawyers and departmental officers to Nauru and Manus Island.[615] In 2003 and 2004, Aladdin Sisalem was the sole asylum seeker on Manus Island for 10 months, at a cost of $250,000 per month.[616]

Apart from paying the cost of running two detention centres on Nauru, as part of the agreement allowing it to send asylum seekers there, Australia has provided Nauru with more than $100 million in aid over the past five years. In 2007, journalist Brendan Nicholson argued, 'Australia is all but running the supposedly independent state of Nauru.' He detailed the cost of Australia providing Nauru with a finance team, a commissioner of police, three police advisers, a director of education, secretary of health, utilities manager and director of nursing at Nauru Hospital.[617] A former staff member of the official Australian aid agency has described aid payments to Nauru as 'an unmitigated bribe' to ensure the continuation of the Pacific Solution.[618]

In April 2003, then immigration minister Philip Ruddock told *Meet the Press*:

> *In relation to the Pacific solution, has it been a success? It has been an enormous success. Has it cost more money? In some respects it did, in other respects it did not.*[619]

Part 4

LIFE AFTER DETENTION

The People's Inquiry heard extensive evidence from asylum seekers and their supporters about their lives after detention. People who spoke to the inquiry were living in the community on a variety of conditions. Some remained technically in detention and were either guarded by or required to report to authorities on a regular basis. Others were granted one of a range of temporary visas with differing entitlements to work, welfare and health care. Some had become permanent residents or Australian citizens. Information provided to the inquiry highlighted the devastating impact detention continued to have on people after their release, particularly on those who had been detained for extended periods, and the difficulties faced by those whose immigration status remained unresolved.

Alternative Places of Detention

Asylum seekers placed in 'alternative places of detention' remain detained outside an actual immigration detention centre. Detainees who require hospitalisation or detainee children who attend schools in the community are deemed to remain detained in these places, and are guarded by actual or 'designated' detention officers. Residential Housing Projects are deemed 'alternative places of detention', as are some homes provided by refugee support organisations or individuals caring for detainees with special needs.

A worker in a refugee assistance organisation told the inquiry the requirement to provide constant supervision of detainees living under this arrangement placed an enormous financial and emotional burden on community groups and volunteers:

> When people are placed in alternative places of detention, DIMIA [Department of Immigration, Multicultural and Indigenous Affairs] has required us to provide accompaniment 24 hours a day, seven days a week. This is a huge undertaking and where children have been involved the school principal or other senior teachers have actually become designated people for the purpose of the Migration Act. It's a very, very complicated and difficult system.
>
> We got to the point last summer where we said we are not doing any more of these unless you give us the money, so they gave us the money. We actually wear out our volunteers doing this and most of our volunteers are people who are retired. They actually do things like go away and we have this huge hole in our volunteer base.

The inquiry also heard evidence that many detainees held in alternative places of detention were placed there because they were seriously mentally ill. Volunteers who cared for them received a pittance from the Department of Immigration for doing so, with concerns being raised about their ability to provide the level of care required. A refugee supporter cared for a refugee who had been in a psychiatric hospital, rather than have him returned to Baxter. The supporter was therefore technically a detention officer and told the inquiry:

> My concern is that particularly for people who are very ill, perhaps I don't provide as much support as they need during the night. I don't know whether I am being a mother duck if I run out and say, 'Are you all right?' or if I should leave them alone. Sometimes you think am I doing as good a job as they need, yet I think I am doing as best a job as I can.
>
> If I can get half a day off just to disappear somewhere, it's appreciated. I've said to DIMA [Department of Immigration and Multicultural Affairs], a trained psychiatric nurse is on duty and then she has time off. I don't. I have been quite willing to let them know. It is not a picnic. One chap was $400 a week and that was fine. The next chap, it was negotiated to $300. It amused me because I know a chap who was in community detention with guards present so there were six guards, eight hour shifts, two each, and this puny little fellow who is not going to hurt a fly and that comes to a lot of money.

Another refugee supporter told the inquiry that an asylum seeker was released into her care from a psychiatric hospital:

> I was a detention officer in my own home for 24 hours, which is very, very hard. It had its toll on me and I had to go away to see my children because they were worried about me. I had been seeing this sick man and he had never asked me for anything. He was still on medication and the doctors hadn't told him or me that he shouldn't drink alcohol. His friends flocked to see him and he had a few drinks and I had two very bad nights with him where I was really scared when he was shouting at me and really upset. He had a girl of his own and he is wanting to get her out. He was seeing her face at night and that came when he was on the alcohol, he got all this dreaming and he couldn't help it, but it was very upsetting.
>
> All the others I had had in my home I could take them straight to

Centrelink, the bank, Medicare and I couldn't do a thing with him. They wouldn't let him put money in the bank. That made him frustrated and he knew I was getting paid for this and he started to want everything he saw. I was getting $400 a week; he spent that. He wanted a new phone, I got that and he wanted one for his friend too. I didn't like to stop doing it because I felt so sorry for him.

You don't realise until you get them in your house that any time you think to pop down to the shop you have got to take him. Any time he wants something you have got to drive him and it's really wearing because they are hoping they can do everything for all their friends and there you are having to say no, you can't do that. It was very difficult because he thought he was going to be more free than he was.

A refugee advocate and social worker told the inquiry that one woman who had twice attempted suicide was released into the care of community volunteers who were unaware of her mental health history:

It was irresponsible of DIMIA to place this woman in the care of volunteers without ascertaining their ability to help her if she again felt she wanted to take her life.

On 21 January 2005, three weeks after detainees reported Cornelia Rau 'screaming incoherently, rolling round on the ground, eating dirt and smearing faeces'[620] the Department of Immigration discussed the possibility of releasing Cornelia Rau into an alternative place of detention with the Australian Refugee Association.[621]

The inquiry also heard that the stringent conditions of this detention arrangement led to a deterioration in people's mental health. A refugee advocate told the inquiry that one man held in an alternative place of detention attempted suicide after telling her that having to have an escort every time he left the house made him feel like a dog awaiting his master to come and walk him in the park. A worker in a refugee assistance organisation told the inquiry another man had also attempted suicide while in this form of detention.

In early 2007, the Human Rights and Equal Opportunity Commission [HREOC] found that alternative detention requirements placed a substantial burden on 'designated officers' and that the requirement for 24-hour accompaniment clearly limited the liberty of those so detained.[622]

Habeas Corpus

Some asylum seekers were released from detention on court order, known as 'habeas corpus'. It applied to people whose detention was deemed illegal by the Federal Court because they had agreed to return to their home country, but there was no practical prospect of that occurring in the foreseeable future. Others had asked to be removed from Australia, but were 'stateless' because they were not recognised as citizens by any country and therefore could not be sent anywhere else.

Australia is signatory to the Convention Relating to the Status of Stateless Persons (1954) and the Convention on the Reduction of Statelessness (1961), both of which require signatories to assist and protect stateless people, including through the granting of nationality. However, these obligations are not incorporated into domestic law and there is no visa available for people who arrive in Australia and are found to be stateless. The only way they can be granted a visa is through the personal intervention of the immigration minister.

On 6 August 2004, the High Court ruled in two cases that asylum seekers released from detention under habeas corpus could be kept in detention indefinitely[623] and some were subsequently re-detained. These decisions meant that a Palestinian man who had been freed almost a year earlier and was due to appear in court again in September 2004 would face re-detention if he attended the court case as required.

Three days before the court case he contacted his lawyer, Abby Hamdan, and told her he would give her his mobile phone number so she could provide him with legal advice, but that she should keep this confidential. A week after he failed to appear at the court hearing, the Department of Immigration issued Hamdan with a notice requiring her to divulge her client's mobile phone number. It is an offence under the *Migration Act* to refuse to comply with such a notice without reasonable excuse. But she refused to provide the telephone number on the grounds that it was subject to legal professional privilege, a position the Federal Court supported.[624]

Asylum seekers released under habeas corpus were utterly dependent on charity, having no visa and no right to any entitlements whatsoever. An asylum seeker who was recognised as a refugee after more than five years in Australia told the inquiry:

I signed for deportation. They said they will deport me within two weeks. But it take three years and they didn't deport me. I said please, send me to Syria, send me to Iraq. They said we can't. I said send me to Somalia, to Sudan, anywhere, I don't like to stay in Australia. I contact the United Nation and Amnesty International. There is no-one can help me. After three years my case in Federal Court and they release me.

I have to report every day to immigration, even in Saturdays and Sundays to the police station. No money from Centrelink, no Medicare. I am not allowed to work, even as a volunteer. Not allowed to study. Two student lawyers working with Amnesty International send my case to over 122 countries to take me as a refugee. I have letters from all these countries. They said that you are already in a country accept refugees, should Australian government accept you as a refugee.

A refugee advocate told the inquiry a refugee released under habeas corpus who stayed with her had to report to officials on the other side of the city seven times a week despite having no source of income. The lack of entitlements and having no certainty about their immigration status made adjusting to life outside detention harder. An asylum seeker released under habeas corpus told the inquiry:

I have been in detention for so long and I have still psychological problems. When I came out I was a little bit happier because of the freedom after a long time. But now it's starting to get worse again. I feel like myself is totally changed.

Residence Determination

In June 2005, the Department of Immigration introduced another form of community detention known as residence determination, which does not require a person to be accompanied by a 'designated officer'. People under residence determination must generally live at a specified address, report to the department regularly and not engage in paid work.[625] Nongovernment organisations are funded to provide casework, housing and financial support to people detained in these conditions.

In January 2007, HREOC found that residence determinations were the best of the alternative detention arrangements because they offer relative autonomy. It urged the Department of Immigration to provide them to all people held in detention centres for three months or longer.[626] The following year it again urged the increased use of residence determinations stating that they offered 'the opportunity to engage in community life, the ability to provide a normal living environment for their children, and privacy and freedom from supervision'.[627]

In a submission to the inquiry, the Brotherhood of St Laurence stated that a national project funded by the department and led by the Red Cross was developing operational guidelines and referral protocols for releasing people under a residence determination.

However, over two years later, residence determinations were granted only in 'exceptional circumstances' by the minister personally. At 30 June 2007, 13 family groups, 13 adults, three unaccompanied minors and 'one accompanied minor whose mother was lawfully in the community' were detained under residence determination arrangements.[628]

Removal Pending Bridging Visa (RPBV)

The RPBV came into effect in May 2005, in the aftermath of the Cornelia Rau scandal. Asylum seekers can only apply for a RPBV after they have been personally invited to do so by the immigration minister. Criteria to be satisfied before an invitation is issued include: the person is in detention; the minister is satisfied their removal is not immediately practical but that they will co-operate with future removal attempts; and that their visa application has been finally determined.[629]

Those invited to apply for the visa have seven days in which to accept the offer before it is withdrawn. The visa allows asylum seekers to live in the community, to work and to access Medicare and income support. RPBVs can be cancelled if the minister decides that removal is now reasonably practicable or if visa conditions are breached.

In a submission to the inquiry, UnitingJustice Australia and Hotham Mission Asylum Seeker Project argued:

> In effect, the RPBV rewards asylum seekers who are willing to forgo a further appeals process in return for a release from detention.

In July 2005, Australia's longest serving immigration detainee, Peter Qasim, was granted a RPBV after six years and 10 months in detention, making him one of just 15 people holding RPBVs as at 30 June 2007.[630] As at January 2008, his future remained uncertain. He told a newspaper:

It has already been a very long time. I don't know what is my future. Maybe I will be deported. I studied and then I left study and then go back to work, and then go back to study ... I don't know what I do. It is very hard to find work and if you get a job, it is very hard to concentrate. [631]

A refugee supporter told the inquiry uncertainty about their future affected the mental health of people on a RPBV:

They keep on hanging on that string, terrified that at any time they could be nabbed. I know one chap who got so frightened that he stopped reporting to DIMIA, so therefore he became a person who was missing and he wasn't missing, he was just psychiatrically unwell and too frightened to front up.

Another refugee supporter told the inquiry:

I contacted employment agencies, but because he had removal pending on his visa he had no priority. On one visit to the doctor he was told his Medicare card had expired. I told him to go to Medicare and ask for a new card. The staff phoned what I think was the Medicare head office, but he thought was DIMIA. He thought he was not issued with a new card because the removal might be close. He constantly lives with the thought that he may not be allowed to remain in Australia. It is difficult for him to form a relationship or live a normal life because of the removal pending visa.

An asylum seeker on a RPBV told the inquiry:

I took my unit, I tried to be a good citizen, to pay my taxes. I started to work and to look at the future. But last month again I received a yellow envelope which we come to know is not good news. It took me almost two hours to open that envelope and when I open it there was a letter from the Department of Immigration that one of the conditions for visa is that you have to comply with the filling this form for passport.

Another asylum seeker on a RPBV, who was later granted a refugee visa, was directed to prepare travel documents to return to his home country. His Australian supporter told the inquiry:

We immediately went into, my husband and I, where are we going to hide him. As we were doing this I thought, we are living in Australia and yet we are thinking about a place to hide someone so that they can be safe. I just found that quite amazing.

Bridging Visas

Bridging visas are visas issued to people in Australia who would otherwise be unlawful and subject to detention. They are issued to keep a person legally in Australia while they await the outcome of a visa application or an appeal against a decision to refuse a visa. Bridging visas are the least beneficial visas that can be granted by the Department of Immigration. There are various categories of bridging visas, all of which confer varying entitlements to work, study and travel. Amnesty International has estimated that 8000 to 10,000 people in Australia hold a bridging visa.[632]

A submission to the inquiry argued that even people on bridging visas which allowed them to work found it difficult to get work, as bridging visas are often issued for a few months at a time. People on bridging visas do not generally have clear time frames about when their immigration status will be resolved, as they do not know when decisions about their visa or appeal will be made.

Some asylum seekers on bridging visas, overwhelmingly those who came to Australia on a valid visa and have never been in detention, are eligible for assistance through the Red Cross administered Asylum Seeker Assistance Scheme. It provides income support (89 per cent of Centrelink's Special Benefit payment), a casework service, counselling, referral and advocacy. Eligibility for assistance ends when the Refugee Review Tribunal (RRT) has made a decision on the protection visa application. One asylum seeker told the inquiry:

I have two hands and two legs and I have the brain and I don't know why should we be assisted by Red Cross instead of working and paying tax and being beneficial for Australia.

Most people on bridging visas are required to report to the Department of Immigration. A refugee advocate told the inquiry:

One family was told to return with tickets and because they were negotiating a further court case, they arrived a day before the visa expired to explain the situation. Their excuse was not accepted despite the fact that the family said they would go and buy the tickets immediately, since their visa still allowed them one more day. An attempt was made to have the parents and child put in detention. The child understood what was happening and she told me she deliberately screamed her head off so the staff took only the husband and dumped him in Villawood.

His wife was not allowed to speak with him for several days. She wasn't even told where he was. She rang the department each day and they wouldn't give her any indication. He was not aware what had happened to his family and began a hunger strike. The wife eventually persuaded DIMIA to allow her to speak to him and after a week in detention he was released on a $20,000 bond. The child could not go to school as the family could not afford overseas fees for her prep year. She taught herself English from the TV which her father found broken on the nature strip and brought home and fixed.

Bridging Visa E (BVE)

The least beneficial bridging visa, the BVE, is held by almost 3000 people in Australia.[633] Following changes to migration regulations in 1997, this visa does not generally allow people to work (including voluntary work), study, travel or access Medicare. People on BVEs include people released from detention and community based asylum seekers (including those originally recognised as refugees, granted a Temporary Protection Visa and refused further protection after three years). BVE holders must generally report to the Department of Immigration on a regular basis.

There are two subclasses of BVE. The only one that people in detention can apply for is a BVE (Subclass 051). To satisfy the criteria for the visa, they must be either over 75, under 18, married to an Australian citizen or have a medical condition that cannot be treated adequately in detention.

But even the limited numbers of asylum seekers in detention who met the criteria for grant of BVE (Subclass 051) found them difficult to obtain, with only 167 of these visas issued between 2001 and 2005.[634] At 30 June 2007, there was only one person living in the community on a BVE (subclass 051) and none were granted during the 2006-07 financial year.[635] Refugee advocate Kate Gauthier told the inquiry:

*There is a child who lost sight in one eye because we were fighting for
a medical bridging visa. He was not getting adequate care in detention
and it was only after court cases that they released the child, who has
ongoing health issues because of the time it took.*

A visitor to detention told the inquiry that BVE applicants also often
needed to provide evidence to the Department of Immigration that their
care needs would be met in the community:

*I was told I had 36 hours to find a doctor, a dentist, all the support
networks for him and so I quickly rang everyone I knew and we got it
all together. We did manage it, but how many people have got someone
on the outside that could do that?*

Despite government reluctance to grant BVEs to those in detention, research
by Hotham Mission, which provides services to asylum seekers living in the
community, found that 43 per cent of BVE holders interviewed (who had
a final decision) were approved as refugees and 57 per cent were rejected
and left the country. No asylum seeker absconded. It also found that being
provided with specialist support through its Asylum Seeker Project reduced
distress for asylum seekers. In contrast to constant critical incidents in
immigration detention, during a two-year period Hotham Mission housing
twice called an ambulance after self-harm attempts and called the mental
health Crisis Assessment Team three times.[636]

A barrister told the inquiry that people on a BVE also found it
difficult being wholly dependent on others:

*I used to see it as a victory getting somebody out on a bridging visa,
but now I don't because they can't work. I have one client awaiting
a decision that's taken 12 months. He's going crazy because he can't
support himself, he has no dignity, he's reliant on handouts.*

A worker from a refugee assistance organisation told the inquiry:

*We have one client who is not allowed to do work or vocational
training. It is challenging to set goals because his future is uncertain and
support is around social visits rather than focusing on tasks to start a
new life in a new country.*

A refugee advocate gave an example of how bridging visa conditions that prohibit even voluntary work impact on people's self-esteem:

> We had a trained theatre sister on a Bridging E looking after her two daughters and she was slowly but surely becoming more frustrated and disturbed with her circumstances. On her own initiative she went to one of the hospitals in Canberra and arranged to take flowers around to those who were ill, just to get herself back in the environment she had originally worked in. I had the tragic job of telling her, having confirmed with the Department of Immigration, that she really shouldn't do that because it would be a breach of her visa condition.

Research carried out by Hotham Mission found that more than two thirds of BVE holders were homeless or at risk of homelessness. It gave case examples of a woman with six children who had been released from detention on psychological grounds with no means of income sharing one flat with another family of four, and of a young woman who lived between friends and was hospitalised for malnutrition.[637]

The requirement that people on BVEs report to the Department of Immigration placed further financial strain on them. Hotham Mission found that of those asylum seekers required to report, over 80 per cent had to report once a week or more frequently. As they had no means of income support, Hotham Mission has spent more than $15,000 per year on travel tickets.[638]

A woman on a BVE told the inquiry:

> This policy has forced us to beg. Day in and day out, from morning until night, we are begging. Begging for our food, begging for housing, begging for transport tickets, begging for clothing. Do we want to work, earn and look after ourselves and our families? The answer to that is a positive yes. We want to feel like humans again.

A former detainee told the inquiry that the government policy of denying work and Medicare rights forced some people to work illegally to survive:

> It is the government that's putting people through criminal activities and makes good people become criminals.

Asylum seekers granted BVEs on the grounds that they needed medical care that could not be provided in detention were some of the most physically and mentally vulnerable cases. They included people with severe burns, failing eyesight and serious psychiatric disorders. Research by Hotham Mission found that BVE holders released from detention were more than three times as likely to seek medical attention as those who had never been in detention, that they had a comparatively high use of medical services and a high dependence on medication. This was especially the case for mental health services.[639]

However their status as BVE holders meant they were not able to access Medicare, placing enormous strain on refugee supporters and organisations to find pro bono health services. A worker in a refugee assistance organisation told the inquiry the Department of Immigration did not even give people in this situation information about community services they could contact for help:

> People are released from Villawood on a Bridging Visa E, often without any English, often without any money. A lot of the people are being released because they have mental health difficulties. In the forums in which I participate with relatively senior DIMIA representation, we have been lobbying to have them give people on their way out just a list of the welfare organisations from which they can seek support. Our argument has been this is publicly available information, you are not really doing anything other than clipping out relevant sections of the White Pages, do that at least.

In 2003, Hotham Mission's report into living conditions for BVE recipients[640] found they lived in abject poverty without mainstream welfare supports:

> The impact of these issues, coupled with the long waiting period and the prolonged passivity of this group, included high levels of anxiety, depression, mental health issues and a general reduction in overall health and nutrition. High levels of family breakdown, including separation and divorce, were also recorded. Problems were compounded by the lack of routine medical care available to expectant mothers, children, victims of torture and trauma, and people with mental illness.

A man who spent 18 months in detention before being released on a bridging visa told the inquiry:

When you are out you are glad, but the depression starts setting in again after a couple of months. Some people in the community have given me a place to stay and some financial assistance and food but you are scared to get 'flu, you are scared to have an upset stomach. I think what happens if I am crossing the road and I get hit by a car? How am I going to get treated?

In a submission to the inquiry, a refugee assistance worker gave an example of how asylum seekers on bridging visas are sometimes refused medical treatment:

The slightest sniffle from the children brought about anxiety in her. One night, she took one of the children to a local medical centre because she was concerned about his fever. She was turned away because she did not have a Medicare card.

More than 24 per cent of BVE holders surveyed by Hotham Mission had been refused medical treatment, including three pregnant women being unable to access obstetric care, a six-year-old child with chronic asthma being denied access to a hospital outpatient clinic[641] and a woman unable to receive remission testing for cancer.[642]

In a submission to the inquiry, UnitingJustice Australia and Hotham Mission Asylum Seeker Project stated that the Victorian Department of Human Services has discovered at least 35 cases of people on BVEs who are HIV positive.

Hotham Mission reported that a single mother discharged herself from hospital the day after a mild heart attack when she was presented with a large hospital bill.[643] A worker in a refugee assistance organisation told the inquiry:

A young man had some back problems and he had to have an operation. He's on a BVE and his wife is Australian and she's a student so they had to borrow $5000 for the surgery. He had the back operation and asked to be discharged from the hospital the day after because of the $750 a day fee.

A GP working in a refugee health service told the inquiry:

Public pronouncements about the release of pregnant women or children

*obscures the reality of their situation which is that they are thrown out
with no resources, utterly dependent on the goodwill of the community.
As a doctor this means that for even the most minor of health concerns
I have to negotiate with pathology laboratories, hospitals, other doctors
and pharmacies to buy the most minimal diagnostic or therapeutic
services.*

BVE holders also had difficulty accessing medications, with one man
unable to buy medication his son needed:

*His son became ill and was taken to hospital ... At one stage the doctors
believed he was suffering from cancer, but he was later diagnosed with
a deadly but treatable virus. He slowly recovered but required constant
check-ups and ... medication. After his son was discharged, [the father]
stopped at the chemist ... The pharmacist asked for the highest price as
the family was not eligible for the Pharmaceutical Benefit Scheme, had
no Medicare or Health Care Card. [He] pleaded with the pharmacist,
offering all that he had: $16.40. The pharmacist refused and only part
of the prescription was purchased at that time.*[644]

In a submission to the inquiry, a worker in a refugee assistance organisation
explained how being on a BVE impacted on social relationships:

*As a 17-year-old, it is extremely difficult for him to have open and
honest relationships with his peers. He is too ashamed to tell them he is
an asylum seeker living in the community entirely reliant on emergency
relief. This support is below the poverty line and does not enable him
to participate in the normal activities of most 17-year-olds. He feels he
cannot invite his friends to where he is living. He looks at his friends
sometimes and thinks they know nothing of the world he knows, they
could never understand.*

Children also found attending school difficult when there was no money
for transport, uniforms, books and excursions. One report gave the
following example:

*Asif is a 13-year-old boy from the Middle East. He stated that he was
ashamed to tell his teacher or his friends that he was an asylum seeker
and that his family had no money. He was constantly being held after*

school for detention for being late and for not attending sports. But Asif did not have any sneakers or a travel ticket to get to school. Instead he had to walk almost two hours to get there. He went without food many days as he had no money for lunch and nothing to take from home. On the days he slept in and raced to school, he would spend so much time walking and then being kept behind that he often wouldn't eat all day until his evening meal. Asif's family was forced to move three times during his four-month stay at high school.[645]

Many people on bridging visas also feared being re-detained when reporting to immigration. A former detainee who spent four months on a bridging visa told the inquiry he took a supporter with him every time he reported. A refugee advocate told the inquiry:

Once the DIMIA computer made a mistake and said that he was illegal and we were so scared that weekend we actually went and stayed at my Mum's house because we thought they might come and get him.

A lawyer told the inquiry about one of her clients who was re-detained:

His bridging visa had been issued on two conditions. One was that he resided at a particular address and the other one was that he not work; and he was found to be doing some work and not living at the address so they brought him into detention.

We took the case to the MRT [Migration Review Tribunal] at which time the member heard all the evidence surrounding both breaches and made a finding that neither was serious enough for this young man to be detained and he should be released. The department was very upset.

There was a day-and-a-half of us on the phone with this particular individual saying, 'It's an order from the Tribunal, you have to abide by that.' And him saying, 'I don't agree with it. I am not going to abide by it.' Then it was getting to his superiors. It took them three days to release him and the only reason they actually did was because we got the ombudsman involved.

But they let him walk out the door and they re-detained him. The paperwork only mentioned one of the conditions being breached so they breached him on the other condition. They hadn't actually officially brought that before the Tribunal even though the member had looked at all the evidence for both breaches.

You think, 'This is just outrageous! Wait until I get in touch with the MRT, they are really going do something about this.' But they said they couldn't do anything because it was within departmental policy and the only way to fight that was to take it back before the MRT which we did. But he was in detention for another seven days.

In a submission to the inquiry, UnitingJustice Australia and Hotham Mission Asylum Seeker Project told how asylum-seeker parents of a child born after their claims had been rejected by the RRT were told to submit a separate refugee application for the child. When the family's case was being considered for ministerial intervention, the child was not included. The next time the father reported to immigration he was told the child was unlawful and would be removed, causing him great stress before he was told it would be sorted out.

Even when aware of the fragile state of some asylum seekers, the department was often insensitive to their anxiety. UnitingJustice Australia and Hotham Mission told the inquiry about one woman's experience:

The social worker spoke to the compliance officer prior to attending with the client to make the department aware of the client's fragile mental state. On attending the interview, the compliance officer took issue with the fact that the client had lost her passport and had lodged a second 417, stating that he found it difficult to believe the client was making preparations to leave the country. He said he might need a bond lodged for security even though the client offered to report frequently.

The client was asked to return to compliance the next day showing evidence that she was making preparations to leave the country. She took an itinerary showing flight bookings and a fax to the Embassy requesting forms to be sent for a replacement passport. The compliance officer said he needed a $10,000 bond to be lodged by 5pm that day. The client only had $2000 available and the compliance officer stated he would detain the mother and separate her from her children.

The client started to become extremely distressed and agitated. The compliance manager was brought in to talk to the client but she became very scared thinking she was going to be detained. She started to scream and become uncontrollable. An ambulance was called as she had difficulty breathing and started to show symptoms of an asthma attack. The client was then hospitalised.

Research undertaken by Hotham Mission's Asylum Seeker Project, which worked with more than 200 BVE holders between February 2001 and February 2003, found that 55 per cent of those interviewed had been waiting for a decision for four years or longer.[646] A refugee supporter told the inquiry the government's general policy of deterring asylum seekers was reflected in the policy of bridging visas:

> It seems to me that part of the strategy of using visas of that type, particularly for protracted periods, is to force people to want to depart Australia. I don't think I can think of any other rationale.

However, even those who did decide they wanted to leave Australia faced difficulties. As they had no work rights, they could not afford the costs of visas, passport renewals and airfares and the Department of Immigration does not pay for people to leave the country unless they are in detention. Hotham Mission told the inquiry that it had paid over $40,000 in airfares in four years to keep its clients out of detention, but no longer had funds to continue this.

In March 2006, the Senate Legal and Constitutional Affairs Committee recommended BVE holders be granted work rights, stating:

> A policy which renders a person destitute is morally indefensible and an abrogation of responsibility by the Commonwealth.[647]

The Department of Immigration has also conducted a review of bridging visas, presenting the findings and recommendations to the then immigration minister, Amanda Vanstone. The results of the review, yet to be made public, were under consideration by the Howard government from January 2007 until it was voted out of office in November 2007.

Temporary Protection Visas (TPVs)

The three-year TPV was introduced in October 1999 with the aim of reducing the number of asylum seekers arriving in Australia by boat. The overwhelming majority of asylum seekers released from detention between then and mid-2008 (when the TPV was abolished by the Rudd Labor government) were granted a TPV. Prior to 1999, all people recognised as refugees, whether they applied onshore or from overseas, were granted permanent residence. People granted a TPV could apply for a permanent visa after 30 months, at which time they needed to show they were still in need of protection.

The preference of John Howard's government for TPV holders to leave Australia was made clear in public comments by then immigration minister Philip Ruddock. In June 2002, he issued a press release stating it was time for the first TPV holders to re-apply if they still wanted protection:

> ... experienced officers of my Department ... will be looking closely at the current situation in the home country. It may be that there is no longer any need for some TPV holders to be in fear of persecution if they return home. As TPV holders reach the 30-month date from the grant of their visas, my Department will write to them to remind them they will need to make another application, or make arrangements to leave Australia.[648]

The press release also suggested that those successful in a further refugee application would be granted another TPV rather than a permanent visa, referring to the 'seven day rule'. Introduced just before the 2001 election, this rule stipulated that asylum seekers who had spent more than seven days in a third country on their way to Australia would only ever be eligible for successive TPVs. It targeted almost all asylum seekers, the overwhelming majority of whom spent weeks in Indonesia, many as a result of 'disruption' activities against people smugglers supported by the Australian government.

In April 2003, Ruddock defended Australia's involvement in the Iraq war while Iraqi refugees remained in detention and on TPVs. He told *Meet the Press*:

> We have had a very generous program. Now when you come to TPVs, they are for people who were not prepared to come through the front door, who sought to access Australia unlawfully, and what we said is, if you need protection – and 4186 people were granted protection – you will not be returned to Iraq, you will be safe, you will be secure, but you will not get a permanent residency outcome.[649]

Two months later, he told ABC Radio:

> Those people, at the expiry of their Temporary Protection Visa, they

will have an opportunity to put a further protection claim ... If at the
end of the process they are a rejected asylum seeker, they'll be treated in
exactly the same way as any other rejected asylum seeker, and they'll be
given an opportunity to make arrangements to leave, and if they don't,
they'll be re-detained.[650]

The TPV created a two-tier refugee system, with those holding it not entitled to important benefits afforded to others recognised as refugees. TPV holders could not sponsor family members to live in Australia and could not re-enter the country if they left. They could not access federally funded settlement services such as migrant resource centres, employment training programs, accommodation and bond assistance. If they wanted to study at university they had to pay full overseas student fees and they were not eligible for the 510 hours of free English tuition provided to other refugees. It was also harder for them to find work due to their temporary visa.

Several studies found that TPVs impacted adversely on the ability of refugees to settle in Australia[651] and that services federally funded for other refugees were provided to TPV holders in an ad-hoc manner by state governments, community organisations and volunteers.

The inquiry heard evidence about the consequences for people released from detention on TPVs abruptly and with little support for coping with life in Australia. Upon being told they had a visa, people were given an hour or two to pack their belongings and leave, often after years of detention. They were usually not allowed to say goodbye to their friends. A man who spent six years in detention told the inquiry:

When I got visa in Baxter I asked five minutes to say hello to everybody,
guards they say no, hurry up take your gear and go totally out and I
couldn't see my friends.

A woman who married an asylum seeker in detention told the inquiry:

My husband had an hour to leave after three years of detention. The
next day he wanted to come with me to visit all his friends and say
goodbye properly, but they wouldn't let him in because he didn't have
three forms of identification.

Although cherishing their freedom, newly released asylum seekers faced enormous challenges. While some had made connections with Australian supporters, they knew there was hostility to them in the broader community. Many could speak little English and were traumatised by their detention experience. A refugee advocate who researched access to support services after detention found that detainees were given an average of $200 and a bus ticket on immediate release. However, some people reported they only received $75 and no bus ticket.[652] A man who spent six months in Woomera told the inquiry:

> They put us on a plane to Adelaide and later that flight to Brisbane. We were accommodated in a hotel, we had no idea why we are going there. We were paying around $150 and I told her, 'Look I can't staying there, I do have some connection with people in Melbourne and I would like to go to Melbourne.' Because they have distributed a small amount of money to every family member, we collected all the money to purchase a ticket to Melbourne.

The inquiry also heard that the lack of comprehensive settlement support for TPV holders left people in vulnerable situations on their release from detention. Baxter visitor David Leach told the inquiry about the release of one of the men he visited:

> When he got released they said he had to go to Adelaide to get his visa stamped. I was going to Adelaide the next day for work. So I said, 'Look, can he come and stay at my house tonight and I'll take him down with me tomorrow?' They said, 'No, he must go on the bus today.' I said, 'But he comes from a village in the middle of Afghanistan. He knows nothing about the big wide world. I visited him for two years. Please let him come with me.' They forced him on the bus under the threat of not giving him his visa. They left him in a flea pit hotel in Hindley Street, which is the diviest mongrel street in Adelaide.

A woman who became friends with a refugee family told the inquiry:

> This little family were put on a bus and a plane. They were met by somebody; they were taken to a Housing Trust place. It was winter, they had no clothes to speak of, no money, no food, and they seemed to be absolutely abandoned from then on. Nobody came back to see that

*they were okay. They had to go to the neighbour to see if they could
borrow a phone to ring whoever was the appropriate person and the
neighbour didn't want to let them in.*

A former detainee told the inquiry that when he was released he was
given accommodation but had no food for two nights until some Japanese
people helped him to get to a shopping centre. Once there, he had no idea
whether the food was for humans or animals because he couldn't read
the labels. Another said that when he was sent to Brisbane with $160, he
was totally confused about where he was. The Immigration Department
provided him with hotel accommodation for a week, and when that ran
out he was asked to leave the hotel.

Teacher Peter Noss told a magazine about the situation for the
family of a year eight student released on a TPV:

*Hawraa came to school one day and I asked her what she'd had for
lunch. She told me she'd had an egg. I said, 'Well, I'm coming around
tonight to see what food you have.' And when I got there and opened
the fridge door, the only thing they had in it was water. That was just
after they'd been released from the detention centre. So I passed the hat
around among the teachers and we raised $500, just to give them a bit
of dignity.*[653]

A psychiatric nurse who worked in a detention centre told the inquiry she
found one detainee a couple of days after his release living in a bare flat
without bedding. At night he was lying on the floor and covering himself
with his clothing. A worker in a refugee assistance organisation told the
inquiry:

*We recently had a client who turned up telling us that he had spent 17
nights sleeping out after being released from Villawood, no English. He
had met somebody who referred him to a legal service who referred him
to us.*

Until 29 August 2000, TPV holders were not eligible for Medicare. One
week after a woman gave birth to premature twins while in detention, her
family was granted a TPV. However the twins required hospitalisation for
three months. Her husband told the inquiry:

They were born before time. In 26 week. More than 13 weeks in special machine. After two week, we got one letter from hospital. I not understand and I take to my friend and he said 'This bill must be wrong, seventy thousand bill for you.' Next day came letter. Seventy thousand dollar each. The other day I got a letter, one thousand dollar, five hundred dollar. All together three-hundred thousand dollar I got billed from hospital. After detention centre, more tension. Very hard days. I think now I work just for hospital, pay this bill. And during three month when they in hospital every day, a doctor check up, any medicine give, any test, X-ray, everyone bills separate. And in three months become 90 page, for each child. One friend, she very support us. She take bill to Red Cross and Medicare and ACM [Australian Correctional Management]. Decided to, when we was in detention ACM pay bill, some pay Medicare, some pay Red Cross.

A visitor to detention centres told the inquiry that newly released asylum seekers were ill-equipped to deal with all the logistical tasks needed to settle into Australian society and that Australian supporters tried to help those they had contact with:

So much readjustment was needed – Centrelink, accommodation, setting up homes, utilities being connected, banking, health care, shopping, using public transport, trying to find employment, language, finding a place for themselves in the community while often homesick, lonely, bewildered and battling with depression and ill health.

A refugee advocate told the inquiry that some of these tasks were made more difficult by people having to account for their time in detention:

There has been the hurdle of finding employment, no work references, where have you been for the last six years? The problem of finding accommodation, no history of tenancy.

The role of Australian supporters was noted in a 2005 study which found that the relationships they formed with refugees played a crucial role in facilitating access to services and support upon release.[654] Refugees without close support sometimes struggled with situations others take for granted. A former teacher in an area where refugee families settled told the inquiry about one family's difficulties in trying to be part of the local community:

One of the boys was chosen to represent the area in district athletics. They were given the sheet that said, 'Be at this oval in Albury at nine on this morning.' How do you get to Albury? When you get to Albury where do you go? What do you have to take? There wasn't provision of all that information that makes it easy for people. The lady went on the internet to find where the oval was and spent time teaching her husband how to ask for directions. They got there in plenty of time but unfortunately didn't hear the announcement for two of the events. He missed them because no-one had thought to say, 'You need to be listening or I will come and get you when your event is on.'

Newly released detainees also had to adjust to the more simple aspects of living outside an institutionalised environment. A woman who married an asylum seeker in detention told the inquiry:

Just after he got released I would catch him looking at himself in mirrors all the time – at home, in the street, everywhere. At first I teased him and told him he was beautiful and didn't need to keep checking. Then it slowly dawned on me that there were no mirrors in detention. He hadn't seen himself for three years.

Another issue the inquiry heard evidence about was that many detainees were dependent on prescription medication when they were released from detention. A GP who works in a refugee health service and has also worked in the prison health sector told the inquiry:

A notable feature of immigration detention health care has been the very poor quality of organising ongoing care after they leave detention. People who are discharged from immigration detention are generally discharged at short notice with little consideration of continuity of care.

In 2001, busloads of detainees were sent across the country at very short notice on medications which were abruptly discontinued. The prime medication in detention centres appears to be antidepressant drugs. Many of these people's drugs were abruptly stopped with absolutely predictable discontinuation reactions which meant that somewhere along the distance from Port Hedland to Canberra, many of the people on that bus began to have gastrointestinal cramping and diarrhoea and acute panic reactions. They arrived in states of extreme distress which could have been predicted. I cannot recall a case when any detainee has ever been given enough medication to tide them over into the community.

She also said it was rare for detainees to have been given their health records and cited the example of a man who had developed diabetes in detention, yet didn't know the name of his medication or how to test his own blood sugar:

We had to go through a textbook and try and match the tablet to work out what he was on. That wouldn't be acceptable in a prison but it appears to be acceptable in detention.

The director of a torture and trauma support service also told the inquiry that detention health services compared unfavourably with prisons:

Ensuring effective continuity of care is a basic principle of good detention and prison health and one which immigration centres do less well than prisons in Australia. As a minimum, a good handover system would ensure that the patient had access to their own notes, that notes contained enough information for continuity of care, and that patients on long-term medication were provided with enough medication until they could make contact with another doctor.

Asylum seekers released from detention on a TPV were eligible for Centrelink benefits. However most wanted to work, with many feeling pressure to send money overseas to family members. A refugee supporter told the inquiry:

He was asked how much money did you have when you were at Baxter and he said this amount. And the Centrelink person drew himself up and said, 'This is not what this paper says. You have this much.' And this chap sank down in his chair and he said, 'I sent it home.' Honestly I nearly burst into tears. This guy had a wife and a couple of kids and whatever money he had made in Baxter emptying bins or cleaning tables, he bundled it up and sent it off.

One man who was detained on Nauru told the inquiry:

> *There are times when I feel a little gloomy, mainly because I am unemployed at the moment. I am thinking of having some income because I have my mother and my brother's widow and his children. I know they are living their lives in difficulties in Pakistan and I am thinking of having some income so I can help them. I am telling this to my doctor and he says you have to be very well because if I go back to work I might be able to work for a couple of days and then I might need a break and I would lose my job anyway. That's what I am praying for now, that I could gain my health back so I can go and get some job.*

A refugee who came to Australia as an unaccompanied minor told the inquiry he had foregone his own chance at study so that he could work and send money home to pay for the education of his younger siblings.

Those who wanted to study and managed to access classes found they also faced difficulties. A teacher in an adult migrant English program told the inquiry:

> *The people we get in our classes who have been in the detention centres have got a lot of problems. We've got one that has poor attendance, suddenly experiencing panic attacks and having to leave the classroom. Trouble socialising where other students are happy to be there. There's that real lack of trust. The people who have been in detention and come into our program don't feel safe. The ones that haven't been in detention come here with a sense of hope, the ones that have been in detention centres still don't – they are not secure.*

A former detainee told the inquiry:

> *My friends told me, 'You crazy going for study, tomorrow they come and kick you out.' I didn't know what's going to happen tomorrow because I was on temporary protection visa. I had really bad time, I couldn't concentrate, sometimes I couldn't sleep, sometimes I don't want to talk to friends, like depression. When I go to school, I see these people, they happy, they got their family. Me, I just go home and cry.*

One refugee told the inquiry when his son wanted to go to university they were told he would have to pay $24,000 in overseas student fees. A refugee advocate told the inquiry that when another refugee boy who looked like doing well in Year 12 approached his MP asking her to advocate for him accessing university without full fees he was told he should think himself lucky to get a secondary education.

Most refugees who wanted to work would take any job they could, whatever their professional background. A man who was a doctor in his home country told the inquiry he applied for jobs in chicken factories and now worked as a meter reader. A refugee advocate told the inquiry:

> I had the temerity to ask if her father was learning English in town because he wasn't at the interview and she said, 'My father is an engineer. He was educated in the United Kingdom and Japan and speaks two languages perfectly. He is looking for a job as a cleaner.'

Some asylum seekers found that their three-year visa also made it harder to find work. A worker in a refugee assistance organisation told the inquiry that one man's apprenticeship was stopped because the apprenticeship was for longer than his visa allowed him to stay in Australia. Another told the inquiry:

> One client has experienced receiving an offer of a job and then the employer pulling out due to temporary visa status.

Many refugees decided to settle in rural areas rather than cities and the inquiry heard from some who lived in Swan Hill, Shepparton and Griffith. A refugee advocate told the inquiry that refugees who wanted to work were welcomed in some areas:

> The first two men who arrived here, a support group found them work in an orchard and accommodation in a backpackers hostel. They arrived here without a word of English, without any idea of the society they were coming in to. The owner of the hostel contacted the multicultural council where there was somebody who spoke Farsi which is very closely related to their language. We helped them find rental accommodation. After they had been here about a month, another two or three men came and eventually there were two households of eight men. We put out an appeal for household goods and for people to help with English and there was work for them. They were filling a place where workers were desperately needed.

A regional organiser of the Australian Workers Union (AWU) told the inquiry that from 1999 newspaper campaigns had been run by the Department of Immigration against farmers and other rural employers hiring illegal workers, which many people equated with refugees. Another refugee advocate told the inquiry that refugees were subject to increased car and license checks by police and that some had returned to cities as a result. A religious worker in a regional town told the inquiry about the experience of one asylum seeker:

> She was taking other families to work. She had just had a baby, and they slammed her in a police van and left her there for two hours and she asked could she go home and feed the baby and they wouldn't let her. She was nearly cooking inside the van, then they brought her into town and I had to fight the immigration people. The police weren't bad, at least they gave her a cup of water but the immigration people, no way. We fought in the police station and she was in the cell. I opened the door and let her out.

In 2002, the far right political party Australia First ran a campaign in Young, in regional NSW, against Afghan refugees working in the meatworks, claiming they were taking the jobs of Australians. But the AWU organiser told the inquiry:

> I have four contractors and they constantly ask me to access the Afghan workers because they have such a good reputation. When you put 40 into one workplace even though it's a 700-person workplace – those places are still calling out for workers. So they are doing work that other people don't want to do. The Young experiment has worked because we have seen people that have gone on and have Australian citizenship now and are still working in those industries. So the industry has benefited as well.

Citrus growers in Griffith also told the inquiry that they had a desperate need for workers to help pick and pack their crops and that often people from overseas were loyal, hard workers who they had grown close to.

After a number of refugees were refused further protection when their TPVs expired, some regional communities argued they had made a valuable contribution and should be allowed to stay. In July 2004, the government introduced changes that allowed TPV holders to apply for mainstream visas, including regional sponsored-migration-scheme visas, an option previously unavailable to them. Refugees who applied but were ineligible for the mainstream visas were issued 18-month RPBVs. These changes prompted some refugees who had settled in cities but been refused further protection to also move to the country. One man told the inquiry:

> DIMIA sent me a letter in 2003 saying I should voluntarily return home. They said the situation had changed in my country. Everyone knows the situation there is bad. This caused me more stress. They gave us option to go to bush to work for one year and we could stay in Australia so I came to Swan Hill but no-one got that visa to stay. I started from zero in Swan Hill. Like the situation I had before. I haven't seen my family for five years. I don't know what is going on for my wife and children.
>
> I contacted immigration and they didn't know anything about bush work. This lady was in Melbourne and every time I speak to her I get different information. First she said if you work for one year in bush you get a visa. Now she says I have to get sponsorship from an employer.

A refugee advocate in a regional town told the inquiry there was confusion amongst refugees, advocates and the Immigration Department about how the visa worked, saying:

> They said that the men would have to come to the country and work for the same employer for 12 months. The men are seasonal workers, they move around different farms, they pick when it's picking, they prune when it's pruning.

Another refugee advocate told the inquiry:

> It's been terribly disruptive for the men to have to come to the country, leave their friends, and in some cases the business they had, employers who loved them, didn't want them to leave, networks. It hasn't been easy to settle here, whether it's a real estate agent, the local newspaper, the schools, the hospital, there's a lot of work to do here, and we haven't really got anywhere yet.

The inquiry also heard that being sponsored for a visa put asylum seekers in a vulnerable position. One man who has been in Australia for five years said:

The boss called me to his office and he said to me, 'Your money now is $17.' In Melbourne they pay for the packer $24, the slicer more but I couldn't say anything to him, because this man sponsored me. With this job I can't say nothing. Everyone in the boning room knows this Afghan guy he comes about visa. Everyone. He comes to me like boss. Just I listen, I say to him nothing. Maybe he says to boss, maybe boss little bit upset. He says, 'You go.'

But the inquiry also heard positive stories of refugees establishing businesses in regional areas, including Griffith, Shepparton and Port Augusta. A refugee living in a regional area who spent six months in detention told the inquiry he volunteered with the organisation White Lion as a mentor to troubled youth:

I talk with them about my experience, how I come, I left my family behind, my friends. Did I give up? I say I not give up because I have a new life.

Family Reunion

For asylum seekers who arrived in Australia without their spouses and children, the most devastating aspect of the TPV was its prohibition on family reunion. Many refugees with families overseas were granted TPVs following years in detention. Had their claims been recognised immediately, they would have been permanent and able to sponsor their family by the time they were released.

But the inquiry heard that in many cases family reunion was further delayed because the Immigration Department slowed the processing of Iraqi and Afghan applications for permanent visas in the hope the situation in those countries would render their further protection unnecessary and allow their return. In September 2001 and November 2002, the Howard government introduced legislation allowing TPV holders whose application for permanency had not been determined within the visa's three-year validity to remain on a TPV until a decision was made.[655] In June 2003, Oxfam Australia noted that by the end of that year, 2200 TPVs would have expired, and that the delay in processing claims was contributing to the anxiety many refugees felt about their future.[656]

The United Nations High Commissioner for Refugees (UNHCR)

has stated, 'The spouses and minor children of recognised refugees should be given refugee status ... and be reunited immediately with the father, mother or child.'[657] However this does not happen for TPV holders in Australia, even if family members outside Australia have been recognised as being 'at risk' by the UNHCR.

In announcing the TPV, then immigration minister Philip Ruddock explained that the government had specifically targeted family reunion to try and deter asylum seekers from coming to Australia:

> These people are trying to exploit Australia's generous arrangements for refugees ... The legislation will prevent unauthorised arrivals from obtaining permanent protection visas and the benefits, particularly family reunion, which appear to attract traffickers and forum shoppers.[658]

The inquiry heard that some people held TPVs for up to five years. Refugee advocate Sue Hoffman has detailed how their temporary visas exacerbated the suffering of men whose families died on the SIEV X:

> Four men living in Perth each lost their wives, all their children, and other family members when SIEV X sank. Conditions of their TPVs did not allow them to leave Australia and return, and Australia does not normally issue tourist visas to people from refugee-generating countries. So despite their tremendous losses, they were unable to gain comfort from meeting with remaining family, who were all overseas. They waited nearly four years for permanent protection visas; four years before they could travel overseas to hug their brothers, sisters, mothers and fathers, having suffered the loss of their wives and children.[659]

However, on the fifth anniversary of the SIEV X sinking, then immigration minister Amanda Vanstone responded to a question in parliament by denying families had travelled on the boat to meet their fathers and husbands in Australia:

> We are sticking with the Temporary Protection Visa policy. We believe it has saved lives. We do not believe it has cost lives. Not one person on this side, and I do not think anybody else on the other side, would have thought to come out on the anniversary of people having lost their lives to assert that 146 children lost their lives because of this policy

> *– a policy that we both supported ... I am told that no evidence led to indicate that the children on the boat were coming to link up with people who had protection here. I am told that the evidence is that family groups were all coming together.[660]*

A former detainee who has been in Australia for five years told the inquiry:

> *I just hope that one day I can see my family again. When I left Afghanistan my daughter was three months old. Now that my family is in Pakistan I can talk to her on the telephone. I talked to her and I told her that I was her father and she just started crying.*

The years in detention also saw family relationships change, particularly for men who came without their families expecting to be recognised as refugees and reunited with their wives and children quickly. A refugee supporter told the inquiry:

> *My friend was almost five years in detention, extremely depressed. Now his wife has divorced him and he will probably never see his little six-year-old daughter again. A Sister who met him on his release said he was extremely distressed. He just went into his church and cried and cried.*

A submission from the Brotherhood of St Laurence to the inquiry stated:

> *After two years in detention and five years on a TPV, an Iranian client was advised of DIMIA's decision to grant him a permanent visa, pending police clearance. He can only begin the process of sponsoring his wife and child to join him in Australia once this is completed. He has now been waiting for eight months for a police clearance. He has been separated from his family by Australian government policy for close to eight years.*

Other refugees had family members die while they were incarcerated. One asylum seeker told the inquiry that both his parents died during his six years in detention. One man who spent five years in detention told the inquiry his wife died of breast cancer in his home country two years before he was recognised as a refugee, leaving his then seven-year-old daughter to live with his parents. He said:

Give me the reason that you rejected my case for five years. I didn't change any single thing in my case. If anyone tell me the human being are at the same level I would say no because my skin colour is darker than the others. Oh, Australia citizen were in Red One isolation! What's different between me and the others? Where is the humanity? Because the others have the drink, have the boyfriend, girlfriends and they have their beautiful weekend and that's it. This is the problem.

Some refugees were not told by their families that loved ones had died until after their release from detention. One man told the inquiry:

I was calling my family in the detention centre and I was thinking a little bit something happened to my father. All the time when I asked where is my father he said your father outside.

A submission to the inquiry from four women living in Swan Hill, where some refugees have settled after detention, states:

Some call TPV 'detention without the wire'. They become more pessimistic about ever obtaining a permanent visa and family reunion. The refugees' wives cannot understand why it is taking so long to bring them here and this is another level of stress for the men. Separations of five to six years is very damaging to marriages and children, some of whom have never met their father. The men work seven days a week to dull the psychological pain. They have done this for over five years and are now exhausted and breaking down. We know of none who aren't suffering from stress, poor sleep, nightmares, anxiety and depression.

A man on a TPV told the inquiry:

Somebody came after us with their family and they got a visa before me. My family criticises me. They think I did something wrong and that's why I don't get a visa when other people did.

The TPV policy also resulted in unaccompanied children facing prolonged separation from their parents. A refugee advocate told the inquiry that children under 18 could sponsor their parents to Australia when they became permanent. But because many of them had to wait years in detention and on a temporary visa, they were often over 18 by the time they became permanent residents, disqualifying them from family reunion.

Other refugees waited so long for permanency that by the time they could sponsor their family to Australia, older children had married, were technically no longer regarded as part of the family unit, and could therefore not be sponsored with the rest of the family.

In February 2003, 46-year-old Dr Habibullah Wahedy killed himself after receiving a letter from immigration offering him $2000 to return to Afghanistan when his TPV expired a few months later. He had spent six months at the Port Hedland Detention Centre, three years on a TPV and had a wife and three children in Afghanistan. Dr Wahedy had attended a Muslim prayer service three weeks earlier for three Afghan refugees who were murdered when returning home from a refugee camp in Pakistan. Philip Ruddock denied his death was related to his visa status saying:

> There is a campaign here by some to try and link his death to issues relating to his status. But I think if there are people who believe they know what his state of mind was, what was influencing him, then I think they bear some culpability.[661]

Legislation introduced in September 2001 also made family reunion more difficult for refugees who had been convicted while in detention of offences such as property damage or escape. The legislation denies permanency to anyone convicted in the previous four years of an offence for which the maximum penalty is 12 months or more imprisonment, regardless of the penalty they received.[662] Even those who did receive permanency faced a long wait for family reunion. The inquiry was told that family sponsorship applications processed through Islamabad took two to three years.

A report released by the Queensland government's Multicultural Affairs Department in 2001 concluded that: 'The prohibition of family reunion and the denial of travel permission have compounded existing torture and trauma symptoms.'[663]

Other Temporary Visas

Migration agent Marion Le told the inquiry that refugees held on Nauru had been granted a range of temporary visas:

> One is a five-year visa which enables them to apply for a protection visa after four-and-a-half years. The other one is a three-year temporary

protection visa which is only renewable as another three-year temporary protection. You can never apply for a permanent visa in Australia. Some of the others got humanitarian visas. Some of those people are on two-year visas, some are on one-year visas.

We've got one Afghan family on a one-year visa that will expire next month, and we don't know what will happen. The conditions on that visa say that no application can be made to the minister, only if she herself approaches them can they make an application and they live with this fear that they may be deported. We certainly intend to be applying to the minister and it will be a very public application because that little girl was the Christmas angel on the front page of the Canberra Times and someone in the department rang me and said good humouredly, 'Marion, don't think we don't know what you are doing.' I said, 'Well it will be very difficult to deport the Christmas angel, won't it!'

STILL ALL THESE THINGS IN MY BRAIN: MENTAL HEALTH

The inquiry heard from a wide range of sources that many refugees who spent years in detention found it difficult to adjust to their new life. Some had spent so long in detention that they were effectively institutionalised upon their release. They had spent years not being able to make decisions about the simplest of things, such as when and what to eat, and this impaired their ability to function independently when they were released without any preparation or support.

The director of a torture and trauma support service told the inquiry that being on a TPV increased anxiety, depression and hopelessness amongst asylum seekers. This compounded their trauma caused by detention experiences, social stigma and ongoing separation from their families. A worker with a refugee assistance organisation told the inquiry the uncertainty associated with the visa also meant they found it difficult to commit to study, loans and relationships, and that family members overseas began to doubt the commitment of those who had 'made it' but were powerless to sponsor family members to Australia.

A GP working in a refugee health service told the inquiry:

The mental health of adults in the community after detention follows a predictable pattern of initial euphoria, which incidentally I don't see in children, and then dysphoria. Although this has been described for many refugees after settlement, in the case of refugees on temporary protection visas the dysphoria becomes quite extreme and often turns into depression.

A Uniting Church minister told the inquiry that far from life being easy after release from detention, many former detainees felt overwhelmed by the problems they faced in the outside world. He told the inquiry one man he knew returned to Baxter asking to be re-detained. Another refugee advocate told the inquiry one man had a serious panic attack immediately after his release while they were driving from Baxter to Adelaide.

A man who spent four years in detention told the inquiry:

I am 28, but I feel I am still not grown up. In detention four years we were treated like babies. If you want to go shopping two officers coming with you and they have money and we have to say I want this one and they buy for us. Everything like a child so in the outside we cannot do anything by ourselves.

Another former detainee told the inquiry:

Four months ago, in the morning up to midday, I was a dangerous person and two officers were taking me from A to B. In the afternoon, I was free and I was told you have to get out straight away. I don't know anybody. I don't know anything. I don't know even how to shop, where to go, what to buy. All I know is the camp for five years, but I had to leave. Now my anxiety has increased more than in the camp. I'm not comfortable in my life and I think I would prefer to be in the camp. I don't mind if they send me back because at least there I know what to do, but outside I am lost.

Refugees who spent years in detention before being released were acutely aware of years of their lives being wasted. One told the inquiry:

Everyone in detention has got a problem with the mental. You cannot say because I get free and I working, I am okay. Sometimes I feel really down. I don't feel talk to anybody. I have a car, I have my house it is not mean I am really good. I have a really terrible time sometimes. I think we lost five years of my life. I don't think this five years is going to come back to me.

The inquiry also heard evidence that the detention of asylum seekers had made them suspicious of authority and fearful of being re-detained. A worker from a refugee assistance organisation that helped detainees released from psychiatric care told the inquiry:

Most clients felt sceptical about our service in the early stages. One client suspected we were ASIO.

A refugee supporter told the inquiry about her first visit to a family:

The day that I met them the husband and wife were out the front washing the car and she ran and hid in the house because she didn't know why we were there. She thought we were from immigration or the police.

A man who spent three years in detention told the inquiry:

Even when we are working, you don't trust who is coming there. Maybe it's him. Maybe it's immigration. It's a very, very, very bad thing to put someone in. Twice I collapsed and I find myself in the hospital.

The fear many asylum seekers held of being re-detained was not unfounded, with Ali Bakhtiyari's re-detention being widely publicised. The inquiry heard people were in danger of being re-detained due to poor record keeping and communication practices within the Department of Immigration. UnitingJustice Australia and Hotham Mission Asylum Seeker Project told the inquiry immigration officers had arrived at one of its properties to wrongfully detain someone. It also reported cases of people being given conflicting information about on which day they would become unlawful, and therefore susceptible to being detained. A refugee advocate told the inquiry about one family's re-detention:

They arrived with five cars outside her home. She was by herself and had taken the day off from her English school because she was preparing for a birthday party. She opened the door and was met with three Federal

Police and a woman and two others from immigration. This woman said, where was her husband, where was her family? And then they just barged in and started searching.

A nine-year-old girl, whose family was falsely accused of being Pakistani and had their visas cancelled, told the inquiry:

We were at school and we were just on normal work, when Mum arrived and took me back home and we had to pack up. We were taken to the airport on this little plane. Then we were taken to Baxter. When we got there we had to get our ID cards ready and after that we went to the compound. It was very hard leaving my friends behind.

The family was released six weeks later while the father remained in detention for another five months. They did not return to their previous house or schools. The girl told the inquiry:

It was really hard leaving my Dad behind. My new school, it was really hard and I had to make new friends and I had a new teacher.

Those who were released from detention while their friends remained also found it hard to enjoy their new-found freedom. A refugee advocate told the inquiry:

I thought it was lovely for him to go to the beach or climb a tree or cook for himself, but he just felt guilty. He wished his friends could be there.

Another visitor to detention told the inquiry a recently released woman was unable to continue with driving lessons because she was thinking about her friends in detention:

She said to me, 'I went for my learners, got out in the car and started having lessons with an instructor.' She just could not do it. She said, 'I felt so guilty because I was on the road and why should I be doing this when other people don't have this privilege?'

Some refugees told the inquiry that they did not tell Australians they had been in detention because they didn't want to be thought of badly. A man who spent five years in detention told the inquiry:

If somebody asks me how long you have been in Australia, I don't know what to say. Five years or four months. I don't know which one is true. I feel that people do not know enough about detention and so if I say that I've been in detention I don't know how they will react.

A woman told the inquiry:

It is something that you feel ashamed to say to people. Some friends of mine don't know I've been there. The Australian don't know what's going on and they say these people are criminals, they went to detention. They are my friends but how could I say I'm one of these people. It's something shameful.

The inquiry also heard extensive evidence of serious mental illness continuing in refugees released after years of detention. A refugee advocate told the inquiry she knew three people who had been in psychiatric hospitals since their release. Another told the inquiry that one man had been hospitalised 10 times for mental health issues. The coordinator of a community organisation supporting people released from detention told the inquiry:

We have had three cases from Nauru. They were four years on Nauru and they came as absolutely broken people. One of them remains in psychiatric care and is happy to be there because he said, 'That is the only place I can survive.'

Another refugee advocate told the inquiry:

In September 2006, I visited a man I had met in Baxter in 2004. This time it was in the Toowong Psychiatric Hospital. Because of the stringent restrictions placed on him, he still felt he was 'locked up' and his situation was no different from being in Baxter.

A former detainee told the inquiry he could not get the experiences of detention out of his mind:

Still I am dreaming I am in Woomera, people they are taking shampoo, they sew their mouth. Kids they crying, they fight with their mum and dad, people razor their body. I saw all these things I never saw in my life, so still all these things in my brain.

In January 2008, 40-year-old Iranian Parviz Yousefi was awarded $800,000 compensation for his experiences while held at Woomera for three years. During his incarceration he sewed his lips together, attempted suicide four times and went on hunger strikes after he was separated from his wife and nine-year-old son, who were held in the detention centre's Residential Housing Project accommodation. He remained in detention despite 15 reports from medical experts and 11 from psychiatrists urging he be moved. His wife told a newspaper her husband was a former oil industry engineer who would never work again and would require medical care for the rest of his life:

> My husband is a shell of the man he used to be. To ignore his cry for help, and his doctors' reports, was not only negligent but it was also inhumane. None of us will ever forget the horror of the detention centres. We will have to learn how to live with what we saw and experienced. We have lost our life.[664]

The inquiry heard from several former detainees who also felt they had lost their sense of self through their experience of detention. One told the inquiry:

> All I've done with the money I get from Centrelink, I have rented somewhere and I've made a little detention for myself because going out is not easy for me. I don't know where to go and I don't know anybody, so fear of unknown keeps me at home. Settlement is difficult for everybody, but at least it is easier for an able body and able mind. I don't have either of them. I have been five years in the camp, not knowing what is going to happen to me, so all this has taken its toll. I actually don't think I am going to ever get better or become somebody like the person I was before.

Another man who spent five years in detention told the inquiry:

> I don't think I'm a normal person right now. The trauma of being in the camp for such a long time has affected me such that I am not the same person who got into the camp. I have reached a point that nothing interests me. All I can feel now is fear and anxiety. Nothing can make me happy.

Another man who spent more than five years in detention told the inquiry:

> *I am a person in front of you who is traumatised, who is devastated. I almost lost my faith in human beings. Before I just joke with everyone but now I become very cynical, pessimistic and all the time I am feeling like there is a conspiracy. I know it is not true but I feel that way. Every night I struggle to sleep, often I got nightmares, panic, frightened.*

Another man who spent five years in detention told the inquiry:

> *My family want a photograph from me. I don't want them to see me this way because I have changed so much, they may not even recognise me. I'm a completely different person. I can't even talk to them. I don't know what to say because, apart from misery and problems that I can't tell them because I am going to worry them unnecessarily, what else can I talk to them, so I am reluctant to ring them either. I have never told my parents that I'm in detention, always told them I'm living in a small town. I felt embarrassed to say that I escaped from the problem in the country and I fell into the worst possible problem imagined.*

A man who spent a year in detention told the inquiry:

> *Now I feel I was better before I came Australia. I don't know what happened to my mind. I am forgetting too much. I felt from time to time to cry. I think is this Australia – I must got a permanent visa, not a permanent sickness. I got a permanent sickness. I know myself it's not going to go out of me.*

Some asylum seekers told the inquiry they wished they had died instead of spending time in detention. A man who spent months in Glenside Psychiatric Hospital told the inquiry:

> *I used to be a social person but I think during this time I lost a lot of things. Sometimes I want to be far away of everything. Sometimes I don't want to call even my family. I was very close to them. And this is one part of my sickness. Now I see myself like a zombie. It is not about TPV, it is not about Curtin. If you put a person in the pressure to time you get suffer. He might be like a person he don't care to anything. He*

wants this life to get finished. I think some of us we get to that feel of life. Sometimes I wish the boat I came on goes under water and finish it. You couldn't see a lot of cruelty. Just things come in the mind because we seen a lot of things.

A man who spent six years in detention told the inquiry:

United Nations says that each person is one life and should be respected with dignity, but we were not respected. We were not treated with dignity and I still feeling that my dignity has gone and it takes years and years to back to normal life. I feel sometimes I have lost myself because they didn't treat us like a human being. Time and time again I thought of the people who were drowned in the ocean and I wish I was one of them rather than going through so much agonising difficulties in prison.

The inquiry also heard evidence from a range of sources about the anger many refugees felt at their treatment. A man who spent four years in detention told the inquiry:

Before I feel that I liked to live and when I go to Baxter I give up everything, I don't care anything even I die. All the time after that I feel angry and prepared to do anything. Still I am the same and I don't feel alive or that it will be a happy life.

Another man said:

I am very disappointed to come to this country. I was very down in detention. I stayed ten months and five days and two hours. I get very, very tired. What about people they stay four years, five years? If I put you in detention for five years, you will become a normal person? They will become in violence, they will become different people, they will come to hate everyone.

A refugee advocate told the inquiry how one man expressed his anger on release from detention:

He had been in detention just over five years and we picked him up and took him out for lunch. We decided to take him where he could look out to the ocean and he started to feel really angry, like why am I released now. There was this whole sea of emotions and then he started to tell these horrible stories. He was at Maribyrnong when that man jumped off the basketball hoop and he was talking about seeing the man with the blood coming out of his face. Honestly, I feel like I have never been the same since. They just came out, all these revolting stories that he had never told us while he was in there. Then he would look out to the ocean and say, 'Oh my eyes are not used to seeing this.' Or he would look at the glass and say, 'I haven't touched a glass for five years, I've only drunk out of a plastic cup and used a plastic fork and knife.'

Refugee advocates trying to assist asylum seekers released from detention with mental health problems were also affected by the damage detention had caused. One told the inquiry:

Carers provide support to refugees who are depressed. We have seen the effect of the mental damage of those recently released on their carers. Some carers are being rung at all times of the day and night. Many carers are in danger of becoming ill themselves. The effects on carers include exhaustion, frustration and anger at the attitude of the federal and state governments and many Australians and a feeling of obsession to solve a problem.

I CAN'T TALK TO PEOPLE AROUND MY AGE: CHILDREN

The inquiry heard evidence from a wide range of sources about the difficulties children faced adjusting to life after detention. The director of a torture and trauma support service told the inquiry:

Children who have spent significant time in immigration detention are more likely to have high levels of anxiety, depression and aggression. We can see particularly detrimental psychological affects on children who have spent years in detention before the age of five. Most have witnessed a range of traumatic events including self-harm, riots and violence.

Psychiatrist Jon Jureidini told the inquiry:

One little boy who spent most of his life in detention was completely wild by the time he came out of detention. He was placed in a foster placement, being cared for by a grandmother-aged woman who he would make lewd sexual suggestions to. He would physically assault her, particularly around her breasts and genitals, and swear obscenely in English (though his parents hardly spoke English). Once he was reunited with his parents, he became this over-compliant little boy who was quite timid and always wanting to please everybody, and everybody thought 'Oh, he's better' which is, I think, a misperception.

A couple of years down the track, some of the aggressive behaviour is beginning to emerge in the school environment, and both the school and the parents have a lot of difficulty making sense of that, so I'm just introducing the notion of the sleeper effect of the detention experience in children. We know that while one population of abused children become disturbed and make their distress obvious at the time they're being abused, there is another cohort of children for whom it doesn't become apparent until their adult life or late adolescence, or maybe in their own parenting.

A general practitioner working in a refugee health service told the inquiry that Temporary Protection Visas impacted on children because they were growing up in environments where their parents were unable to provide security for them. A study of families who had been in detention noted:

There is evidence in adult populations that TPV holders in the community have higher levels of distress than those granted permanent residency, and that they may in fact suffer 'anticipatory post traumatic stress disorder'.[665]

However the inquiry also heard from several mental-health professionals that the detention experience continued to affect children after their release, even if the family was granted permanent residency. A child and adolescent psychiatrist told the inquiry:

I continue to see children who now are living in a community with Permanent Protection Visas who are extremely developmentally delayed, who continue to suffer from nightmares, whose parents are irrevocably changed by their experience.

A child psychologist told the inquiry that the impact of detention on their parents affected the resilience of children, as the parents were unable to help their children process and move on from their distressing experiences. This put the children at increased risk of mental illness in adolescence and adulthood, and seriously impaired their capacity to form and sustain healthy relationships. A GP working in a refugee health service told the inquiry:

I have got two shampoo overdoses. There is no reason why anybody would overdose on shampoo unless they had learnt that as behaviour in detention centres. It is isolated to that particular environment, but we are seeing children in the community, who have been in detention, now doing that.

A refugee advocate who worked with a family while the father remained in detention told the inquiry that when he was released the children were extremely clingy:

The boy, who was six at the time, refused to go to school because he was worried that his father would be taken away again in his absence. The girl, who was only two, would scream hysterically if her father disappeared from her view for any length of time. After extensive torture and trauma counselling, the boy's health seemed to improve and the bed-wetting gradually ceased. However, the counsellors said he couldn't get the detention scenes out of his mind.

Two years later the ghosts of the past seemed to be gaining ground and he was becoming more and more withdrawn and listless. On one visit the lawyer accompanying me saw a bird flying around the lounge room and asked where the cage was. His mother replied that a friend of the family gave the boy the bird and when he saw the cage he insisted that the bird be taken out. He would regularly ask his mother why other children were still in detention.

A former teacher at a school attended by refugee children described some of the difficulties children had in settling into school. The school initially wasn't told the children had been in detention because family members were not sure how this would be viewed:

> Those who had been in detention centres didn't like voices to be raised. If the teachers did raise their voice, they were frightened. People in a uniform frightened them as well. There were some fights because they didn't know how to play, how to share things. That's in the context of what little they had might have been precious. And because they were the newest children in, there were others who had arrived in previous years who were ready to pick on them.

The inquiry heard that an Afghan boy in a regional town was bashed at school after being called a terrorist by other children, and that older children found it difficult to relate to their schoolmates. A teenager who spent three years in detention told the inquiry:

> When I was in my country I was a really social person. I had heaps of really good, loyal friends. When I came to Baxter I was isolated for at least three years so that had a bad affect on my mind because right now seriously I can't talk to people around my age. I talk to them, laugh with them, but I can't be friends with them because I just don't know what to talk about to them. I remember talking to a girl and she told me I talk like a 40-year-old. I felt really bad and I laughed, but it really hurt.
>
> I didn't get a lot of friends in my school at the beginning because I was really a grumpy person and I would fight without any reason because there was so much pressure. One of my friends told me I am going through a lot of pressure. I said I went through a lot of pressure. I have seen people around me suffer; you have just broke off with your boyfriend, it is nothing to what other people suffer.

It was also more difficult for refugee children to complete schoolwork. A man who spent six months in Woomera told the inquiry his son had problems learning at school:

> One of my children didn't really do a good progress report because of the fears that he had been through in all these places and the interrupted life. He suffered a lot until finally he has been referred to a specialist at

the hospital. The initial assessment took them to believe that he had a mental problem but it seems that it is all the accumulated difficulties through the life.

A child psychologist told the inquiry that children released from detention found it difficult to concentrate at school:

Many of them were experiencing extreme difficulty with learning because they couldn't participate in classrooms. Children often show hyper-vigilance because they needed it to survive before, but this persists and it impairs their capacity to learn. They're in this heightened state of arousal and they can't settle to concentrate on learning new things or taking risks. You can't learn if you are in danger and these children can't leave behind that feeling because it's become neurologically wired in.

A boy who spent three years in detention told the inquiry:

My mind is jumping around because the only way I could survive that place was not caring and not caring is not that easy. When I came out of the detention I can't concentrate any more. I was one of the best students in my school. I went to the class and I could not learn. I have to read over and over to actually understand one point and that has made my studies far harder in Year 12.

Some children feared that they would be returned to detention. A woman whose family was held in Port Hedland told the inquiry her eight-year-old son had behavioural difficulties in school:

They called me and said come and pick up your son because he is so angry, we can't calm him down and he is throwing things and trying to break down his bag. I ask him what is going on and he said my teacher forced me to do music and I don't want to do music. Principal said to me maybe something in his past. I told he was in detention and probably start from there. When we came home he asked me, 'Mum, will my teacher put me in detention because I have been very upset at school and I've been naughty?' I said, 'No, you was naughty, but no one is going to put you in detention any more.'

A refugee advocate told the inquiry another child was similarly affected:

This child got to the school and they said on Monday you are going to camp and she absolutely flipped because she thought that was back to detention. She had to leave school that day. I was asked to collect her and at that stage nobody's English was good so it was a matter of comforting and reassuring her and the school had an interpreter to explain.

The inquiry heard that some children took on adult worries and responsibilities. One refugee supporter told the inquiry about a 17-year-old girl who sacrificed her chance to go to school so she could help her family:

I managed to get her placed in one of the private secondary schools here. When I went that morning, as I had arranged an interview with the principal, she didn't open her front door. I made another arrangement later and the same thing happened. She didn't want to tell me that she didn't want to go to school, she wanted to get a job and help her family to get here. She got the whole family out. There were 13 people in that flat and they've only got two bedrooms.

The inquiry also heard some positive stories from children who had been in detention. A boy who spent one year on Nauru said:

I am getting on with my life. I am happy, I've got Australian friend, Italian, Iraqi and we have a small community. I'm happy, I'll finish school, move to Melbourne.

A boy who spent six months in Woomera told the inquiry:

I am studying and I am planning to finish Year 12 and go to uni. I want to start aeroplane engineering. I know I will have to work hard.

One man who was detained on Nauru told the inquiry:

I am extremely thankful when my children are coming to me and telling me that they want to be a doctor. I didn't have that much freedom in my own country but here my children are making decisions about their future and that makes me extremely happy.

A former teacher at a school where refugee families settled told the inquiry that refugee families were slowly becoming part of community life:

> *The school held a concert recently, and the Afghan children were performing on stage with everybody else and the parents were there watching. They didn't necessarily mix with any other parents but they were very proud that they were there, so they are becoming more comfortable.*
>
> *They all came along to the multicultural festival. The aim was to have the different ethnic groups march around with a flag and the Afghan group were by far the largest and in the course of the afternoon's activities the young men danced just impromptu.*

THIS MUST BE A JOKE:
DEBTS

The inquiry heard that another issue that made it difficult for some asylum seekers to settle in Australia after release from detention was being issued with enormous bills for the cost of their detention. Under Section 209 of the *Migration Act*, people held in detention can be charged by the Commonwealth for the cost of detaining them and for appealing adverse legal decisions. These provisions were inserted by the Labor government in 1992.[666]

Generally, asylum seekers who are later recognised as refugees have the debts waived. However, a number who were granted humanitarian, spouse or other visas after the immigration minister intervened in their cases received bills demanding hundreds of thousands of dollars. Those unable to pay or make an arrangement to pay off the debts face difficulties gaining permanency and citizenship, and travelling out of the country. Refugee advocate Julian Burnside has commented on Australia's unique detention billing system:

> *It is a remarkable thing that an innocent person, who is incarcerated, is made liable for the financial cost of his own incarceration. No other country on earth makes innocent people liable for their own detention.*[667]

However, a constitutional challenge to the legality of these debts was unsuccessful in the Federal Court.[668] A former detainee told the inquiry:

> I was in detention for four years but now I got a bill for more than $200,000 and I don't think even if you were staying in a five-star hotel on Gold Coast you never get this bill. Immigration should pay me and not I should pay for the bill.

Eighteen per cent of asylum seekers interviewed by Hotham Mission had incurred debts relating to detention and legal costs.[669] One asylum seeker told the inquiry:

> I thought I was really free. Until today I am not free, because three months after my release I received this letter from immigration saying I owed more than $80,000 for my detention. I told myself this must be a joke. Then I rang DIMIA and they told me you have to pay. I was shocked, I wouldn't even imagine that this would happen. That bill is still hanging there. It's a burden because I don't think I will ever be able to pay it. And even I could pay it, I wouldn't pay it. I am getting married in a couple of weeks and I did try to get my mother and my sister here to visit me. But I was told that my mum can't come, my sister can't come because I owe money to the government.

The inquiry heard of seven cases where Australian women who had married asylum seekers were asked to supply their full financial details to the Immigration Department, although technically they are not liable for the debts presented to their husbands.

One Australian woman who married an asylum seeker told the inquiry that a week after receiving a letter from the minister granting him a spouse visa and wishing him all the best in Australia, her husband received a bill for over $100,000. Their request for the debt to be waived was initially refused, despite her being pregnant and her husband working casually in a low-paid job, on the grounds that he was relatively young and his circumstances might improve in the future.

Another Australian woman who married an asylum seeker granted a spouse visa told the inquiry:

> We received a letter from DIMIA saying that he had to pay all of his detention expenses. So we now have a Commonwealth debt of over

$200,000. We have appealed that debt and we just got a letter last week saying, 'We won't waive the debt, come back to us when you apply for your Permanent Visa.' He was hoping to be able to visit his parents in a third country because they are getting older and he's a bit concerned about missing them entirely, but he won't be able to travel now because of the Commonwealth debt preventing his returning.

A FEW OF US GOT TOGETHER:
REFUGEE ADVOCACY

As well as supporting asylum seekers in detention, ordinary Australians created community organisations that helped asylum seekers once they had been released. They raised and distributed millions of dollars in direct assistance and utilised thousands of volunteers to provide other services. These included health services, accommodation, English classes, food banks, recreational programs, computer classes, counselling and advocacy.

The Bridge for Asylum Seekers Foundation, established in June 2003, has distributed $450,000 to people released from detention, without work rights, for living expenses. One of its founding members told the inquiry how it had been established:

A man on a Bridging Visa E who had been released from Villawood Detention Centre in Sydney and whom I was helping to resettle told me that he was going to try to find work now that he was out of detention. I realised that he was not allowed to work and I advised him that if he worked he would be put back into Villawood. So a few friends got together to set up an organisation to raise funds for asylum seekers living in the community on BVEs. We don't have an office as such; it's my spare bedroom and we live on the smell of an oily rag. Everything is either owned by me or lent to me and I only claim for expenses. Without the assistance of UnitingCare NSW ACT we would not continue to exist. UnitingCare provides banking and tax-deductibility assistance.

More formal organisations were able to lobby mainstream institutions to provide services to asylum seekers. Rosemary Hudson-Miller told the inquiry about the Western Australian organisation Coalition for Asylum Seekers, Refugees and Detainees (CARAD), which has provided housing, health and monetary support to over 4000 people released from detention:

> When they were releasing the first groups of people they arrived in Perth with enough to last them for three days and then they were wandering the city. There was no formal arrangement with any nongovernment organisation to provide support. They were only granted TPVs and at that time they had fewer rights and no access to Medicare.
>
> We were very pleased to have the Children's Hospital in Western Australia decide at an executive level that every child in Western Australia would be treated in the same way. And we've had terrific support from many in the WA health network who set up the WA Health Refugee Network.

Other mainstream institutions also adopted policies to assist asylum seekers adversely affected by government policy. RMIT University established the Refugee and Asylum Seeker Project to provide a limited number of places for tertiary study to asylum seekers who would otherwise be liable for full overseas student fees. Lucy Fiske, a founding member of community legal centre CASE for refugees, said:

> While the Howard government refused to allow any federal funds to be allocated to TPV holders, teachers in classrooms around the country enrolled children on TPVs in intensive language classes. Curtin University and many other universities developed scholarships and fee waiver places for students on TPVs. Volunteers organised English classes in church halls, community centres and private homes around the country.[670]

A refugee advocate told the inquiry how a boy who had spent 12 months on Nauru scored 95.5 on his VCE after just two years of school in Australia. He would have had to pay overseas student fees, making university unaffordable, but supporters were able to organise a scholarship for him to study Commerce and Civil Engineering at Melbourne University and for him to stay at a university college.

A member of a refugee support group told the inquiry that in the previous financial year it had expended about 17,000 hours of volunteer time and given over $50,000 to asylum seekers.

A worker with the Asylum Seeker Centre in Sydney told the inquiry that government policy which did not allow asylum seekers to work created unnecessary tasks for underfunded charities choosing to support this community:

> We have a current active caseload of 180 asylum seekers, and 4½ full-time staff. We don't have time to do anything but the basics. We get people into short-term accommodation, refer people to pro bono health practitioners and counsellors, and do some individual advocacy. We work with schools to get discounts so children can attend in a normal way. We organise lunch for people. It's not a given that people are going to eat every day if it's not provided. We get no government funding, and funding is a constant struggle. Over 70 per cent of the people we've interviewed have had skills which are on the skilled occupations list on the DIMIA website.

Part 5

THE GOLDEN CAGE:
POST-CORNELIA CHANGES

Following the Cornelia Rau scandal and the release of the damaging Palmer Inquiry report, the Howard government initiated changes in the Department of Immigration. According to the new head of the department, Andrew Metcalfe, the three key aims of the changes were: to develop and maintain an open and accountable culture, to promote fair and reasonable dealings with clients, and to ensure well-trained and supported staff.[671]

In line with this philosophy, senior officials in the department contacted the People's Inquiry into Detention after the release of its first report, and offered to help provide information and facilitate detention centre inspections on request. However, while it did host visits of Inquiry representatives to the Perth and Northern detention centres and responded to initial written questions, the department later failed to provide the inquiry with answers to many questions put to it over almost a year.

The changes in the Immigration Department have brought about positive practical outcomes for some asylum seekers. In June 2005, then immigration minister Amanda Vanstone announced that all families with children under 18 would be held in community detention rather than detention centres.[672] Most long-term detainees who arrived by boat were released from detention by the end of 2005.[673]

But almost five and a half thousand people were put into immigration detention at some time during 2006–07, with the highest number held on any one day being 847.[674] As at 30 June 2007, over half of the 441 people held in immigration detention had been there for more than six months, with 22 per cent of these (97 people) being detained for more than two years.[675]

Asylum seekers who have been in detention for more than two years now have their cases reviewed by the Commonwealth ombudsman, who recommends courses of action to the immigration minister. The minister must table the ombudsman's report and recommendations in parliament, but is under no obligation to follow them.

As at 30 June 2007, the department had reported to the ombudsman the circumstances of 367 people who had been detained for two years or more. Of these, 275 were no longer in detention. This number included 106 people who had been granted temporary visas, 102 people who had been granted permanent visas, and 39 others living in the community on a variety of conditions.[676]

However, despite a February 2006 ombudsman's report recommending then immigration minister Amanda Vanstone make a decision 'as soon as possible' in the case of a mentally ill Turkish man in detention, the man was still detained (and had been for four and a half years) when the Howard government was voted out of office in November 2007.[677]

In March 2007, then immigration minister Kevin Andrews rejected a recommendation from the acting Commonwealth ombudsman that another mentally ill man, who had spent almost seven years in detention, be granted a permanent visa. The man's condition was such that at one time he had set fire to a bed before lying on it. The ombudsman's office concluded that, although the man had been released from detention, his temporary visa status was having a continuing adverse impact on his health.[678]

The physical environment and conditions in most detention centres has improved. In 2006, the year before its closure, Baxter underwent a $5.5 million upgrade. Announcing the upgrade in September 2005, then immigration minister Amanda Vanstone said it would make Baxter 'friendlier' and that improvements would include a new visitor centre, cafeteria, a 'fabulous' floodlit oval, plus basketball and volleyball courts.[679] A former detention officer told the inquiry:

> There's a new oval out there. It's not very often used. I believe initially it was to get people from the outside to come in to play. They can't get insurance for that oval, there are no external gates so the other sporting teams can't come in. At one stage there were only Aussie Rules posts put at either end and Indonesians and Middle Easterners wouldn't have a clue what that meant, so that was quite sad.

In August 2006, Amanda Vanstone announced that a new $5.4 million accommodation wing at Villawood could 'store' up to 40 detainees and that:

> There are a lot of Australians who don't have houses anywhere near as good as these houses are.[680]

However, a visitor who attends church services at Villawood told the inquiry some detainees did not want to use the new area:

> They have built this brand new place and it is less coercive and you can go out and shop but you have a guard with you, of course. They have asked a number of people who have refused to go because they have community inside that they have developed over two or three years and

because they are afraid that, if they go there, it is just a ruse to get them into another place and then whisk them off at midnight on a plane home. Because they have seen it happen.

Despite the new accommodation, in January 2008 the Human Rights and Equal Opportunity Commission (HREOC) described the part of Villawood that accommodates some of the longest term detainees as 'the most prison-like of all facilities' and recommended it be demolished.[681]

A visitor to Villawood described visiting shortly after razor wire had been removed from the centre perimeter:

This is my second visit to Villawood. The razor wire was gone, but they were a bit glum. Was it because of the elderly lady, new in here, who cried for the duration of our visit? Was it because of the fire the night before? Was it because of the two people who have been on a hunger strike for two months now? An ambulance arrived while we were there – was it for them? Was it because of the detainee who had recently attempted suicide?

Maybe it was because of the call for one of our new friends to collect something from the property section. When the guard came the request was met with a direct refusal. We were told when they call you to property, sometimes they send you to Baxter or deport you. They do it on Friday afternoons so you can't contact anyone to help you. All of our friends became quiet and anxious. The one who was called paled, developed a tremor and was very distracted. Later the guard encouraged her away with assurances that it was all good. Those remaining watched a panel van in the car park. If that van comes this way it will be very bad. But the razor wire was gone.

In late 2006, Commonwealth ombudsman Professor John McMillan said Immigration Minister Amanda Vanstone had mostly been responsive to his recommendations, and that he had noticed 'a significant culture change' in the Immigration Department.[682]

Around the same time, HREOC visited detention centres, releasing a report in early 2007. Human rights commissioner Graeme Innes said:

There have been substantial efforts to improve the physical environment, reduce the tension levels, enhance the programs and activities available to detainees and improve mental health services. DIMA [Department of Immigration and Multicultural Affairs] and the detention services provider (GSL) also seem more open to requests, suggestions and concerns voiced by detainees.[683]

The report found that Maribyrnong had introduced internet access for detainees and that the Immigration Department intended this to be available in all other detention centres. Villawood detainees also have access to the internet, although the inquiry was told there were four computers for about 200 detainees until late December 2007, when another five computers were made available for four hours a day. If a computer is available, a detainee can use it for one hour per day. Many websites are filtered out, including the Global Solutions Limited (GSL) website, and those for shopping, banking and social networking. Detainees are also now allowed a personal mobile phone. Before it closed, Baxter detainees could also buy and cook a limited amount of their own food. HREOC found this arrangement to be very popular because it occupied people constructively and allowed detainees some autonomy.

HREOC also reported that detainees at Villawood could be selected to go on a 'Mystery Tour' which ran approximately every two months. However, detention officers selected who could go and the destination for that excursion. There was no transparency as to how participants were selected and those chosen were only told shortly before the tour took place. The program was suspended one year later. Instead of having detainees earn points for performing labour within detention centres, the Immigration Department introduced the Purchasing Allowance Scheme. All detainees receive 25 merit points per week, but can earn up to 200 points per month, at a rate of two points per hour. The points can then be used to make purchases, but cannot be cashed out when people leave detention. Points are earned for participation in 'meaningful activities' such as life-skills classes, sport, computer training and English classes, but not labour.

However, a Villawood detainee told the inquiry that three detainees there performed duties that could be categorised as labour in return for merit points, including two who worked at the detainee shop. He also criticised the scheme, saying the poverty of those in detention forced many of them to participate in activities they did not want to undertake and the monitoring associated with the activities unreasonably intruded into their privacy. He added that people who were sick, introverted, seeing visitors, studying privately or preparing their legal cases lost the opportunity to earn merit points.

He also said that the system promoted corruption, with records of participation in activities, such as gym, being falsified. These false records were then used to create reports under Section 486N of the *Migration Act*, which states the Department of Immigration must make a report every six months to the Commonwealth ombudsman relating to the circumstances of a person's detention. The ombudsman considers the department's report when making an assessment about the appropriateness of the arrangements for an individual's detention. Detainees reported as participating in recreational, sporting and religious activities may not have actually done so, or may have done so only because they needed the merit points to buy items such as cigarettes.

The same detainee also told the inquiry that as detainees were not allowed to accumulate more than 200 points they could therefore not buy anything more expensive than $200. However, he said that detainees often bought cigarettes and sold them to others at lower prices, including to detention officers, in order to accumulate extra money and circumvent this restriction.

In its 2006 inspections of detention centres, HREOC found very few of its posters displayed, except in Maribyrnong. Detainees told HREOC staff that posters at the Northern centre and Baxter had been put up only a week before their visit. At the Northern centre it found a structured program for internal activities had only been developed the week before its visit, and that one of these activities was the washing of staff cars by detainees.

HREOC also found evidence that disturbing practices continued in detention centres. Detainees in Baxter and Villawood reported delays in accessing health procedures. Some mental health staff told them that the suicide and self-harm system was sometimes used as a behaviour, rather than mental health, management tool.[684]

Despite Department of Immigration brochures stating, 'There are no children in immigration detention centres',[685] HREOC also stated:

It was disappointing to find 13 unaccompanied children in the Northern centre when HREOC visited on 1 November. All of these children were Indonesian boys found on illegal fishing boats. As at 1 November, those 13 children had been detained for between eight and 15 days. We understand that all 13 children had been returned to Indonesia as at 1 December ... HREOC saw no evidence of any effort to provide the children detained at the Northern centre with appropriate education or recreation activities. There was no teacher to conduct classes for them;

no contingency arrangements for the children to be placed in external schools in the event that they could not be turned around quickly; no special activities for the children inside the centre; and no efforts to take the children on external excursions.[686]

HREOC concluded that despite efforts to improve the environment inside detention facilities 'the fundamental problem with immigration detention has not changed – namely the length of detention and the uncertainty about how much longer that detention will last'.[687] It stated:

It is for this reason that HREOC reiterates its call for the repeal of the mandatory detention laws. In the absence of repealing mandatory detention, there should be greater efforts to promptly release detainees and resolve visa decisions.[688]

In late 2006, then immigration minister Amanda Vanstone announced that management of health and psychological services in detention would be transferred from the detention contractor to the direct control of the Immigration Department.[689] In briefing potential providers of these services, the department stated that health promotion and preventative health services such as health screening and education should be provided in detention.[690] A later departmental briefing to potential providers acknowledges that detention harms mental health, but does not seem to have a clear understanding of why:

Understanding the effect detention has on emotional well-being, health services include the provision of mental health services, such as screening or access to specialists … When an individual's well-being is maintained, a sense of collective well-being will follow. This will help facilitate a positive and healthy detention environment. The aim of the detention system is to ensure that the only change to an individual's well-being as a result of being in detention is the restriction of freedom of movement … The detention services provider/s and DIAC [Department of Immigration and Citizenship] must have a comprehensive understanding of the factors that underpin well-being in order to administer the appropriate services. This includes normalising the detention environment to the greatest extent possible.[691]

However, many health professionals and detainees have argued that mental health promotion efforts in detention are ineffective as they do not address the main sources of mental distress for detainees. Psychiatrist Jon Jureidini told the inquiry that working with the Department of Immigration to meet the mental health needs of detainees risked being collusive with the detention system:

> ...because we will take the sickest of your detainees and get them back into health just to stop the whole system from collapsing. Well, it might be better to just let the whole system collapse. Are we doing more harm than good by being seen to be providing top quality mental health services to people so that DIMIA [the Department of Immigration, Multicultural and Indigenous Affairs] can say we are looking after these people really well, when in fact what we're doing is from a mental health perspective completely useless. When we talk about the adequacy of mental health services there are two ways of talking about it. One is the quantity and quality of it is grossly deficient, the other is the impossibility of providing meaningful mental health services in that environment.

A boy who spent three years in detention told the inquiry:

> That was the worst thing – people coming to tell me, 'How can we fix your problems?' The only way you could help me was to release me. There was no other way. They said you should talk about it, it will help you, and I talked about it. It doesn't, it just doesn't. This is not something that will be helped by just talking about it.

A man detained in Villawood told the inquiry:

> The 'better conditions' discussed by HREOC are meaningless when you are depressed over your lack of freedom and your life is run by management who hail from a corrective services background and mentality.

Public health researcher Pauline McLoughlin has argued that immigration detainees face an uncertain future, loss of control over their daily lives, boredom, a lack of services, constant scrutiny and public demonisation. This puts the detention system intrinsically at odds with the central principle of health promotion – enabling people to increase control over, and to improve, their health.[692]

McLoughlin argues that detention health service providers who do not challenge the detention itself risk aligning themselves with the detention system and perpetuating the mental distress of those detained.[693] She concludes that refugee advocates and health professionals working outside the system have been far more effective in promoting the mental health of detainees as they have worked both to improve conditions in detention, and to ultimately remove people from it by pursuing legal and policy reform. The alliance of these advocates is very clearly with the detained and as such challenges the dehumanisation the detention system subjects them to.

Several people who had worked in detention centres told the inquiry that efforts to improve the physical conditions or material items available in detention were ineffective in terms of alleviating mental health problems. Former Woomera teacher Tom Mann told the inquiry:

> *Detainees will continue to deteriorate in their mental state, especially if kept longer than three months. I don't believe it is possible to prevent this downhill slide by improving conditions in the detention centre.*

A nurse told the inquiry:

> *I was working in Baxter for three months and, even within this time, the deteriorating mental and physical health of most of the detainees was patently obvious. These individuals craved some identification of a definite period they must serve and then freedom would be their reward. But every person within the system was acutely aware of the permanent absence of time frames. This was the root of their despair.*

A former Woomera worker told the inquiry:

> *Detainees didn't want what we call material stuff, such as soccer balls, Nintendo's, computers, books, all sorts of things. They would demonstrate against receiving this sort of help and all they would say is they wanted their freedom, or they wanted information from immigration about how their freedom would come about.*

Visitors who tried to make life easier for those in detention also reached the same conclusion. One refugee advocate told the inquiry:

*I had all this Afghan food because Ramadan finished and they could eat
all this special food. I had brought all this stuff. People had given me all
these gifts. You know, it didn't matter. All this stuff didn't mean a thing.
All their hope was they needed to get out.*

Refugee advocate Kate Gauthier, who was an early visitor to Curtin
detention centre, told the inquiry:

*We met a family who had completely broken down. I spoke to the
mother – this was just prior to them moving to Baxter – telling her
there will be better conditions in Baxter and you will have visitors and
everything. She looked at us and she said, 'We don't want your golden
cage.'*

Despite improvements implemented since the Cornelia Rau scandal, the
inquiry also heard evidence of disturbing incidents continuing within
detention centres. For instance, in August 2005, the Australian government
attempted for the second time to deport a Palestinian man without
informing his lawyers or the UN Human Rights Committee, which was
reviewing his case. As the man's plane departed, the Federal Court granted
an injunction against the deportation and he was returned to Australia
from Dubai. He was later recognised as a refugee.

In January 2006, the Federal Court intervened to stop the deportation
of 45-year-old Turkish Kurd Ali Beyazkilinc, ruling that such a move
would significantly worsen his already severe mental condition, after his
psychiatrist claimed the man was unfit to travel.[694] The airline that was to
be used in the deportation had allocated 140 seats on a flight to Istanbul
to prevent disruption to other passengers.[695] Then immigration minister
Amanda Vanstone responded to the court injunction, saying:

*If we come to the state or situation where if someone can be designated
as being mentally ill and not removed, I think you will find there will
be a lot of people who are very stressed and therefore seeking not to be
removed on that basis.*[696]

On 27 March 2007, a Chinese democracy activist was deported after
three years in detention and a Chinese Falun Gong practitioner due to be
deported was taken to Auburn Hospital with head injuries.[697]

The next day a 35-year-old Falun Gong practitioner was dragged screaming from her bed at 4am by at least six guards. Her deportation prompted about 35 other mainly Chinese detainees, many of whom were interviewed by Chinese authorities inside Villawood in 2005, to start a hunger strike. Thirty five days later, three women and one man were still refusing food, with one woman having been hospitalised about six times. Four other Chinese asylum seekers were deported during the hunger strike.[698]

In September 2007, the Immigration Department attempted to deport to China an asylum seeker who had been in detention for four years, despite a UN Human Rights Committee request to stay his removal pending their investigation. His removal was proposed despite the fact that Australia has no extradition treaty with China.

The asylum seeker's visa had been cancelled on the basis of an unsigned, undated Chinese arrest warrant, which would be dismissed in an Australian court. While the name on this warrant was the same as the asylum seeker's, the surname is the fourth most common in China. The warrant also had no other data such as date of birth, address or occupation, which could prove he was the same man. An internal Immigration Department memo said of conflicting address information: 'Not an exact match but clearly in the neighbourhood.'

In public correspondence, the Immigration Department stated it had received assurances the man would not be executed upon return to China. However, in an internal memo dated 17 March 2006, an officer in the Removals Support Section, Canberra, stated the section had not sought an assurance about the death penalty and were not aware it was an issue. The day he was due to be deported the asylum seeker was admitted to Bankstown Hospital for surgery to remove a razor blade from his oesophagus.[699]

In October 2007, Federal Court judge Margaret Stone described the deportation of Timothy Borstrok to New Zealand, despite him lodging an appeal against a decision to cancel his visa, as 'truly disgraceful', telling the lawyer acting for then immigration minister Kevin Andrews:

The applicant is not here so he does not have legal representation. It is inevitable it will be dismissed and it is exactly, one would assume, what your client has intended, that he has no effective right of appeal. When the law allows for a right, this is just flagrant violation of his rights and it is all the more disgraceful because this court can do nothing about it.[700]

A spokeswoman for the minister justified the removal on the basis that Mr Borstrok, who did not have a lawyer, had not lodged an injunction against his removal.

Three days later, a Sri Lankan man, who claimed to have been tortured by having his penis burnt with hot irons, his legs beaten and his lips torn from repeatedly being punched in the face, was deported from Maribyrnong detention centre. His claim for asylum had been rejected, and he was handcuffed and injected with a chemical sedative at around 4am in preparation for his removal, despite a medical report stating:

> The scars on the legs are consistent with being beaten. The scars on his lips are consistent with being punched in the face. The areas of pigmentation on his penis are consistent with being burnt.[701]

In February 2007, a Villawood detainee complained to NSW Police that he had been assaulted by another detainee. NSW Police reluctantly took an incomplete statement from him and told him that as the alleged assault had occurred on Commonwealth land, NSW Police could not investigate. Three months later, after sending two letters to NSW police, the detainee was told his allegation 'will be forwarded to the Australian Federal Police (AFP) for further investigation'.[702]

In July 2007, after having sent another letter to NSW Police, the detainee received a response from them. It stated that a confidential Memorandum of Understanding (MOU) regarding offences committed at Villawood placed responsibility for investigations with the Immigration Department, supported by the AFP.[703]

Two weeks later, following yet another letter from the detainee, NSW Police told him that although no MOU actually existed, one was being negotiated and that Crown Law advice provided to the NSW ombudsman supported the view that the AFP was responsible for policing Villawood.[704] When the detainee requested this Crown Law advice from the NSW ombudsman he was told:

> Section 34 of the Ombudsman Act 1974 prevents this office from disclosing this information. Consequently the NSW Police Force is the appropriate authority from which you should be seeking such information. I appreciate that you may be disappointed that this office cannot further assist you.[705]

Six months after the detainee first complained of the assault, he responded to the ombudsman's office by writing that Section 34 of the act allowed disclosure of information if it was believed necessary to prevent harm, including self-harm, being done to any person:

> I am not only disappointed; I am furious and am prepared to pave the way for removing any perceived restriction which s34 of the Ombudsman Act 1974 might pose ... My question is that should I slash my throat or jump from the roof or commit suicide or take the law in my own hands by punishing the person who has assaulted me as I may consider fit as the government's response in my case is nothing but harassment, harassment and continual harassment. Please let me know if my proposal is able to satisfy s34 (1) (b2) of the Ombudsman Act 1974 or should I act in a manner as suggested above.

In late November 2007, a member of the NSW Police visited the detainee in Villawood and told him that in the near future two NSW Police officers would be stationed there, paid for by the federal government. They would investigate some matters, referring others to the AFP.

The inquiry was also told that police did not seem to have any problem investigating complaints from detention authorities. In April 2007, a Baxter detainee with bi-polar disorder was due in court to face charges of property damage. He had broken fluorescent tubes in frustration after waiting nearly five months to see a specialist. However, detention officers denied the man transport to the court, saying they had no record of him being due there and refusing to speak to a supporter waiting for him. A jail order was issued against the detainee before the magistrate was told what had happened.

In June 2007, a North Korean couple in Baxter attempted suicide by taking a drug overdose and were transferred to hospital after their asylum claims were rejected. The week before Christmas 2007, two detainees who had been receiving psychiatric care at Toowong Private Hospital were discharged to detention against medical advice. One of the men was given six days supply of medication, which he took on his first night in detention. Found unconscious in the morning, he was taken back to hospital.[706]

In June 2007, the government presented its response to a Senate committee report. It stated that a senior immigration officer must endorse any detainee being placed in a management unit within 24 hours, and that the management units at Villawood and Baxter had not been used since February and October 2006 respectively.[707] However, a Villawood detainee told the inquiry that while the management unit had not been used for a time, from about September 2007 it was again being used, albeit less frequently and for shorter periods. He said it was primarily used to punish detainees who had assaulted others or instigated protests.

The inquiry also received information that in October 2007, a man released from hospital following a serious suicide attempt was kept in an isolation room at Villawood with nothing but a blanket and two guards in the room watching him. When he requested a second blanket, he did not receive it for 20 hours and Catholic nuns and a priest who asked to visit him were denied access.[708]

Senior immigration officials have continued to distort the reality of detention. In June 2007, Andrew Metcalfe, the secretary of the Immigration Department, gave an address on detention reforms in which he stated, 'What is not always clearly understood is that the power of detention is not punitive in nature' and that one of the policy purposes of immigration detention is to ensure that noncitizens who arrive unlawfully 'are provided with access to appropriate services, such as health or counselling'.[709]

According to the Department of Immigration, it is developing alternative detention arrangements and, in the future, detainees may be held in Residential Housing centres, immigration transit accommodation centres (once established) and in the community.[710] In late 2005, a worker with a refugee assistance organisation told the inquiry:

> There are many more opportunities for community agencies to have open and frank dialogue with senior DIMIA personnel. We are being consulted a lot more. Yesterday in Canberra one of the things discussed with us was the possibility of a community care program. It's a model where people who arrive in Australia from 1 February 2006 and end up in detention could be released into the community.

However as at 11 January 2008, about 93 per cent of immigration detainees were still held under guard, the overwhelming majority in immigration detention centres.[711]

A May 2006 Department of Immigration information paper defines operating principles for detention, including that facility-based detention should be for the shortest possible time. Yet it also seeks to blame detainees who exercise their legal rights for prolonging their own incarceration, stating, 'A decision by a detainee to appeal their removal from Australia may result in an extension of their stay in facility-based detention.'[712]

In a 2007 Industry Briefing to potential detention and health services providers, the department states that:

Immigration detention is an option of last resort for people while their status as unlawful noncitizens within Australia is under review.[713]

But UnitingJustice Australia and Hotham Mission Asylum Seeker Project argued in a submission to the inquiry that while the *Migration Act*'s new Statement of Intent notes that children should be detained as a last resort, the retention of mandatory detention rendered the sentiment meaningless. An immigration officer must, as a matter of first resort, detain any person, including any child, they suspect to be an unlawful noncitizen. Community detention options can only be granted by the minister personally, a process that generally takes four to six weeks.[714]

Despite the former Howard government talking about alternative detention arrangements, in January 2007 it was reportedly considering building a new 800-bed detention centre in Sydney to replace Villawood.[715] It also constructed a high security 800- bed detention centre on Christmas Island, 1000kms from the Australian mainland, at an estimated cost of $400 million.[716]

The Christmas Island detention centre was built to process boat arrivals that land on the Australian mainland, even though just 226 people arrived by boat without authorisation between 2002 and 2007,[717] only about 100 of whom reached the mainland.[718]

The centre has an eight cot nursery, a childcare centre, play area, classrooms, hospital, operating theatre, visiting rooms with noncontact glass panels and management units, which include facilities for families. The centre is surrounded by electric fences and microwave movement detectors, and in every room there are cameras with microphones, linked to a control room in Canberra, behind heavy metal grilles. Detainees will wear electronic ID tags which will identify them wherever they are in the complex by locator beacons.[719] Refugee advocate Pamela Curr told *The Age*:

It's at the far end of an island that is 24kms long, surrounded by impenetrable cliffs. What's the point of all this security?[720]

A resident of Christmas Island told the inquiry:

> *Islanders are constantly raising money to assist the refugees in their court bids. They are quite certain now how they stand and they are not happy about how the island is used to abuse people's rights. They want tourism to be the backbone of the economy, not a prison. The new detention centre is becoming an obscene blot on our island.*

The Howard government also continued to tighten legislation relating to asylum seekers after the Cornelia Rau scandal. In July 2005, a further 5000 islands around the entire northern half of the Australian coastline were excised from the migration zone, despite a motion by Democrats senator Andrew Bartlett to disallow the legislation.

In January 2006, 43 West Papuan asylum seekers evaded detection by Australian authorities and arrived on the Australian mainland in a traditional boat. Their recognition as refugees caused a diplomatic row with Indonesia and in a move widely seen as an attempt to appease a furious Indonesian government, then prime minister John Howard sought to harden policy further.

He proposed sending all asylum seekers who arrived by boat offshore for processing, effectively excising the whole of Australia from its migration zone. Even those found to be refugees were to be settled in countries other than Australia – a process which could have resulted in their indefinite detention.[721]

Liberal MP Petro Georgiou called it 'the most profoundly disturbing piece of legislation I have encountered since becoming a member of parliament'.[722] Howard only withdrew the legislation after government backbenchers Georgiou, Russell Broadbent and Judi Moylan crossed the floor to vote against it in the lower house and it was clear that government senator Judith Troeth would do the same to defeat it in the Senate.

However, in September and October 2006, eight Burmese asylum seekers were sent to Nauru, on a flight that cost $225,000,[723] after they had arrived at Ashmore Reef in August. In December 2006, they received letters from the Australian government telling them their only chance to be accepted for settlement in Australia was if they agreed to return to Malaysia, where they feared arrest and deportation, while their refugee status was being assessed.

If they remained in Nauru, they would not be accepted by Australia even if found to be refugees. Instead, Australia would look at finding them a third country 'which may take some time'.[724] In April 2007, immigration officials visiting Nauru refused to interview the asylum seekers for refugee visas. In May 2007, their lawyers took the Australian government to the High Court over the refusal to consider their applications for refugee status[725] and, two months later, the Immigration Department agreed to interview the men.[726]

A year after the Burmese asylum seekers had been sent to Nauru, then immigration minister Kevin Andrews refused a HREOC request to visit them on the basis that it had no jurisdiction over offshore facilities.[727] Human Rights Commissioner Graeme Innes told *The Australian* he was reluctant to visit without permission, saying:

> *If I didn't have their approval there are doubts as to whether I would get a visa to Nauru, and if I would get permission to inspect the detention centre.*[728]

In late September 2007, Burma was shaken by protests in which dozens of people were believed killed by security forces. John Howard described the country as being run by:

> *... a thoroughly loathsome regime and the repression is appalling. I'm glad that the United Nations is saying something about it and I hope that it can take some concerted action through the Security Council. But it's a closed country, it's a very unforgiving regime and it's very resistant to outside pressure. Nothing changes in the mind of the regime. [But] equally the people are resilient and there's a real spark of freedom there and there is a desire to enjoy that freedom.*[729]

In March 2007, *The Australian* reported that the then immigration minister Kevin Andrews had proposed that Indonesia become part of Australia's offshore immigration processing regime despite the fact Indonesia has not signed the UN's Refugee Convention.[730] Earlier that month, 83 Sri Lankan asylum seekers, including Tamils from the east of the country, were intercepted off Christmas Island. Australian and Indonesian immigration officials negotiated a plan to return them to Indonesia for repatriation to Sri Lanka without being allowed to make claims for asylum, possibly breaching international refugee conventions.[731]

A recent United Nations High Commissioner for Refugees (UNHCR) report on Tamils in the east of Sri Lanka stated:

Harassment, intimidation, arrest, detention, torture, abduction and killing ... are frequently reported to be inflicted.[732]

Sri Lankan ambassador to Indonesia, Janaka Perera, who was consulted by Australian and Indonesian officials about the plans for the asylum seekers, said they were probably economic migrants who had nothing to fear. But as reporter Mike Steketee argued:

Perera's involvement breaches the fundamental tenet of refugee law that the country from which asylum seekers flee should play no part in deciding their future.[733]

When the plan to return them to Indonesia was dismissed, an immigration official left open the idea that they could be allowed to settle in Australia if found to be refugees before they were flown to Nauru. However, at the same time Kevin Andrews declared they would be settled in a third country if they were found to be refugees.[734] A spokesperson for the UNHCR said:

Anyone recognised as a refugee is going to need state protection somewhere and we'd hope that Australia will play its part.[735]

It having taken five years for refugees from the *Tampa* to be removed from detention in Nauru, Nauruan government officials stated publicly, after the Sri Lankans were transferred there, that they wanted their applications processed within six to 12 months.[736] The Refugee and Immigration Legal Centre (RILC) flew a team of lawyers and interpreters to Nauru to assist 27 of the Sri Lankans in May 2007, much of which was paid for by private donations. Six months after their arrival on Nauru, 55 of the Sri Lankans started a hunger strike, during which seven were hospitalised, to protest the inaction on their claims. It was called off a week later after the Immigration Department promised their claims would be decided 'within days'.[737]

Shortly afterwards, Kevin Andrews announced that 72 of the Sri Lankans had been found to be refugees, but that Australia would not be settling them and they would remain on Nauru until another country agreed to take them, saying:

The successful reduction in the number of people seeking to enter Australia unlawfully has been a direct result of the Howard government's clear policy that persons who seek to enter Australia illegally will not be settled in Australia.[738]

However, an editorial in *The Age* newspaper argued:

What kind of country has Australia become? The men are in for a long and possibly fruitless wait ... other countries are reluctant to accept people they consider, with justification, to be Australia's responsibility.[739]

Almost two weeks after they were found to be refugees, the Howard government had made no approach to the countries most likely to consider resettling them – Norway, Denmark, Sweden, the United States, Canada and New Zealand.[740] This is despite Kevin Andrews announcing months earlier that Australia and the US had signed an agreement allowing third country resettlement of up to 200 refugees claiming asylum in those countries each year, saying at the time that the 83 Sri Lankan and eight Burmese asylum seekers on Nauru could be the first to be resettled in the US.[741]

In August 2007, the Howard government secretly returned five Papuan asylum seekers to Papua New Guinea, without allowing them to apply for refugee status despite them raising 'protection concerns' with authorities. They had landed at Saibai Island, which had been excised from the migration zone, and were held in immigration detention for almost a month, during which time two of the men were flown to Cairns for medical treatment. Despite usually announcing the arrival of asylum seekers in boats, the government did not make a public announcement in this case. Refugee lawyer David Manne told a newspaper that returning the men was 'profoundly concerning and scandalous' and questioned whether Australia had violated its international obligations to protect refugees.[742]

During his time as immigration minister, Philip Ruddock repeatedly claimed that African refugees were more deserving of refugee places than the mainly Middle Eastern asylum seekers who arrived by boat between 1999 and 2002. However, in early October 2007, shortly after three white youths had been charged with the bashing and death of Sudanese refugee Liep Gony, Kevin Andrews claimed the proportion of Africans in the 2007–08 refugee intake was being cut due to concerns about their ability to integrate into Australian society.

He released a dossier, allegedly based on 'anecdotal' feedback from the community, claiming that African refugees formed gangs, fought in nightclubs and attacked other families. When Victorian Police commissioner Christine Nixon stated that Sudanese people were not over-represented in crime statistics, Andrews dismissed it saying, 'You can use data in all sorts of ways.'[743] In a previous press release, he had explained the changed composition of the refugee intake as a result of improved conditions in some African countries, and a need to help Iraqis displaced by the war and Burmese refugees in camps near the Thai border.

A week after the seven Burmese asylum seekers had spent one year in detention in Nauru with no indication of when their claims would be processed, former foreign affairs minister Alexander Downer supported Andrews, saying:

> When you see the situation in Burma today, the brutality of what the regime has done in recent times, you can't help but appreciate the priority we need to give to Burma.[744]

In October 2007, the Howard government introduced a 20-question computer-based citizenship test, available only in English. Applicants for citizenship had to correctly answer 12 questions, including three about the responsibilities and privileges of Australian citizenship. The booklet applicants read to prepare for the test provided information on Australian history, geography, national emblems, the parliamentary system of government and the responsibilities and privileges of being an Australian citizen. It described the values important in modern Australia as including: respect for the equal worth, dignity and freedom of the individual, equality under the law, and tolerance, mutual respect and compassion for those in need.[745]

In January 2008, it was revealed that of 10,636 people who had sat the citizenship test in the three months since its introduction, 2,311 had failed, prompting new Labor immigration minister Chris Evans to promise a review of it.[746] The inquiry was informed of one man's experience of the test:

> A refugee friend of mine today sat the ludicrous citizenship test. This cultured, honourable man failed. He has his own business in Australia, built from nothing, and employs others. He is law-abiding, of courage and high morals ... just the sort of person we should welcome into this country. Should the fact that he didn't remember the date of Federation or the names of a couple of sportspeople stand in the way of his gaining a passport?

Despite many positive reforms introduced to the Immigration Department in the wake of the Cornelia Rau scandal, evidence gathered by the inquiry into Detention shows that the fundamental problems with Australian government policy remain.

The inquiry heard that significant numbers of people continue to be incarcerated for considerable periods in immigration detention, despite having committed no criminal offence. As at the end of June 2007, over half of the people held in immigration detention had been there for more than six months, with almost a quarter being detained for more than two years.[747]

Evidence presented to the inquiry from a range of sources indicates that this deprivation of liberty is the primary cause of the serious damage inflicted on people by immigration detention, and that despair has resulted in continuing incidents of self-harm within detention centres.

The inquiry heard that many people released after spending years in detention centres continue to have serious mental health problems and that a lack of certainty about their future exacerbates these. Some have been released on visas conditional on the person agreeing to present themselves for removal from Australia at any time. Others hold visas which render them dependent on charity or unable to see family members they have been separated from for years.

The inquiry heard that there are still serious issues of accountability regarding immigration detention, with authorities such as the Commonwealth ombudsman powerless to enforce its recommendations. Evidence was also presented outlining the attempted deportation of people suffering from serious mental illness or later recognised as refugees, and the actual deportation of people for whom credible safety and humanitarian concerns existed.

A CHANGE OF GOVERNMENT:
SOME CHANGE OF HEART?

The election of the Rudd Labor government in late November 2007 offered many asylum seekers and their supporters hope that policies would change. In April 2007, the Australian Labor Party national conference adopted a refugee policy which it took to the election. It included the use of mandatory detention only for the purpose of initial health, identity and security checks, with children and family groups housed under supervision in the community during these; making the length and conditions of detention subject to review; public sector management of detention centres; abolishing the 'Pacific Solution'; reviewing the '45 day rule', which removes work rights from many asylum seekers in the community; establishing a new refugee determination tribunal; and providing permanent protection to people found to be refugees.[748]

Within weeks of victory, the new government had granted refugee status to the Burmese held for over a year on Nauru and resettled them in Australia. In January 2008, the first of 75 Sri Lankans on Nauru, recognised as refugees but not offered resettlement by the Howard government, also arrived in Australia.[749] The following month, the Labor government announced that the detention centres on Nauru and Manus Island would be permanently closed. It also moved to grant humanitarian visas to a number of Afghan asylum seekers who had been stranded in Indonesia for up to seven years.[750]

In the May 2008 Budget, Labor announced the abolition of the Temporary Protection Visa. After less than three months as immigration minister, Chris Evans told a Senate committee he was uncomfortable with the ministerial intervention powers accorded to him under the *Migration Act*:

> *I have formed the view that I have too much power ... I am uncomfortable with that not just because of a concern about playing God, but also because of the lack of transparency and accountability for those ministerial decisions, the lack in some cases of any appeal rights against those decisions and the fact that what I thought was to be a power that was to be used in rare cases has become very much the norm. There is an industry in appealing to the minister for immigration and citizenship, I have noticed ... there is a real sense of the appeal to the minister becoming very much part of the process. Rather than being a check on the system it has become institutionalised.*[751]

However, in May 2008 refugee advocates expressed disappointment at the minister's refusal to intervene in some cases, with the Asylum Seeker Resource Centre saying 42 of its 43 cases before the minister had been rejected in five weeks. Some cases turned down included a Bangladeshi man married to and caring for a disabled Australian citizen, and a 63-

year-old East Timorese woman with no home in East Timor but three Australian citizen children and six grandchildren here.[752]

The same month, a Chinese asylum seeker was deported from Villawood a day after spending a week in hospital for swallowing an ID card, the head of a toothbrush and an iron button. However, two other Chinese men whose cases had been reviewed by the minister and who were told they were being deported were granted government funding to submit a further application to the minister after they protested on the roof of Villawood for three days.[753]

In May 2008, the Joint Standing Committee on Migration announced an inquiry into immigration detention in Australia. Its terms of reference include reviewing the appropriate length of detention, the options for community based detention and for the provision of services to immigration detainees. However, more than seven months after coming to power, Labor had yet to make any changes to the mandatory detention regime, institute a review process for immigration detention, grant work rights to all community-based asylum seekers or establish a new refugee determination tribunal.

Labor has also indicated it intends to continue some of the Howard government's policies. The day before the election Kevin Rudd told a newspaper that Labor would turn back boats of asylum seekers and continue to use detention as a deterrent, saying:

> You cannot have anything that is orderly if you allow people who do not have a lawful visa in this country to roam free. That's why you need a detention system. Deterrence is effective through the detention system but also your preparedness to take appropriate action as the vessels approach Australian waters on the high seas.[754]

In January 2008, immigration minister Chris Evans told ABC Radio that the Labor government would continue the people-smuggling disruption program in Indonesia[755] and that no decision had yet been made on whether to reverse the excision of 5000 islands from Australia's migration zone.[756]

Under Labor policy, asylum seekers who arrive by boat will be processed outside Australian law on Christmas Island, 2600 kilometres from Perth. In January 2008, refugee lawyer David Manne told a newspaper those found to be refugees may not be resettled in Australia:

It's a matter of profound concern that the government appears to be replacing the Pacific Solution with an Indian Ocean Solution.[757]

Swinburne University researcher Michelle Dimasi told a newspaper that Christmas Island locals are mystified at the resources that have gone into the detention centre, saying its facilities are equivalent to those found in a small town. They include a medical centre 'believed to be better equipped than the island's own medical centre'.[758]

In February 2008, Chris Evans told the Senate that he was considering how to deal with the renewal of the detention centre contracts, given the advanced stages of negotiations begun under the Howard government policy. The secretary of the department, Andrew Metcalfe, told the Senate:

Yes, it is fair to say that we are well advanced. We are at the evaluation stage and, as the minister alluded to, this has been a very expensive exercise. It is a very complex series of contracts and a great deal of effort has been put into getting us to the stage that we are currently at.[759]

Part 6

A FRESH START

The evidence presented to the People's Inquiry into Detention stands as a clear condemnation of government policies which damaged and, in some cases, destroyed the men, women and children who fled brutal regimes and asked for help. It condemns those politicians who, in the face of overwhelming evidence of the destruction such policies were causing, not only failed to change them, but continued to defend them.

The evidence provided to the inquiry offers the Rudd Labor government a unique opportunity to draw inspiration from the thousands of ordinary Australians and the few brave politicians (from several political parties) who stood against these policies and to close a chapter on a shameful era of Australian history.

It can choose to offer a fresh start, based on compassion and decency, to thousands of people whose resilience and courage enabled them to survive both the dangers they faced in their own countries and their disgraceful treatment in Australia. It can grant the wish that many former detainees expressed to the inquiry, that the practices that brutalised so many people are not repeated. One said:

> I'm asking the government to treat the people who came legal or illegal to Australia as a human being, not like an animal or to keep them in detention centres for all that time. That's all I hope for these people because I faced that and I don't want it to be the same for another person. We've been an example and that's it. We want just to finish it.

The inquiry recommends that three fundamental changes are needed to address the human rights issues arising from the evidence presented to it. These are to remove racism from, restore human rights to and reinstate accountability for immigration policy.

REMOVING RACISM

The inquiry has heard extensive evidence that many elements of migration policy disproportionately penalise people who are not Australian citizens in a way that is completely inconsistent with the way Australians would expect to be treated in similar circumstances.

In particular, the policy of mandatory detention deprives people of their liberty for an indefinite period. Deprivation of liberty is one of the most serious sanctions a state can issue against a human being and is ordinarily proscribed except where authorised by a court. The people imprisoned in Australia's detention centres have committed no crime and have not been charged with any offence.

Detained asylum seekers are incarcerated because they crossed a national border without documentation in order to seek asylum. The right to seek asylum is named in the Universal Declaration of Human Rights and guaranteed under the Refugee Convention; both are documents that Australia supports. Australians fleeing natural disasters from other states or suburbs could equally pose threats to an area's health or security, yet any attempt to indefinitely detain people crossing these internal borders would rightly be met with outrage.

The inquiry therefore recommends that asylum seekers should be treated with compassion and decency while their claims for refugee status are assessed. They should be held in open reception centres for a maximum of 48 hours for health and security checks upon arrival, after which they should be transferred to community housing and provided with health and welfare services. If the government believes individuals pose a threat to the community, the onus should be on it to prove this before a court. In these very exceptional cases, where a court agrees, immigration detention should be strictly monitored and continue to be judicially reviewed.

The inquiry further recommends that other aspects of immigration policy be amended to address concerns raised during the inquiry about their racist nature. During the past two decades, successive governments have introduced legislation specifically aimed at restricting the legal appeal rights of non-Australian citizens: they are routinely denied legal aid; their detention is not judicially reviewable; they have no legally enforceable right to a minimum standard of care while in detention; and some are made to pay for their incarceration. People who have been granted permission to stay in Australia permanently can suffer the double punishment of having this revoked if they subsequently serve a jail sentence. This treatment should not be tolerated just because the people it affects are not Australians.

The inquiry recommends the Rudd Labor government:

- Abolishes mandatory detention;
- Immediately releases all immigration detainees under residence determination provisions, ensuring they receive comprehensive health and welfare assessments and services unless they have been

judicially determined to be a security risk;

- Legislates to restore full access to judicial review of migration decisions, including access to legal aid;

- Legislates to ensure any immigration detention longer than 48 hours is judicially reviewed;

- Legislates to guarantee minimum standards in detention and a legal right to enforce them;

- Abolishes the practice of charging people for their detention and waives all debts currently outstanding;

- Legislates to remove the ability for Australian permanent visa holders to have their visas cancelled on character grounds.

RESTORING HUMAN RIGHTS

The Universal Declaration of Human Rights states that all people have the right to seek and enjoy asylum from persecution; that no-one should be subjected to arbitrary detention, cruel, inhuman or degrading treatment or interference in their family unit; and that all people have the right to work.[760] By endorsing this and as a signatory to other human rights conventions, Australia holds itself out as a compassionate and decent member of the international community. National leaders often invoke the 'Australian ethos' of mateship, helping those in need and 'a fair go'. However, the inquiry heard that the reality of Australian immigration policy was often diametrically opposed to these concepts.

The inquiry recommends the Rudd Labor government:

- Incorporates human rights conventions to which Australia is a signatory into Australian domestic law;

- Repeals legislation which allows excisions of Australian territory from the 'migration zone' and escorts asylum seekers intercepted at sea or in Australian territory to the Australian mainland for processing;

- Closes all isolation facilities in detention centres;

- Provides all people recognised as refugees with expedited family reunion, including all children who came to Australia as unaccompanied minors;

- Provides work rights, Medicare, income support, eligibility for concession cards and settlement assistance to all asylum seekers;
- Provides fully funded legal advice to all asylum seekers and immigration detainees;
- Offers non-detention-based repatriation assistance to failed asylum seekers;
- Conducts pre-removal assessments of failed asylum seekers and provides complementary protection where there are safety, humanitarian or welfare concerns;
- Grants Australian citizenship to asylum seekers found to be stateless.

REINSTATING ACCOUNTABILITY

Despite the Howard government claiming immigration as one of the most highly scrutinised portfolios, the inquiry heard that a number of factors allowed the Immigration Department to develop a culture which resulted in the gross abuses detailed in this report.

The public demonisation of asylum seekers and their supporters by ministers and senior officials encouraged their mistreatment by more junior officers. The remote locations in which asylum seekers were detained made it difficult for lawyers, human rights groups and supporters to offer effective assistance. The privatisation of detention centres and the imposition of fines for failing to meet standards created a conflict of interest for both the private operators and the department to accurately report on conditions in detention. Finally, the preparation undertaken by the department in advance of visits to detention centres by media, religious leaders and others, and the inability of human rights watchdogs such as the Human Rights and Equal Opportunity Commission (HREOC) and the Commonwealth ombudsman to enforce their recommendations, rendered the scrutiny ineffective.

The inquiry recommends the Rudd Labor government:

- Establishes a Royal Commission into the four aspects of immigration policy covered by this report: journeys into detention, the refugee assessment process, life in detention, and life for people after release from detention – in particular the role played by Australian government ministers and organisations including the Department of Immigration, the Royal Australian Navy and the Australian Federal Police;

- Holds a coronial investigation into the deaths of asylum seekers, immigration detainees and those refused asylum in Australia;
- Closes the Christmas Island detention centre;
- Restores government control of detention centres;
- Abolishes the ministerial intervention powers under the *Migration Act* and replaces them with reviewable administrative decisions;
- Allows media, human rights groups, religious leaders and politicians to make unannounced visits to detention centres;
- Resources an independent authority to effectively investigate immigration detainee complaints and make binding recommendations for their resolution.

RIGHTING THE WRONGS

Only by the full implementation of all these recommendations will men, women and children be protected from further abuse. The Australian Council of Heads of Schools of Social Work, in conjunction with the Centre for Human Rights Education (Curtin University) and Child Abuse Research Australia (Monash University) will closely monitor these areas. Royalties from the sales of this book will be used for this purpose.

APPENDICES

1. ACKNOWLEDGEMENTS

There are many people, from all walks of life and from all around Australia, who worked tirelessly for the People's Inquiry. The inquiry captured their hearts and minds and gave voice to those who bore witness to events that debased the nation. The generosity and passion of people affronted by immigration detention made the inquiry possible. As a collaborative project over a three-year time frame, it is not easy to single out individual contributions but we would particularly like to acknowledge the following people and organisations.

Among those who bestowed inspiration and guidance from the outset are Catherine Forsayeth, Marcus Einfeld, Madeleine Byrne and the Melbourne-based steering committee. Lyn Mitchell garnered a team of volunteers who were undaunted by the heartrending material with which they were confronted as they transcribed hundreds of hours of evidence to the inquiry. The legal firm Holding Redlich provided invaluable advice. Staff at Lonely Planet enthusiastically volunteered their time for editing, formatting and preparing the manuscript for publication. Many students were on placements or internships with the inquiry or volunteered their time in other ways including fund-raising. The inquiry ran on a small budget and the funding grants we received were greatly appreciated.

Crucial assistance and support was provided by: Zaid Alamiri, Adnan Alghazal, Kandie Allen-Kelly, Margaret Alston, Alperhan Babacan, Abdul Baig, Kerrie Barry, Alex Bhathal, Thea Birss, Jenny Bilos, Bridget Blair, Robert Bland, Neda Bojnordi, Jenny Bourne, Lydia Brown, Rob Bryant, Trish Bryant, Peter Cahill, Lesley Cambell, Ashlee Cannon, Peter Camilleri, Ellie Cobb, Barney Cooney, Laura Crawford, Rob Croser, Sophie Cunningham, Pamela Curr, Melanie Dankel, Azadeh Dastyari, Gillian Davy, Anna Demant, Simon Doyle, Nobesuthu Dumezweni, Jan Ellemor, Sophie Ellis, Bruce Evans, Marcus Finlay, Beth Flenley, Lucy Fiske, Christine Gamble, Kate Gauthier, Ardeshir Gholipour, Rosie Glow, Sian Gooden, Penelope Goodes, Diane Gosden,

Andrea Gowers, Paddy Hall, Jocelyn Harewood, Sue Hoffman, Pam Hewitt, John Highfield, Trish Highfield, Jim Hsu, Amin Houvedar Sefed, Richard Hugman, Carol Irizarry, Mary Ivec, Jon Jureidini, Mary-Anne Kenny, Liz Kirk, Anne Leith, Helen Lewers, Callum MacDonald, Kate Maclurcan, Margaret McGregor, Jaclyn McKew, Kath O'Connor, Nick Maguire-Rosier, Lily Master, Annelies Mertens, Maryanne Netto, Margaret Ng, Carolyn Noble, Damien Norris, Jill Pattenden, Anne Pedersen, Deborah Quin, Chris Rau, Kirsten Rawlings, Fiona Redding, Erin Richards, Ellen Roberts, Ngareta Rossell, Kerry Rotumah, Mik Ruff, Diane Schallmeiner, Amin Houvedar Sefed, Marilyn Shepherd, Charandev Singh, Diane Sisely, Jack Smit, Cara Smith, Neil Smith, Louisa Syme, Charlene Thompson, Bernadette Wauchope, Hugh Webb and Mohsen Soltany Zand.

We also thank the following organisations for their contributions: ASeTTS (WA), Australian Association of Social Workers, Avant Card, Centacare, Independent Theatre, Institute of Postcolonial Studies, Canberra Southern Cross Club, Cutting Edge Youth Services Shepparton, Law Society of South Australia, Loss and Grief Centre (partnership between Anglicare SA and Flinders University Department of Social Work), Project Safecom, RMIT Foundation, Rural Australians for Refugees, SIEV X Memorial Project and Spark and Cannon.

The work of students was highly valued including from Jessica Brooks, Lydia Brown, Chikwanda Mya Chiti, Inge Christanti, Sophie Ellis, Sally Fitzmaurice, Amanda Haury, Cassandra Hawkins, Kelly Hinton, Jaclyn McKew, Ann Megalla, Peter Pullicino, Carol Plunkett, Fiona Redding, Cara Rotherey, Sarah Rubenach, Melissa Sanders, Vicki Saunders, Florence Seow, Lauren Stockbridge, Andrea Symons, Stacey Walker and Emma Wynack.

We give our heartfelt thanks to the many people and organisations who gave testimony to the inquiry at the public hearings and through written submissions. Although telling personal stories is painful we were told time and again that people felt validated after speaking and that it helped in the healing process for those who had been in detention, had worked in detention or who had advocated on behalf of those in detention. As much as possible we have used the words of former detainees, their supporters and advocates, workers and others to tell the story. It was impossible to include every word given so generously but we believe that the book builds an accurate and collective story of this shameful time.

In working collaboratively with a vast pool of volunteers we may have omitted some people from our acknowledgements. Please accept our sincere apologies and appreciation.

Finally we thank Henry Rosenbloom and Scribe for publishing the book and for sharing with us the belief that it is important to place these stories of shame on the public record.

The People's Inquiry at a Glance

Auspice:	Australian Council of Heads of Schools of Social Work
President:	The Hon Marcus Einfeld, AO, QC
Transcribing coordinator:	Lyn Mitchell
Legal advice:	Holding Redlich (Nicholas Pullen, Sarah Talbot, Ian Robertson)
Media advice:	Madeleine Byrne
Ethics advice:	Richard Hugman
Mental health advice:	Robert Bland
Inquiry logo:	Catherine Forsayeth
Website:	Tatiana Lenz and Nathan Keatch

Hearing Locations & Convenors:

Melbourne	RMIT University
Sydney	University of New South Wales
Canberra	Australian Catholic University
Perth	Curtin University and Edmund Rice Centre
Launceston	University of Tasmania
Swan Hill	Uniting Church Community Issues Group
Griffith	Charles Sturt University
Port Augusta	Rural Australians for Refugees (RAR)
Shepparton	RAR and Cutting Edge Youth Services
Adelaide	Flinders University

Panel Members Who Heard Evidence:

Kandie Allen-Kelly

Yasmine Ahmed

Mary Allstrom

Margaret Alston

Julia Anaf

Chiks Anyanwu

Heather Barton

Peter Bayne

Thea Birss

Robert Bland

Natalie Bolzan

Linda Briskman

Lydia Brown

Margaret Brown

Mike Bull

Peter Camilleri

Stephanie Cauchi

Mike Clare

Terry Cleary

Fran Crawford

Tina Dolgopol

Marcus Einfeld

Sophie Ellis

Barbara Fawcett

Angela Fielding

Lucy Fiske

Graham Flenley

Catherine Forsayeth

Christine Gamble

Chris Goddard

Donald Grey-Smith

Lorna Hallahan

Janine Harrison

Rhonda Hawtin

Richard Hugman

Jim Ife

Carol Irizarry

Sabina Leitman

William Maley

Marika Mannik

Sue Maywald

Jennifer McKinnon

Keith Miller

Gavin Moonie

Carolyn Noble

Lynelle Osburn

Diane Sisely

Maurice Todd

Adam Tretheway

Vicki Waller

John Warhurst

Ailsa Watkinson

Jerzy Zubrzycki

Joanna Zubrzycki

Funding Received From:

Australian Association of Social Workers

Australian Council of Heads of Schools of Social Work

Becher Foundation

Donkey Wheel

Great Lakes Rural Australians for Refugees

MacKillop Family Services

RMIT Refugee and Asylum Seeker Project

Ron Gray Human Rights Foundation

Reichstein Foundation

Search Foundation

Maureen and Tony Wheeler

2: PEOPLE'S INQUIRY INTO DETENTION TERMS OF REFERENCE

This is an open inquiry into the practices and procedures related to the observance of the human rights of those detained in immigration detention facilities, whatever their ethnic background. It is a transparent process in which people can tell their stories and give evidence of their experiences of detention. In particular, we will investigate and assess:

- The question of the accountability of immigration detention policy and practices to government and community;
- The impact of detention on the wellbeing and mental health of detainees;
- The adequacy of and accountability of services provided for detainees;
- Issues relating to privatisation of the operations of detention;
- The question of whether duties of care have been breached and the process of redress and potential civil liability of those involved;
- The behavioural management policies, procedures and techniques used with detainees;
- Deportation methods and outcomes;
- Decision making practices of the Department of Immigration and private detention operators in relation to detainees;
- The financial costs of detention;
- The efficacy of alternative models of processing asylum seekers; and
- Any other matters at the discretion of the convenor.

3: VOLUNTEERS WITH THE PEOPLE'S INQUIRY

When the inquiry was announced, many people volunteered to assist. Below are some of the reasons volunteers wanted to help.

Fiona Redding: *Over the last few years, I found myself becoming increasingly disturbed by the attitude of the government towards asylum seekers, and the promotion of concepts like 'being un-Australian'. The*

Tampa, *the ensuing promotion of a 'fear of invasion', mandatory detention and the almost complete lack of any public debate really concerned me. When it was eventually found that an Australian resident and an Australian citizen were detained and deported, it seemed that finally the situation was going to be appropriately addressed.*

It soon became apparent that this was not the case, and I heard about the People's Inquiry into Detention. I felt that this was an excellent outlet to focus my concerns, and maybe get the information to a wider audience. Additionally, I felt that I had some useful skills that I could bring to the inquiry. I got to work with some amazing people, who I never would have met otherwise, and to speak with people first-hand about their experiences – as asylum seekers, as detainees, as Temporary Protection Visa holders and as people trying to make a new life in a new country.

The inquiry is enabling the stories of everyone involved with the system, not just those Australians 'accidentally' detained or deported, to be heard and placed on the public record. While this, clearly, is not a discussion that Australians are willing to have now, at some point in the future the inquiry will mean that the people involved with the system and their experiences will be appropriately remembered and reflected upon.

Lyn Mitchell: *It must have started with the* Tampa, *but then later being told people threw their children overboard – I felt that either they must have been so desperate or something else was wrong. I decided I needed to find out more about what was going on. So I went to a forum held in Collins St chaired by Carmen Lawrence with other speakers such as Louise Newman and Marie Tehan. The speeches made me realise what was going on and how distressed I felt about it. I also went to another talk by Julian Burnside which made me so upset that this was going on in my country.*

Then I was given an email address on a piece of paper and told that a group were putting together a report on asylum seekers and needed someone to do transcripts. I took that piece of paper home and within two days knew I must make contact even though I was sure they would have so many typists it wouldn't be necessary for me to go onboard. How wrong I was! So I was able to commence on the work and got more and more familiar with what was really happening and just how terrible the situation was. Sometimes I sat at the computer for so long I nearly fell over when I got up. It was as though I was listening to something that was happening right at that moment and I couldn't get up and leave it. It was emotional and a big learning curve for me.

I used to wonder why the German people didn't do or say anything if they knew what was happening in their country during Nazi rule. I no longer ask that question. I feel so ashamed of what is happening in my country. My voice goes unheard, so one way of helping is to type up these horrendous stories. I am often distressed with what I am reading and then get so angry that our leaders can be so cold and heartless. They do not seem to realise that asylum seekers are human beings with feelings and emotions, and treat them in a way that is far worse than that of criminals. Certainly no-one would ever think of treating animals in that way. What is happening in this country and why are people so uncaring? I don't understand that at all.

Sophie Ellis: *It was recently, while I was trawling through DIMIA media releases, that I realised with intensity what the People's Inquiry was all about. I had stumbled across a plethora of articles on Griffith including: 'Operation nets 22 near Griffith' and 'Nine illegals located in Griffith'. The headlines didn't surprise me; I've grown accustomed to them as they pop up everyday in our media. It was their content that took me aback. For the first time, the 'two south Koreans' transferred to Villawood and deported meant something to me. I was familiar with their story and their circumstances. I felt I knew them, and the human tragedy of it all suddenly replicated before me, in the lives of all the other unknown, faceless people who have shared the barbaric experience of detention as well. The public hearings in Griffith, like those that have been conducted all over Australia, bring these stories into the open. They allow brandings such as 'illegals', 'detainees', 'South Koreans', 'Indians', and numbers to dissolve, and for the stories of people to be heard and told. Stories that I have been both shocked and deeply humbled by.*

Lydia Brown: *I first heard about the People's Inquiry into Detention about 18 months ago. At that time I understood asylum-seeker policy in terms of news flashes. Images of barbed wire, hunger strikes and suited, fierce-looking politicians glaring through my TV screen shouting 'children overboard!' In my mind, asylum seeker policy was a confusing, impersonal, political haze. It felt detached from the safe, giving community I was used to and I felt there was nothing I could do.*

Then I heard about the People's Inquiry. People from across the nation were being invited to tell their own stories relating to Australia's immigration detention policy. Those on temporary protection, people who have experienced detention, asylum seeker advocates, health care professionals, friends, employers, public servants and interested citizens were all invited to speak about what they knew.

No twisted political message, few impersonal facts, just simple human stories. At the Canberra hearings earlier this year I think everyone who attended experienced a sharp mix of feelings. People who had experienced detention spoke of the fear, frustration, uncertainty and abuse connected to their time in detention. Breakdowns, deaths and deceit – at times the reality painted seemed like some twisted, stylised, sadistic novel.

Others spoke of small things. Someone was not allowed to give their homemade banana cake to a detained friend on their birthday. Many spoke about their life post detention. Family reunion, work, recognition. Piecing together a strong new life. Documenting the human stories of detention and temporary protection helps people overcome that confused, impersonal, news-flash haze that used to veil immigration policy in my mind. It helps people understand in human terms.

Ailsa Watkinson (University of Regina, Canada): *With my involvement I felt like a lobster plunged into the boiling water. I was truly shocked. I had no idea this was going on. We have not heard about it. Even now when I talk about it in my classes, no-one has ever heard about the way Australia's government treats those seeking asylum.*

When I was on the panel in Perth, my reaction and feelings were similar to the feelings I felt when listening to the stories of sexual abuse survivors. It left me raw and I experienced the same feelings I had then – the same feeling of dread (I didn't want to know what they were about to tell me), distress and despair.

I have checked my diary on those days and made such notes as: 'I was struck by many things – it's such a devastating time. But in particular I was struck by the fear of the people we heard from. When describing their journey to what they thought was safety they said, "I was scared," over and over. They said the same thing when describing their treatment once here. We heard from many volunteers/agency workers who, it seems to me, are also traumatised by this. They are "unsung heroes". Every detainee we spoke to is mentally damaged as well. It's draining.'

I was particularly outraged to hear how people could be dragged back into the detention centres for working. It is so ludicrous! They have no means to support themselves. But they do have the wherewithal to find work, and rather than consider it an accomplishment or something to celebrate, they are punished for it! The costs, both monetary and mental, surrounding the mental health of all the people detained also had me fixated. It is beyond cruel to do what the Australian government is doing to those already traumatised by having to leave their country and family. It's torture. And the effects will rest with the asylum seekers and the Australian people. What is to be gained? I wondered about the possibility of suing the government for the deterioration of mental health. I was happy to see it succeed for young Shayan. But he will never be the same and neither will his family and all the others who worked with him.

ENDNOTES

1   This inquiry has included deaths that occurred during Australian naval intervention under Operation Relex, Immigration Department compliance raids, and the death of an asylum seeker held on behalf of the Australian government in Nauru.

2   Australian minister for immigration, Philip Ruddock, to the Australian Anglican Synod, 27/7/2001.

3   Australian minister for immigration, Philip Ruddock, to the Australian Parliament, 19/2/2002, quoted in Brennan, Frank 2000 & 2002, 'Australia's Refugee Policy — Facts, Needs and Limits', from Brennan F., Carlton J., et al. 2002, *Refugees, Morality and Public Policy: The Jesuit Lenten Seminars*, David Lovell Publishing, p. 9–10

4   UNHCR Executive Committee (EXCOM) Conclusion No. 44 (XXXVII) — 1986

5   Jackson, A., 'Mystery woman held at Baxter could be ill', *The Age*, 31/1/2005, http://www.theage.com.au/news/National/Mystery-woman-held-at-Baxter-could-be-ill/2005/01/30/1107020257062.html, viewed 27/5/2008

6   For the terms of reference see http://pandora.nla.gov.au/pan/31543/20050430-0000/www.minister.immi.gov.au/media_releases/media05/v05030.htm, viewed 15/1/2008

7   Rau, C. & MacDonald, J., 'My sister lost her mind, and Australia lost its heart', *Sydney Morning Herald*, 7/2/2005, http://www.smh.com.au/articles/2005/02/06/1107625064599.html, viewed 13/10/2006

8   Baxter detainees statement to refugee advocates, 2005

9   Redding, F. 2005, *What is the Point of a Citizen Led Inquiry?*, international field study report, RMIT, Melbourne

10 The Australian Immigration Department has undergone several name changes during the period this report addresses. For ease of reading, the term 'Immigration Department' or 'Department of Immigration' is used in the text. It appears in direct quotes as DIMA (Department of Immigration and Multicultural Affairs), DIMIA (Department of Immigration and Multicultural and Indigenous Affairs) and DIAC (Department of Immigration and Citizenship) — its current name.

11 Australasian Correctional Management (ACM) held the contract to manage Australian detention centres from 1997 until Global Solutions Limited (GSL) was awarded the contract in August 2003

12 Department of Immigration and Citizenship, 'Fact Sheet 7 — Managing the Border', quoted in Oxfam 2007, *A price too high: The cost of Australia's approach to asylum-seekers*, Oxfam, Melbourne, p. 13

13   Gordon, M., 'Damaged souls caught in third wave of suffering', *The Age,*
     9/8/2008, p. 9

14   The final report was: Palmer M. 2005, 'Inquiry into the circumstances of
     the immigration detention of Cornelia Rau: Report', Commonwealth of
     Australia, Canberra. The report can be found at http://www.minister.immi.
     gov.au/media_releases/media05/palmer-report.pdf, viewed 3/12/2006

15   'Detention policy changes "meaningful"', *Insiders*, ABC Television,
     19/6/2005, http://www.abc.net.au/insiders/content/2005/s1395397.htm,
     viewed 18/10/2006

16   Department of Immigration and Citizenship, Detention and Offshore
     Services Division, *Detention Statistics Summary as at 9/11/2007*, available
     at http://www.immi.gov.au/managing-australias-borders/detention/_pdf/
     immigration-detention-statistics-09-11-07.pdf, viewed 25/11/2007

17   Smith, M. 2001, 'Asylum-seekers in Australia', *The Medical Journal of
     Australia*, no. 175, pp. 587–89, available at http://www.mja.com.au/public/
     issues/175_12_171201/smith/smith.html, viewed 25/11/2007

18   Jackson, A., 'Academics to hold alternative inquiry', *The Age*, 14/2/2005,
     http://www.theage.com.au/news/Immigration/Academics-to-hold-
     alternative-inquiry/2005/02/13/1108229858789.html, viewed 3/11/2006

19   Department of Immigration and Citizenship, 'Fact Sheet 7 — Managing the
     Border', quoted in Oxfam 2007, *A price too high: The cost of Australia's
     approach to asylum-seekers*, Oxfam, Melbourne, p. 13

20   Stratton, J. 2007, 'Dying to Come to Australia: Asylum-seekers, Tourists
     and Death', *Our Patch: Enacting Australian Sovereignty Post-2001*,
     Network Books, Perth

21   Advertisements to dissuade would-be boat people, 2000, *The 7.30 Report*,
     ABC Television 15 June, available at http://www.abc.net.au/7.30/stories/
     s140871.htm, viewed 14/6/2007

22   ibid.

23   ibid.

24   'Ruddock defends inaction on refugees lost at sea', *The World Today,* ABC
     Radio, 14/12/2000 http://www.abc.net.au/worldtoday/stories/s223968.htm
     viewed 2/10/2006

25   Ruddock P. 2002, *Ministerial Statements: Managing Migration*,
     available at http://parlinfoweb.aph.gov.au/piweb//view_document.
     aspx?TABLE=hansardr&ID=2195377, viewed 4/1/2008

26   Department of Immigration and Citizenship, 'Fact Sheet 7 — Managing the
     Border', quoted in Oxfam 2007, *A price too high: The cost of Australia's
     approach to asylum-seekers*, Oxfam, Melbourne, p. 13

27   Marr, D. 'PM's move to block *Tampa* made "despite legal advice"', *The
     Age*, 23/7/2007, p. 6

28   'To Deter and Deny', *Four Corners*, ABC Television 15/4/2002 http://www.
     abc.net.au/4corners/stories/s531993.htm, viewed 2/10/06

29   Marr, D., op. cit.

30   Nicholson B., 'Labor recruit hopes to show how the west can be won', *The Age*, 29/9/2007, p. 5

31   'To Deter and Deny', *Four Corners*, op. cit.

32   Smith Dr H. 2004, 'Border Protection and the Limits of Obedience', *Defender: The National Journal of the Australia Defence Association*, p. 26, http://www.ada.asn.au/defender/Defender%20Autumn%202004.pdf, viewed 2/10/2006

33   'To Deter and Deny', *Four Corners*, op. cit.

34   Gettler, L. 'Voyage of the Damned: a disturbing lesson from history', *The Age*, 5/9/2001

35   Senate Select Committee on A Certain Maritime Incident, ch. 2, par. 5, available at http://www.aph.gov.au/Senate/committee/maritime_incident_ctte/report/c02.htm, viewed 2/10/2006

36   Operation Relex was replaced by Operation Relex II and is currently known as Operation Resolute

37   Quoted in Wilkie, A., *People Smuggling: national myths and realities*, a speech delivered at the Charles Darwin Symposium on irregular immigration on 30/9/2003, available at http://www.smh.com.au/articles/2003/10/02/10 64988327625.html, viewed 24/11/2007

38   Interview: defence minister Peter Reith, on *Sunday*, Channel Nine, Sydney, 30/9/2001, available at http://sunday.ninemsn.com.au/sunday/political_transcripts/article_934.asp?s=1, viewed 24/11/2007

39   Wilkie, A., op. cit.

40   Quoted in Sidoti, C., *Truth Overboard: One Year After Tampa – Refugees, Deportees and TPVs*, paper presented at Deakin University 5/12/2002, available at http://www.hrca.org.au/one%20year%20after%20tampa.htm, viewed 28/10/2006

41   Leser, D., 'Children overboard: Two women, two stories', *The Australian Women's Weekly*, August 2007, p. 63

42   'Children overboard: the view from the sea', *Sunday*, Channel Nine, Sydney, 29/8/2004, available at http://sunday.ninemsn.com.au/sunday/cover_stories/article_1634.asp?s=1, viewed 2/10/2006

43   'To Deter and Deny', *Four Corners*, op. cit.

44   Senate Select Committee on A Certain Maritime Incident, op. cit. ch. 2, par. 66 & 67

45   Senate Select Committee on A Certain Maritime Incident, op. cit. ch. 3, par. 16

46   'Navy chief enters asylum-seeker debate', *7.30 Report*, ABC Television, 8/11/2001, http://www.abc.net.au/7.30/content/2001/s412083.htm, viewed 2/10/2006

47   'Children overboard: the view from the sea', *Sunday*, op. cit.

48   Leser, D., op. cit., p. 64

49   To Deter and Deny, *Four Corners*, op. cit.

50   ibid.

51   ibid.

52   Senate Select Committee on A Certain Maritime Incident, op. cit., ch. 2, par. 66 & 67

53   Smith, Dr. H., op. cit., p. 25

54   Senate Select Committee on A Certain Maritime Incident, op. cit., ch. 3, par. 30

55   Senate Select Committee on A Certain Maritime Incident, op. cit., ch. 3, par. 33

56   Senate Select Committee on A Certain Maritime Incident, op. cit., ch. 3, par. 41

57   ABC Radio 2001, cited in Mares, P. 2002, *Borderline: Australia's response to refugees and asylum-seekers in the wake of Tampa*, 2nd ed., UNSW Press, Sydney, p. 135

58   Senate Select Committee on A Certain Maritime Incident, op. cit., ch. 3, par. 42

59   Smith, Dr H., op. cit., p. 26

60   'Children overboard: the view from the sea', *Sunday*, op. cit.

61   Senate Select Committee on A Certain Maritime Incident, op. cit., ch. 2, par. 56

62   Leser, D. op.cit., p. 64

63   'To Deter and Deny', *Four Corners*, op. cit.

64   Quoted in Rose, A., 'The forgotten people', *Dissent: Sydney University Law Society's Social Justice Journal*, July 2006, p. 111

65   Zable, A., 'Scorning those in need', *The Age*, 27/6/2006, available at http://www.theage.com.au/news/opinion/scorning-those-in-need/2006/06/26/1151174130006.html?page=fullpage#contentSwap1, viewed 27/10/2006

66   'To Deter and Deny', *Four Corners*, op. cit.

67   Senate Select Committee on A Certain Maritime Incident, op. cit., ch. 2, par. 69

68   Quoted in Rose, A. op. cit.

69   'To Deter and Deny', *Four Corners*, op. cit.

70   See *Four Corners* and Rose, A. op. cit.

71   'To Deter and Deny', *Four Corners*, op. cit.

72   Rose, A. op. cit.

73   Rose, A. op. cit.

74   Hyland, T., 'Morale overboard', *The Sunday Age*, 22/7/2007, p. 13

75   ibid.

76   Senate Select Committee on A Certain Maritime Incident, op. cit. Appendix 1, par. 39–43

77   Hyland, T., op. cit.

78   'To Deter and Deny', *Four Corners*, op. cit.

79   Kingston, M., 'More threads in SIEV-X caper', *Sydney Morning Herald*, 16/6/2002, available at http://www.smh.com.au/articles/2002/06/16/1023 864379714.html

80   Manne, R., 'The Tragedy of Indifference', *The Age*, 24/6/2002, available at http://www.theage.com.au/articles/2002/06/23/1023864527315.html, viewed 2/10/2006

81   ibid.

82   Kingston, M., op. cit.

83   Zable, A., 'Perilous journeys', *Eureka Street*, April 2003 available at http://www.eurekastreet.com.au/articles/0304zable.html viewed 2/10/2006 and Debelle, P., 'Survivor saw ships in rescuing distance', *Sydney Morning Herald*, 20/6/2002 http://www.smh.com.au/articles/2002/06/20/10238644 60509.html, viewed 2/10/2006

84   Jannah — The SIEV X Memorial, http://sievxmemorial.org/accounts.htm/ viewed 2/10/2006

85   Kevin, T. 2004, reprinted 2008, *A Certain Maritime Incident: The sinking of the SIEV X*, Scribe Publications, Melbourne

86   Marr and Wilkinson are the authors of *Dark Victory*, published in 2004 by Allen and Unwin.

87   Faulkner, Senator John, *A Certain Maritime Incident — the aftermath*, address to Australian Fabian Society, Victoria, 23/7/2003, available at http://www.fabian.org.au/910.asp, viewed 21/5/07

88   'The Federal Police and People Smugglers', *Sunday*, Channel Nine, 1/9/2002 available at http://www.sievx.com/articles/challenging/20020901_SundayEnniss.html, viewed 4/7/2007

89   Senate Select Committee on A Certain Maritime Incident, op. cit. additional comments by Senator John Faulkner

90   Faulkner, Senator John, 26/9/2002, in Senate Hansard 2002, no. 10, p. 5007, available at http://www.aph.gov.au/HANSARD/senate/dailys/ds260902.pdf, viewed 6/2/2008

91   Official Committee Hansard, Senate Legal and Constitutional Legislation Committee, Consideration of Supplementary Estimates, 20/11/2002, p. 127, available at http://www.aph.gov.au/hansard/senate/commttee/s6002.pdf, viewed 8/2/2008

92   ibid., p. 127–28,

93   ibid., p. 133–35

94   Banham, C., 'Federal police won't talk tracking devices — it's against the public interest', *Sydney Morning Herald*, 23/11/2002, available at http://www.smh.com.au/articles/2002/11/22/1037697872793.html, viewed 18/1/2008

95   Morris, S., 'No surveillance on SIEV X; Keelty', *The Australian*, 23/11/2002, available at http://sievx.com/articles/challenging/20021123Australian.html, viewed 6/2/2008

96   Minister for foreign affairs, Alexander Downer and Minister for justice and customs, Senator Chris Ellison, *People Smuggler Abu Quassey Found Guilty*, media release, 28/12/2003, available at http://foreignminister.gov.au/releases/2003/joint_ellison_abuquassey.html, viewed 6/2/2008

97   Faulkner, Senator John, *A Certain Maritime Incident — the aftermath*, address to Australian Fabian Society, Victoria, 23/7/2003, available at http://www.fabian.org.au/910.asp, viewed 21/5/07

98   Extracted from Senate Hansard, 11 August 2003, pp. 13092–3 Justice and Customs: Indonesia (Question no. 1229), available at http://sievx.com/testimony/2003/20030811EllisonAnswertoQoN.html, viewed 9/7/2007

99   Mares, P., 'Sending them home', *The Age*, 10/4/2004, available at http://www.theage.com.au/articles/2004/04/06/1081222458223.html, viewed 18/9/2007

100   Quoted in Lygo, I. 2004, *News Overboard: The Tabloid Media, Race Politics and Islam*, Southerly Change Media, p. 56

101   Mares, P., 'Sending them home', *The Age*, 10/4/2004, available at http://www.theage.com.au/articles/2004/04/06/1081222458223.html, viewed 18/9/2007

102   'Beazley accuses PM of twisting his words', *The World Today*, ABC Radio, 23/10/01, available at http://www.abc.net.au/worldtoday/stories/s398163.htm, viewed 17/5/07

103   Transcript of the prime minister, the Hon. John Howard MP, press conference, Melbourne, 7/11/2001, available at http://pandora.nla.gov.au/pan/10052/20020221-0000/www.pm.gov.au/news/interviews/2001/interview1452.htm, viewed 21/1/2008

104   Liberals questioned over asylum-seeker stance, *Lateline*, ABC Television, 7/11/2001, www.abc.net.au/lateline/content/2001/s412177.htm, viewed 30/12/2006

105   Quoted in Hyland, T., 'Morale overboard', *The Sunday Age*, 22/7/2007, p. 13

106   'To Deter and Deny', *Four Corners*, op. cit.

107   'Liberals accused of trying to rewrite history', *Lateline*, ABC Television, 21/11/2001, http://www.abc.net.au/lateline/content/2001/s422692.htm, viewed 30/10/2006

108 Wilkinson, M., 'The near fiasco of the Pacific Solution', *The Age*, http://
www.theage.com.au/articles/2002/10/27/1035683304533.html, viewed
2/10/2006

109 *Perspective*, ABC Radio National, 8/11/2001, http://www.abc.net.au/rn/
talks/perspective/stories/s411582.htm, viewed 27/10/2006

110 Smith, Dr H., op. cit., p. 26

111 Quoted in Hyland, T., op. cit.

112 Hyland, T., 'Revealed: how Howard's way threatened security', *The Sunday
Age*, 22/7/2007, p. 1

113 ibid.

114 Quoted in Marr, D., & Wilkinson, M. 2005, *Dark Victory*, Allen and
Unwin, Sydney, p. 367

115 'Claims Navy staff disagree with asylum-seeker policy', *The World
Today*, ABC Radio, 7/11/2006, http://www.abc.net.au/worldtoday/
stories/s410695.htm, viewed 30/10/2006, and Tippet, G., 'Navy officer
condemns "despicable" treatment of boat people', *Sydney Morning Herald*,
7/11/2001, p. 4

116 Zable, A., 'Scorning those in need', *The Age*, 27/6/2006, http://www.theage.
com.au/news/opinion/scorning-those-in-need/2006/06/26/1151174130006.
html?page=fullpage#contentSwap1, viewed 27/10/2006

117 Forbes, M., 'The families no one wants', *The Age*, 2/12/2006, available
at http://www.theage.com.au/news/world/the-families-no-one-
wants/2006/12/01/1164777791814.html, viewed 26/9/2007

118 Rose, A., op. cit.

119 Forbes, M., 'Entry for 120 asylum-seekers', *The Age*, 5/5/2007, available
at http://www.theage.com.au/news/national/entry-for-120-asylum-
seekers/2007/05/04/1177788401796.html, viewed 18/6/2007

120 Immigration Department and Citizenship, 'Fact Sheet 60 — Australia's
Refugee and Humanitarian Program', available at http://www.immi.gov.au/
media/fact-sheets/60refugee.htm, viewed 28/12/2007

121 In very few cases the minister for immigration has exercised discretion under
section 417 of the *Migration Act* to grant permanent protection visas to
people in this group.

122 Working Group on Arbitrary Detention, no. 85, [62] quoted in New
South Wales Council for Civil Liberties, *Shadow report prepared for the
United Nations Committee Against Torture on the occasion of its review of
Australia's Third Periodic Report under the Convention Against Torture and
other Cruel, Inhuman or Degrading Treatment or Punishment*, 27/7/2007,
par. 105, available at http://www.nswccl.org.au/docs/pdf/CAT%20
shadow%20report.pdf, viewed 25/9/2007

123 Amnesty International, Australia, *The impact of indefinite detention: the
case to change Australia's mandatory detention regime*, AI Index: ASA
12/001/2005

124   Including Human Rights and Equal Opportunity Commission 1998, *Those who've come across the seas*, and Human Rights and Equal Opportunity Commission 2004, *A last resort?* National Inquiry into Children in Immigration Detention

125   Flood, P. 2001, *Inquiry into Immigration Detention Procedures*, Commonwealth of Australia

126   Report of Justice Bhagwati, regional advisor for Asia and the Pacific of the United Nations High Commissioner for Human Rights, *Mission to Australia*, 24/5–2/6/2002

127   'Report of an Own Motion Investigation into the Immigration Department and Multicultural Affairs Immigration Detention Centres', March 2001

128   Millet, M. 'Worst I've seen says UN asylum inspector', *Sydney Morning Herald*, 6/6/2002, available at http://www.smh.com.au/articles/2002/06/05/1022982721514.html, viewed 10/7/2007

129   UN Economic and Social Council, 'Detention of Asylum-seekers, Sub-Commission on Human Rights Resolution 2000/1', E/CN.4/SUB.2/RES/2000/21, 18/8/2000

130   Detailed in Justice for Asylum-seekers (JAS) Alliance Detention Working Group, 'Submission to National Inquiry into Children in Immigration Detention', available at http://www.hreoc.gov.au/human_rights/children_detention/submissions/jas.html#6, viewed 25/9/2007

131   Senate Legal and Constitutional Committee, 'Administration and Operation of the *Migration Act 1958*', par. 5.4, available at http://www.aph.gov.au/senate/committee/legcon_ctte/Migration/report/c05.htm, viewed 11/7/2007

132   York, B., *Australia and Refugees, 1901–2002 Annotated Chronology Based on Official Sources: Summary, 16/6/2003*, available at http://www.aph.gov.au/library/pubs/chron/2002-03/03chr02.htm#nineteen, viewed 6/10/2007

133   Ker, P., 'Bob Hawke plays own race card in Bennelong', *The Age*, 5/10/2007, available at http://www.theage.com.au/handheld/articles/2007/10/04/1191091281220.html, viewed 12/10/2007

134   Gerry Hand: 'Migration Amendment Bill 1992, Second Reading', *Hansard*, 5/5/1992, http://parlinfoweb.aph.gov.au/piweb/view_document.aspx?ID=108158&TABLE=HANSARDR, viewed 18/8/2003, quoted in Whyte, J. *Life in the camp: Giorgio Agamben and Australia's Mandatory Detention of Asylum-seekers*, Honours Thesis, School of Social Science and Planning, RMIT University, October 2003

135   Senate Legal and Constitutional Committee, 'Administration and Operation of the *Migration Act 1958*', op. cit., par 5.5

136   *Chu Kheng Lim v Commonwealth (Minister for Immigration, Local Government and Ethnic Affairs) (1992)* 176 CLR 1

137   *Chu Kheng Lim and Others v The Minister for Immigration, Local Government and Ethnic Affairs and Another (1992)* **176 CLR 1**, Quoted in Whyte, J. *Life in the camp: Giorgio Agamben and Australia's Mandatory Detention of Asylum-seekers*, Honours Thesis, School of Social Science and Planning, RMIT University, October 2003

138   Crock, M., Saul, B. & Dastyari, A. 2006, *Future Seekers II: Refugees and Irregular Migration in Australia*, The Federation Press, p. 176

139   The Hon. Gerry Hand, MP, *Migration Amendment Bill 1992*, Second Reading Speech, House of Representatives, *Debates*, 5/5/1992, p. 2370, quoted in Whyte, J. *Life in the camp: Giorgio Agamben and Australia's Mandatory Detention of Asylum-seekers*, Honours Thesis, School of Social Science and Planning, RMIT University, October 2003

140   Cited in Brennan, F. 2003, *Tampering with Asylum: A universal humanitarian problem*, University of Queensland Press, St Lucia, p. 87

141   Whyte, J. *Life in the camp: Giorgio Agamben and Australia's Mandatory Detention of Asylum-seekers*, Honours Thesis, School of Social Science and Planning, RMIT University, October 2003

142   Department of Immigration and Citizenship, 'Fact Sheet 61 — Seeking Asylum within Australia', available at http://www.immi.gov.au/media/fact-sheets/61asylum.htm, viewed 10/8/2007

143   Response by Minister Philip Ruddock to the ACBC Statement on Refugees and Asylum Seekers with Comments by the Australian Catholic Migrant and Refugee Officer, available at http://www.acmro.catholic.org.au/policies/docs/ruddock.pdf, viewed 11/7/2007

144   Aiton, D, 'Foreword: 10 things you didn't know about Philip Ruddock, Attorney General', *The Weekend Australian Magazine*, 27–28/1/2007, p. 10

145   Money, J., 'Xenophobia and Xenophilia: Pauline Hanson and the Counterbalancing of Electoral Incentives in Australia', *People and Place*, vol. 7, no. 3, p. 12, available at http://elecpress.monash.edu.au/pnp/free/pnpv7n3/v7n3_2money.pdf, viewed 8/1/2008

146   Quoted in Mansouri, F. & Leach, M., *Temporary Protection of Refugees: Australian Policy and International Comparisons*, p. 1, available at http://www.deakin.edu.au/arts/cchr/rsg/pdfs/Fethi%20Mansouri.pdf, viewed 23/10/2007

147   Highfield, J. 2007, 'Timeline of events', *Acting from the Heart: Australian advocates for asylum-seekers tell their stories*, (eds) S. Mares & L. Newman, Finch Publishing, Sydney

148   *Al Kateb v Godwin (2004)* 219 CLR 562, and *Minister for Immigration v Al Khafaji (2004)* 219 CLR 664

149   Council for Civil Liberties, Conferral of life membership on John Marsden, Julian Burnside speech, 'You can't fight city hall, can you?' March 2005, available at http://www.users.bigpond.com/burnside/marsden.htm, viewed 6/9/2007

150   'Suspected asylum-seekers arrive in Melville Island', *Lateline*, ABC Television, 4/11/2003, available at http://www.abc.net.au/lateline/content/2003/s982197.htm, viewed 5/11/2007

151   *NATB v Minister for Immigration and Multicultural and Indigenous Affairs [2003]* FCAFC 292 (16/12/2003)

152   189 U.N.T.S. 150, entered into force 22/4/1954

153   Article 1A(2) of the Convention Relating to the Status of Refugees

154   Department of Immigration and Citizenship, 'Fact Sheet 63 — Immigration Advice and Application Assistance Scheme', available at http://www.immi. gov.au/media/fact-sheets/63advice.htm, viewed 10/8/2007

155   Crock, M., Saul, B. & Dastyari, A. 2006, op. cit., p. 203

156   Leser, D., 'Children overboard: Two women, two stories', *The Australian Women's Weekly*, August 2007, p. 64

157   Committees: Reports: Government Responses, *Senate Hansard*, 14/6/2007, available at http://parlinfoweb.aph.gov.au/piweb/view_document. aspx?id=2451613&table=HANSARDS, viewed 23/1/2008

158   Crock, M. 2006, *Seeking asylum alone: a study of Australian law, policy and practice regarding unaccompanied and separated children*, Themis Press, p. 126

159   Crock, M., op. cit. pp. 40–41

160   Bilboe, H., 'Statement to the National Inquiry into Children in Immigration Detention', available at http://www.hreoc.gov.au/Human_Rights/children_detention/statements/bilboe.html, viewed 13/3/07

161   Macken, J., 'Lost in translation', *Australian Financial Review*, 25–26 September, p. 24–25

162   Eades, D. 2005, 'Applied Linguistics and Language Analysis in Asylum-seeker Cases', Applied Linguistics, vol. 26, no. 4, December 2005, pp. 503–26

163   Eades, D., Fraser, H., Siegel, J., McNamara, T., Baker, B. 2003, *Linguistic identification in the determination of nationality: A preliminary report*, p. 8

164   Eades, D. op. cit., p. 510–11

165   Eades, D. op cit., p. 8

166   'Immigration official gives insight into department', *Lateline*, ABC Television, 13/6/2005, available at http://www.abc.net.au/lateline/content/2005/s1391140.htm, viewed 4/6/2007

167   Refugee Review Tribunal Reference: N00/34605 22/11/2000, par. 40

168   Refugee Review Tribunal Reference: V01/12919 20/7/2001

169   Refugee Review Tribunal Reference: V97/07726 30/5/2000

170   Eades, D. op. cit., p. 14

171   *SBAN v Minister for Immigration & Multicultural & Indigenous Affairs* [2002] FCA 591 (10 May 2002)

172   *SBAU v Minister for Immigration & Multicultural & Indigenous Affairs* [2002] FCA 1076 (13 September 2002)

173   *Minister for Immigration Multicultural Indigenous Affairs v NASS* [2003] FCA 477 (20 May 2003)

174   Quoted in Austin J. & Burnside, J. (eds) 2003, *From Nothing to Zero:*

Letters from Refugees in Australia's Detention Centres, Lonely Planet, Melbourne, p. 110

175 The term 'set aside rates' refers to the rates of Immigration Department decisions being overturned.

176 Legomsky, S., 'Refugees, Administrative Tribunals and Real Independence: Dangers Ahead for Australia', *Washington University Law Quarterly* vol. 4, no. 76, Spring 1998, p. 250

177 Quoted in Legomsky, S., 'Refugees, Administrative Tribunals and Real Independence: Dangers Ahead for Australia', *Washington University Law Quarterly*, vol. 4, no. 76, Spring 1998, p. 250

178 Walsh, K. 'Visa staff pressured in appeals decision', *Sydney Morning Herald*, 29/6/2003, available at http://www.smh.com.au/articles/2003/06/28/1056 683950237.html, viewed 17/7/2007

179 Official Committee Hansard, Senate Select Committee on Ministerial Discretion in Migration Matters, 17/11/2003, p. 52, available at http://www.aph.gov.au/hansard/senate/commttee/S7143.pdf, viewed 22/5/2007

180 ibid., p. 58

181 ibid., p. 56

182 Refugee Review Tribunal, *Annual Report 2005–2006*, available at http://www.rrt.gov.au/publications/annrpts/0506/PDFs/Part-4.pdf, viewed 23/7/2007 and Parliament of Australia, 'The Senate Inquiry into the Administration and Operation of the *Migration Act 1958*', Table 3.6, available at http://www.aph.gov.au/Senate/committee/legcon_ctte/migration/report/c03.htm, viewed 18/7/2007

183 Refugee Review Tribunal, *Annual Report 2004–2005*, p. 19.

184 Refugee Review Tribunal, *Annual Report 2005–2006*, available at http://www.rrt.gov.au/publications/annrpts/0506/PDFs/Part-4.pdf, viewed 23/7/2007

185 Parliament of Australia: Senate Legal and Constitutional References Committee, *A Sanctuary under Review: an Examination of Australia's Refugee and Humanitarian Determination Processes*, June 2000, available at http://www.aph.gov.au/Senate/committee/legcon_ctte/completed_inquiries/1999-02/refugees/report/contents.htm, viewed 12/9/2007

186 Haslem, B. 'Justices Hammer *Tampa* Laws', *The Australian*, 5/9/2002, available at http://www.law.mq.edu.au/Units/law404/Aust%20Tampa%20judges%20HCA.htm, viewed 16/7/2007

187 'Hot issue — minister Ruddock and the Federal Court', *Legal Information Access Centre — Hot Topics*, available at http://beta.austlii.edu.au/au/other/liac/hot_topic/hottopic/2002/3/7.html, viewed 15/5/2007

188 Refugee Review Tribunal, *Annual Report 2005–2006*, op. cit., p. 33,

189 From Human Rights Council of Australia, *It's broke and it needs fixing: The Case for Reforming Administration of Refugees and Asylum-seekers Programs* (draft discussion paper), available at: http://www.hrca.org.au/dimiaper cent20changes.htm, viewed 23/1/2008

190   Senate Select Committee on Ministerial Discretion on Migration Matters, March 2004, ch. 3, 'Table 3.2: Ministerial Interventions on RRT and MRT Decisions', available at http://www.aph.gov.au/Senate/committee/minmig_ctte/report/c03.htm, viewed 23/1/2008

191   Jackson, A., 'Our lives are in limbo: former detainees', *The Age*, 5/1/2008, p. 6

192   Senate Select Committee on Ministerial Discretion in Migration Matters, March 2004, ch. 1, par. 6, available at http://www.aph.gov.au/SEnate/committee/minmig_ctte/report/c01.htm, viewed 12/9/2007

193   Senate Select Committee on Ministerial Discretion in Migration Matters, March 2004, ch. 6, par. 46–49

194   Correspondence from Mr Alistair Sands, DIMIA secretary, to Senate Select Committee on Ministerial Discretion in Migration Matters, available at http://www.aph.gov.au/Senate/committee/minmig_ctte/rel_links/040903.doc, viewed 23/1/2008

195   Senate Select Committee on Ministerial Discretion on Migration Matters, March 2004, available at http://www.aph.gov.au/Senate/committee/minmig_ctte/report/b01.htm, viewed 26/9/2007

196   Senate Legal and Constitutional Committee, 'Inquiry into the Administration and Operation of the *Migration Act 1958*', 2006, [3.27], available at http://www.aph.gov.au/senate/committee/legcon_ctte/Migration/report/index.htm quoted in New South Wales Council for Civil Liberties, *Shadow report prepared for the United Nations Committee Against Torture on the occasion of its review of Australia's Third Periodic Report under the Convention Against Torture and other Cruel, Inhuman or Degrading Treatment or Punishment*, 27/7/2007, par. 149, available at http://www.nswccl.org.au/docs/pdf/CAT%20shadow%20report.pdf, viewed 25/9/2007

197   *S v Secretary, Department of Immigration & Multicultural & Indigenous Affairs* [2005] FCA 549, par. 144

198   Crock, M., op. cit., p. 113

199   Amanda Vanstone, *Minister Message to Baxter Protestors*, media release 23/3/2005, available at http://pandora.nla.gov.au/pan/31543/20060430-0000/www.minister.immi.gov.au/media_releases/media05/v05047.html, viewed 23/1/2008

200   Commonwealth of Australia, Official Committee Hansard, Joint Standing Committee on Foreign Affairs, Defence and Trade, Human Rights Subcommittee, 22 August 2002, available at http://www.aph.gov.au/hansard/joint/commttee/j5748.pdf, viewed 10/5/2007

201   Gordon, M., 'Freedom for Nauru Man', *The Age*, 1/2/2007, p. 3

202   Clennell, A., 'Go home, Ruddock tells Afghan protesters', *Sydney Morning Herald*, 21/1/2002

203   'Afghan detainees end hunger strike', *The 7.30 Report*, ABC Television, available at http://www.abc.net.au/7.30/content/2002/s469902.htm, viewed 23/1/2008

204   *Minister for Immigration & Multicultural & Indigenous Affairs v VFAD of 2002* [2002] FCAFC 390

205   On the 26th and 27th of September the Commonwealth Parliament passed the following bills: Migration Amendment (Excision from Migration Zone) Act 2001; Migration Amendment (Excision from Migration Zone) (Consequential Provisions) Act 2001; Border Protection (Validation and Enforcement Powers) Act 2001; Migration Legislation Amendment (Judicial Review) Act 2001; Migration Legislation Amendment Act (No 1) 2001 ; Migration Legislation Amendment Act (No 5) 2001; Migration Legislation Amendment Act (No 6) 2001

206   Department of Immigration and Citizenship, 'Fact Sheet 76 — Offshore Processing Arrangements', available at http://www.immi.gov.au/media/fact-sheets/76offshore.htm, viewed 17/10/2007

207   Oxfam 2007, *A price too high: The cost of Australia's approach to asylum-seekers*, Oxfam, Melbourne, p. 14

208   Abayasekara, S. 'Julian Burnside: On Refugees, Rights and the Rule of Law', *Dissent*, Sydney University Law Society's Social Justice Journal, July 2006, p. 106

209   Francis, A., 'Submission to the Senate Legal and Constitutional Legislation Committee, Inquiry into the Migration Amendment (Designated Unauthorised Arrivals) Bill 2006', available at http://www.aph.gov.au/SEnate/committee/legcon_ctte/migration_unauthorised_arrivals/submissions/sub60.pdf, viewed 17/10/2007

210   Parliament of Australia, 'The Senate Inquiry into the Administration and Operation of the Migration Act 1958', Table 3.6, available at http://www.aph.gov.au/Senate/committee/legcon_ctte/migration/report/c03.htm, viewed 18/7/2007 and Refugee Review Tribunal, *Annual Report 2001–02*, p. 3, available at http://www.mrt-rrt.gov.au/annrpts/rrt/RRTAR0102.pdf, viewed 17/10/2007

211   Burnside, J., 'A layperson's guide to some aspects of Australian refugee law', available at http://www.users.bigpond.com/burnside/layguide.htm#_ftnref4, viewed 10/8/2007

212   Jackson, A., 'Nauru bars boat people's lawyers', *The Age*, 27/4/2004, available at http://www.theage.com.au/articles/2004/04/26/1082831498329.html, viewed 3/10/2007

213   'Nauru Government turns detainees' lawyers away', *Lateline*, ABC Television, 26/04/2004, available at http://www.abc.net.au/lateline/content/2004/s1095201.htm, viewed 23/10/2007

214   Jackson, A., op. cit.

215   *Ruhani v Director of Police [2005]* HCA 42; (2005) 222 CLR 489; (2005) 219 ALR 199; (2005) 79 ALJR 1431 (31 August 2005)

216   Abayasekara, S. op. cit., p. 107

217   'Nauru sets asylum-seeker deadline', *PM*, ABC Television, 19/3/2007, available at http://www.abc.net.au/pm/content/2007/s1876105.htm, viewed 18/9/2007

218   Crock, M. op. cit. p. 178

219   Gordon, M. 'Suicide warning led to visas for Nauru refugees', *The Age*,
       6/11/2006, p. 3

220   UNHCR, *Asylum Levels and Trends in Industrialised Countries*, 2006,
       available at http://www.unhcr.org/statistics/STATISTICS/460150272.pdf,
       quoted in Oxfam 2007, *A price too high: The cost of Australia's approach
       to asylum-seekers*, August, Oxfam, Melbourne

221   Oxfam, op. cit.

222   Lygo, I. 2004, *News Overboard: The Tabloid Media, Race Politics and
       Islam*, Southerly Change Media, p. 116

223   Taylor, S. 2006, 'Immigration detention reforms: A small gain in human
       rights', *Agenda*, vol. 13, no. 1, p. 49

224   'UNHCR goes up against government in plight of refugees', *The 7.30
       Report*, ABC Television, 19/6/2001, available at http://www.abc.net.
       au/7.30/content/2001/s315568.htm, viewed 7/1/2008

225   *Australia Now*, ABC Radio, June 2003, available at http://www.
       radioaustralia.net.au/australia/now/program_13.htm, viewed 7/1/2008

226   Taylor, S. op. cit., p. 49–50

227   Crock, M., Saul, B. & Dastyari, A. 2006, *Future Seekers II: Refugees and
       Irregular Migration in Australia*, The Federation Press, Sydney

228   'If this is a Man? Men and Mandatory Detention', *All in the Mind*, ABC
       Radio, 21/1/2006, available at http://www.abc.net.au/rn/allinthemind/
       stories/2005/1473868.htm, viewed 4/6/2007

229   'DIMIA Submission to Senate inquiry in Migration Amendment (Designated
       Unauthorised Arrivals) Bill 2006', available at http://www.aph.gov.au/
       senate/committee/legcon_ctte/migration_unauthorised_arrivals/submissions/
       sub118.pdf, quoted in Oxfam 2007, *A price too high: The cost of Australia's
       approach to asylum seekers*, Oxfam, Melbourne

230   Dongas are small, transportable accommodation huts.

231   'About Woomera', *Four Corners*, ABC Television, 19/5/2003, available at
       http://www.abc.net.au/4corners/content/2003/transcripts/s858341.htm,
       viewed 2/7/2007

232   Carey, C. 'Woomera: Victims of the war zone', *The Age*, 25/2/2007, p. 11

233   Huxstep, M., 'Statement to the National Inquiry into Children in
       Immigration Detention', available at http://www.hreoc.gov.au/human_
       rights/children_detention/statements/huxstep. html, viewed 12/3/07

234   'Maggots found in food at detention centre', *Sydney Morning Herald*,
       24/8/2004 http://www.smh.com.au/news/Immigration/Maggots-found-
       in-food-at-detention-centre/2004/08/24/1093246511221.html, viewed
       9/10/2006

235   'ACM Detention Services Operating Manual, Policy 19.9 Issue 8', *Merits
       Point System*, 12/8/2002

236   *Hussein v Secretary of the Department of Immigration and Multicultural Affairs (No. 2)* [2006] FCA 1263 (21 September 2006)

237   Singh, C. 'Map of Detention Health Service Provision', Accountability and Regulation, 4/9/2007

238   Spencer, M., 'Doctors unite to slam refugee policy', *The Australian*, 24/1/2002, p. 1, 4, cited in Singh, C. 2002, 'We are Human Beings, We are Not Animals: The Relentless Commodification and Obliteration of Lives Within Australia's Privatised Immigration Detention Centres', unpublished paper

239   Huxstep, M. op. cit.

240   Oxfam 2007, *A price too high: The cost of Australia's approach to asylum-seekers*, Oxfam, Melbourne

241   Professional Alliance for the Health of Asylum Seekers and their Children, 'Submission to the National Inquiry into Children in Immigration Detention', available at http://www.cpmc.edu.au/docs/hreoc_submission.pdf, viewed 16/5/07

242   'Ruddock denies "disgraceful" condition of detention centres', ABC News Online, available at http://www.abc.net.au/news/regionals/northwa/monthly/regnwa-30oct2001-2.htm, viewed 13/10/2006

243   'Ruddock under pressure', *Lateline*, ABC Television, 29/7/2003, available at http://www.abc.net.au/lateline/content/2003/s912987.htm, viewed 19/6/2007

244   Professional Alliance for the Health of Asylum Seekers and their Children, 'Submission to the National Inquiry into Children in Immigration Detention', available at http://www.cpmc.edu.au/docs/hreoc_submission.pdf, viewed 16/5/07

245   Soldatic, K. & Fiske, L., 'Bodies "Locked Up": Intersections of Disability and Race in Australian Immigration', unpublished paper, p. 16–17

246   Byrne, M., 'Tales from the desert camps', *Griffith Review*, ABC Books, ed. 8, May 2005, p. 191

247   Taylor, P., 'Private guards "abused" detainees', *The Australian*, 2/2/2008, available at http://www.theaustralian.news.com.au/story/0,25197,23146909-5006789,00.html, viewed 4/2/2008

248   Crock, M., Saul, B. & Dastyari, A. op. cit. p. 194

249   Global Solutions Limited, 'Items not permitted into a facility', reviewed 14/6/2005

250   'Family still in limbo after Bali bombing', *The 7.30 Report*, ABC Television, 26/3/2003, available at http://www.abc.net.au/7.30/content/2003/s817253.htm, viewed 21/9/2007

251   'Aussie magistrate goes into bat for Indonesian children', *The 7.30 Report*, ABC Television, 21/5/2003, available at http://www.abc.net.au/7.30/content/2003/s860730.htm, viewed 9/10/2007

252   ibid.

253 'Publicity the key for visa-less Bali orphans', *Lateline*, ABC Television, 15/10/2003, available at http://www.abc.net.au/lateline/content/2003/s967845.htm, viewed 21/9/2007

254 Julian Burnside Q.C., *16th Lionel Murphy Memorial Lecture*, 20/11/2002, NSW Parliament House Theatrette http://lionelmurphy.anu.edu.au/16th%20Memorial%20Lecture%20WEB%20EDITION.doc, viewed 30/10/2006

255 Human Rights and Equal Opportunity Commission, 'Summary of Observations following the Inspection of Mainland Immigration Detention Facilities, January 2007', available at http://www.humanrights.gov.au/human_rights/asylum_seekers/inspection_of_mainland_idf.html, viewed 3/7/2007

256 'Anna's Story', *Four Corners*, ABC Television, 4/4/2005, available at http://www.abc.net.au/4corners/content/2005/s1338239.htm, viewed 16/5/07

257 'Baxter psychologists unregistered, letter reveals', ABC News Online, 1/7/2005 available at http://www.abc.net.au/news/newsitems/200507/s1404501.htm, viewed 11/10/2006

258 Mares, S. & Jureidini, J. 2004, 'Psychiatric Assessment of children and families in immigration detention — clinical, administrative and ethical issues', *Australian and New Zealand Journal of Public Health*, vol. 28, no. 6, p. 522

259 *S v Secretary, Department of Immigration & Multicultural & Indigenous Affairs* [2005] FCA 549, par. 181

260 ibid., par. 230

261 ibid., par. 147

262 'About Woomera', *Four Corners*, ABC Television, 19/5/2003, available at http://www.abc.net.au/4corners/content/2003/transcripts/s858341.htm, viewed 2/7/2007

263 Dudley, M., 'Contradictory Australian National Policies on Self-harm and Suicide', *Australasian Psychiatry*, 11 (Supplement October), 2003, p. S102

264 'Philip Ruddock responds to UN immigration detention scrutiny', *Lateline*, ABC Television, 6/6/2002, available at http://www.abc.net.au/lateline/stories/s575825.htm, viewed 26/7/2007

265 'Mohammed and Juliet — A Modern Tragedy', *Insight*, SBS Television, 8/5/2003, available at http://news.sbs.com.au/insight/trans.php?transid=522, viewed 13/8/2007

266 Wroe, D. 'Canberra paid $30,000 for report to discredit studies', *The Age*, 12/2/2005, available at http://www.theage.com.au/articles/2005/02/11/1108061874526.html, viewed 12/3/07

267 'Our work has been undermined, researchers say', *Lateline*, ABC Television, 9/2/2005, available at http://www.abc.net.au/lateline/content/2005/s1299518.htm, viewed 27/7/2007

268 'Government accused of biased detention centre research', *AM*, ABC Radio, 10/2/2005, available at http://www.abc.net.au/am/content/2005/s1299812.

htm, viewed 7/2/2006

269   ibid.

270   Jackson, A., 'The lost people of Villawood', *The Age*, 23/2/2008, p. 4

271   'About Woomera', *Four Corners*, 19/5/2003, available at http://www.abc.
      net.au/4corners/content/2003/transcripts/s858341.htm, viewed 2/7/2007

272   ibid.

273   'Senate Committee Inquiry into the Operation and Administration of the
      Migration Act 1958', ch. 6, par. 21, available at http://www.aph.gov.au/
      senate/Committee/legcon_ctte/migration/report/c06.pdf, viewed 23/1/2008

274   Crock, M., Saul, B. & Dastyari, A., op. cit., p. 201

275   Global Solutions Limited, *Baxter IDF Generic Management Plan — Daily
      Routines/Behaviour*, reviewed 7/6/2004

276   *S v Secretary, Department of Immigration & Multicultural & Indigenous
      Affairs* [2005] FCA 549

277   'Senate Committee Inquiry into the Operation and Administration of the
      Migration Act 1958', ch. 6, par. 26, available at http://www.aph.gov.au/
      senate/Committee/legcon_ctte/migration/report/c06.pdf, viewed 23/1/2008

278   Human Rights and Equal Opportunity Commission 2002, 'Report of an
      inquiry into complaints by five asylum-seekers concerning their detention
      in the separation and management block at the Port Hedland Immigration
      Reception and Processing Centre', available at http://www.hreoc.gov.au/
      human_rights/human_rights_reports/hrc_24.html quoted in New South
      Wales Council for Civil Liberties, *Shadow report prepared for the United
      Nations Committee Against Torture on the occasion of its review of
      Australia's Third Periodic Report under the Convention Against Torture and
      other Cruel, Inhuman or Degrading Treatment or Punishment*, 27/7/2007,
      par. 115, available at http://www.nswccl.org.au/docs/pdf/CAT%20
      shadow%20report.pdf, viewed 25/9/2007

279   Quoted in Marr, D. 'Purgatory in Baxter', *Sydney Morning Herald*,
      19/7/2005, available at http://www.smh.com.au/news/national/purgatory-
      in-baxter/2005/07/18/1121538922305.html, viewed 13/8/2007

280   O'Connor, C., 'The impact of detention on the mental health of detainees in
      immigration detention, and the implications for failing to deliver adequate
      Mental Health Services: Who Cares?', paper presented at the Inaugural
      Women Lawyers Conference, Sydney, September 2006, available at http://
      www.safecom.org.au/claire-o-connor.htm, viewed 22/1/2008

281   Rau, C. 'My sister lost her mind and Australia lost its heart when it
      imprisoned her', *The Age*, 7/2/05, pp. 1, 8

282   *S v Secretary, Department of Immigration & Multicultural & Indigenous
      Affairs* [2005] FCA 549, par. 10

283   ibid., par. 183

284   ibid., par. 108

285   ibid., par. 110

286   ibid., par. 144

287   ibid., par. 178

288   ibid., par. 174

289   ibid., par. 253

290   ibid., par. 231

291   O'Connor, C., op. cit.

292   Australasian Correctional Management, 'Incident Log', 2001

293   Professional Alliance for the Health of Asylum Seekers and their Children, 'Submission to the National Inquiry into Children in Immigration Detention', available at http://www.cpmc.edu.au/docs/hreoc_submission. pdf, viewed 16/5/07

294   *S v Secretary, Department of Immigration & Multicultural & Indigenous Affairs* [2005] FCA 549, par. 126

295   'Prison watchdog slams refugee conditions', *CNN*, 30/10/2001, available at http://archives.cnn.com/2001/WORLD/asiapcf/auspac/10/30/aust.refugees. disgrace/index.html, viewed 9/10/2006

296   *Background Briefing*, ABC Radio National, op. cit.

297   ibid.

298   ibid.

299   ChilOut Information Night, 3/6/2002, available at http://www.ChilOut. org/information/first_hand_account_of_woomera.html, viewed 9/10/2006

300   Huxstep, M. 'Statement to the National Inquiry into Children in Immigration Detention', available at http://www.hreoc.gov.au/human_ rights/children_detention/statements/huxstep. html, viewed 12/3/07

301   Quoted in Lygo, I. 2004, *News Overboard: The Tabloid Media, Race Politics and Islam*, Southerly Change Media, p. 97

302   'Refugee riot', *AM*, ABC Radio, 12/5/2001, available at http://www.abc. net.au/am/stories/s295268.htm, viewed 25/9/2007

303   Dudley, M., 'Contradictory Australian National Policies on Self-harm and Suicide', *Australasian Psychiatry*, 11 (Supplement October), 2003, p. S102

304   Crock, M., Saul, B. & Dastyari, A., op. cit., p. 200

305   Topsfield, J., 'Vanstone plays down self-harm', *The Age* 20/9/2005, available at http://www.theage.com.au/news/immigration/vanstone-plays-down-selfharm/2005/09/19/1126982001952.html, viewed 9/10/2006

306   'Woomera detention centre doctor speaks out', *Lateline*, ABC Television, 27/10/2004, available at http://www.abc.net.au/lateline/content/2004/ s1229335.htm, viewed 25/10/2006

307   Ruddock, P., 'Migration Act 1958, Direction Under Section 499, Strip Search Of Immigration Detainees, Direction no. 25', 27/9/2001,

available at http://www.comlaw.gov.au/ComLaw/Legislation/
LegislativeInstrument1.nsf/0/CED5FEF886C849D7CA25723C00149A18/$
file/copydirection+no.25.doc, viewed 19/6/2007

308 ibid.

309 Gray, D. '39 detainees moved to jails to stop riots', *The Age*, 3/1/2003,
     available at http://www.theage.com.au/articles/2003/01/02/104119673861
     7.html, viewed 19/6/2007

310 Senate Legal and Constitutional Legislation Committee, Official Committee
     Hansard, Consideration of Budget Estimates, 11/2/2003, available at http://
     www.aph.gov.au/hansard/senate/commttee/s6144.pdf, viewed 19/6/2007

311 National Community Legal Centre Conference 2003, 'Conference
     Resolutions', available at http://www.naclc.org.au/docs/03_%20conf_
     resolutions.pdf, viewed 19/6/2007

312 'Worse than prisons? Managing Detention Centres', *Background Briefing*,
     ABC Radio National, 6/10/2002, available at http://www.abc.net.au/rn/
     talks/bbing/stories/s697195.htm, viewed 13/10/2006

313 Steel, Z. et al. 2004, 'Psychiatric status of asylum-seeker families held for a
     protracted period in a remote detention centre in Australia', *Australian and
     New Zealand Journal of Public Health*, vol. 28, no. 6. p. 532

314 Byrne, M. 2005, 'Tales from the desert camps', *Griffith Review*, ABC
     Books, ed. 8, May, p. 184

315 Byrne, M. 2005, 'Detention centre workers', *New Matilda*, available at
     http://www.newmatilda.com/home/articledetailmagazine.asp?ArticleID=62
     7&CategoryID=-1, viewed 29/5/2007

316 Davies, J. A. & Byrne, M., 'Black and Blue Justice', *The Bulletin*, 5/7/2005,
     p. 16

317 Jackson, A., 'Baxter inmate alleges assault', *The Age*, 26/8/2005, available
     at http://www.theage.com.au/news/national/baxter-inmate-alleges-
     assault/2005/08/25/1124562981868.html, viewed 18/9/2007

318 Australasian Correctional Management Woomera Residential Housing
     Project, 'Operating Procedure, Procedure 10.14RHP, Use of Force and
     Restraints', 7/11/2002

319 Highfield, J., 2007, 'Timeline of events', *Acting from the Heart: Australian
     advocates for asylum-seekers tell their stories*, (eds) S. Mares & L. Newman,
     Finch Publishing, Sydney

320 Article 37 (b), available at http://www.austlii.edu.au/au/other/dfat/
     treaties/1991/4.html, viewed 23/1/2008

321 'Letting the children go', *Sydney Morning Herald*, 10/7/2004, available
     at http://www.smh.com.au/news/Immigration/Letting-the-children-
     go/2004/07/09/1091065972725.html, viewed 9/10/2006

322 *Minister for Immigration and Multicultural and Indigenous Affairs v B*
     [2004] HCA 20; 219 CLR 365; 206 ALR 130; 78 ALJR 737 29/4/2004

323 United Nations Human Rights Committee, 'International Covenant on Civil

and Political Rights', Communication no. 1069/2002

324 Goddard, C. & Briskman, L., 'By any measure, it's official child abuse', *The Herald Sun*, 19/2/2004, p. 17

325 'Iranian refugee seeks compensation', *AM*, ABC Radio, 27/8/2005, available at http://www.abc.net.au/am/content/2005/s1447376.htm, viewed 27/8/2007

326 'Immigration pay boy $400,000', *Sydney Morning Herald*, available at http://www.smh.com.au/news/national/immigration-pay-boy-400000/2006/03/03/1141191820943.html, viewed 19/6/2007

327 Highfield, J., op. cit.

328 Murphy, D., 'Record payout for refugee who sewed lips', *Sydney Morning Herald*, 12/1/2008, available at http://www.smh.com.au/news/national/record-payout-for-refugee/2008/01/11/1199988590128.html, viewed 14/1/2008

329 'Child refugee sues over detention trauma'. ABC News Online, 27/8/2005, available at http://www.abc.net.au/news/newsitems/200508/s1447392.htm, viewed 22/1/2008

330 Steel, Z. et al. op. cit.

331 Human Rights and Equal Opportunity Commission 2004, 'Summary of the important issues, findings and recommendations of the National Inquiry into Children in Immigration Detention', available at http://www.hreoc.gov.au/HUMAN_RIGHTS/children_detention_report/summaryguide/7_safety.htm, viewed 14/9/2007

332 Mares, S. & Jureidini, J. 2004, 'Psychiatric Assessment of children and families in immigration detention — clinical, administrative and ethical issues', *Australian and New Zealand Journal of Public Health*, vol. 28, no. 6, p. 520

333 Steel, Z. et al. op. cit.

334 Mares, S. & Jureidini, J., op. cit., p. 523

335 Davies, J. A., 'Child abuse experts act on Woomera', *The Age*, 21/3/2002

336 United Nations Human Rights Committee, 'International Covenant on Civil and Political Rights', communication no. 1069/2002, par. 5.14

337 Purcell, M., 'Damaging children, in our name', *The Age*, 17/2/2004, available at http://www.theage.com.au/articles/2004/02/16/1076779903107.html, viewed 29/5/2007

338 'Philip Ruddock responds to UN immigration detention scrutiny', *Lateline*, ABC Television, 6/6/2002, available at http://www.abc.net.au/lateline/stories/s575825.htm, viewed 26/7/2007

339 *Australia Now*, ABC Radio, June 2003, available at http://www.radioaustralia.net.au/australia/ now/program_13.htm, viewed 7/1/2008

340 Council for Civil Liberties, conferral of life membership on John Marsden, Julian Burnside speech, 'You can't fight city hall, can you?' March 2005,

available at http://www.users.bigpond.com/burnside/marsden.htm, viewed 6/9/2007

341 'Immigration Detention Standards and Performance Measures — Part Two: Detainees', available at http://www.immi.gov.au/managing-australias-borders/detention/standards_two.htm, viewed 13/9/2007

342 Szewczyk, K., *The Impacts of Detention on Family Relationships*, Victorian Women's Trust, available at http://www.vwt.org.au/docs/KateSzweczykImpacts.pdf, viewed 15/3/07

343 Huxstep, M., 'Statement to the National Inquiry into Children in Immigration Detention', available at http://www.hreoc.gov.au/human_rights/children_detention/statements/huxstep. html, viewed 12/3/07

344 Professional Alliance for the Health of Asylum Seekers and their Children, 'Submission to National Inquiry into Children in Immigration Detention', available at http://www.cpmc.edu.au/docs/hreoc_submission.pdf, viewed 16/5/07

345 National Scientific Council on the Developing Child, *Excessive Stress Disrupts the Architecture of the Developing Brain*, Working Paper #3, Summer 2005

346 Human Rights and Equal Opportunity Commission 2004, *A Last Resort?* — The Report of the National Inquiry into Children in Immigration Detention, ch. 3, sec. 5.3, available at http://www.hreoc.gov.au/Human_Rights/children_detention_report/report/chap. 03.htm, viewed 2/11/2006

347 Goddard, C., 'Baby Ghazal's got a new name: No. 390', *The Age*, 13/4/2004, available at http://www.theage.com.au/articles/2004/04/12/108 1621892083.html, viewed 1/11/2006

348 Professional Alliance for the Health of Asylum Seekers and their Children, op. cit., p. 27–28, available at http://www.cpmc.edu.au/docs/hreoc_submission.pdf, viewed 16/5/07

349 Mares, S. & Jureidini, J., op. cit.

350 Crock, M., Saul, B. & Dastyari, A., op. cit., p. 198

351 Mares, S. & Jureidini, J., op cit, p. 523

352 'Claims of drug running in Nauru detention centre', *AM*, ABC Radio, 13/8/2003, available at http://www.abc.net.au/am/content/2003/s923059. htm, viewed 24/10/2007

353 'School's out for asylum seekers', *The 7.30 Report*, ABC Television, 10/4/2002, available at http://www.abc.net.au/7.30/content/2002/s528365. htm, viewed 25/9/2007

354 Leser, D., 'Children overboard: Two women, two stories', *The Australian Women's Weekly*, August 2007, p. 66

355 Highfield, T. 'Nowhere to go', *Bedrock*, vol. 8, no. 3, Publication of the Early Childhood Services Independent Education Union, November 2003

356 Department of Immigration and Citizenship, 'Fact Sheet 69 — Caring for Unaccompanied Minors', available at http://www.immi.gov.au/media/fact-

sheets/69unaccompanied.htm, viewed 24/1/2008

357 Human Rights and Equal Opportunity Commission 2004, *A Last Resort?* —
The Report of the National Inquiry into Children in Immigration Detention,
op. cit., viewed 09/02/07

358 Crock, M. 2006, *Seeking asylum alone: a study of Australian law, policy and
practice regarding unaccompanied and separated children*, Themis Press, p.
42

359 ibid., p. 46

360 Professional Alliance for the Health of Asylum Seekers and their Children,
op. cit.

361 Department of Immigration and Citizenship, 'Detention Reforms', *Detention
Placement Options*

362 *Australia Now*, ABC Radio, June 2003, available at http://www.
radioaustralia.net.au/australia/now/program_13.htm, viewed 7/1/2008

363 Survivors of Torture and Trauma Assistance and Rehabilitation Service
2005, 'Submission to the Senate Inquiry into the Administration and
Operation of the Migration Act 1958', available at http://www.aph.gov.au/
senate/committee/legcon_ctte/migration/submissions/sub138.pdf, viewed
13/3/2007

364 Steel, Z. et al., op. cit.

365 Bilboe, H., 'Statement to the National Inquiry into Children in Immigration
Detention', available at http://www.hreoc.gov.au/Human_Rights/children_
detention/statements/bilboe.html, viewed 13/3/07

366 *Mr Omar Sharif Baban v. Australia*, Communication no. 1014/2001, UN
Doc CCPR/C/78/D/1014/2001 (2003)

367 ChilOut Information Night, 3/6/2002, available at http://www.ChilOut.
org/information/first_hand_account_of_woomera.html, viewed 09/10/2006

368 Professional Alliance for the Health of Asylum Seekers and their Children,
op. cit.

369 Skelton, R., 'Woomera Assault Error Admitted', *The Age*, 16/6/2002,
quoted in Whyte, J. *Life in the camp: Giorgio Agamben and Australia's
Mandatory Detention of Asylum-seekers*, Honours Thesis, School of Social
Science and Planning, RMIT University, October 2003

370 Skelton, R., 'Sacked guards who assaulted boy reinstated', *The Age*,
20/4/2002, available at http://www.theage.com.au/articles/2002/04/19/101
9020706643.html, viewed 24/9/2007

371 ibid.

372 Skelton, R., 'The Case of a Bashed Boy and Three Missing Guards', *The
Age*, 5/10/2002, quoted in Whyte, J. *Life in the camp: Giorgio Agamben
and Australia's Mandatory Detention of Asylum-seekers*, Honours Thesis,
School of Social Science and Planning, RMIT University, October 2003

373 Senate Legal and Constitutional Legislation Committee, Official Committee

Hansard, Consideration Of Budget Estimates, 11/2/2003, available at http://www.aph.gov.au/hansard/senate/commttee/s6144.pdf, viewed 19/6/2007

374   Suicide Prevention Australia, 'Two Australian National Policies on Self-Injury and Suicide: A Submission to the Human Rights Commission on Children in Detention', available at http://www.hreoc.gov.au/Human_Rights/children_detention/submissions/suicide_prevention.html, viewed 25/10/2007

375   Mares, S. & Jureidini, J., op. cit., p. 523

376   Bilboe, H., op. cit.

377   Rogalla, B. 2003, 'Modern-day torture: Government-sponsored neglect of asylum-seeker children under the Australian mandatory immigration detention regime', *Journal of South Pacific Law*, vol. 7, iss. 1, available at http://www.paclii.org/journals/fJSPL/vol07no1/11.shtml, viewed 17/9/2007.

378   Australian Democrats, 'Issue Sheet, Immigration and Multicultural Affairs, Children in Detention'

379   'Mandatory detention fair: government tells UN', *Sydney Morning Herald*, 7/4/2005, available at http://www.smh.com.au/news/National/Mandatory-detention-fair-Govt-tells-UNs/2005/04/07/1112815658191.html, viewed 13/6/2007

380   Immigration minister Senator Amanda Vanstone and attorney general Phillip Ruddock, *Human Rights and Equal Opportunity Commission Inquiry into Children in Immigration Report Tabled*, media release, 13/5/2004, available at http://pandora.nla.gov.au/pan/31543/20050430-0000/www.minister.immi.gov.au/media_releases/media04/v04068.htm, viewed 14/11/2007

381   Hoffman, S., *Temporary Protection Visas & SIEV X*, 6/2/2006, available at http://sievx.com/articles/challenging/2006/20060206SueHoffman.html, viewed 24/1/2008

382   ibid.

383   ibid.

384   Hamilton-Smith, A., 'Statement to the National Inquiry into Children in Immigration Detention', available at http://www.hreoc.gov.au/human%5Frights/children%5Fdetention/statements/hamilton.html, viewed 24/1/2008

385   Department infrastructure manager at Woomera in 2000, 'Statement to the National Inquiry into Children in Immigration Detention', available at http://www.hreoc.gov.au/human_rights/children_detention/submissions/infrastructure.html#facilities, viewed 24/1/2008

386   'He Lost 14 Members of his Family in the Ship Catastrophe', *El Telegraph*, iss. #3792, November 2001, English translation available at http://sievx.com/articles/disaster/200111xxElTelegraph.html, viewed 6/10/2007

387   'UN Convention against Torture and Other Cruel, Inhuman and Degrading Treatment or Punishment', available at http://www.austlii.edu.au/au/other/

dfat/treaties/1989/21.html, viewed 1/8/2007

388   Question taken on notice, Supplementary Budget Estimates Hearing: 30/10/2006, Immigration and Multicultural Affairs Portfolio (222) Output 1.3: Enforcement of Immigration Law

389   'Deportee incident causes human rights concerns', *AM*, ABC Radio, 27/1/05

390   ibid.

391   'Botched deportation cost thousands', *The Age*, available at http://www. theage.com.au/news/immigration/botched-deportation-costs-thousands/200 5/09/06/1125772499023.html, viewed 26/9/2007

392   Jackson, A., 'Cornelia Rau set to get $2.4 million compo payout', *The Age*, 18/2/2008, p. 7

393   Cazzulino, M., 'Get Out – And leave your baby behind', *The Daily Telegraph*, 12/10/2002, p. 1

394   ibid., p. 4

395   Walker, F., 'Mother's painful sacrifice', *The Sun-Herald*, 7/11/2004

396   *Winata v Australia (930/2000) 18 August 2001*, UN Doc. CCPR/C/72/ D/930/2000, quoted in Charlesworth, H., *Human Rights: Australia versus the UN*, discussion paper 22/06, August 2006, available at http:// democratic.audit.anu.edu.au/papers/20060809_charlesworth_aust_un.pdf, viewed 19/10/2007

397   Williams, J., Minute: Ministerial Intervention under Section 417 of the *Migration Act 1958*, file no.: CLF2001/8664, 28/2/2002

398   McGeogh, P., 'Mrs Bakhtiyari is one of ours, say Afghan', *Sydney Morning Herald*, 28/9/2005, available at http://www.smh.com.au/news/world/mrs-Bakhtiyari-is-one-of-ours-say-afghan/2005/09/27/1127804478530.html, viewed 20/6/2007

399   DIMIA Minute, 'Notice of Intention to Cancel — Ali Bakhtiyari', 21/3/2002

400   *Bakhtiyari v Australia* (1069/2002) 6/11/2003, UN Doc. CCPR/C/79/ D/1069/2002, available at http://www.bayefsky.com/./html/australia_t5_ iccpr_1069_2002.php, viewed 31/7/2007

401   McGeogh, P., op. cit.

402   Williams, J., op. cit.

403   Williams, J., op. cit.

404   *Bakhtiyari v Australia* (1069/2002) 6/11/2003, UN Doc. CCPR/C/79/ D/1069/2002, available at http://www.bayefsky.com/./html/australia_t5_ iccpr_1069_2002.php, viewed 31/7/2007

405   Refugee Review Tribunal ref: NO2/45217

406   *Bakhtiyari v Australia* (1069/2002) 6/11/2003, UN Doc. CCPR/C/79/ D/1069/2002, op. cit.

407   ibid.

408   ibid.

409   ibid.

410   Refugee Review Tribunal ref: NO2/45217

411   *Bakhtiyari v Australia* (1069/2002) 6/11/2003, UN Doc. CCPR/C/79/
D/1069/2002, op. cit.

412   Question taken on notice, Supplementary Budget Estimates Hearing
1/11/2005, Immigration and Multicultural Affairs Portfolio (114) Output
1.3: Enforcement of Immigration Law

413   *Bakhtiyari v Australia* (1069/2002) 6/11/2003, UN Doc. CCPR/C/79/
D/1069/2002, op. cit.

414   'Detained children release decision overruled', *Sydney Morning Herald*,
29/4/2004, available at http://www.smh.com.au/articles/2004/04/29/1083
103589964.html, viewed 24/5/2008

415   'Bakhtiyaris remain in limbo', *The Age*, 27/12/2004, available at
http://www.theage.com.au/news/National/Bakhtiyaris-remain-in-
limbo/2004/12/27/1103996484781.html, viewed 24/5/2008

416   'Bakhtiyari family moved', ABC News Online, 18/12/2004, available at
http://www.abc.net.au/news/newsitems/200412/s1268193.htm, viewed
24/5/2008

417   McGeogh, P., op. cit.

418   Quoted in McGeogh, P., 'Mrs Bakhtiyari is one of ours, say
Afghan', *Sydney Morning Herald*, 28/9/2005, available at http://
www.smh.com.au/news/world/mrs-Bakhtiyari-is-one-of-ours-say-
afghan/2005/09/27/1127804478530.html, viewed 20/6/2007

419   ibid.

420   ibid.

421   Minchin, L., 'Bakhtiyari family goes "missing"', *The Age*, 3/1/2005,
available at http://www.abc.net.au/news/newsitems/200412/s1268193.htm,
viewed 24/5/2008

422   ibid.

423   Question taken on notice, Supplementary Budget Estimates Hearing
1/11/2005, Immigration and Multicultural Affairs Portfolio (114) Output
1.3: Enforcement of Immigration Law

424   Amanda Vanstone, former minister for immigration and multicultural
affairs, *Bakhtiyari Family*, media release, 1/1/2005, available at http://
pandora.nla.gov.au/pan/31543/20050430-0000/www.minister.immi.gov.au/
media_releases/media05/v05001.htm, viewed 19/6/2007

425   Letter from DIMIA sent to Iranian detainees in early April 2003

426   'Trading with Iran', *Background Briefing*, ABC Radio, 8/6/2003, available
at http://www.abc.net.au/rn/talks/bbing/stories/s877364.htm, viewed
15/1/2008

427   ibid.

428   ibid.

429   Phillips, J. & Millbank, A., 'The detention and removal of asylum-seekers', e-brief, Parliament of Australia, Parliamentary Library, 5/7/2005, available at http://www.aph.gov.au/library/INTGUIDE/SP/asylum_seekers.htm, viewed 27/11/2007

430   Oxfam 2007, *A price too high: The cost of Australia's approach to asylum-seekers, Oxfam*, Melbourne, Table six

431   Parliament of Australia, 'The Senate Inquiry into the Administration and Operation of the Migration Act 1958', Table 3.6, available at http://www.aph.gov.au/Senate/committee/legcon_ctte/migration/report/c03.htm, viewed 18/7/2007

432   Crock, M., op. cit., p. 42

433   Edmund Rice Centre 2004, *Deported to Danger: A study of Australia's treatment of 40 rejected asylum seekers*, ERC, Sydney.

434   'Group claims returned asylum-seekers killed', *Lateline*, ABC Television, 7/8/2006, available at http://www.abc.net.au/lateline/content/2006/s1708870.htm, viewed 13/6/2007

435   Banham, C. 'Rejected refugees sent home to die: families tell harrowing stories', *Sydney Morning Herald*, 8/8/2006, available at http://www.smh.com.au/news/world/rejected-refugees-sent-home-to-die/2006/08/07/1154802823160.html, viewed 13/6/2007

436   ibid.

437   Shaw, M., 'Australia denies blame for asylum-seeker deaths', *The Age*, 10/10/2002, available at http://www.theage.com.au/articles/2002/10/09/1034061256063.html, viewed 1/8/2007

438   Banham, C. 'This man asked for our help — now he's dead', *Sydney Morning Herald*, 9/10/2002, available at http://www.smh.com.au/articles/2002/10/08/1034061209982.html, viewed 13/6/2007

439   Quoted in Browning, J. 2006, *States of Exclusion: Narratives from Australia's Immigration Detention Centres, 1999–2003*, PhD Thesis, p. 193

440   Nicholls, G. 2007, *Deported: A History of Forced Departures from Australia*, University of NSW Press, Sydney, p. 147

441   Irwin, J. 'Save us: family's plea', *Preston Leader*, 17/10/2006, p. 1

442   Senate Legal and Constitutional Legislation Committee, *Hansard*, 1/11/2005, available at http://www.aph.gov.au/hansard/senate/commttee/S8860.pdf, viewed 16/4/07

443   *Secretary, Department of Immigration, Multicultural and Indigenous Affairs v Mastipour* [2004] FCAFC 93 (29 April 2004), par. 31

444   ibid., par. 62

445   ibid.

446   ibid., par. 68

447   ibid., par. 69, 71, 72

448   ibid., par. 93, 94, 106

449   ibid., par. 122, 123, 125, 126

450   ibid., par. 12

451   Australasian Correctional Management, 'Singleton Immigration Reception and Processing Centre, Emergency Management Plan, Emergency Procedure: 5.16, Issue Date: 08.10.01, Death of a Detainee'

452   Byrne, P., 'Record of Investigation into Death', 28/11/2003, case no. 4162/00, pages 13, 17

453   ibid., p. 18

454   'Mohammed and Juliet — A Modern Tragedy', *Insight*, SBS Television, 8/5/2003, available at http://sbs.com.au/sbsmain/insight/archive. php3?daysum=2003-05-08#, viewed 24/5/2008

455   ibid.

456   Coroner's Court of Western Australia, 'Inquest into the Death of Mohammed Yousef Saleh', ref. no. 27/02, p. 19

457   'Mohammed and Juliet — A Modern Tragedy', *Insight*, op. cit.

458   Coroner's Court of Western Australia, op. cit.

459   Coroner's Court of Western Australia, op. cit.

460   Coroner's Court of Western Australia, op. cit.

461   'Mohammed and Juliet — A Modern Tragedy', *Insight*, op. cit.

462   ibid.

463   Wynhausen, E., 'A deadly shock to our system', *The Australian*, 12/102002, pp. 1–2

464   Coroner's Court of Western Australia, op. cit., p. 24

465   Wynhausen, E., op. cit.

466   'Accident linked to alleged illegal work scheme', *The World Today*, ABC Radio, 30/10/2002, available at http://www.abc.net.au/worldtoday/stories/ s714987.htm, viewed 4/9/2007

467   'No more investigating visa fraud: Ruddock', *PM*, ABC Radio, 31/10/2002, available at http://www.abc.net.au/pm/stories/s716067.htm, viewed 5/9/2007

468   'Investigation into Villawood detainee death', *PM*, ABC Radio, 27/7/2001, available at http://www.abc.net.au/pm/stories/s336835.htm, viewed 4/9/2007

469   'Philip Ruddock responds to UN immigration detention scrutiny', *Lateline*, ABC Television, 6/6/2002, available at http://www.abc.net.au/lateline/ stories/s575825.htm, viewed 26/7/2007

470 'Ruddock denies "disgraceful" condition of detention centres', *ABC News Online,* available at http://www.abc.net.au/news/regionals/northwa/ monthly/regnwa-30oct2001-2.htm, viewed 13/10/2006

471 Lamont, L., 'Sex slave inquest looks at detention', *Sydney Morning Herald*, 13/3/2003, available at http://www.smh.com.au/cgi-bin/common/ popupPrintArticle.pl?path=/articles/2003/03/12/1047431095513.html, viewed 5/9/2007

472 Project Respect media kit, 'Phuongtong Simpalee — the Death of a Trafficked woman in Villawood', available at http://www.projectrespect.org. au/resources/simaplee.pdf, viewed 5/9/2007

473 Costello, G. 'Trafficking of women and children', *Themis*, no. 5, November 2004, p. 5, available at http://www.womenlawyers.org.au/documents/ Themis_November_2004.pdf, viewed 24/10/2007

474 Milovanovich, C., *Inquest into the death of Puongtong Simpalee*, 24/4/2003, p. 11

475 Clennell, A., 'Detainee's fatal balcony fall believed to be suicide', *Sydney Morning Herald*, 15/01/2002, p. 3

476 Project Respect, 'Stop The Traffic Symposium on Trafficking of Women for Prostitution', *Through Our Eyes Bulletin 24*, 21/2/2002, available at https://www.nwjc.org.au/avcwl/lists/public/through-our-eyes/msg00024. html, viewed 24/10/2007

477 Quoted in Browning, J. 2006, *States of Exclusion: Narratives from Australia's Immigration Detention Centres, 1999–2003*, unpublished PhD thesis, UTS Sydney p. 220

478 ibid.

479 'Group claims returned asylum-seekers killed', *Lateline*, ABC Television, 7/8/2006, available at http://www.abc.net.au/lateline/content/2006/ s1708870.htm, viewed 13/6/2007

480 Jacobsen, G., 'Immigration death sparks training queries', *The Age* 29/8/2005, available at http://www.smh.com.au/news/national/ immigration-death-sparks-training-queries/2005/08/28/1125167552329. html, viewed 17/5/07

481 Therin, F. & Kerin, J., 'French fury over detainee's death', *The Australian*, 9/9/2004, available at http://groups.yahoo.com/group/archive-laonews/ message/9007, viewed 8/5/07

482 'Villawood may be scrapped and replaced', AAP, 14/1/2008, available at http://www.villagevoice.com.au/article/20080114/NWS02/801140301/0/ EVENTS/Villawood+may+be+scrapped+and+replaced, viewed 4/2/2008

483 'Detention Services Contract, Schedule 2: Detention Services, Section 17.1.7', cited in PIAC 2006, 'Immigration Detention in Australia: The loss of decency and humanity, submission to the People's Inquiry into Detention'

484 Harding, R. 1997, 'Private Prisons and Public Accountability', p. 33, cited in PIAC 2006, 'Immigration Detention in Australia: The loss of decency and humanity, submission to the People's Inquiry into Detention'

485 *Background Briefing*, ABC Radio National, op. cit.

486 *S v Secretary, Department of Immigration & Multicultural & Indigenous Affairs* [2005] FCA 549, par. 223

487 ibid. par. 224

488 ibid. par. 237

489 'Ruddock responds', *The Age*, 1/2/2002, available at http://www.safecom. org.au/ruddockspeak.htm, viewed 10/7/2007

490 'Behind Closed Doors', *Insight*, SBS Television, 26/4/2005, available at http://news.sbs.com.au/insight/archive.php?daysum=2005-04-26#, viewed 13/8/2007

491 ibid.

492 Jackson, A., 'Apology ordered for former detainee', *The Age*, 18/2/2008, p. 7

493 Metcalfe, A., secretary, Department of Immigration and Citizenship, address on 'Designing public policy and programs: Case study in compliance and detention reforms', The Australian and New Zealand School of Government, Canberra, 15/6/2007, p. 9, available at http://www.immi.gov. au/about/speeches-pres/_pdf/2007-06-15-ANZSOG-transcript.pdf, viewed 18/6/2007

494 Press conference, 'Rau family and University of Newcastle Legal Centre response to Mick Palmer's report into the detention of Cornelia Rau', NSW Parliament House, 15/7/2005.

495 Human Rights and Equal Opportunity Commission, 'HRC Report no. 12, Report of an Inquiry into a Complaint of Acts or Practices Inconsistent With or Contrary to Human Rights in an Immigration Detention Centre', available at http://www.hreoc.gov.au/human_rights/asylum_seekers/index. html#port_headland, viewed 14/9/2007

496 *A v Australia (1997)* UN Doc. CCPR/C/59/D/560/1993; *C v Australia (2002)* UN Doc. CCPR/C/76/D/900/1999; *Baban v Australia (2003)* UN Doc. CCPR/C/78/D/1014/2001; *Bakhtiyari v Australia (2003)* UN Doc CCPR/C/79/D/1069/2002; *D & E v Australia 2006* UN Doc. CCPR/ C/87/D/1050/2002; and, *Shafiq v Australia (2006)* UN Doc. CCPR/C/88/ D/1324/2004, quoted in New South Wales Council for Civil Liberties, *Shadow report prepared for the United Nations Committee Against Torture on the occasion of its review of Australia's Third Periodic Report under the Convention Against Torture and other Cruel, Inhuman or Degrading Treatment or Punishment*, 27/7/2007, par. 107, available at http://www. nswccl.org.au/docs/pdf/CAT%20shadow%20report.pdf, viewed 25/9/2007

497 Official Records of the General Assembly, 53rd session, UN Doc. CCPR/ A/53/40, vol. 1 (1998), quoted in Charlesworth, H., *Human Rights: Australia versus the UN*, Discussion Paper 22/06 (August 2006), available at http://democratic.audit.anu.edu.au/papers/20060809_charlesworth_aust_ un.pdf, viewed 19/10/2007

498 United Nations Economic and Social Council, 'Report of the Working Group on Arbitrary Detention', 2002, available at http://www.unhchr.ch/

Huridocda/Huridoca.nsf/0/6035497b015966fec1256cc200551f19?Opendo cument, viewed 24/9/2007

499   Australian minister for foreign affairs, *Government Rejects UN Report on Arbitrary Detention*, media release, 13/12/2002, available at http://www. foreignminister.gov.au/releases/2002/fa184a_02.html, viewed 24/9/2007

500   United Nations Human Rights Committee, International Covenant on Civil and Political Rights, communication no. 1069/2002

501   Lygo , I. 2004, *News Overboard: The Tabloid Media, Race Politics and Islam*, Southerly Change Media, Sydney, p. 112

502   Bender, L. 2007, 'Compelled to Act', *Acting from the Heart: Australian advocates for asylum-seekers tell their stories*, (eds) S. Mares & L. Newman, Finch Publishing, Sydney, p. 209

503   'About Woomera', *Four Corners*, op. cit.

504   'Mohammed and Juliet — A Modern Tragedy', *Insight*, op. cit.

505   'Senator denied Nauru visa', news.com.au, available at http://www.news. com.au/story/0,23599,15991649-1702,00.html, viewed 3/10/2007

506   'Detention Services Contract, schedule 3: Immigration Detention Standards, Performance Measures and the Performance Linked Fee Matrix, Attachment A: Incidents', cited in PIAC 2006, 'Immigration Detention in Australia: The loss of decency and humanity, submission to the People's Inquiry into Detention'

507   Quoted in Marr, D., 'Yes, Prime Minister — we're a nation in authority's grip', *The Age*, 2/6/2007, p. 5

508   ibid.

509   Quoted in Lygo, I. 2004, *News Overboard: The Tabloid Media, Race Politics and Islam*, Southerly Change Media, p. 102. One year later, having been taken to visit Villawood 10 times by refugee advocate Ngareta Rossell, the author of the original article, David Penberthy, wrote another exposing the reality of life in detention. The second article is available at http://www. safecom.org.au/daily-telegraph.htm, viewed 24/9/2007

510   Mares, S. & Jureidini, J., op cit. p. 524

511   Marr, D., 'Purgatory in Baxter', *Sydney Morning Herald*, 19/7/2005, available at http://www.smh.com.au/news/national/purgatory-in-baxter/2005/07/18/1121538922305.html, viewed 13/8/2007

512   ibid.

513   Interview with immigration and indigenous affairs minister Philip Ruddock, *Meet the Press*, Channel Ten, 20/4/2003, available at http://legacy.ten.com. au/library/documents/Mtp20_04.doc, viewed 29/8/2007

514   Some of this footage can be viewed at http://www.youtube.com/ watch?v=ftP6VTSD21k, viewed 22/11/2007

515   'Woomera detention centre doctor speaks out', *Lateline*, op. cit.

516   ibid.

517   Burnside, J., 'Speech at the Melbourne Rotary Breakfast', 17/2/2004, available at http://www.safecom.org.au/burnside4.htm, viewed 16/7/2007

518   Simons, M., 'In the name of the father', *The Age*, 22/11/2003, available at http://www.theage.com.au/articles/2003/11/22/1069027346572.html, viewed 12/11/2007

519   ibid.

520   Adams, P., 'Mr Anathema International', *The Australian Magazine*, 28/6/2003, p. 13

521   'Backbenchers defy Howard on asylum bill', *Sydney Morning Herald*, 9/8/2006, available at http://www.smh.com.au/news/national/new-asylum-laws-profoundly-disturbing/2006/08/09/1154802942102.html?page=fullpage#contentSwap1, viewed 18/10/2006

522   ibid.

523   *A Current Affair*, 28/8/2001, quoted in Highfield, T., 'Someone's Beloved Child', *Rattler*, Publication of Community Child Care Cooperative, no. 60, Summer 2001, p. 2

524   Dodson, L., 'Immigration levels sufficient, poll finds', *Sydney Morning Herald*, 25/3/2005, quoted by Gosden, D., *What if no one had spoken out against this policy?: The Rise of Asylum-seeker and Refugee Advocacy in Australia*, presented at Other Worlds: Social Movements and the Making of Alternatives conference, University of Technology Sydney, April 2005

525   Reynolds, M., 'The Untold Story: A report to the 60th Session of the United Nations Commission on Human Rights April 2004', United Nations Association of Australia Inc, quoted by Gosden, D. op cit

526   Newman, L., & Mares, S., (eds) 2007 *Acting from the Heart: Australian advocates for asylum-seekers tell their stories*, Finch Publishing, Sydney

527   Gosden, D. op. cit.

528   Zable, A., 'In Search of Refuge: Two Tales', Craven, P. (ed.) *Best Australian Essays 2001*, Black Inc, Melbourne, p. 63

529   Debelle, P., 'Love in detention', *The Age*, 15/12/2003, available at http://www.theage.com.au/articles/2003/12/14/1071336811465.html, viewed 23/1/2008

530   Australasian Correctional Management, Memorandum 29/8/2002, 'Alleged Overfamiliarity with Detainee'

531   ChilOut Information Night, op. cit.

532   Huxstep, M., 'Statement to the National Inquiry into Children in Immigration Detention', available at http://www.hreoc.gov.au/human_rights/children_detention/statements/huxstep. html, viewed 12/3/2007

533   Quoted in Carey, C. 'Woomera: victims of the war zone', *The Sunday Age*, 25/2/2007

534   ibid.

535   Migration Litigation Reform Bill 2005, *Migration Litigation Reform:*

Better Access, More Integrity, media release, 10/3/2005, available at http://pandora.nla.gov.au/pan/31543/20050430-0000/www.minister.immi.gov.au/media_releases/media05/v05041.htm, viewed 19/11/2007

536 Australian Lawyers for Human Rights, 'Submission to the Senate Legal and Constitutional Affairs Committee Inquiry into the Migration Litigation Reform Bill 2005', 1/4/2005, available at http://www.aph.gov.au/senate/committee/legcon_ctte/mig_litigation/submissions/sub19.pdf, viewed 19/11/2007

537 Lamattina, M., 'Migration reforms: A slippery slope?', *Lawyers Weekly Online*, available at http://www.lawyersweekly.com.au/articles/Migration-reforms-A-slippery-slope_z66873.htm, viewed 19/11/2007

538 Balint, R., 'A death in the Harbour: Policing Australia's northern waters', *The Monthly*, April 2007, p. 34

539 'Business Affairs cast doubt on CLP Senator's future', *The 7.30 Report*, ABC Television, 9/5/2002, available at http://www.abc.net.au/7.30/content/2002/s552133.htm, viewed 10/7/2007

540 Shaw, B.J., The President of the Senate, Re: Senator Scullion Advice, 18/12/2003, available at http://wopared.aph.gov.au/library/intguide/POL/Scullion.pdf, viewed 6/2/2008

541 ibid.

542 *Inquest into the death of Mansur La Ibu* [2004] NTMC 020, available at http://www.nt.gov.au/justice/docs/courts/coroner/findings/2004/mansur.pdf, viewed 10/7/2007

543 ibid.

544 Balint, R., op. cit., p. 35

545 ibid., p. 34

546 *Inquest into the death of Mansur La Ibu* [2004] op. cit.

547 Balint, R., 'A death in the Harbour: Policing Australia's northern waters', *The Monthly*, April 2007, p. 38

548 Murdoch, L., 'Help too late for illegal fishermen', *The Age*, 19/1/2006, available at http://www.theage.com.au/news/national/help-too-late-for-illegal-fisherman/2006/01/18/1137553651598.html, viewed 9/7/2007

549 Human Rights and Equal Opportunity Commission, 'Summary of Observations following the Inspection of Mainland Immigration Detention Facilities', January 2007, available at http://www.humanrights.gov.au/human_rights/asylum_seekers/inspection_of_mainland_idf.html, viewed 3/7/2007

550 ibid.

551 Murdoch, L., op. cit.

552 Balint, R., op. cit., p. 34

553 Department of Immigration and Citizenship, *Annual Report 2006–07*, p. 121, available at http://www.immi.gov.au/about/reports/annual/2006-07/

html/index.htm, viewed 10/1/2008

554   Balint, R., op. cit., p. 34

555   Fitzpatrick, S. & Taylor, P., 'Fishing crackdown forced boat people to seek asylum', *The Mercury*, 22/11/2007, available at http://www.news.com.au/mercury/story/0,22884,22799736-421,00.html?from=public_rss, viewed 27/11/2007

556   Department of Immigration and Multicultural Affairs, public information paper, *Onshore Detention Strategy*, May 2006

557   'Illegal boats caught in Australian waters', *The Daily Telegraph*, 19/5/2007, available at http://www.news.com.au/dailytelegraph/story/0,,21759369-5001028,00.html, viewed 9/7/2007

558   Balint, R., op. cit., p. 37

559   Department of Immigration and Citizenship, *Population Flows: Immigration Aspects 2005–06 Edition*, p. 79, available at http://www.immi.gov.au/media/publications/statistics/popflows2005-6/Ch5pt4.pdf, viewed 28/12/2007

560   Department of Immigration and Citizenship, 'Fact Sheet 86 — Overstayers and People in Breach of Visa Conditions', available at http://www.immi.gov.au/media/fact-sheets/86overstayers.htm, viewed 23/1/2008

561   ibid.

562   Department of Immigration and Citizenship, *Managing the Border: Immigration Compliance 2004–2005 Edition*, p. 37, available at http://www.immi.gov.au/media/publications/compliance/managing-the-border/pdf/mtb-chapter5.pdf, viewed 28/12/2007

563   See pp. 235-6

564   See p. 216

565   Department of Immigration and Citizenship, *Annual Report 2006–07*, p. 117, available at http://www.immi.gov.au/about/reports/annual/2006-07/html/index.htm, viewed 10/1/2008

566   PhillipsKPA and LifeLong Learning Associates, *Evaluation of the Education Services for Overseas Students Act 2000*, June 2005, available at http://www.dest.gov.au/sectors/international_education/publications_resources/profiles/evaluation_report.htm, sec. 8.1.1

567   Tippet, G. & Sexton, R., 'Opportunity's knocks', *The Age*, 16/12/2007, p. 16

568   Department of Immigration and Citizenship, *Annual Report 2006–07*, op. cit., p. 119

569   Quoted in 'Attachment A, Supplementary Information for the Submission to The Senate Inquiry into The Migration Act 1958 Re: "The Detention of International Students"', available at http://www.aph.gov.au/SENATE/committee/legcon_ctte/migration/submissions/sub220a.pdf, viewed 17/9/2007

570 Rost, M., 'Indian student billed $97,000 for detention in Baxter', *South Asia Times*, February 2005, p. 19

571 'Judges slam Immigration Department over student's treatment', *PM*, ABC Radio, 27/7/2005, available at http://www.abc.net.au/pm/content/2005/ s1423848.htm, viewed 17/9/2007

572 Bayman, R., Burton, G., D'Cruz, D., Gebhard, F., Humphries, J., Kenny, J., King, K., Matijas-Kezer, J., Mavor, C., Searle, G., Talikowski, E., Vicary, D. & Wettinger, M., Western Australian Department of Family and Children's Services, *Operation Safe Haven — disaster recovery management with the Kosovar refugees*, 1999, available at http://www.nationalsecurity.gov.au/ agd/EMA/rwpattach.nsf/viewasattachmentpersonal/(C86520E41F5EA5C8 AAB6E66B851038D8)~Operation_Safe_Haven.pdf/$file/Operation_Safe_ Haven.pdf, viewed 10/10/2007

573 NSW Service for the Treatment and Rehabilitation of Torture and Trauma Survivors, 2002, *Documentation and evaluation of Service Provision at Singleton Haven Centre — from the point of view of service providers*, available at http://www.swsahs.nsw.gov.au/areaser/Startts/publications/ article_8.asp, viewed 10/10/2007.

574 Nicholls, G., 'Election 2007: It's time to reform deportation policy', *Australian Review of Public Affairs*, September 2007, available at http:// www.australianreview.net/digest/2007/election/nicholls.html, viewed 31/12/2007

575 Parliament of Australia, 2006, 'The Senate Inquiry into the Administration and Operation of the Migration Act 1958', ch. 9, par. 63, available at http:// www.aph.gov.au/senate/Committee/legcon_ctte/migration/report/c09.htm, viewed 18/7/2007

576 Department of Immigration and Citizenship, 'Fact Sheet 79 — The Character Requirement', available at http://www.immi.gov.au/media/fact-sheets/79character.htm, viewed 1/1/2008

577 ibid.

578 Department of Immigration and Citizenship, *Annual Report 2006–07*, op. cit., p. 113

579 Parliament of Australia, 2006, 'The Senate Inquiry into the Administration and Operation of the *Migration Act 1958*', ch. 9, par. 37, available at http:// www.aph.gov.au/senate/Committee/legcon_ctte/migration/report/c09.htm, viewed 18/7/2007

580 Parliament of Australia, 2006, op. cit., ch. 9, par. 50

581 Parliament of Australia, 2006, op. cit., ch. 9, par. 80-81

582 Parliament of Australia, 2006, op. cit., ch. 9, par. 80

583 Parliament of Australia, 2006, op. cit., ch. 9, par. 77

584 Parliament of Australia, 2006, op. cit., ch. 9, par. 85

585 Davis, M., 'Serial offender asks to be deported to Sweden', *The Daily Telegraph*, 15/11/2006, available at http://www.news.com.au/ dailytelegraph/story/0,22049,20758736-5005941,00.html, viewed

31/12/2007

586 *Nystrom v Minister for Immigration and Multicultural and Indigenous Affairs* [2005] FCAFC 121

587 Quoted in Davis, M., op. cit.

588 Quoted in Bamford, P., 'Stefan Nystrom and "The Kafka Principle"' *On Line Opinion*, 15/12/2006, available at http://www.onlineopinion.com.au/view.asp?article=5284, viewed 31/12/2007

589 *Minister for Immigration and Multicultural and Indigenous Affairs v Nystrom* [2006] HCA 50

590 Nicholls, G., op. cit.

591 'Bring Jovicic home, family pleads', *Lateline*, ABC Television, 30/11/2005, available at http://www.abc.net.au/lateline/content/2005/s1520349.htm, viewed 31/12/2007

592 'Robert Jovicic's uncertain return home', *ABC Sydney*, ABC Radio, 13/3/2006, available at http://www.abc.net.au/sydney/stories/s1590439.htm, viewed 31/12/2007

593 Nicholls, G., op. cit.

594 Cooke, D., 'Life in limbo ends as man told he can stay', *The Age*, 23/2/2008, p. 4

595 'Terror Suspect loses Visa', *The Age*, 16/7/2007 available at http://www.theage.com.au/news/national/haneef-detained-at-villawood/2007/07/16/1184438205768.html, viewed 27/5/2008

596 Thomas, H., 'AFP insisted Haneef was no threat', *The Australian*, 3/11/2007

597 'Profile: Julian Burnside', *Sunday*, Channel Nine, 4/11/2007, http://www.abc.net.au/sundayprofile/stories/s2080576.htm, viewed 6/11/2007

598 'Visa returned to Mohamed Haneef', *PM*, ABC Radio, 21/12/2007, available at http://www.abc.net.au/pm/content/2007/s2125844.htm, viewed 1/1/2008

599 Commonwealth Ombudsman 2006 Department of Immigration and Multicultural Affairs, 'Administration of section 501 of the *Migration Act 1958* as it applies to Long-Term Residents', pp. 2-5, available at http://www.ombudsman.gov.au/commonwealth/publish.nsf/attachmentsbytitle/reports_2006_01.pdf/$file/s501_immigration_feb-2006.pdf, viewed 17/1/2008

600 ibid.

601 Australian National Audit Office 2004, 'Management of the Detention Centre Contracts', available at http://www.anao.gov.au/director/publications/auditreports/2003-2004.cfm?item_id=1EB0C496C2A17F68C5194FF0D6972A70, viewed 12/11/2007

602 'Detention Manager gets $5.7 million payout', *The Age*, 2/3/2006 http://www.theage.com.au/news/National/Detention-manager-gets-57m-

payout/2006/03/02/1141191798603.html, viewed 16/10/2006

603 Australian National Audit Office, 'Preparations for the Re-tendering of DIAC's Detention and Health Services Contracts', audit report no. 35 2006–07

604 Crock, M., Saul, B. & Dastyari, A., op. cit., p. 204

605 Australian Greens, *Transferring Sri Lankans to Nauru could cost $60 million*, media release, 2/3/2007, available at http://www.greens.org.au/media/releases/release.php?release_id=21, viewed 19/6/2007

606 'Bizarre footage of detention centre', *The Age*, 17/5/07, available at http://www.theage.com.au/articles/2007/05/17/1178995303970.html?s_cid=rss_age, viewed 17/5/07

607 Senate Standing Committee on Legal and Constitutional Affairs Estimates (Budget Estimates) 21/5/2007, 118–119, available at http://www.aph.gov.au/hansard/senate/commttee/S10246.pdf, viewed 23/5/07

608 Jackson, A., 'Burmese Asylum-seekers sent to Nauru', *The Age*, 19/9/06, available at http://www.theage.com.au/news/national/burmese-asylum-seekers-sent-to-nauru/2006/09/18/1158431645273.html, viewed 17/5/07

609 'Greens want detention centre closures made an election issue', *ABC News Online*, 25/5/2007, available at http://www.abc.net.au/news/newsitems/200705/s1933245.htm, viewed 19/6/2007

610 Metherell, M., 'Costs cited to justify refugee swap with US', *Sydney Morning Herald*, available at http://www.smh.com.au/news/national/costs-cited-to-justify-refugee-swap-with-us/2007/04/18/1176696916766.html, viewed 26/9/2007

611 Justice for Asylum-seekers, 'Alternative approaches to asylum-seekers: Reception and Transitional processing System', June 2002, pp. 6, 7

612 Metcalfe, A., secretary, Department of Immigration and Citizenship, address on 'Designing public policy and programs: Case study in compliance and detention reforms', op. cit.

613 Oxfam 2007, op. cit.

614 Burnside, J., 'Speech at the Melbourne Rotary Breakfast', op. cit.

615 Oxfam 2007, op. cit.

616 Jackson, A. 'Aladdin Sisalem released from Manus Island', *The Age*, 1/6/2004, available at http://www.theage.com.au/articles/2004/05/31/1085855499159.html, viewed 19/6/2007

617 Nicholson, B., 'DFAT asked to explain Nauru aid blow-out', *The Age*, 2/3/2007, available at http://www.theage.com.au/news/national/dfat-asked-to-explain-nauru-aid-blowout/2007/06/01/1180205515179.html, viewed 13/8/2007

618 Corlett, D., 'Border protection comes at too high a price', *The Age*, 4/9/2007, available at http://www.theage.com.au/news/national/border-protection-comes-at-too-high-a-price/2007/09/03/1188783152824.html?page=fullpage, viewed 24/10/2007

619   Interview with Immigration and Indigenous Affairs Minister Philip Ruddock, *Meet the Press*, Channel Ten, 20/4/2003, available at http://legacy.ten.com.au/library/documents/Mtp20_04.doc, viewed 29/8/2007

620   Information provided to the inquiry by Chris Rau, Cornelia Rau's sister

621   Senate Legal and Constitutional Legislation Committee Estimates 15/2/2005, p. 118, available at http://www.aph.gov.au/hansard/senate/commtte/S8082.pdf, viewed 28/8/2007

622   Human Rights and Equal Opportunity Commission, 'Summary of Observations following the Inspection of Mainland Immigration Detention Facilities', January 2007, available at http://www.humanrights.gov.au/human_rights/asylum_seekers/inspection_of_mainland_idf.html, viewed 3/7/2007

623   *Al Kateb v Godwin* (2004) 208 ALR 124, and *Minister for Immigration v Al Khafaji* (2004) 208 ALR 201

624   See *Hamdan v Minister for Immigration & Multicultural & Indigenous Affairs* [2004] FCA 1267 and *Minister for Immigration & Multicultural & Indigenous Affairs v Hamdan* [2005] FCAFC 113

625   Department of Immigration and Citizenship, 'Fact Sheet 83a — Residence Determination', available at http://www.immi.gov.au/media/fact-sheets/83aResidence_determination.html, viewed 28/8/2007

626   Human Rights and Equal Opportunity Commission, op. cit.

627   Human Rights and Equal Opportunity Commission, op. cit.

628   Department of Immigration and Citizenship, *Annual Report 2006–07*, p. 127, available at http://www.immi.gov.au/about/reports/annual/2006-07/html/index.htm, viewed 10/1/2008

629   Department of Immigration and Citizenship, 'Fact Sheet 85 — Removal Pending Bridging Visa', available at http://www.immi.gov.au/media/fact-sheets/85removalpending.htm, viewed 26/9/2007

630   Department of Immigration and Citizenship, *Annual Report 2006–07*, op. cit., p. 128

631   Jackson, A., 'Our lives are still in limbo: former detainees', *The Age*, 5/1/2008, p. 6

632   Quoted in McNevin, A., 'Seeking Safety, not Charity: A report in support of work-rights for asylum-seekers living in the community on Bridging Visa E', March 2005

633   Editorial, 'A visa that lowers the bridge on asylum-seekers', *The Age*, 14/12/2007, p. 16

634   Quoted in New South Wales Council for Civil Liberties, *Shadow report prepared for the United Nations Committee Against Torture on the occasion of its review of Australia's Third Periodic Report under the Convention Against Torture and other Cruel, Inhuman or Degrading Treatment or Punishment*, 27/7/2007, par. 147, available at http://www.nswccl.org.au/docs/pdf/CAT%20shadow%20report.pdf, viewed 25/9/2007

635 Department of Immigration and Citizenship, *Annual Report 2006–07*, op. cit., p. 128

636 Hotham Mission Asylum Seeker Project, 'Welfare issues and immigration outcomes for asylum-seekers on Bridging Visa E: Research and Evaluation', April 2003

637 Quoted in McNevin, A., op. cit.

638 McNevin, A., op. cit.

639 ibid.

640 Hotham Mission Asylum Seeker Project, op. cit.

641 Quoted in McNevin, A., op. cit.

642 Hotham Mission Asylum Seeker Project, op. cit.

643 Hotham Mission Asylum Seeker Project, op. cit.

644 Quoted in McNevin, A., op. cit.

645 McNevin, A., op. cit.

646 Hotham Mission Asylum Seeker Project, op. cit.

647 Quoted in Green, M., 'Asylum-seekers: No Work and No Play', *New Matilda*, available at http://www.newmatilda.com/home/articledetailmagazine.asp?ArticleID=2321&HomepageID=206, viewed 13/8/2007

648 Philip Ruddock, former minister for immigration and multicultural affairs, *Decision Time for TPV Holders*, media release, 11/6/2002, available at http://pandora.nla.gov.au/pan/31543/20040430-0000/www.minister.immi.gov.au/media_releases/ruddock_media02/r02047.htm, viewed 23/1/2008

649 Interview with immigration and indigenous affairs minister Philip Ruddock, *Meet the Press*, Channel Ten, 20/4/2003, available at http://legacy.ten.com.au/library/documents/Mtp20_04.doc, viewed 9/2/2008

650 'Trading with Iran', *Background Briefing*, ABC Radio, 8/6/2003, available at http://www.abc.net.au/rn/talks/bbing/stories/s877364.htm, viewed 15/1/2008

651 Mann, R., 'Temporary Protection Visa Holders in Queensland', Multicultural Affairs Queensland, February 2001; Curran, L., 'Forgotten People — Asylum in Australia', occasional Paper no. 10, Catholic Commission for Justice, Development and Peace, February 2001; Mansouri, F. & Bagdas, M., 'Politics of Social Exclusion: Refugees on Temporary Protection Visa in Victoria', Victorian Arabic Social Services & Deakin University, 2002; 'Temporary Protection Visa Holders in Queensland — A Year On, Findings from a consultation held by Brisbane City Council's Social Action and Equity Team', May 2002. All quoted on Human Rights and Equal Opportunity Commission website — 'Erace: a web forum on Race Discrimination Issues, Temporary Protection Visas: operation and impacts', available at http://www.humanrights.gov.au/racial_discrimination/forum/Erace/tpvs/tpvs.html, viewed 3/7/07

652   Stockbridge, L. 2005, 'How the abuse continues after detention', unpublished paper

653   Leser, D., 'Children overboard: Two women, two stories', *The Australian Women's Weekly*, August 2007, p. 66

654   Stockbridge, L., op. cit.

655   Department of Immigration and Citizenship, 'TPV Holders: Applications for further protection visas', July 2003, p. 13, available at http://www.immi. gov.au/refugee/_pdf/tpv_faq.pdf, viewed 31/10/2007

656   Oxfam Australia, 'Temporary Protection Visas: Urgent Response no. 30', June 2003, available at http://www.oxfam.org.au/campaigns/urgent/tpvs. html, viewed 27/1/2007

657   Quoted in Amnesty International Australia booklet, *Australia: Human Rights Denied*, available at https://www.amnesty.org.au/__data/assets/pdf_file/40585/Refugee_Campaign_Avant_Card_booklet.pdf, viewed 19/9/2007

658   Philip Ruddock, former minister for immigration and multicultural affairs, *Ruddock Announces Tough New Initiatives*, media release, 13/10/1999, available at http://pandora.nla.gov.au/pan/31543/20040430-0000/www. minister.immi.gov.au/media_releases/ruddock_media99/r99143.htm, viewed 23/1/2008

659   Hoffman, S., *Temporary Protection Visas & SIEV X*, 6/2/2006, available at http://sievx.com/articles/challenging/2006/20060206SueHoffman.html, viewed 24/1/2008

660   Senate Hansard, 17/10/2006, p. 24, available at http://www.aph.gov.au/ HANSARD/senate/dailys/ds171006.pdf, viewed 13/5/2008

661   Shaw, M., 'Visa status blamed for suicide', *The Age*, 8/2/2003, available at http://www.theage.com.au/articles/2003/02/07/1044579934925.html, viewed 28/5/2007

662   Department of Immigration and Citizenship, 'TPV Holders: Applications for further protection visas', op. cit., p. 4,

663   Mann, R., op. cit., p. 21

664   Murphy, D., 'Record payout for refugee who sewed lips', *The Sydney Morning Herald*, 12/1/2008, available at http://www.smh.com.au/news/ national/record-payout-for-refugee/2008/01/11/1199988590128.html, viewed 14/1/2008

665   Mares, S. & Jureidini, J., op. cit., p. 524

666   Migration Reform Act 1992 (Cth). Quoted in New South Wales Council for Civil Liberties, *Shadow report prepared for the United Nations Committee Against Torture on the occasion of its review of Australia's Third Periodic Report under the Convention Against Torture and other Cruel, Inhuman or Degrading Treatment or Punishment*, 27/7/2007, paragraph 158, available at http://www.nswccl.org.au/docs/pdf/CAT%20shadow%20report.pdf, viewed 25/9/2007

667   Burnside, J., *The Art of Dissent*, The Third Annual MCA Address, 27/9/2004, available at http://www.mca.org.au/fileadmin/user_upload/

PDFs/BurnsideAddress2004.pdf, viewed 31/10/2007

668   *Shahid Kamran Qureshi v Minister For Immigration Multicultural Indigenous Affairs* [2005] FCA 11 (17 January 2005)

669   McNevin, A., 'Seeking Safety, not Charity: A report in support of work-rights for asylum-seekers living in the community on Bridging Visa E', March 2005

670   Fiske, L. 2006, 'Politics of Exclusion, Practice of Inclusion: Australia's Response to Refugees and the Case for Community Based Human Rights Work', *International Journal of Human Rights* 10 (3): 219–29

671   Metcalfe, A., *An overview of organisational change within the Department of Immigration and Multicultural Affairs and its implications for other agencies*, Australian Public Service Commission SES Breakfast Series, 2/5/2006

672   Highfield, J. 2007, 'Timeline of events', *Acting from the Heart: Australian advocates for asylum-seekers tell their stories*, (eds) S. Mares & L. Newman, Finch Publishing, Sydney

673   Grattan, M., & Topsfield, J., 'Dramatic plunge in number of detainees', *The Age*, 4/9/2005, available at http://www.theage.com.au/news/immigration/dramatic-plunge-in-number-of-detainees/2005/09/03/1125302782280.html, viewed 5/11/2007

674   Department of Immigration and Citizenship, *Annual Report 2006–07*, op. cit., p. 123

675   ibid., p. 126

676   ibid., p. 128

677   Jackson, A., 'Mentally ill man's detention attacked', *The Age*, 26/11/2007, p. 16

678   Topsfield, J., 'Minister ignores plea on sick detainee', *The Age*, 23/3/2007, p. 7

679   Topsfield, J., 'Vanstone plays down self-harm', *The Age*, 20/9/2005, available at http://www.theage.com.au/news/immigration/vanstone-plays-down-selfharm/2005/09/19/1126982001952.html, viewed 9/10/06

680   'New detention centre "better" than home', *The Age*, 1/8/2006, available at http://www.theage.com.au/news/national/new-detention-centre-better-than-home/2006/08/01/1154198122904.html, viewed 9/10/2006

681   Human Rights and Equal Opportunity Commission, 'Summary of Observations following the Inspection of Mainland Immigration Detention Facilities', January 2007, available at http://www.hreoc.gov.au/human_rights/idc/idc2007.html, viewed 14/1/2008

682   Jackson, A. 'Needless detention rises', *The Age*, 2/11/2006, available at http://www.theage.com.au/news/national/needless-detention-rises/2006/11/01/1162339918843.html, viewed 3/11/2006

683   Human Rights and Equal Opportunity Commission, *Substantial improvements, but it's still detention*, media release, 19/1/2007, available

at http://www.hreoc.gov.au/about/media/media_releases/2007/4_07.html, viewed 29/8/2007

684   Human Rights and Equal Opportunity Commission, 'Summary of Observations following the Inspection of Mainland Immigration Detention Facilities', op. cit.

685   Department of Immigration and Citizenship, 'Detention Reforms' and Detention and Offshore Services Division, 'Detention Statistics Summary — as at 26 January 2007'

686   Human Rights and Equal Opportunity Commission, 'Summary of Observations following the Inspection of Mainland Immigration Detention Facilities', op. cit.

687   Human Rights and Equal Opportunity Commission, *Substantial improvements, but it's still detention*, op. cit.

688   Human Rights and Equal Opportunity Commission, 'Summary of Observations following the Inspection of Mainland Immigration Detention Facilities', op. cit.

689   Amanda Vanstone, former minister for immigration and multicultural affairs, *Immigration Takes Direct Control of Detention Health Services*, media release, 30/10/2006, available at http://pandora.nla.gov.au/pan/31543/20070124-0000/www.minister.immi.gov.au/media_releases/media06/v06248.html, viewed 19/6/2007

690   Department of Immigration and Multicultural Affairs, *Industry Briefing: Detention and Health Services Contract Re-tender*, available at http://www.immi.gov.au/about/contracts-tenders/detention-services/_pdf/Industry-Briefing.pdf, viewed 18/9/2007

691   Department of Immigration and Citizenship, 'The Service Delivery Model', available at http://www.dimia.gov.au/about/contracts-tenders/detention-services/_pdf/SDM.pdf, viewed 26/9/2007

692   McLoughlin, P., 'Serve, subvert or emancipate? Promoting mental health in immigration detention', *Australian e-Journal for the Advancement of Mental Health*, vol. 5, no. 2, 2006, p. 3

693   ibid., p. 4

694   'Court stops sick man's deportation', *The Age*, 19/1/2006, available at http://www.theage.com.au/news/national/court-stops-sick-mans-deportation/2006/01/18/1137553651604.html, viewed 14/11/2007

695   Department of Immigration, *Removal costs misrepresented*, media release, 19/1/2006, available at http://www.immi.gov.au/media/media-releases/2006/d06004.htm, viewed 26/11/2007

696   'Vanstone considers deportation challenge', *The Age*, 19/01/2006, online edition, quoted in Sampson, R., Correa-Velez, I. & Mitchell, G. 2007, *Removing seriously ill asylum-seekers from Australia*, Melbourne: Refugee Health Research Centre

697   'Villawood detainees on hunger strike', *National Nine News*, Channel Nine, 28/3/2007, available at http://news.ninemsn.com.au/article.

aspx?id=257135&rss=yes, viewed 26/2/2008

698 Rintoul, I., email correspondence, Villawood Hunger Strike — 35 Days, Hunger Strike Refugee Supporters To Picket DIAC Offices, 28/4/2007

699 Curr, P., email correspondence, urgent grave concerns Chinese man — deportation tomorrow.

700 Topsfield, J., 'Minister condemned for "abuse of rights"'. *The Age*, 13/10/2007, available at http://www.theage.com.au/news/national/judge-savages-andrews/2007/10/12/1191696179057.html?page=fullpage#content Swap1, viewed 14/11/2007

701 Curr, P., 'Just Freedom blog', available at http://justfreedom.org.au/, viewed 14/11/2007

702 Letter from D.G. Tucker, acting crime manager, Bankstown Local Area Command, NSW Police Service, to Villawood detainee, 22/5/2007

703 Letter from David Darcy, superintendent, Bankstown Local Area Command, NSW Police Service, to Villawood detainee, 19/7/2007

704 Letter from David Darcy, superintendent, Bankstown Local Area Command, NSW Police Service, to Villawood detainee, 30/7/2007

705 Letter from NSW Ombudsman's office to Villawood detainee, 14/8/07

706 Curr, P., email correspondence, 7/1/2008

707 Committees: Reports: Government Responses, *Senate Hansard*, 14/6/2007, available at http://parlinfoweb.aph.gov.au/piweb/view_document. aspx?id=2451613&table=HANSARDS, viewed 23/1/2008

708 Curr, P., email correspondence 12/10/2007 and 15/10/2007

709 Metcalfe, A., secretary, Department of Immigration and Citizenship, *Designing public policy and programs: Case study in compliance and detention reforms*, The Australian and New Zealand School of Government, Canberra, 15/6/2007, p. 3, available at http://www.immi.gov.au/about/ speeches-pres/_pdf/2007-06-15-ANZSOG-transcript.pdf, viewed 18/6/2007

710 Department of Immigration and Multicultural Affairs response to Human Rights and Equal Opportunity Commission Report on Annual Visits to Immigration Detention Centres, available at http://www.humanrights.gov. au/human_rights/asylum_seekers/DIMAresponse.html, viewed 4/7/2007

711 Department of Immigration and Citizenship, Detention and Offshore Services Division, 'Detention Statistics Summary — as at 11/1/2008', available at http://www.immi.gov.au/managing-australias-borders/ detention/_pdf/immigration-detention-statistics-11-01-08.pdf, viewed 28/1/2008

712 Department of Immigration and Multicultural Affairs public information paper, *Onshore Detention Strategy*, May 2006, p. 2

713 Department of Immigration and Citizenship, 'The Service Delivery Model', op. cit.

714 Department of Immigration and Multicultural Affairs, 'Detention Reforms'

715   Hart, C., 'Plan for new detention centre', *The Australian*, 31/1/2007, p. 2

716   'Bizarre footage of detention centre', *The Age*, 17/5/07, available at http://www.theage.com.au/articles/2007/05/17/1178995303970.html?s_cid=rss_age, viewed 17/5/07

717   Department of Immigration and Citizenship, 'Fact Sheet 7 — Managing the Border', quoted in Oxfam 2007, *A price too high: The cost of Australia's approach to asylum-seekers*, Oxfam, Melbourne

718   Including 53 Vietnamese people who landed at Port Hedland in July 2003 and 43 West Papuans who landed at Cape York in January 2006

719   Black, S., 'Christmas Island — building our own private Guantanamo', *Crikey.com.au*, available at http://www.crikey.com.au/Politics/20070328-Christmas-Island-the-full-plans.html, viewed 24/9/2007

720   Gordon, M., 'Island plan rekindles child detention fears', *The Age*, 25/11/2006

721   Migration Amendment (Designated Unauthorised Arrivals) Bill 2006

722   'Backbenchers defy Howard on asylum bill', *The Age*, 9/8/2006, available at http://www.smh.com.au/news/national/new-asylum-laws-profoundly-disturbing/2006/08/09/1154802942102.html?page=fullpage#contentSwap1, viewed 18/10/2006

723   Australian Greens, *Transferring Sri Lankans to Nauru could cost $60 million*, media release, 2/3/2007, available at http://www.greens.org.au/media/releases/release.php?release_id=21, viewed 19/6/2007

724   Steketee, M., 'Return to sender', *The Australian*, 1/3/2007, available at http://theaustralian.news.com.au/story/0,20867,21303571-7583,00.html, viewed 2/7/07

725   Topsfield, J., 'Nauru seven aim for High Court', *The Age*, 26/5/2007, p. 7

726   Oxfam 2007, op. cit.

727   'Government rejects Nauru inspections', *The Australian*, 3/9/2007, available at http://www.news.com.au/story/0,23599,22352284-29277,00.html, viewed 5/9/2007

728   Hart, C., 'Ban on Nauru rights inspection', *The Australian*, 3/9/2007, p. 5

729   'UN wants Burma envoy, Howard flags more sanctions', *ABC News*, ABC Television, 27/9/2007, available at http://www.abc.net.au/news/stories/2007/09/27/2044748.htm, viewed 12/11/2007

730   Hart, C., 'Indonesia "may join Pacific Solution"', *The Australian*, 30/3/2007, available at http://www.theaustralian.news.com.au/story/0,20867,21472437-601,00.html, viewed 26/9/2007

731   Forbes, M., 'Asylum-seekers to be sent back to Sri Lanka', *The Age*, 24/2/2007, available at http://www.theage.com.au/news/world/asylum-seekers-to-be-sent-back-to-sri-lanka/2007/02/23/1171734021621.html, viewed 19/6/2007

732   Steketee, M., 'Return to sender', *The Australian*, 1/3/2007, available at

http://theaustralian.news.com.au/story/0,20867,21303571-7583,00.html, viewed 2/7/07

733   ibid.

734   Murphy, K., 'Sri Lankans are left in Nauru limbo', *The Age*, 19/3/2007, p. 2

735   King, R., 'UN critical of refugee stance', *The West Australian*, 17/3/2007, p. 66

736   'Nauru sets asylum-seeker deadline', *PM*, ABC Radio, 19/3/2007, available at http://www.abc.net.au/pm/content/2007/s1876105.htm, viewed 18/9/2007

737   'Hunger strike ends', *The Age*, 8/9/2007

738   Department of Immigration and Citizenship, *Status of Sri Lankan Asylum-seekers*, media release, 12/9/2007, available at http://pandora.nla.gov.au/pan/67564/20071110-0000/www.minister.immi.gov.au/media/media-releases/2007/ka07087.html, viewed 24/1/2008

739   Editorial, 'Australia must not lose its way on the rights of refugees', *The Age*, 14/9/2007, p. 12

740   Levett, C., 'Refugees languish on Nauru', *The Age*, 24/9/2007, available at http://www.theage.com.au/news/national/refugees-languish-on-nauru/2007/09/23/1190486137325.html, viewed 2/10/2007

741   Hart, C., 'Refugee swap not binding, says US', *The Australian*, 20/4/2007, available at http://www.theaustralian.news.com.au/story/0,20867,21588498-601,00.html, viewed 19/6/2007

742   Hart, C., 'Returning asylum-seekers "scandalous"', *The Australian*, 27/9/2007, available at http://www.theaustralian.news.com.au/story/0,25197,22489350-2702,00.html, viewed 1/10/2007

743   Topsfield, J., 'Minister scoffs at *Tampa* talk', *The Age*, 6/10/2007, p. 4

744   'Downer opens door for Burmese refugees', *ABC News*, ABC Television, 23/10/2007, available at http://www.abc.net.au/news/stories/2007/10/23/2067334.htm, viewed 12/11/2007

745   Department of Immigration and Citizenship, *Becoming an Australian Citizen*, p. 5, available at http://www.citizenship. gov.au/test/resource-booklet/citz-booklet-pt-1.pdf, viewed 14/11/2007

746   Butterly, N., 'Migrants flunk citizenship test', *The Age*, 2/1/2008, available at http://www.theage.com.au/news/national/migrants-flunk-citizenship-test/2008/01/01/1198949817046.html, viewed 2/1/2008

747   Department of Immigration and Citizenship, *Annual Report 2006–07*, p. 126, available at http://www.immi.gov.au/about/reports/annual/2006-07/html/index.htm, viewed 10/1/2008

748   ALP National Platform and Constitution 2007, available at http://www.alp.org.au/platform/, viewed 31/12/2007

749   Topsfield, J., 'Refugees' long wait set to end', *The Age*, 12/1/2008, p. 3

750   Jackson, A., 'Australia accepts stranded Afghans', *The Age*, 2/2/2008, p. 13

751 Senate Standing Committee on Legal and Constitutional Affairs: Department of Immigration and Citizenship: Discussion, 19/2/2008, available at http://parlinfoweb.aph.gov.au/piweb/view_document. aspx?id=103720&table=ESTIMATE, viewed 26/2/2008

752 Jackson, A., 'Labor "tougher" on asylum seekers', *The Age*, 12/5/2008, p. 5

753 Email correspondence with Ian Rintoul, Refugee Action Coalition

754 Kelly, P. & Shanahan, D., 'Rudd to turn back boat people', *The Australian*, 23/11/2007, available at http://www.theaustralian.news.com.au/ story/0,25197,22806913-601,00.html, viewed 25/11/2007

755 Topsfield, J., 'People smuggler blocks to continue, says minister', *The Age*, 17/1/2008, available at http://www.theage.com.au/news/national/people-smuggler-blocks-to-continue-minister/2008/01/16/1200419885329.html, viewed 17/1/2008

756 Transcript of interview, Radio National, ABC Radio, 16/1/2008, available at http://www.chrisevans.alp. org.au/news/0108/ immiinterviewtranscripts16-01.php, viewed 26/2/2008

757 Topsfield, J., 'Labor urged to end offshore asylum seeker processing', *The Age*, 22/1/2008, available at http://www.theage.com.au/news/national/ labor-urged-to-end-offshore-asylum-seeker-processing/2008/01/21/1200764 171351.html

758 Johnson, C., 'Is this a $400m white elephant?', *The West Australian*, 24/5/2008, p. 6

759 Senate Standing Committee on Legal and Constitutional Affairs: Department of Immigration and Citizenship: Discussion, 19/2/2008, available at http://parlinfoweb.aph.gov.au/piweb/view_document. aspx?id=103720&table=ESTIMATE, viewed 26/2/2008

760 Adopted and proclaimed by General Assembly resolution 217 A (III) of 10 December 1948, available at http://www.un.org/Overview/rights.html, viewed 5/2/2008